A Reader's
Hebrew-English Lexicon
of the Old Testament

A Reader's Hebrew-English Lexicon of the Old Testament

Volume III Isaiah—Malachi

Terry A. Armstrong

Douglas L. Busby

Cyril F. Carr

Regency
Reference Library
Zondervan Publishing House
Grand Rapids, Michigan

A Reader's Hebrew-English Lexicon of the Old Testament.
Volume III (Isaiah–Malachi)

Regency Reference Library is an imprint of Zondervan
Publishing House, 1415 Lake Drive, S.E.,
Grand Rapids, Michigan 49506

Copyright © 1986 by The Zondervan Corporation
Grand Rapids, Michigan

Library of Congress Cataloging in Publication Data
(Revised for volume III)

Armstrong, Terry A., 1944–
    A reader's Hebrew-English lexicon of the Old Testament.

    Vol.   originally issued in 2 v.
    Contents: [1] Volumes I and II, Genesis–2 Kings.
v. 3. Isaiah–Malachi.
    1. Bible. O.T. Hebrew—Glossaries, vocabularies, etc.
2. Hebrew language—Dictionaries—English.
3. Hebrew language—Word frequency.
I. Busby, Douglas, L., 1946–   .   II. Carr, Cyril F., 1949–82.
III. Title.
[PJ4833.A69   19844m221.4'4   84-5180
ISBN 0-310-37040-X (v. 1)
ISBN 0-310-37010-8

Printed in the United States of America

CONTENTS

PREFACE

A Reader's Hebrew-English Lexicon of the Old Testament is an attempt to meet the need for an Old Testament translation tool on the level of Sakae Kubo's *Reader's Greek-English Lexicon of the New Testament.* With the student and pastor in view, it has been developed as a means to a more rapid reading of the Hebrew text. The *Reader's Lexicon* should not, therefore, be considered a replacement to a standard lexicon.

The format of the *Reader's Lexicon,* then, serves the purpose of eliminating most of the time-consuming lexical work from basic translation. The appendix contains words occurring over fifty times in the Old Testament. For speed and convenience the reader is encouraged to master this list. In the body of the book, words that occur fifty or fewer times in the Old Testament are listed verse by verse in the order of their occurrence. Nouns and adjectives appear in their vocabulary form. Verbs appear in the perfect third person masculine singular form of the stem used at that point in the text (e.g., וַיַּבְדֵּל appears in Genesis 1:4; in the *Reader's Lexicon* it is listed as הִבְדִּיל). This allows the reader to identify both the root (בדל)and the stem (hiphil). When these verb forms are not pointed, it simply means that the specific form is not extant.

In rare situations, forms other than those described will appear in the *Reader's Lexicon.* In each case clarity is the governing principle. This lexicon does not include numerals or proper nouns.

Along with the definition of the Hebrew words, their respective frequencies are given. For words other than verbs, the first number indicates the frequency of that word in the entire Old Testament. In the case of verbs the first number indicates the frequency of the given stem in the Bible book in which it is being studied. The second number gives the number of occurrences of that stem in the entire Old Testament. The third number gives the frequency of all the stems of a given verb in the entire Old Testament.

Example: Genesis 1:22 פרה (10-22-29)

> 10—The Qal stem occurs ten times in Genesis.
>
> 22—The Qal stem occurs twenty-two times in the Old Testament.
>
> 29—The cumulative occurrence of all stems in the Old Testament is twenty-nine.

Konkordanz zum Hebräischen Alten Testament by Gerhard Lisowsky has been relied on for verb, noun, and adjective frequencies. Frequencies for words in other categories come from *Veteris Testamenti Concordantiae Hebraicae Atque Chaldaicae* by Solomon Mandelkern. Occasionally Lisowsky departs from *A Hebrew and English Lexicon of the Old Testament* by Francis Brown, S. R. Driver, and Charles A. Briggs (hereafter designated BDB) in accepting one root, whereas BDB sees two roots (or vice versa). An example of this is Genesis 3:15. Lisowsky assumes the two occurrences of שׁוּף to be two different words, while BDB lists but one root. When a question mark follows the frequency, it indicates this disharmony.

For the sake of ease in rapid reading, the compound form of particles appears in the *Reader's Lexicon* even when the simple form exists in excess of fifty times (e.g., מִלְמַעְלָה, Genesis 6:16, which occurs only twenty-four times, though its basic part, מַעְלָה, occurs more than fifty times). Thus each compound is treated on its own and the numbers appearing with it indicate the frequency of that particle or compound only.

Definitions have been taken from BDB and checked against the text for meaning in context. Question marks following definitions indicate the interrogative. Suggested meanings are indicated by "perh.," while questionable definitions are designated as [dub.]. The number at the end of the entry gives the page number in BDB carrying a discussion of the word.

As an exegetical tool, this work allows the user to (1) estimate the work involved in any given word study he might wish to pursue, (2) appraise the degree of certainty of a given definition, and (3) go directly to the correct page of a standard lexicon for further investigation. As a translational tool, this lexicon has the primary function of making rapid reading of the Hebrew text possible. Students of Hebrew will be enabled to examine the syntax of the language and, by extensive reading of the text, acquire an understanding of the contexts in which a given word occurs.

It is our prayer that this tool will make Hebrew reading and Hebrew exegesis more delightful and more common among students and pastors who have a high regard for the Word of God as given in the Old Testament.

ISAIAH

Chapter 1

חָזוֹן 1 vision (2 · 35) 302
הַאֲזִין 2 to give ear, listen (8 · 41 · 41) 24
פָּשַׁע to rebel (9 · 40 · 41) 833
קֹנֶה 3 owner (2 · 7) 888 קנה
אֵבוּס crib (1 · 3) 7
כָּבֵד 4 heavy (3 · 40) 458
מֵרַע evildoer (4 · 18) 949
נָאַץ to spurn (3 · 15 · 24) 610
נָזוֹר to be estranged (1 · 2 · 6[?]) 266
אָחוֹר backwards (9 · 41) 30
סָרָה 5 apostasy (3 · 7[?]) 694
חֳלִי sickness (4 · 24) 318
דַּוָּי faint (1 · 3) 188
מְתֹם 6 soundness (1 · 4) 1071
פֶּצַע bruise, wound (1 · 8) 822
חַבּוּרָה stripe, blow (2 · 7) 289
מַכָּה wound (5 · 48) 646
טָרִי fresh (1 · 2) 382
זוֹר to press out (1 · 1 · 1[?]) 266 III. זור
חבש to be bound up (1 · 2 · 32) 289
רכך to be softened (1 · 1 · 8) 939
לְנֶגֶד 7 in front of, before (1 · 32) 617
מַהְפֵּכָה overthrow (2 · 6) 246
סֻכָּה 8 booth (2 · 31) 697
מְלוּנָה hut (2 · 2) 534
מִקְשָׁה field of cucumbers (1 · 2) 903
לוּלֵי 9 unless (1 · 10) 530
שָׂרִיד survivor (1 · 28) 975
דָּמָה to be like (2 · 13 · 27) 197
קָצִין 10 ruler (4 · 12) 892
הַאֲזִין to give ear, listen (8 · 41 · 41) 24
מְרִיא 11 fatling (2 · 8) 597
עַתּוּד he-goat (3 · 29) 800
רָמַס 12 to trample (4 · 17 · 18) 942
מִקְרָא 13 convocation (2 · 22) 896
עֲצָרָה assembly (1 · 11) 783

טֹרַח 14 burden (1 · 2) 382
נִלְאָה to be weary (3 · 10 · 19) 521
הֶעְלִים 15 to hide, conceal (1 · 11 · 29) 761
הִתְזַכָּה 16 to make oneself clean (1 · 1 · 8) 269
רֹעַ evil, badness (1 · 19) 947
מַעֲלָל practice (3 · 41) 760
מִנֶּגֶד from, from before (1 · 26) 617
אשר 17 to set right (3 · 5 · 7) 80
חָמוֹץ the ruthless [coll.] (1 · 1) 330
יָתוֹם orphan (4 · 42) 450
חֵטְא 18 sin, guilt of sin (4 · 33) 307
שָׁנִי scarlet (1 · 42) 1040
שֶׁלֶג snow (2 · 20) 1017
הִלְבִּין to grow white (1 · 4 · 5) 526
הֶאְדִּים to emit [show] redness (1 · 1 · 10) 10
תּוֹלָע scarlet stuff (1 · 2) 1068
צֶמֶר wool (2 · 16) 856
טוֹב 19 good things, produce; goods (3 · 32) 375
מֵאֵן 20 to refuse (2 · 45 · 45) 549
מָרָה to be stubborn (3 · 21 · 43) 598
אֵיכָה 21 how! (1 · 18) 32
זוֹנָה harlot (3 · 33[?]) 275
קִרְיָה town, city (10 · 30) 900
מְרַצֵּחַ assassin (1 · 2) 954
סִיג 22 dross (2 · 8) 691
סֹבֶא liquor (1 · 3) 685
מהל to weaken (1 · 1 · 1) 554
סָרַר 23 to be stubborn (3 · 17 · 17) 710
חָבֵר associate, companion (2 · 12) 288
גַּנָּב thief (1 · 17) 170
שֹׁחַד bribe (4 · 23) 1005
שַׁלְמֹן reward, bribe (1 · 1) 1024
יָתוֹם orphan (4 · 42) 450
אָבִיר 24 strong [one] (3 · 6) 7
נקם to avenge oneself (1 · 12 · 34) 667
צָרַף 25 to smelt away (3 · 19 · 22) 864
בֹּר lye (1 · 7) 141
סִיג dross (2 · 8) 691
בְּדִיל alloy, tin, dross (1 · 1[?]) 95

יוֹעֵץ 26 counselor (5 · 22) 419

תְּחִלָּה beginning (1 · 22) 321

קִרְיָה town, city (10 · 30) 900

שֶׁבֶר 28 breaking (9 · 45) 991

פֶּשַׁע to transgress, rebel (9 · 40 · 41) 833

חַטָּא sinners (3 · 19) 308

אַיִל 29 terebinth [a deciduous tree] (3 · 4) 18

חָמַד to desire, take pleasure in (3 · 16 · 21) 326

חָפֵר to be ashamed (2 · 13 · 17) 344

גַּנָּה garden (5 · 16) 171

אֵלָה 30 terebinth [a deciduous tree] (2 · 17) 18

נָבֵל to wither, fall (11 · 21 · 25) 615

עָלֶה leaf, leafage (3 · 18) 750

גַּנָּה garden (5 · 16) 171

חָסֹן 31 strong (1 · 2) 340

נִיצוֹץ spark (1 · 1) 665

נְעֹרֶת tow [fiber of flax, hemp, or jute] (1 · 2) 654

פֹּעַל work, thing made (6 · 37) 821

כבה to extinguish (2 · 10 · 24) 459

Chapter 2

נהר 2 to stream (1 · 3[?] · 3[?]) 625

הורה 3 to teach (4 · 45[?] · 45[?]) 434

כָּתַּת 4 to hammer (1 · 5 · 17) 510

אֵת cutting instrument of iron, usu. plowshare (1 · 5) 88

חֲנִית spear (1 · 46) 333

מַזְמֵרָה pruning knife (2 · 4) 275

נָטַשׁ 6 to abandon (2 · 33 · 40) 643

עוֹנֵן to practice soothsaying (2 · 10 · 11) 778

נָכְרִי foreigner (2 · 45) 648

הִשְׂפִּיק to cause to clap (1 · 1 · 2[?]) 706 ספק

קָצֶה 7 end (2 · 5) 892

מֶרְכָּבָה chariot (3 · 44) 939

אֱלִיל 8 worthlessness, worthless gods, idols (10 · 20) 47

לַאֲשֶׁר that which (4 · 38) 81 אֲשֶׁר 4.c.

אֶצְבַּע finger (4 · 31) 840

נִשְׁחַח 9 to be humbled (3 · 4 · 18[?]) 1005

שָׁפֵל to become low, be humiliated (10 · 11 · 30) 1050

נטמן 10 to hide oneself (1 · 1 · 31) 380

פַּחַד dread (5 · 49) 808

הָדָר splendor, majesty (7 · 30) 214

גָּאוֹן exaltation, majesty (12 · 49) 144

גַּבְהוּת 11 haughtiness (2 · 2) 147

שָׁפֵל to become low, be humiliated (10 · 11 · 30) 1050

שַׁח to be humbled (3 · 12 · 18[?]) 1005

רוּם haughtiness, height (3 · 6) 927

נִשְׂגָּב to be exalted (6 · 10 · 20) 960

לְבַדּוֹ alone (2 · 36) 94

גֵּאֶה 12 proud (1 · 8) 144

רָם high, exalted (7 · 31[?]) 926 רום

שָׁפֵל to become low, be humiliated (10 · 11 · 30) 1050

רָם 13 high, exalted (7 · 31[?]) 926 רום

אַלּוֹן oak (3 · 9) 47

רָם 14 high, exalted (7 · 31[?]) 926 רום

מִגְדָּל 15 tower (4 · 49) 154

גָּבֹהַּ tall, high, lofty (6 · 41) 147

בָּצוּר cut off, made inaccessible; i.e., fortified (5 · 25[?]) 130 בצר

אֳנִיָּה 16 ship (5 · 31) 58

שְׂכִיָּה standard, ship, watchtower [very dub.] (1 · 1) 967

חֶמְדָּה desire, delight (1 · 16) 326

שַׁח 17 to be humbled (3 · 12 · 18[?]) 1005 שחח

גַּבְהוּת haughtiness (2 · 2) 147

שָׁפֵל to become low, be humiliated (10 · 11 · 30) 1050

רוּם haughtiness, height (3 · 6) 927

נִשְׂגָּב to be exalted (6 · 10 · 20) 960

לְבַדּוֹ alone (2 · 36) 94

אֱלִיל 18 worthlessness, worthless idols (10 · 20) 47

כָּלִיל entirety (1 · 15) 483

חָלַף to vanish, pass away (4 · 14 · 26) 322

מְעָרָה 19 cave (1 · 40) 792

מְחִלָּה hole (1 · 1) 320

פַּחַד dread (5 · 49) 808

הָדָר splendor, majesty (7 · 30) 214

גָּאוֹן exaltation, majesty (12 · 49) 144

עָרַץ to cause to tremble (3 · 11 · 14) 791

אֱלִיל 20 worthlessness, idols (10 · 20) 47

חָפַר to dig, search for (1 · 23 · 23) 343

חֲפֹר פֵּרוֹת → חֲפַרְפָּרוֹת mole (1 · 1) 344

עֲטַלֵּף bat (1 · 3) 742

נִקְרָה 21 hole, crevice (1 · 2) 669

סָעִיף cleft (2[?] · 4[?]) 703

פַּחַד dread (5 · 49) 808

הָדָר splendor, majesty (7 · 30) 214

גָּאוֹן exaltation, majesty (12 · 49) 144

עָרַץ to cause to tremble (3 · 11 · 14) 791

נְשָׁמָה 22 breath (4 · 24) 675

בַּמֶּה in what (1 · 29) 552

Chapter 3

מִשְׁעֵן 1 support (1 · 1) 1044

מַשְׁעֵנָה staff (2 · 12) 1044

מַשְׁעֵן support, staff (2 · 4) 1044

קֹסֵם 2 diviner (1 · 9[?]) 890 קסם

יוֹעֵץ 3 counselor (5 · 22) 419

חָרָשׁ magic art, or perh. magic drug (1 · 1) 361

נָבוֹן intelligent, discerning (3 · 21) 106

לַחַשׁ serpent charming (3 · 5) 538

תַּעֲלוּלִים 4 caprice (2 · 2) 760

נָגַשׂ 5 to tyrannize over each other (2 · 3 · 7) 620

רהב to storm against (1 · 2 · 4) 923

נִקְלָה to be lightly esteemed (2 · 5 · 6) 885

שִׂמְלָה 6 wrapper, mantle (4 · 29) 971

קָצִין dictator (4 · 12) 892

מַכְשֵׁלָה overthrown mass (1 · 2) 506

חֹבֵשׁ 7 one who binds (1 · 1[?]) 289

שִׂמְלָה wrapper, mantle (4 · 29) 971

קָצִין dictator (4 · 12) 892

מַעֲלָל 8 practice (3 · 41) 760

הִמְרָה to show disobedience, rebellious-ness (1 · 22 · 43) 598

הַכָּרָה 9 a look, expression (1 · 1) 648

כִּחֵד to hide (1 · 15 · 30) 470

אוֹי Woe! Alas! (4 · 25) 17

גָּמַל to deal out to, to do (6 · 34 · 37) 168

מַעֲלָל 10 practice (3 · 41) 760

אוֹי 11 Woe! Alas! (4 · 25) 17

גְּמוּל dealing, recompense, benefit (5 · 19) 168

נֹגֵשׂ 12 ruler (5 · 15) 620

עוֹלֵל to play the child (1 · 1 · 1) 760

אִשֵּׁר to lead on (3 · 5 · 7) 80

הִתְעָה to mislead (6 · 21 · 50) 1073

בִּלַּע to swallow up, engulf (2 · 3 · 6[?]) 118

דִּין 13 to minister judgment (1 · 23 · 24) 192

בִּעֵר 14 to consume, devour (4 · 26 · 28[?]) 129

גְּזֵלָה plunder, spoil (1 · 6) 160

דָּכָא 15 to crush (2 · 11 · 18) 194

טחן to grind (2 · 7 · 7) 377

גָּבַהּ 16 to be haughty, be high (5 · 24 · 34) 146

גָּרוֹן neck, throat (2 · 8) 173

שִׁקֵּר to ogle, to eye (1 · 1 · 1) 974

טפף to take quick little steps (1 · 1 · 1) 381

עכס to shake bangles (1 · 1 · 1) 747

שִׂפַּח 17 to smite with a scab (1 · 1 · 1) 705

קָדְקֹד crown of head, scalp (1 · 11) 869

פֹת   secret parts [dub.] (1 · 1) 834

עָרָה   to lay bare (2 · 9 · 15) 788

תִּפְאֶרֶת   18   beauty, finery (18 · 50) 802

עֶכֶס   anklet, bangle (1 · 2) 747

שָׁבִיס   front band (1 · 1) 987

שַׂהֲרֹן   crescent, moon [ornaments] (1 · 3) 962

נְטִיפָה   19   drop, pendant (1 · 2) 643

שֵׁרָה   bracelet (1 · 1) 1057

רְעָלָה   veil (1 · 1) 947

פְּאֵר   20   turban (3 · 7) 802

צְעָדָה   armlet (1 · 3) 857

קִשֻּׁרִים   bands, sashes (1 · 2) 905

לַחַשׁ   charms, amulets (3 · 5) 538

טַבַּעַת   21   signet ring (1 · 49) 371

נֶזֶם   ring, nose ring (1 · 17) 633

מַחֲלָצָה   22   robe of state (1 · 2) 323

מַעֲטָפָה   overtunic (1 · 1) 742

מִטְפַּחַת   cloak (1 · 2) 381

חָרִיט   bag, purse (1 · 2) 355

גִּלָּיוֹן   23   tablet, tablets of polished metal, mirrors [dub.] (2 · 2) 163

סָדִין   linen wrapper (1 · 4) 690

צָנִיף   turban (2 · 5) 857

רְדִיד   wide wrapper, large veil (1 · 2) 921

בֹּשֶׂם   24   perfume (2 · 30) 141

מַק   rottenness (2 · 2) 597

חֲגוֹרָה   loin covering, girdle, belt (1 · 5) 292

נִקְפָּה   encircling rope (1 · 1) 669

מִקְשֶׁה   artistic hair arrangement (1 · 1) 904

קָרְחָה   bald spot (3 · 11) 901

פְּתִיגִיל   rich robe [dub.] (1 · 1) 836

מַחֲגֹרֶת   a girdling (1 · 1) 292

שַׂק   sackcloth (8 · 48) 974

כִּי   burning, branding (1 · 1) 465

יֳפִי   beauty (2 · 19) 421

מַת   25   man, male (3 · 21) 607

אנה   26   to mourn (2 · 2 · 2) 58

אָבַל   to mourn (5 · 18 · 38) 5

נִקָּה   to be cleaned out (1 · 23 · 37) 667

Chapter 4

שִׂמְלָה   1   clothes (4 · 29) 971

צֶמַח   2   sprouting, growth (2 · 12) 855

צְבִי   beauty (7 · 18) 840

גָּאוֹן   majesty, exaltation (12 · 49) 144

תִּפְאֶרֶת   glory (18 · 50) 802

פְּלֵיטָה   escaped remnant (5 · 28) 812

צֹאָה   4   filth (3 · 5) 844

הֵדִיח   to cleanse by washing (1 · 4 · 4) 188

בָּעֵר   to consume, devour (4 · 26 · 28[?]) 129

בָּרָא   5   to create, shape (20 · 38 · 48) 135

מָכוֹן   established place (2 · 17) 467

מִקְרָא   convocation (2 · 22) 896

עָשָׁן   smoke (7 · 25) 798

נֹגַהּ   brightness (5 · 19) 618

לֶהָבָה   flame (5 · 19) 529

חֻפָּה   canopy, chamber (1 · 3) 342

סֻכָּה   6   booth (2 · 31) 697

חֹרֶב   parching heat (5 · 16) 351

מַחְסֶה   shelter (4 · 20) 340

מִסְתּוֹר   hiding place (1 · 1) 712

זֶרֶם   rain storm, flood of rain, downpour (7 · 9) 281

מָטָר   rain (3 · 38) 564

Chapter 5

יָדִיד   1   beloved (2 · 8) 391

שִׁירָה   song (2 · 13) 1010

עֹזַק   2   to dig about (1 · 1 · 1) 740

סִקֵּל   to free from stones (2 · 4 · 22) 709

שֹׂרֵק   choice species of vine (1 · 2) 977

מִגְדָּל   tower (4 · 49) 154

יֶקֶב   wine vat (2 · 16) 428

חָצֵב   to hew out (4 · 14 · 17) 345

קִוָּה   to wait (13 · 39 · 45) 875

עֵנָב   grape (2 · 19) 772

בְּאֻשִׁים   stinking or worthless things, wild grapes (2 · 2) 93

4

קַוָּה	4 to wait (13 · 39 · 45) 875
עֵנָב	grape (2 · 19) 772
בְּאֻשִׁים	stinking or worthless things, wild grapes (2 · 2) 93
מְשׂוּכָה	5 hedge (1 · 1) 968
בָּעַר	to consume, devour, burn (4 · 26 · 28) 129
פָּרַץ	to break down (2 · 46 · 49) 829
גָּדֵר	wall, fence (1 · 13) 154
מִרְמָס	trampling (4 · 7) 942
בָּתָה	6 end, destruction (1 · 1) 144
נִזְמַר	to be pruned (1 · 1 · 3) 274
נֶעְדַּר	to be hoed (2 · 2 · 2) 727
שָׁמִיר	thorns (8 · 11) 1038
שַׁיִת	thorn bushes (7 · 7) 1011
עָב	dark cloud (7 · 30) 728
הִמְטִיר	to send rain (1 · 16 · 17) 565
מָטָר	rain (3 · 38) 564
נֶטַע	7 plantation (3 · 4) 642
שַׁעֲשׁוּעִים	delight (1 · 9) 1044
קַוָּה	to wait (13 · 39 · 45) 875
מִשְׂפָּח	bloodshed (1 · 1) 705
צְעָקָה	cry of distress (1 · 21) 858
אֶפֶס	8 an end of (14 · 43) 67
שַׁמָּה	9 a waste (3 · 39) 1031
מֵאֵין	without (6 · 48[?]) 34 אֵין 6.d.
צֶמֶד	10 square measure of land (3 · 15) 855
בַּת	bath [liquid measure] = 40 liters (1 · 13) 144
חֹמֶר	homer [dry measure] = 10 ephahs = 393.9 liters (1 · 13[?]) 330
אֵיפָה	ephah [grain measure] (1 · 38) 35
שֵׁכָר	11 strong drink (8 · 23) 1016
אִחֵר	to tarry (2 · 15 · 17) 29
נֶשֶׁף	twilight (3 · 12) 676
הִדְלִיק	to inflame (1 · 2 · 9) 196
כִּנּוֹר	12 lyre (5 · 41) 490
נֶבֶל	harp (2 · 27) 614
תֹּף	timbrel (3 · 17) 1074
חָלִיל	flute, pipe (2 · 6) 319

מִשְׁתֶּה	feast (3 · 45) 1059
פֹּעַל	deed (6 · 37) 821
מִבְּלִי	13 from want of; here = unawares, suddenly (1 · 25) 115
מַת	man, male (3 · 21) 607
צִחֵה	parched (1 · 1) 850
צָמָא	thirst (3 · 17) 854
הִרְחִיב	14 to enlarge (5 · 21 · 25) 931
פָּעַר	to open wide (1 · 4 · 4) 822
לִבְלִי	without (1 · 3) 115
הָדָר	splendor (7 · 30) 214
שָׁאוֹן	uproar (8 · 18) 981
עָלֵז	jubilant (1 · 1) 759
נִשְׁחַח	15 to be humbled (3 · 4 · 18[?]) 1005
שָׁפֵל	to be humiliated (10 · 11 · 15) 1050
גַּבְהַּ	haughty (6 · 41) 147
גָּבַהּ	16 to be exalted, be high (5 · 24 · 34) 146
דֹּבֶר	17 pasture (1 · 2) 184
חָרְבָּה	waste, waste place amid ruins (9 · 42) 352
מֵחַ	fatling (1 · 2) 562
מָשַׁךְ	18 to draw (2 · 30 · 36) 604
חֶבֶל	cord (3 · 49) 286
עֲבֹת	rope (1 · 24) 721
עֲגָלָה	cart rope (3 · 25) 722
חַטָּאָה	sin, sinful thing (1 · 2) 308
הֵחִישׁ	19 to hasten (3 · 6 · 21) 301
מַר	20 bitter, injurious, hurtful (6 · 38) 600
מָתוֹק	sweet (2 · 12) 608
נָבוֹן	21 intelligent, discerning (3 · 21) 106 בין niph.
מָסַךְ	22 to mix (2 · 5 · 5) 587
שֵׁכָר	strong drink (8 · 23) 1016
הִצְדִּיק	23 to declare righteous (3 · 12 · 41) 842
עֵקֶב	because of (1 · 15) 784
שֹׁחַד	bribe (4 · 23) 1005
קַשׁ	24 stubble, chaff (5 · 16) 905
חֲשַׁשׁ	chaff (2 · 2) 366
לֶהָבָה	flame (5 · 19) 529

רָפָה to sink down (2 · 14 · 45) 951

שֹׁרֶשׁ root (7 · 33) 1057

מַק rottenness (2 · 2) 597

פֶּרַח bud (2 · 17) 827

אָבָק dust (2 · 6) 7

אִמְרָה word[s] (5 · 30) 57

נָאֵץ spurn (3 · 15 · 24) 610

רָגַז 25 to quake (6 · 30 · 41) 919

נְבֵלָה corpse (2 · 48) 615

סוּחָה offal (1 · 1) 691

מֵרָחֹק 26 at a distance (12 · 34) 935

נֵס standard (10 · 21) 651

שָׁרַק to hiss (2 · 12 · 12) 1056

מְהֵרָה hastily, quickly; haste (2 · 20) 555

קַל swift, swiftly (4 · 13) 886

עָיֵף 27 faint, weary (5 · 17) 746

נוּם to be drowsy, to slumber (2 · 6 · 6) 630

יָשֵׁן to sleep (1 · 15 · 16[?]) 445

אֵזוֹר waistcloth, girdle (3 · 14) 25

חָלָץ loins (3 · 10) 323

נִתַּק to be torn apart (2 · 10 · 27) 683

שְׂרוֹךְ [sandal] thong (1 · 2) 976

נַעַל sandal (3 · 22) 653

שָׁנַן 28 to sharpen (1 · 7 · 9) 1041

פַּרְסָה hoof (1 · 21) 828

צַר flint (1 · 1) 866

גַּלְגַּל wheel (2 · 11) 165

סוּפָה storm wind (5 · 15) 693

שְׁאָגָה 29 roaring (1 · 7) 980

שָׁאַג to roar (1 · 20 · 20) 980

לָבִיא lioness (2 · 11) 522

כְּפִיר young lion (3 · 31) 498

נהם to growl (2 · 5 · 5) 625

טֶרֶף prey (2 · 17) 383

הִפְלִיט to bring into security (1 · 2 · 27) 812

נהם 30 to growl (2 · 5 · 5) 625

נְהָמָה growling (1 · 2) 625

צַר straits, distress (5[?] · 20[?]) 865

חָשַׁךְ to be or grow dark (2 · 11 · 17) 364

עָרִיף cloud (1 · 1) 791

Chapter 6

רָם 1 high, exalted (7 · 31[?]) 926   רום

שׁוּל skirt [of robe] (1 · 11) 1002

שְׂרָפִים 2 seraphim (4[?] · 7[?]) 977

מִמַּעַל with ל = on the top of, above (2 · 29) 751   II מעל 1.b.

עוֹפֵף to fly about (3 · 5 · 25) 733

מְלֹא 3 fullness, entire contents (5 · 38) 571

נוּעַ 4 to tremble (6 · 22 · 38) 631

אַמָּה support, foundation [dub.] (1 · 1) 52

סַף threshold (1 · 25) 706

עָשָׁן smoke (7 · 25) 798

אוֹי 5 Alas! Woe! (4 · 25) 17

נִדְמָה to be ruined, cut off, undone (3 · 12 · 16) 198

עוּף 6 to fly (4 · 18 · 25) 733

שְׂרָפִים seraphim (4[?] · 7[?]) 977

רִצְפָה glowing stone (1 · 2) 954

מֶלְקָחַיִם tongs (1 · 6) 544

הִשְׁמִין 10 to make fat (1 · 2 · 5) 1031

הָשַׁע to besmear (1 · 1 · 3) 1044

מָתַי when? (1 · 42) 607

שָׁאָה 11 to crash into ruin (1 · 1 · 6) 980

מֵאֵין without (6 · 48[?]) 34   אִי 6.d.

נִשְׁאָה to be ruined (3 · 3 · 6) 980

רבב 12 to become great (4 · 23 · 24) 912

בָּעֵר 13 to consume, devour, burn (4 · 26 · 28[?]) 129

אֵלָה terebinth [deciduous tree] (2 · 17) 18

אַלּוֹן oak (3 · 9) 47

שַׁלֶּכֶת felling [of tree] (1 · 1) 1021

מַצֶּבֶת stump (2 · 2) 663

Chapter 7

נוּעַ 2 to tremble (6 · 22 · 38) 631

תְּעָלָה 3 conduit, trench (2 · 9) 752

בְּרֵכָה pool (4 · 17) 140

מְסִלָּה highway (9 · 27) 700

הַשְׁקֵט 4 to show quietness (4 · 10 · 41) 1052

רכך to be fearful (1 · 6 · 8) 939

זָנָב end, stump (4 · 11) 275

אוּד firebrand (1 · 3) 15

חֳרִי burning (1 · 6) 354

עָשֵׁן smoking (1 · 2) 798

הָקִיץ 6 to cause sickening dread (1[?]-1[?]-1[?]) 880

בְּעוֹד 8 within yet (3 · 20) 728 עוֹד 2.a.

הַעֲמִיק 11 to make deep (4 · 8 · 9) 770

שְׁאָלָה underworld (1 · 1) 982

הַגְבֵּהַ to make high, exalt (1 · 10 · 34) 146

לְמַעְלָה upward (3 · 34) 751 מַעַל 2.c.

נִסָּה 12 to test (1 · 36 · 36) 650

הִלְאָה 13 to exhaust (2 · 6 · 19) 521

עַלְמָה 14 young woman (1 · 9) 761

הָרָה pregnant (2 · 15) 248

חֶמְאָה 15 curd (3 · 10) 326

בְּטֶרֶם 16 before (7 · 39) 382

קוּץ to feel a sickening dread (1 · 8 · 8 [?]) 880

שָׁרַק 18 to hiss (2 · 12 · 12) 1056

זְבוּב fly (1 · 6) 256

דְּבוֹרָה bee (1 · 4) 184

בַּתָּה 19 precipice, steep (1 · 1) 144

נָקִיק cleft of rock (1 · 3) 669

נַעֲצוּץ thorn bush (2 · 2) 654

נַהֲלֹל pasture (1 · 1) 625

גִּלַּח 20 to shave off (1 · 18 · 23) 164

תַּעַר razor (1 · 13) 789

שָׂכִיר hired (3 · 18) 969

שֵׂעָר hair (1 · 28) 972

זָקָן beard (2 · 18) 278

ספה to sweep away (2 · 8 · 18) 705

עֶגְלָה 21 heifer (1 · 12) 722

חָלָב 22 milk (4 · 44) 316

חֶמְאָה curd (3 · 10) 326

שָׁמִיר 23 thorns (8 · 11) 1038

שַׁיִת thorn bushes (7 · 7) 1011

שָׁמִיר 24 thorns (8 · 11) 1038

שַׁיִת thorn bushes (7 · 7) 1011

מַעְדֵּר 25 hoe (1 · 1) 727

נעדר to be hoed (2 · 2 · 2) 727

יִרְאָה fear, terror (5 · 45) 432

שָׁמִיר thorns (8 · 11) 1038

שַׁיִת thorn bushes (7 · 7) 1011

מִשְׁלַח place of letting loose (1 · 7) 1020

מִרְמָס trampling place (4 · 7) 942

שֶׂה a sheep [or goat] (4 · 45) 961

Chapter 8

גִּלָּיוֹן 1 tablet [for writing] (2 · 2) 163

חֶרֶט stylus, graving tool (1 · 2) 354

אֱנוֹשׁ men, man, mankind (8 · 42) 60

חָשׁ to make haste (2 · 15 · 21) 301 חוּשׁ

בַּז plunder, spoil (5 · 27) 103

הֵעִיד 2 to take as witness (1 · 39 · 44) 729

נְבִיאָה 3 prophetess (1 · 6) 612

הָרָה to conceive, become pregnant (4 · 38 · 40) 247

חָשׁ to make haste (2 · 15 · 21) 301 חוּשׁ

בַּז plunder, spoil (5 · 27) 103

בְּטֶרֶם 4 before (7 · 38) 382

אַט 6 gentleness; with ל = gently (1 · 5) 31

מָשׂוֹשׂ exultation (10 · 17) 965

עָצוּם 7 mighty (3 · 31) 783

אָפִיק channel, stream bed (1 · 18) 67

גָּדָה bank of river (1 · 4) 152

חָלַף 8 to move or sweep on, pass on quickly (4 · 14 · 26) 322

שָׁטַף to overflow (9 · 28 · 31) 1009

צַוָּאר neck (4 · 41) 848

7

מַטֶּה   outspreading (1 · 1) 642

מְלֹא   fullness, entire contents (5 · 38) 571

הַאֲזִין   9 to give ear, hear, listen (8 · 41 · 41) 24

מֶרְחָק   distant place (7 · 18) 935

הִתְאַזַּר   to gird oneself (2 · 3 · 16) 25

עוּץ   10 to plan (1 · 2 · 2) 734

הוּפַר   to be frustrated (1 · 3 · 45) 830

חֶזְקָה   11 strength, force (1 · 4) 305

יסר   to discipline (1 · 30 · 41) 415

קֶשֶׁר   12 conspiracy (2 · 16) 905

מוֹרָא   object of reverence (2 · 12) 432

הֶעֱרִיץ   to treat with awe (2 · 2 · 14) 791

מוֹרָא   13 object of reverence (2 · 12) 432

מַעֲרִיץ   awe inspirer (1 · 1) 793 ערץ

נֶגֶף   14 striking (1 · 7) 620

מִכְשׁוֹל   stumbling (2 · 14) 506

פַּח   bird trap (3 · 25) 809

מוֹקֵשׁ   lure (1 · 27) 430

נוּקַשׁ   15 to be ensnared (2 · 4 · 8) 430

תְּעוּדָה   16 testimony (2 · 3) 730

חתם   to seal up (3 · 23 · 27) 367

לִמֻּד   taught (4 · 6) 541

חִכָּה   17 to await, wait for (3 · 13 · 14) 314

קִוָּה   to wait for (13 · 39 · 45) 875

מוֹפֵת   18 sign [of future event] (2 · 36) 68

אוֹב   19 necromancer; i.e., medium (3 · 16) 15

יִדְּעֹנִי   familiar spirit (2 · 11) 396

צפצף   to chirp, peep (4 · 4 · 4) 861

הֶהְגָּה   to mutter; ptc. = one who makes mutterings (1 · 1 · 25) 211

תְּעוּדָה   20 testimony (2 · 3) 730

שַׁחַר   dawn (3 · 23) 1007

נקשה   21 to be hard pressed (1 · 1 · 28) 904

רָעֵב   hungry (5 · 19) 944

רָעֵב   to be hungry (5 · 12 · 14) 944

הִתְקַצֵּף   to put oneself in a rage (1 · 1 · 34) 893

לְמַעְלָה   upward (3 · 34) 75 מעל 2.c.

חֲשֵׁכָה   22 darkness, distress (2 · 6) 365

מְעוּף   gloom (1 · 1) 734

צוּקָה   distress (2 · 3) 848

אֲפֵלָה   darkness; fig. of calamity (3 · 10) 66

נדח   to be thrust (1 · 1 · 43) 623

מוּעָף   23 gloom (1 · 1) 734

לַאֲשֶׁר   to whom (4 · 38) 81 אֲשֶׁר 4.c.

מוּצָק   distress (1 · 3) 848

Chapter 9

צַלְמָוֶת   1 deep shadow, darkness (1 · 18) 853

נָגַהּ   to shine (1 · 3 · 6) 618

קָצִיר   2 harvest, time of harvest (7 · 49) 894

גִּיל   to rejoice (11 · 45 · 45) 162

עֹל   3 yoke (5 · 40) 760

סֹבֶל   burden (3 · 3) 687

שְׁכֶם   shoulder (5 · 22) 1014

נֹגֵשׂ   oppressor (5 · 15) 620

סְאוֹן   4 sandal, boot of soldier (1 · 1) 684

סאן   to tread, tramp (1 · 1 · 1) 684

רַעַשׁ   shaking (2 · 17) 950

שִׂמְלָה   wrapper, mantle (4 · 29) 971

גלל   to be rolled (1 · 1 · 17) 164

שְׂרֵפָה   burning (2 · 13) 977

מַאֲכֹלֶת   fuel (2 · 2) 38

מִשְׂרָה   5 rule, dominion (2 · 2) 976

שְׁכֶם   shoulder (5 · 22) 1014

פֶּלֶא   wonder (3 · 13) 810

יוֹעֵץ   counselor (5 · 22) 419

עַד   eternal, everlasting (8 · 48) 723 I & II עַד

מַרְבֵּה   6 increase (1 · 2) 916

מִשְׂרָה   rule, dominion (2 · 2) 976

סָעַד   to support (1 · 12 · 12) 703

קִנְאָה   zeal (7 · 43) 888

גַּאֲוָה   8 pride, haughtiness (5 · 19) 144

גֹּדֶל   greatness, pride, insolence [of heart] (2 · 14) 152

לְבֵנָה   9 brick (2 · 12) 527

גָּזִית	hewing, hewn stones (1 · 11) 159
שִׁקְמָה	sycamore tree (1 · 7) 1054
גָּדַע	to be hewn down (1 · 1 · 22) 154
הֶחֱלִיף	to substitute, cause to succeed (3 · 10 · 26) 322
שָׂגַב	10 to exalt (1 · 6 · 20) 960
סִכְסֵךְ	to prick or spur on (2 · 2 · 4[?]) 968, 1127
מֵאָחוֹר	11 behind [= on the west] (1 · 2[?]) 30
זָנָב	13 tail (4 · 11) 275
כִּפָּה	branch, frond (2 · 4[?]) 497
אַגְמוֹן	rush, bulrush [used as metaph. of the lowly] (3 · 5) 8
הוֹרָה	14 to teach (4 · 45[?] · 45[?]) 434
זָנָב	tail, end, stump (4 · 11) 275
אִשֵּׁר	15 to lead on (3 · 5 · 7) 80
הִתְעָה	to mislead (6 · 21 · 50) 1073
אֻשַּׁר	to be led on (1 · 1 · 7) 80
בֻּלַּע	to be swallowed up (1 · 1 · 6) 118
בָּחוּר	16 young man (6 · 45) 104
יָתוֹם	orphan (4 · 42) 450
רִחַם	to have compassion (12 · 42 · 47) 933
חָנֵף	profane, godless man (3 · 13) 338
מֵרַע	evildoer (4 · 18) 949
נְבָלָה	disgraceful folly (2 · 13) 615
רִשְׁעָה	17 wickedness (1 · 15) 958
שָׁמִיר	thorns (8 · 11) 1038
שַׁיִת	thorn bushes (7 · 7) 1011
יָצַת	to kindle (2 · 4 · 27) 428
סְבַךְ	thicket (2 · 3) 687
הִתְאַבֵּךְ	to roll, roll up (1 · 1 · 1) 5
גֵּאוּת	column, lifting up (5 · 8) 145
עָשָׁן	smoke (7 · 25) 798
עֶבְרָה	18 fury (6 · 34) 720
נֶעְתַּם	to be scorched, burned up [dub.] (1 · 1 · 1) 801
מַאֲכֹלֶת	fuel (2 · 2) 38
חָמַל	to spare, have compassion (22 · 40 · 40) 328
גָּזַר	19 to cut off (1 · 1 · 1[?]) 160

רָעֵב	to be hungry (5 · 12 · 14) 944

Chapter 10

חָקַק	1 to engrave, enact, decree (4 · 8 · 11) 349
דִּין	2 cause, plea, judgment (1 · 19) 192
דַּל	helpless, poor (5 · 48) 195
גָּזַל	to seize, rob, tear away (1 · 29 · 30) 159
יָתוֹם	orphan (4 · 42) 450
בָּזַז	to spoil, plunder (7 · 37 · 41) 102
פְּקֻדָּה	3 visitation (3 · 32) 824
שׁוֹאָה	devastation (2 · 12) 996
מֶרְחָק	distance מִמֶּרְחָק = from afar (7 · 18) 935
עֶזְרָה	help (4 · 26) 740
אָנָה	whither? (1 · 39) 33 אָן
בִּלְתִּי	4 except (2 · 24) 116
כָּרַע	to bow down (5 · 30 · 36) 502
אַסִּיר	[coll.] prisoners (4 · 17[?]) 64
זַעַם	5 indignation (5 · 22) 276
חָנֵף	6 profane, godless (3 · 13) 338
עֶבְרָה	fury (6 · 34) 720
שָׁלָל	to plunder (1 · 13 · 15) 1021
בָּזַז	to spoil, plunder (7 · 37 · 41) 102
בַּז	booty, spoil (5 · 27) 103
מִרְמָס	trampling (4 · 7) 942
חֹמֶר	clay, mire (5 · 17) 330
דָּמָה	7 to think, intend (5 · 13 · 27) 197
אֱלִיל	10 idolatrous, worthlessness (10 · 20) 47
פָּסִיל	idol (4 · 23) 820
אֱלִיל	11 pl. = worthless gods (10 · 20) 47
עָצָב	idol (2 · 17) 781
בָּצַע	12 to finish, complete, cut off (2 · 6 · 16) 130
גֹּדֶל	greatness, pride, insolence of heart (2 · 14) 152
תִּפְאֶרֶת	glorying, boasting (18 · 50) 802

רוּם loftiness, height; fig. of haughtiness (3 · 6) 927

גְּבוּלָה 13 border, boundary (2 · 10) 148

עָתִיד Q עָתִיד prepared; i.e., stores (1 · 1) 800

שׁוֹשֵׂתִי "I plundered"; שׁסה to plunder (1 · 1 · 5) 1042

אַבִּיר mighty (3 · 17) 7

קֵן 14 nest (2 · 13) 890

בֵּיצָה egg (3 · 6) 101

נדד to flutter, elsewhere = to flee, retreat (8 · 20 · 24) 622

פצה to open, part (1 · 15 · 15) 822

צפצף to chirp, peep (4 · 4 · 4) 861

הִתְפָּאר 15 to glorify oneself (5 · 7 · 13) 802

גַּרְזֶן axe (1 · 4) 173

חָצֵב to hew wood (4 · 14 · 17) 345

מַשּׂוֹר saw (1 · 1) 673

הֵנִיף to wield (5 · 32 · 34[?]) 631

מִשְׁמָן 16 fatness; stout, vigorous ones (2 · 4) 1032

רָזוֹן leanness (1 · 3) 931

יקד to be kindled (2 · 3 · 8) 428

יְקוֹד a burning (2 · 2) 423

לֶהָבָה 17 flame (5 · 19) 529

שַׁיִת thorn bushes (7 · 7) 1011

שָׁמִיר thorns (8 · 11) 1038

כַּרְמֶל 18 plantation, garden land (8 · 14[?]) 502

מסס to melt (1 · 1 · 21) 587

נסס to be sick (1 · 1 · 3[?]) 651

שְׁאָר 19 remainder (12 · 26) 984

שְׁאָר 20 remnant (12 · 26) 984

פְּלֵיטָה escaped remnant (5 · 28) 812

נִשְׁעָן to lean (5 · 22 · 22) 1043

שְׁאָר 21 remnant (12 · 26) 984

חוֹל 22 sand (2 · 22) 297

שְׁאָר remnant (12 · 26) 984

כִּלָּיוֹן annihilation (1 · 2) 479

חָרַץ to decide (1 · 5 · 10) 358

שָׁטַף to overflow (9 · 28 · 31) 1009

כָּלָה 23 complete destruction (2 · 22) 428

נֶחֱרָץ ptc. = decisive (2 · 5 · 10) 358

מִזְעָר 25 a little (4 · 4) 277

זַעַם indignation (5 · 22) 276

תַּבְלִית destruction (1 · 1) 115

שׁוֹט 26 scourge (1[?] · 8[?]) 1002

מַכָּה beating, scourging (5 · 48) 646

עֹרֵב raven (2 · 12) 788, 1126

סֵבֶל 27 burden (3 · 3) 687

שְׁכֶם shoulder (5 · 22) 1014

עֹל yoke (5 · 40) 760

צַוָּאר neck (4 · 41) 848

חֻבַּל to be ruined, broken (1 · 2 · 10) 287

מַעְבָּרָה 29 pass (2 · 8) 721

מָלוֹן lodging place (1 · 8) 533

חָרַד to be terrified (4 · 23 · 39) 353

צהל 30 to cry shrilly (1 · 1 · 8) 843

הִקְשִׁיב to give attention (8 · 45 · 46) 904

נדד 31 to retreat, flee (8 · 20 · 24) 622

העיז to bring into safety (1 · 4 · 5) 731

נוֹפֵף 32 to brandish (1 · 1 · 34[?]) 631

סֵעֵף 33 to lop off (1 · 1 · 1) 703

פֻּארָה [coll.] boughs (1 · 1) 802

מַעֲרָצָה awful shock, crash (1 · 1) 792

רָם high, exalted (7 · 31[?]) 926 רום

קוֹמָה height (2 · 45) 879

גָּדַע to hew, cut in two (1 · 5 · 22) 154

גָּבֹהַּ high, haughty (6 · 41) 147

שָׁפֵל to become low (10 · 11 · 30) 1050

נִקַּף 34 to be struck away (1 · 2[?] · 2) 668

סְבַךְ thicket (2 · 3) 687

אַדִּיר majestic one (3 · 27) 12

Chapter 11

חֹטֶר 1 branch, twig (1 · 2) 310

גֶּזַע stem, stock (2 · 3) 160

נֵצֶר sprout, shoot (3 · 4) 666

שֹׁרֶשׁ root (7 · 33) 1057

פָּרָה to bear fruit (4 · 22 · 29) 826

בִּינָה 2 understanding, object of knowledge (5 · 37) 108

יִרְאָה fear of God, reverence, piety (5 · 45) 432

הֵרִיחַ 3 to smell; metaph. = delight in [cf. Am 5:21] (1 · 11 · 14) 926

יִרְאָה fear, reverence, piety (5 · 45) 432

מִשְׁמָע thing heard (1 · 1) 1036

דַּל 4 reduced, weak, helpless (5 · 48) 195

מִישׁוֹר uprightness, level place (3 · 23) 449

עָנָו poor and weak (3[?] · 21[?]) 776

אֵזוֹר 5 waistcloth (3 · 14) 25

מָתְנַיִם loins (4 · 47) 608

חֲלָץ dual = loins (3 · 10) 323

זְאֵב 6 wolf (2 · 8) 255

נָמֵר leopard (1 · 6) 649

גְּדִי kid (1 · 16) 152

רָבַץ to lie down, stretch out (6 · 24 · 30) 918

עֵגֶל calf (2 · 35) 722

כְּפִיר young lion [old enough to hunt] (3 · 31) 498

מְרִיא fatling (2 · 8) 597

נָהַג to drive, conduct (3 · 20 · 30) 624

פָּרָה 7 heifer, cow (1 · 26) 831

דֹּב bear (2 · 12) 179

רָבַץ to lie down, stretch out (6 · 24 · 30) 918

אַרְיֵה lion (6 · 45) 71

תֶּבֶן straw, food for livestock (2 · 17) 1061

שִׁעֲשַׁע 8 to sport, take delight (1 · 3 · 6) 1044

יוֹנֵק suckling, babe (2[?] · 11[?]) 413 ינק

חֻר hole (2 · 2[?]) 359

פֶּתֶן venomous serpent, perh. cobra (1 · 6) 837

מְאוּרָה light-hole = den of great viper (1 · 1) 22

צִפְעוֹנִי a poisonous serpent (3 · 5) 861

גָּמַל to wean; ptc. pass. = weaned child (6 · 34 · 37) 168

הָדָה to stretch out (1 · 1 · 1) 213

דֵּעָה 9 knowledge (2 · 6) 395

שֹׁרֶשׁ 10 root (7 · 33) 1057

נֵס standard, ensign (10 · 21) 651

מְנוּחָה resting place (4 · 21) 629

שְׁאָר 11 remnant, remainder (12 · 26) 984

אִי coastlands [and islands] (17 · 36) 15

נֵס 12 standard, ensign (10 · 21) 651

נָדַח to be thrust out, banished; ptc. = banished one, outcast (5 · 11) 623

נָפַץ to disperse, be scattered (1 · 5 · 21 [?]) 659

קִנְאָה jealousy, rivalry (7 · 43) 888

צֹרֵר vexer, harasser (1 · 17) 865 III צור

קִנֵּא to be jealous of (1 · 30 · 34) 888

צָרַר to show hostility toward, treat with enmity (1 · 10 · 10) 865

עוּף 14 to fly (4 · 18 · 25) 733

בָּזַז to plunder, despoil (7 · 37 · 41) 102

מִשְׁלוֹחַ outstretching, sending (1 · 3) 1020

מִשְׁמַעַת subjects, obedient band (1 · 4) 1036

הֶחֱרִים 15 to devote to destruction, destroy (3 · 46 · 49) 355

הֵנִיף to shake, wave, brandish against (5 · 32 · 34) 631

עָיָם [dub.] glow (1 · 1) 744

נַעַל sandal, shoe (3 · 22) 653

מְסִלָּה 16 highway, public road (9 · 27) 700

שְׁאָר remnant, residue, remainder (12 · 26) 984

Chapter 12

אָנַף 1 to be angry (1 · 8 · 14) 60

פָּחַד 2 to be in dread (7 · 23 · 26) 808

זִמְרָה melody, song (1[?] · 4[?]) 274

שָׁאַב 3 to draw [water] (1 · 14 · 14) 980

שָׂשׂוֹן exultation, rejoicing, joy (6 · 22) 965

11

מַעְיָן spring (2 · 23) 745

עֲלִילָה 4 deed (1 · 24) 760

נִשְׂגָּב to be exalted, high (6 · 10 · 20) 960

זִמֵּר 5 to praise in song (1 · 43 · 43) 274

גֵּאוּת majesty; here as adv. = majestical-
ly (5 · 8) 145

צָהַל 6 to cry shrilly (3 · 7 · 8) 843

Chapter 13

מַשָּׂא 1 utterance, oracle (11 · 21) 672

נִשְׁפָּה 2 to be windswept, bare (1 · 1 · 2) 1045

נֵס standard, ensign (10 · 21) 651

הֵנִיף to wave [as a signal] (5 · 32 · 34) 631

נָדִיב noble, princely, generous (3 · 27)
622

עַלִּיז 3 exultant, jubilant (5 · 7) 759

גַּאֲוָה proud one, pride, haughtiness
(5 · 19) 144

דְּמוּת 4 likeness, similitude; here adverbial-
ly = in likeness of, like (2 · 25) 198

שָׁאוֹן roar, uproar, din (8 · 18) 981

מֶרְחָק 5 distant place, distance (7 · 18) 935

זַעַם indignation (5 · 22) 276

חִבֵּל to ruin, destroy (3 · 6 · 10) 287

הֵילִיל 6 to utter or make a howling, give a
howl (11 · 30 · 30) 410

שֹׁד devastation, ruin (6 · 25) 994

שַׁדַּי name of God = (1) self-sufficient,
(2) almighty, or (3) my sovereign
(1 · 48) 994 · 995

רָפָה 7 to sink, drop; of hands = to lose
heart, energy (2 · 14 · 45) 951

אֱנוֹשׁ man, mankind (8 · 42) 60

נָמֵס to melt, dissolve; of heart = faint,
grow fearful (3 · 19 · 21) 587

נִבְהַל 8 to be disturbed, dismayed, terrified
(2 · 24 · 39) 96

צִיר pang [writhing] (3 · 5) 852

חֵבֶל pains of travail, anguish (3 · 7) 286

חִיל to twist, writhe; fig. = be in
severe pain, anguish (9 · 30 · 47) 296

תָּמַהּ to be astounded (2 · 8 · 9) 1069

לַהַב flame; w. פֶּה = hot with excite-
ment (4 · 12) 529

אַכְזָרִי 9 cruel, cruelty (1 · 8) 470

עֶבְרָה overflowing rage, fury (6 · 34) 720

חָרוֹן [burning of] anger (2 · 41) 354

שַׁמָּה waste [of land] (3 · 39) 1031

חַטָּא sinner[s], sinful (3 · 19) 308

כּוֹכָב 10 star (3 · 37) 456

כְּסִיל Orion, or constellations of same
brilliancy (1 · 4) 493

הֵהֵלִיל to flash forth light, shine (1 · 4 · 4)
237

חָשַׁךְ to be dark, grow dark (2 · 11 · 17)
364

יָרֵחַ moon (3 · 27) 437

הִגִּיהַ to cause to shine (1 · 3 · 6) 618

תֵּבֵל 11 world (9 · 36) 385

גָּאוֹן exaltation, majesty, excellence
(12 · 49) 144

זֵד insolent one, insolent, presumptuous (1 · 13) 267

גַּאֲוָה pride, haughtiness (5 · 19) 144

עָרִיץ ruthless, terror-striking (7 · 20[?])
792

הִשְׁפִּיל to lay low, humiliate (6 · 19 · 30)
1050

הוֹקִיר 12 to make rare, precious (1 · 2 · 11)
429

אֱנוֹשׁ man (8 · 42) 60

פָּז refined, pure gold (1 · 9) 808

כֶּתֶם gold (1 · 9) 508

הִרְגִּיז 13 to cause to quake (3 · 7 · 41) 919

רָעַשׁ to quake, shake (2 · 21 · 29) 950

עֶבְרָה overflowing rage, fury (6 · 34) 720

חָרוֹן [burning of] anger (2 · 41) 354

צְבִי 14 gazelle (1 · 11) 840

הֻדָּח ptc. = chased, hunted (1 · 1 · 43) 623

12

נִדְקָר 15 to be pierced through, slain
(1 · 1 · 11) 201

נִסְפָּה to be caught up, captured; to be
swept away (1 · 9 · 18) 705

עוֹלֵל 16 child (1 · 11) 760

רֻטַּשׁ to be dashed in pieces (1 · 4 · 6) 936

נִשַׁסַּס to be plundered, rifled (1 · 2 · 5)
1042

נִשָּׁגַל to violate, ravish [Mass. regarded
verb obscene and subst. שכב]
(1 · 2 · 4) 993

רָטַשׁ 18 to dash in pieces (1 · 2 · 6) 936

רָחַם to have compassion, be compassionate (12 · 42 · 47) 933

חוּס to look with compassion or pity on
(1 · 24 · 24) 299

צְבִי 19 beauty, honor (7 · 18) 840

תִּפְאָרָה gloryïng, boasting, beauty, glory
(18 · 50) 802

גָּאוֹן exaltation, majesty, excellence
(12 · 49) 144

מַהְפֵּכָה overthrow (2 · 6) 246

נֵצַח 20 everlastingness; w. ל = forever
(7 · 43) 664

אהל to pitch one's tent (1 · 1 · 3) 14

הרביץ to cause to lie down (2 · 6 · 30)
918

רָבַץ 21 to lie down = make lair, abode
(6 · 24 · 30) 918

צִי a wild beast, desert-dweller, yelper
(3 · 6) 850

אֹחַ jackal (1 · 1) 28

יַעֲנָה ostrich (3 · 8) 419

שָׂעִיר satyr, demon [with he-goat form]
(2 · 4) 972 Note: שָׂעִיר is often used
as merely a he-goat 972 II

רקד to dance, leap (1 · 5 · 9) 955

ענה 22 to sing (1 · 13 · 16) 777 IV; but
perh. to dwell 732 עון

אִי jackal (2 · 3) 17

אַלְמוֹן → אַרְמוֹן castle, palace, citadel (5 · 33)
74

תַּן jackal (4 · 14) 1072

עֹנֶג daintiness, exquisite delight (2 · 2)
772

נִמְשַׁךְ to be prolonged, postponed, drawn
out (1 · 3 · 36) 604

Chapter 14

רִחַם 1 to have compassion, be compassionate (12 · 42 · 47) 933

נִלְוָה to join oneself or be joined [to]
(3 · 11 · 12) 530

נספח to attach oneself to (1 · 1 · 5) 705

שָׁבָה 2 to take captive; ptc. = captive,
captor (1 · 30 · 38) 985

שֹׁבֶה captive, captor (2 · 9) 985

רדה to have dominion, rule (2 · 22 · 23)
921

נֹגֵשׂ oppressor, tyrant (5 · 15) 620 נגשׂ

עֹצֶר 3 pain (1 · 3) 780

רֹגֶז disquiet, turmoil (1 · 7) 919

קָשֶׁה severe, hard (6 · 36) 904

מָשָׁל 4 parable, proverb (1 · 39) 605

נֹגֵשׂ oppressor, tyrant (5 · 15) 620 נגשׂ

מַדְהֵבָה → מַרְהֵבָה boisterous, raging behavior
(1 · 1) 923

מֹשֵׁל 5 ruler (4 · 24) 605 III (משׁל)

עֶבְרָה 6 overflowing rage, fury (6 · 34) 720

מַכָּה conquest, defeat [of enemy],
slaughter (5 · 48) 646

בִּלְתִּי not; here w. סרה = never-ceasing
(2 · 24) 116

סָרָה withdrawal, turning aside (1[?] · 1
[?]) 694

רדה to have dominion, rule (2 · 22 · 23)
921

מֻרְדָּף persecution (1 · 1) 923

בְּלִי adv. of negation, not (3 · 23) 115

13

חָשַׂךְ to hinder, withhold, refrain (3 · 26 · 28) 362

שָׁקַט 7 to be at peace, quiet (3 · 31 · 41) 1052

פצח to break forth with (6 · 7 · 7[?]) 822

רִנָּה ringing cry (9 · 33) 943

בְּרוֹשׁ 8 cypress, fir (5 · 20) 141

מֵאָז since, from that time (8 · 18) 23

רָגַז 9 to be excited, perturbed, agitated (6 · 30 · 41) 919

רְפָאִים shades, ghosts; name of dead in She ól (3 · 8) 952

עַתּוּד he-goat; here fig. of chiefs or princes (3 · 29) 800

נִמְשַׁל 10 to be like, similar (1 · 5 · 15) 605

גָּאוֹן 11 exaltation, majesty, excellence (12 · 49) 144

הֶמְיָה sound, music (1 · 1) 242

נֶבֶל portable harp, lute (2 · 27) 614

הוּצַע to be laid, spread (1 · 2 · 4) 426

רִמָּה worm [that feeds on the dead] (1 · 7) 942

מְכַסֶּה covering (2 · 4) 492

תּוֹלֵעָה worm, grub (3 · 41) 1069

הֵילֵל 12 shining one; i.e., star of the morning (1 · 1) 237

שַׁחַר dawn (3 · 23) 1007

נִגְדַּע to be hewn off, severed (2 · 7 · 22) 154

חלשׁ to disable, prostrate (1 · 3 · 3) 325

מִמַּעַל 13 with ל = on the top of, above (3 · 29) 751

כּוֹכָב star (3 · 37) 456

יַרְכָה remote part, extreme part, recesses (3 · 28) 438

עָב 14 dark cloud (7 · 30) 728

הדמה to make oneself like, become like (1 · 1 · 27) 198

יַרְכָה 15 remote part, recesses or innermost part (3 · 28) 438

הִשְׁגִּיחַ 16 to gaze (1 · 3 · 3) 993

הִרְגִּיז to cause to quake (3 · 7 · 41) 919

הִרְעִישׁ to cause to quake (1 · 7 · 29) 950

תֵּבֵל 17 world (9 · 36) 385

הָרַס to throw down, tear down (2 · 30 · 43) 248

אָסִיר prisoner (4 · 17[?]) 64

נֵצֶר 19 sprout, shoot (3 · 4) 666

נִתְעָב to be abhorred, rejected (1 · 3 · 22) 1073

לְבוּשׁ garment, clothing (3 · 47) 528

טען to be pierced; ptc. = pierced (1 · 1 · 1) 381

פֶּגֶר corpse, carcass (4 · 22) 803

הבוס to be trodden down; ptc. = trodden down (1 · 1 · 12) 101

יחד 20 to be united (1 · 2 · 3) 402

קְבוּרָה burial, grave (1 · 14) 869

מֵרַע evildoer (4 · 18) 949 רעע vb. de-nom.

מַטְבֵּחַ 21 place of slaughter (1 · 1) 371

תֵּבֵל world (9 · 36) 385

שְׁאָר 22 rest, residue, remainder (12 · 26) 984

נִין offspring, posterity (1 · 3) 630

נֶכֶד progeny, posterity (1 · 3) 645

מוֹרָשׁ 23 possession (1 · 3) 440

קִפֹּד porcupine (2-3) 891

אֲגַם troubled or muddy pool, marsh (4 · 8) 8

טאטא to sweep (1 · 1 · 1) 370

מַטְאֲטֵא broom (1 · 1) 370

דָּמָה 24 to imagine, think, intend (5 · 13 · 27) 197

בוס 25 to tread down, trample (2 · 7 · 12) 100

עֹל yoke (5 · 40) 760

סֹבֶל burden [always fig. of tyranny] (3 · 3) 687

שְׁכֶם shoulder (5 · 22) 1014

הֵפֵר 27 to frustrate, make ineffectual (4 · 42 · 45) 830

מַשָּׂא 28 utterance, oracle (11 · 21) 672 III

שֹׁרֶשׁ 29 root (7 · 33) 1057

נָחָשׁ serpent (4 · 31) 638

צֶפַע poisonous serpent (3 · 5) 861

שָׂרָף fiery serpent (4 · 7[?]) 977

עוֹפֵף to fly about, to and fro (3 · 5 · 25) 733

דַּל 30 reduced, poor; בכורי ד׳ = poor (5 · 48) 195

בֶּטַח security; with ל = securely (4 · 43) 105

רָבַץ to lie down, repose (6 · 24 · 30) 918

שֹׁרֶשׁ root (7 · 33) 1057

הֵילִיל 31 to make a howling, give a howl (11 · 30 · 30) 410

נָמוֹג to melt away, be helpless (1 · 8 · 17) 556

עָשָׁן smoke (7 · 25) 798

בדד to be separate, isolated; ptc. = straggler (1 · 3 · 3) 94

מוֹעֵד appointed place (1 · 1) 418

יסַד 32 to found (2 · 10 · 41) 414

חָסָה to seek refuge (3 · 37 · 37) 340

Chapter 15

מַשָּׂא 1 utterance, oracle (11 · 21) 672 III

נִדְמָה to be cut off, destroyed, ruined (3 · 12 · 16) 198

בְּכִי 2 weeping (8 · 32) 113

הֵילִיל to make a howling, to give a howl (11 · 30 · 30) 410

קָרְחָה baldness, bald spot [made in mourning] (3 · 11) 901

זָקָן beard (2 · 18) 278

גרע to diminish; ptc. pass. = diminished, clipped (1 · 14 · 22) 175

חגר 3 to gird on, bind on (3 · 44 · 44) 291

שַׂק sackcloth (8 · 48) 974

גָּג roof (3 · 29) 150

רְחוֹב broad open place, plaza (2 · 43) 932

הֵילִיל to make a howling, give a howl (11 · 30 · 30) 410

בְּכִי weeping (8 · 32) 113

חלץ 4 to equip for war; ptc. pass. = equipped one, warrior (1 · 17[?]) 323

הֵרִיעַ to cry out in distress (3 · 40 · 44) 929

ירע to quiver (1 · 1 · 1) 438

בָּרִיחַ 5 fugitive, fleeing (3 · 4[?]) 138

בְּרִיחַ bar [of city gates] (2 · 41) 138; but perh. בריח = fleeing, fugitive 138 I

מַעֲלֶה ascent (1 · 19) 751

בְּכִי weeping (8 · 32) 113

זְעָקָה cry, cry of distress (3 · 18) 227

שֶׁבֶר shattering, crushing, breaking (9 · 45) 991

עער = Pilp. form of עור, to rouse 735

מְשַׁמָּה 6 devastation, waste (1 · 8) 1031

חָצִיר grass (8 · 18) 348

דֶּשֶׁא grass (3 · 14) 206

יָרָק green thing, grass (2 · 8) 438

יִתְרָה 7 abundance, riches (1 · 2) 452

פְּקֻדָּה store, things laid up (3 · 32) 824

עֲרָבָה poplar, Euphrates poplar (2 · 5) 788

הִקִּיף 8 to go about, go around (1 · 16 · 17) 669

זְעָקָה cry of distress, outcry (3 · 18) 277

יְלָלָה howling (2 · 5) 410

פְּלֵיטָה 9 escaped remnant (5 · 28) 812

אַרְיֵה lion (6 · 45) 71

Chapter 16

כַּר 1 he-lamb; here lamb of ruler = tribute lamb (2 · 11) 503

מֹשֵׁל ruler (4 · 24) 605 III משל

נדד 2 to wander, stray (8 · 20 · 24) 622

קֵן nestling, nest (2 · 13) 890

מַעְבָּרָה ford, pass, passage (2 · 8) 721

פְּלִילָה 3 office of judge or umpire (1 · 1) 813

צָהֳרַיִם noon, midday (3 · 23) 843

נִדָּח banished one, outcast (5 · 11) 623
נדח

נָדַד to retreat, flee, stray; ptc. = fugitive (8 · 20 · 24) 622

נִדָּח 4 banished one, outcast (5 · 11) 623
נדח

הָוָה to become (1 · 5 · 5) 217

סֵתֶר hiding place (5 · 35) 712

אָפֵס to cease, fail, come to an end (2 · 5 · 5) 67

מֵץ squeezer, extortioner, oppressor (1 · 1) 568

שֹׁד devastation, ruin (6 · 25) 994

רֹמֵס trampler (1 · 1) 942 רָמַס

מָהִיר 5 prompt, quick, ready (1 · 4) 555

גָּאוֹן 6 pride [in bad sense] (12 · 49) 145

גֵּא proud, = גאה (1 · 1[?]) 144

גַּאֲוָה . majesty, pride (5 · 19) 144

עֶבְרָה arrogance, fury (6 · 34) 720

כֵּן veritable, true (1 · 24) 467

בַּד empty, idle talk (2 · 6) 95

הֵילִיל 7 to make a howling, give a howl (11 · 30 · 30) 410

אֲשִׁישָׁה raisin cake (1 · 5) 84

הָגָה to moan for, sigh (7 · 23 · 25) 211

נָכָא stricken (1 · 1) 644

שְׁדֵמָה 8 field (2 · 6) 995

אֻמְלַל to be or grow feeble, languish (6 · 15[?] · 15[?]) 51

הָלַם to smite, strike down, hammer (3 · 8 · 8) 240

שָׂרֵק vine tendrils [or clusters] (1 · 2) 977

תָּעָה to wander about, err (8 · 27 · 50) 1073

שְׁלֻחָה shoot, branch (1 · 1) 1020

נָטַשׁ to be spread abroad, let go (2 · 6 · 40) 644

בְּכִי 9 weeping (8 · 32) 113

רִוָּה to drench, water abundantly (3 · 6 · 14) 924

דִּמְעָה tears (3 · 23) 199

קַיִץ summer fruit, summer (2 · 20) 884

קָצִיר harvested crop, harvest (7 · 49) 894

הֵידָד shouting, shout (2 · 7) 212

גִּיל 10 rejoicing (1 · 8) 162

כַּרְמֶל garden land (8 · 14) 502

רֵעַע to utter a shout (1 · 1 · 44) 929

יֶקֶב wine press, wine vat (2 · 16) 428

הֵידָד shout, shouting (2 · 6) 212

מֵעֶה 11 internal organs, inward parts (4 · 32) 588

כִּנּוֹר lyre, stringed instrument (5 · 41) 490

הָמָה to murmur, growl, roar (5 · 33 · 33) 242

נִלְאָה 12 to weary oneself (3 · 10 · 19) 521

מֵאָז 13 in time past = of old (8 · 18) 23

שָׂכִיר 14 hireling, hired laborer (3 · 18) 969

נִקְלָה to be lightly esteemed (2 · 5 · 6) 885

שְׁאָר rest, residue, remainder, remnant (12 · 26) 984

מִזְעָר a remnant, very few, a little (4 · 4) 277

כַּבִּיר much, great, mighty (3[?] · 10[?]) 460

Chapter 17

מַשָּׂא 1 utterance, oracle (11 · 21) 672 III

מְעִי = עי ruin heap (1 · 1) 590

מַפֵּלָה ruin (3 · 3) 658

עֵדֶר 2 flock (3 · 39) 727

רָבַץ to lie down, lie (6 · 24 · 30) 918

הֶחֱרִיד to terrify (1 · 16 · 39) 353

מִבְצָר 3 fortress, stronghold (3 · 37) 131

שְׁאָר rest, remainder, residue (12 · 26) 984

נָדַל 4 to be brought low (1 · 8 · 8[?]) 195
דלל

מִשְׁמָן fatness (2 · 4) 1032

נָרְזָה to be made lean (1 · 1 · 2) 931

קָצִיר 5 what is harvested, crop (7 · 49) 894

קָמָה standing grain (2 · 10) 879

שִׁבֹּלֶת ear of grain (3[?] · 20[?]) 987 II

קצר to reap (2 · 24 · 24) 894 II

לקט to glean, gather up, pick up (1 · 21 · 37) 544

רְפָאִים shades, ghosts (3 · 8) 952 I

עוֹלֵלוֹת 6 gleaning [fig. of remnant] (2 · 6) 760

נֹקֶף striking off (2 · 2) 668

זַיִת olive tree, olive (2 · 38) 268

גַּרְגַּר berry (1 · 1) 176

אָמִיר top, summit (2 · 2[?]) 57

סָעִיף branch (2 · 2) 703

פרה to bear fruit; ptc. = fruit bearer (4 · 22 · 29) 826

שָׁעָה 7 to regard [w. trust], gaze [at] (5 · 12 · 15) 1043

שָׁעָה 8 to regard, gaze [at] (5 · 12 · 15) 1043

אֶצְבַּע finger (4 · 31) 840

אֲשֵׁרָה sacred tree or pole (2 · 40) 81

חַמָּן sun pillar [used in idolatrous worship] (2 · 8) 329

מָעוֹז 9 refuge, place of safety (10 · 36) 731

עֲזוּבָה ptc. as subst. = deserted region (>50) 737; 736 I עזב, Qal. 2.a.

חֹרֶשׁ wooded height (1 · 3) 361

אָמִיר top, summit (2 · 2)[?]) 57

יֵשַׁע 10 salvation, deliverance (5 · 36) 447

מָעוֹז place of safety (10 · 36) 731

נֶטַע plantation (3 · 4) 642

נַעֲמָן pleasantness; but perh. epithet of Adonis (1 · 1) 654

זְמוֹרָה twig, branch, shoot; זר = twigs of a strange one; i.e., of strange god (1 · 5) 274

נֶטַע 11 act of planting (3 · 4) 642

שגשג to fence carefully about (1 · 1 · 1[?]) 691 סוג ג

הפריח to cause to bud or sprout (1 · 5 · 34) 827

נֵד heap (1 · 6) 622

קָצִיר what is reaped, harvested; crop (7 · 49) 894 I

נַחֲלָה severe, sore (1 · 5[5]) 317 I

כְּאֵב pain (2 · 6) 456

אנש to be weak, sick; ptc. pass. = incurable (1 · 8 · 8[?]) 60

המה 12 to roar, murmur, growl (5 · 33 · 33) 242

שָׁאוֹן roar, din (8 · 18) 981

לְאֹם people (11 · 35) 522

כַּבִּיר great, mighty, much (3[?] · 10[?]) 460

נשאה to be in uproar (3 · 3 · 6) 980

לְאֹם 13 people (11 · 35) 522

שָׁאוֹן roar, din (8 · 18) 981

נשאה to be in uproar (3 · 3 · 6) 980

גָּעַר to rebuke (2 · 14 · 14) 172

מֶרְחָק distance, distant place; to a distance (7 · 18) 935

מֹץ chaff (3 · 8) 558

גַּלְגַּל whirl [of dust or chaff], whirlwind; dust (2 · 11) 165

סוּפָה storm wind (5 · 15) 693

בַּלָּהָה 14 calamity, destruction, terror (1 · 10) 117

בְּטֶרֶם before (7 · 39) 382

שֹׁסֶה plunderer, spoiler (1 · 7) 1042 שסה

בָּזַז to plunder, despoil (7 · 37 · 41) 102

Chapter 18

צִלְצָל 1 whirring, buzzing (1 · 1) 852

צִיר 2 envoy, messenger (2 · 6) 851

גֹּמֶא papyrus, paper reed (2 · 4) 167

קַל swift, fleet (4 · 13) 886

מֻשָּׁךְ to be long, drawn out; of persons = tall (2 · 3 · 36) 604

מרט ptc. = polished, smooth pual ptc. [G.K. 52S] (2 · 5 · 14) 599

17

נוֹרָא   fearful, wonderful (4 · 44) 431   ירא

הָלְאָה   onwards, further (2 · 13) 229

קַו   might [dub.] (16 · 25[?]) 876   קוקו

מְבוּסָה   downtreading, subjugation (3 · 3) 101

בזא   to divide, cut through (2 · 2 · 2) 102

תֵּבֵל   3 world (9 · 36) 385

נֵס   standard, ensign (10 · 21) 651

שָׁקַט   4 to be quiet, inactive (3 · 31 · 41) 1052

מָכוֹן   fixed place, established place (2 · 17) 467

חמם   חם = heat; to be or grow warm (5 · 23 · 26[?]) 328   חם

צַח   glowing, dazzling (2 · 4) 850

עָב   dark cloud (7 · 30) 728

טַל   mist, dew (3 · 31) 378

קָצִיר   harvest, time of harvest (7 · 49) 894

קָצִיר   5 time of harvest, harvest (7 · 49) 894

פֶּרַח   bud, sprout (2 · 17) 827

בֹּסֶר   unripe grapes (1 · 5) 126

גָּמַל   to become ripe (6 · 34 · 37) 168

נִצָּה   blossom (1 · 4) 665

זַלְזַל   tendrils (1 · 1) 272

מַזְמֵרָה   pruning knife (2 · 4) 275

נְטִישָׁה   twig, tendril (1 · 3) 644

הֵתַז   to strike away (1 · 1 · 1) 1064   תזז

עַיִט   6 bird[s] of prey (3 · 8) 743

קָץ   to spend the summer (1 · 1 · 23[?]) 884   II קיץ

חרף   to remain in harvest time (1 · 1 · 2 [?]) 358

הוֹבִיל   7 to be borne [carried] along (3 · 11 · 18) 384   יבל

שַׁי   gift [offered as homage] (1 · 3) 1009

מְשֻׁךְ   to be long, drawn out; of persons = tall (2 · 3 · 36) 604

מרט   polished, smooth; pual ptc. [G.K 52S] (2 · 5 · 14) 598

נוֹרָא   fearful, dreadful, wonderful (4 · 44) 431   ירא

הָלְאָה   onwards, further (2 · 13) 229

קַו   might [dub.] (16 · 25[?]) 876   קוקו

מְבוּסָה   downtreading, subjugation (3 · 3) 101

בזא   to divide, cut through (2 · 2 · 2) 102

Chapter 19

מַשָּׂא   1 utterance, oracle (11 · 21) 672   III

עָב   dark cloud (7 · 30) 728

קַל   swift, fleet (4 · 13) 886

נוּע   to tremble (6 · 22 · 38) 631

אֱלִיל   idolatrous worthlessness, worthless gods, idols (10 · 20) 47

נָמֵס   to melt, dissolve; of heart = to be faint, grow fearful (3 · 19 · 21) 587   מסס

סִכְסֵךְ   2 to prick or spur on [pilpel סכך] (2 · 2 · 4[?]) 1127

נבק   3 to be emptied [laid waste] (2 · 2 · 7) 132   בקק

בִּלַּע   to swallow up, engulf; i.e., confuse, confound (2 · 3 · 6[?]) 118

אֱלִיל   idolatrous worthlessness, worthless gods, idols (10 · 20) 47

אִטִּי   mutterer, whisperer of charms (1 · 1) 31

אוֹב   necromancer, one who seeks the dead for instruction (3 · 16) 15

יִדְּעֹנִי   familiar spirit (2 · 11) 396

סִכַּר   4 to shut up, deliver (1 · 1 · 3) 698

קָשֶׁה   severe, rough, hard (6 · 36) 904

עַז   formidable, fierce, mighty (4 · 22) 738

נשׁת   5 to be dried up (1[?] · 1[?] · 3[?]) 677

חרב   to be dried up (6 · 17 · 37[?]) 351

הִזְנִיחַ   6 to stink, emit stench (1 · 1 · 1) 276

דָּלַל   to be low (2 · 8 · 8[?]) 195

חרב   to be dried up (6 · 17 · 37[?]) 351

סוּף   rushes, reeds (1 · 4) 693

קָמַל to be decayed (2 · 2 · 2) 888

עָרָה 7 bare place [dub., LXX, reeds] (1 · 1) 788

מִזְרָע place of sowing, seedland (1 · 1) 283

נָדַּף to be driven, driven about (2 · 6 · 9) 623

אָנָה 8 to mourn (2 · 2 · 2) 58

דַּיָּג fisherman (1 · 2[?]) 186

אָבַל to mourn, lament (5 · 18 · 38) 5

חַכָּה hook, fishhook (1 · 3) 335

מִכְמֹרֶת net, fishing net (1 · 3) 485

אָמְלַל to languish, grow feeble (6 · 15 [?] · 15[?]) 51

פֵּשֶׁת 9 flax, linen (1 · 16) 833

שָׂרִיק carded, combed (1 · 1) 977

אָרַג to weave; ptc. = weaver (2 · 10[?]) 70

חוֹרָי white stuff (1 · 1) 301

שָׁת foundation, stay [of society] (2 [?] · 4[?]) 1011

דָּכָא to be crushed; ptc. = crushed, broken (2 · 4 · 18) 194

שֶׂכֶר hire, wages (1 · 2) 969

אָגֵם sad (1 · 1) 8

אֱוִיל 11 fool, foolish (2 · 26) 17

יוֹעֵץ counselor (5 · 22) 419

נִבְעַר to be brutish, stupid; ptc. = stupid, brutish (1 · 4 · 7) 129

אֵי 12 where? אַיָּם = where are they? (4 · 39) 32 אֵי

אֵפוֹא pray (2 · 15) 66

נוֹאַל 13 to become fools (1 · 4 · 4) 383 I יאל

נִשָּׁא to be beguiled (1 · 1 · 16) 674 II

הִתְעָה to cause to wander about (6 · 21 · 50) 1073

פִּנָּה corner [fig. for support, defense] (2 · 30) 819

מָסַךְ 14 pour, mix (2 · 5 · 5) 587

עִוְעִים distorting, רוח ע׳ = warped judgment (1 · 1) 730

הִתְעָה to cause to wander about (6 · 21 · 50) 1073

נִתְעָה to be made to wander about (1 · 2 · 50) 1073

שִׁכּוֹר drunken one, drunkard (4 · 13) 1016

קִיא vomit (2 · 3) 883

זָנָב 15 tail, end (4[?] · 11[?]) 275

כִּפָּה branch, frond [prob. of palm tree] (2 · 3) 497

אַגְמוֹן rush, bulrush [fig. = lowly persons] (3 · 5) 8

חָרַד 16 to be terrified, tremble (4 · 23 · 39) 353

פָּחַד to be in dread, to dread (7 · 23 · 26) 808

תְּנוּפָה a brandishing, swinging (2 · 30) 632

הֵנִיף to shake, wave, brandish against (5 · 32 · 34) 631 נוף

חָגָּא 17 reeling (1 · 1) 291

פָּחַד to be in dread, to dread (7 · 23 · 26) 808

הֶרֶס 18 overthrow, destruction; [word-play allusion to On–Heliopolis] (1 · 1) 249

מַצֵּבָה 19 pillar, sacred stone (1[?] · 36[?]) 663

לֹחֵץ 20 oppressor (1 · 4[?]) 537 לחץ

מוֹשִׁיעַ savior (9 · 27[?]) 446 ישב

נָדַר 21 to vow (1 · 31 · 31) 623

נָגַף 22 to strike, smite (2 · 25 · 48) 619

נֶעְתַּר to be supplicated, entreated (1 · 8 · 20) 801

מְסִלָּה 23 highway (9 · 27) 700

Chapter 20

תַּרְתָּן 1 field marshal, title of Assyrian general (1 · 2[?]) 1077

שַׂק 2 sackcloth (8 · 48) 974

מָתְנַיִם loins (4 · 47) 608

נַעַל sandal, shoe (3 · 22) 653

חָלַץ to draw, draw off (1 · 5 · 27) 322

עָרוֹם naked (4 · 16) 736

יָחֵף barefoot (3 · 5) 405

עָרוֹם 3 naked (4 · 16) 736

יָחֵף barefoot (3 · 5) 405

מוֹפֵת sign, token of future event, symbolic act (2 · 36) 68

נָהַג 4 to drive away, off; to conduct (3 · 20 · 30) 624

שְׁבִי captives [coll.] (4 · 49) 985

גָּלוּת exiles [coll.] (2 · 15) 163

עָרוֹם naked (4 · 16) 736

יָחֵף barefoot (3 · 5) 405

חֲשׂוּפַי stripped, bared (1 · 1[?]) 362 חשׂף

שֵׁת seat, buttocks (2[?] · 4[?]) 1059

מַבָּט 5 expectation, thing looked to for hope (2 · 3) 613

תִּפְאָרָה glorying, boasting; beauty, glory (18 · 50) 802

אִי 6 coast, border, region (17 · 36) 15

מַבָּט expectation, thing looked to for hope (2 · 3) 613

עֶזְרָה help, succor (4 · 26) 740

Chapter 21

מַשָּׂא 1 utterance, oracle (11 · 21) 672

סוּפָה storm wind (5 · 15) 693

חָלַף to move on, sweep on (4 · 14 · 26) 322

נוֹרָא fearful, dreadful; wonderful (4 · 44) 431

חָזוּת 2 vision (3 · 5) 303

קָשֶׁה severe, hard (6 · 36) 904

בָּגַד to act treacherously (12 · 49 · 49) 93

צוּר to shut in, besiege (3 · 31 · 31) 848

אֲנָחָה sighing, groaning (3 · 11) 58

מָתְנַיִם 3 loins [seat of keenest pain] (4 · 47) 608

חַלְחָלָה anguish (1 · 4) 298

צִיר pang, writhing (3 · 5) 852

נַעֲוָה to be bent, bowed down (1 · 4 · 17) 730

נִבְהַל to be disturbed, dismayed, terrified (2 · 24 · 39) 96

תָּעָה 4 to wander about (8 · 27 · 50) 1073

פַּלָּצוּת shuddering (1 · 4) 814

בָּעַת to overwhelm (1 · 13 · 16) 130

נֶשֶׁף twilight (3 · 12) 676

חֵשֶׁק desire (1 · 4) 366

חֲרָדָה trembling, fear, anxiety (1 · 9) 353

צָפֹה 5 to lay out (1 · 9 · 18) 860

צָפִית rug, carpet (1 · 1) 860

צָפָה 6 to keep watch; ptc. = watchman (1 · 9 · 18) 859

צֶמֶד 7 pair, couple (3 · 15) 855

הִקְשִׁיב to give attention [or cause to give attention] (8 · 45 · 46) 904

קֶשֶׁב attentiveness (2 · 4) 904

אַרְיֵה 8 lion (6 · 45) 71

מִצְפֶּה watchtower (1 · 2) 859

צֶמֶד 9 pair, couple (3 · 15) 855

פָּסִיל idol, image (4 · 23) 820

מְדֻשָׁה 10 that which is threshed (1 · 1) 190

גֹּרֶן threshing floor (1 · 34) 175

מַשָּׂא 11 utterance, oracle (11 · 21) 672

דּוּמָה = Edom [name of Edom with a mystic ring; e.g., silence of death, desolation] 189

מַה מִּלַּיְלָה [idiom] how much of the night is past? 552 מַה 1.a.

אָתָה 12 to come (9 · 19 · 21) 87

בָּעָה to seek, inquire (2 · 2 · 4) 126

מַשָּׂא 13 utterance, oracle (11 · 21) 672

אֹרְחָה traveling company, caravan (1 · 3) 73

צָמֵא 14 thirsty one, thirsty (5 · 9) 854

הֵאֵתָה to bring (1 · 2 · 21) 87

קִדֵּם to come to meet (2 · 24 · 26) 869

נָדַד to retreat, flee; ptc. = fugitive (8 · 20 · 24) 622

נָדַד 15 to retreat, flee (8 · 20 · 24) 622

נָטַשׁ to leave, forsake, permit (2 · 33 · 40) 643

כֹּבֶד vehemence, heaviness (2 · 4) 458

בְּעוֹד 16 within yet (3 · 20) 728   עוֹד, 2.a.

שָׂכִיר hireling, hired laborer (3 · 18) 969

שְׁאָר 17 rest, residue, last remnant (12 · 26) 984

מעט to become few, small (1 · 8 · 22) 589

Chapter 22

מַשָּׂא 1 utterance, oracle (11 · 21) 672

גַּיְא valley (5 · 47) 161

חִזָּיוֹן vision (2 · 9) 303

אֵפוֹא pray [enclitic part.] (2 · 15) 66

גַּג roof (3 · 29) 150

תְּשֻׁאוֹת 2 noise (1 · 4) 996   תְּשֻׁאָה

הָמָה to be in commotion, stir [roar, murmur] (5 · 33 · 33) 242

קִרְיָה town, city (10 · 30) 900

עַלִּיז jubilant, exultant (5 · 7) 759

קָצִין 3 ruler, chief (4 · 12) 892

נדד to retreat, flee (8 · 20 · 24) 622

יַחַד all together (7 · 44) 403

מֵרָחֹק to a distance, at a distance (12 · 34) 935   רָחֹק 2.a.(3).

שָׁעָה 4 to gaze; w. מִן = to turn gaze away (5 · 12 · 15) 1043

מרר to show bitterness (1 · 3 · 16) 600

בְּכִי weeping (8 · 32) 113

האיץ to hasten (1 · 2 · 10) 21

שֹׁד devastation, ruin (6 · 25) 994

מְהוּמָה 5 discomfiture, disquietude (1 · 12) 223

מְבוּסָה downtreading, subjugation (3 · 3) 101

מְבוּכָה confusion (1 · 2) 100

גַּיְא valley (5 · 47) 161

חִזָּיוֹן vision (2 · 9) 303

קרקר to tear down (1 · 1 · 3) 903   II קרר

שׁוֹעַ cry; perh. war cry, cry for help (1 · 1) 1003

אַשְׁפָּה 6 quiver for arrows (2 · 6) 80

עֵרָה to lay bare (2 · 9 · 15) 788

מִבְחַר 7 choicest, best (2 · 12) 104

מָסָךְ 8 covering, fig. for protection; eye-screen (1 · 25) 697

נֶשֶׁק equipment, weapons (1 · 10) 676

בְּקִיע 9 fissure, breach (1 · 2) 132

רבב to be [become] many (4 · 23 · 24) 912   I רבב

בְּרֵכָה pool, pond (4 · 17) 140

תַּחְתּוֹן lower (1 · 13) 1066

נָתַץ 10 to pull down (1 · 31 · 42) 683

נבצר to fortify (1 · 2 · 4[?]) 130

מִקְוָה 11 reservoir (1 · 1) 876

בְּרֵכָה pool, pond (4 · 17) 140

יָשָׁן old (1 · 8) 445

עֹשֶׂה maker, creator (6 · 24[?]) 793   I עשה

יָצַר to form, fashion; fig. for frame, preordain, plan (22 · 41 · 44) 427

מֵרָחֹק long ago, at a distance (12 · 34) 935

בְּכִי 12 weeping (8 · 32) 113

מִסְפֵּד wailing (1 · 16) 704

קָרְחָה baldness (3 · 11) 901

חגר to gird on, bind on (3 · 44 · 44) 291

שַׂק sackcloth (8 · 48) 974

שָׂשׂוֹן 13 exultation, joy (6 · 22) 965

סֹכֵן 15 servitor, steward (1 · 3[?]) 698   סכן

פֹּה 16 here (2 · 44) 805

מַה לְּךָ פֹה [idiom] what have you here? 552   מה, 1.a.(d).

מִי לְךָ פֹה [idiom] who do you have here? 552

חָצֵב to hew out (4 · 14 · 17) 345

חקק to cut in, inscribe (4 · 8 · 11) 349

טלטל 17 to hurl, cast (1 · 1 · 14) 376,   טול

טַלְטֵלָה a hurling (1 · 1) 376

עטה to grasp; inf. abs. + ptc. = grasp forcibly (2 · 4 · 4) 742

צָנַף 18 to wind up, wrap (2 · 3 · 3) 857

צְנֵפָה winding (1 · 1) 857

דּוּר ball, circle (2 · 2) 189

רָחָב — wide, broad (2 · 21) 932

רַחֲבָה יָדַיִם — [idiom] = wide on both hands = wide in both directions 388 יָד 3.d.

מֶרְכָּבָה — chariot (3 · 44) 939

קָלוֹן — dishonor, disgrace (1 · 17) 885

הָדַף — 19 to depose, thrust out (1 · 11 · 11) 213

מַצָּב — station, office (1 · 10) 662

מַעֲמָד — station, office, post (1 · 5) 765

הָרַס — to cast down, throw down (2 · 30 · 43) 248

כֻּתֹּנֶת — 21 tunic (1 · 29) 509

אַבְנֵט — girdle (1 · 9) 126

מֶמְשָׁלָה — rule, dominion (2 · 17) 606

מַפְתֵּחַ — 22 key (1 · 3) 836

שְׁכֶם — shoulder (5 · 22) 1014

יָתֵד — 23 peg (4 · 23) 450

תָּלָה — 24 to hang, hang up (1 · 23 · 27) 1067

צֶאֱצָא — offspring (7 · 11) 425

צְפִיעָה — offshoot [dub.] (1 · 1) 861

קָטָן — small size, small (2 · 47) 881

אַגָּן — bowl (1 · 3) 8

נֵבֶל — [earthen] jar, pitcher (2 · 11) 614

מוּשׁ — 25 to depart, remove (5 · 20[?] · 20[?]) 559

יָתֵד — peg (4 · 23) 450

נִגְדַּע — to be hewn off (2 · 7 · 22) 154

מַשָּׂא — load, burden (3 · 42) 672

Chapter 23

מַשָּׂא — 1 utterance, oracle (11 · 21) 672

הֵילִיל — to howl (11 · 30 · 30) 410

אֳנִיָּה — ship (5 · 31) 58

דָּמַם — 2 to be struck dumb, be astounded, be silent (1 · 23 · 30) 198 דָּמַם I

אִי — coast, region (17 · 36) 15

סֹחֵר — trafficker, trader (3 · 16) 695 סחר

שִׁיחוֹר — 3 Nile (1 · 4) 1009

קָצִיר — harvested crop, harvest (7 · 49) 894

תְּבוּאָה — income, revenue (2 · 43) 100

סַחַר — traffic, gain from traffic (4 · 8) 695

מָעוֹז — 4 place of safety, harbor (10 · 36) 731

חוּל — to twist, writhe (9 · 30 · 47) 297

בָּחוּר — young man (6 · 45) 104

בְּתוּלָה — virgin (5 · 50) 143

שֵׁמַע — 5 report, tidings (3 · 17) 1034

חוּל — to be in severe pain, anguish (9 · 30 · 47) 297

הֵילִיל — 6 to howl (11 · 30 · 30) 410

אִי — coast, region (17 · 36) 15

עַלִּיז — 7 exultant, jubilant (5 · 7) 759

קַדְמָה — antiquity, beginning (1 · 6) 870

הֵיבִל — to carry away (1 · 7 · 18) 384

מֵרָחֹק — to a distance, at a distance (12 · 34) 935

הֶעֱטִיר — 8 to bestow a crown (1 · 1 · 7) 742

סֹחֵר — trafficker, trader (3 · 16) 695 סחר

כְּנַעֲנִי — trader, merchant (1 · 4) 489, 1124

גָּאוֹן — 9 exaltation, majesty, excellence; pride (12 · 49) 144

צְבִי — beauty, decoration (7 · 18) 840

מֵזַח — 10 girdle [dub.]; fig. for restraint (1 · 1) 561

הִרְגִּיז — 11 to shake, cause to quake (3 · 7 · 41) 919

מָעוֹז — place of safety, fastness (10 · 36) 731

עָלַז — 12 to exult, triumph (1 · 16 · 16) 759

עָשַׁק — to be crushed (1 · 1 · 37) 798

בְּתוּלָה — virgin (5 · 50) 143

יָסַד — 13 to appoint, establish (5 · 20 · 41) 413

צִי — wild beast, desert dweller (3 · 6) 850

בָּחוּן — siege tower (1 · 1) 103

עוֹרֵר — to lay bare (1 · 1 · 4) 792 II

אַרְמוֹן — palace, castle, citadel (5 · 33) 74

מַפֵּלָה — ruin (3 · 3) 658

הֵילִיל — 14 to howl (11 · 30 · 30) 410

אֳנִיָּה — ship (5 · 31) 58

מָעוֹז — place of safety, fastness (10 · 36) 731

22

שִׁירָה 15 song, ode (2 · 13) 1010

זוֹנָה harlot (3 · 33[?]) 275 זנה

כִּנּוֹר 16 lyre (5 · 41) 490

זוֹנָה harlot (3 · 33[?]) 275 זנה

נִגֵּן to play a stringed instrument (2 · 13 · 14) 618

אֶתְנַן 17 hire of harlot (2 · 11) 1072

סַחַר 18 traffic, gain (4 · 18) 695

אֶתְנַן hire of harlot (2 · 11) 1072

נֶאֱצַר to be stored up (1 · 1 · 5) 69

נֶחְסָן to be treasured up, hoarded (1 · 1 · 1) 1123   (340 b)

שָׂבְעָה satiety, one's fill (3 · 7[?]) 960

מְכַסֶּה covering (2 · 4) 492

עָתִיק eminent, surpassing (1 · 1) 801

Chapter 24

בקק 1 to empty, lay waste (1 · 4 · 7) 132

בלק to lay waste [Pual ptc.] (1 · 1 · 2) 118

עָוָּה to distort, twist (1 · 2 · 17) 730

גְּבֶרֶת 2 mistress (3 · 15) 150

קוֹנֶה buyer (2 · 7) 888 קנה

הלוה to cause to borrow, lend (1 · 9 · 14) 530   II לוה

לוה to borrow (1 · 5 · 14) 530   II

נשה to lend; ptc. = creditor (1 · 10 · 12) 674 I

נשא creditor (1 · 5) 673 נשא

נבק 3 to be emptied (2 · 2 · 7) 132   II בקק

תִּבּוֹז to be spoiled, plundered; here = Niph. impf. 2 ms. (2 · 3 · 41) 102 בזז

אָבַל 4 to mourn (5 · 18 · 38) 5

נָבֵל to droop, wither and fall, fade (11 · 21 · 25) 615

אֻמְלַל to be or grow feeble, languish (6 · 15[?] · 15[?]) 51

תֵּבֵל world (9 · 36) 385

חנף 5 to be polluted (1 · 6 · 10) 337

חָלַף to overstep, transgress, pass on (4 · 14 · 26) 322

הֵפֵר to break, violate (4 · 42 · 45) 830   I פור

אָלָה 6 curse (1 · 36) 46

אָשֵׁם to be held guilty, be guilty (1 · 31 · 33) 79

חר to burn, be burned (1 · 3 · 9) 359   I חרר

אֱנוֹשׁ men (8 · 42) 60

מִזְעָר a little; מְעַט מִזְעָר = a very little while (4 · 4) 277

אָבַל 7 to mourn (5 · 18 · 38) 5

תִּירוֹשׁ fresh or new wine (4 · 38) 440

אֻמְלַל to be or grow feeble, languish (6 · 15[?] · 15[?]) 51

נֶאֱנַח to sigh (1 · 12 · 12) 58

שָׂמֵחַ glad, joyful, merry (1 · 21) 970

מָשׂוֹשׂ 8 exultation (10 · 17) 965

תֹּף timbrel, tambourine (3 · 17) 1074

שָׁאוֹן uproar (8 · 18) 981

עַלִּיז exultant, jubilant (5 · 7) 759

כִּנּוֹר lyre (5 · 41) 490

מַר 9 to be bitter (1 · 6 · 16) 600 מרר

שֵׁכָר intoxicating drink, strong drink (8 · 23) 1016

קִרְיָה 10 town, city (10 · 30) 900

תֹּהוּ formlessness, primeval chaos (11 · 20) 1062

צְוָחָה 11 outcry (1 · 4) 846

ערב to grow dark, become evening (1 · 2 · 3) 788

מָשׂוֹשׂ exultation (10 · 17) 965

שַׁמָּה 12 a waste (3 · 39) 1031

שְׁאִיָּה ruin (1 · 1) 981

הֻכַּת to be crushed (1 · 4 · 17) 510 כתת

נֹקֶף 13 striking off (2 · 2) 668

זַיִת olive tree (2 · 38) 268

עוֹלֵלוֹת gleaning (2 · 6) 760

בָּצִיר vintage (2 · 7) 131

23

גָּאוֹן   14 exaltation, majesty (12 · 49) 144

צהל   to cry shrilly (3 · 7 · 8) 843

אֻרִים 15 region of light, East (5 · 6[?]) 22

אִי   coastland, island (17 · 36) 15

זָמִיר 16 song (2 · 6) 274

צְבִי   honor (7 · 18) 840

רָזִי   leanness, wasting (2 · 2) 931

אוֹי   Woe! Alas! (4 · 25) 17

בָּגַד   to act treacherously; ptc. = treacherous one (12 · 49 · 49) 93

בֶּגֶד   treachery (1 · 2) 93

פַּחַד 17 dread (5 · 49) 808

פַּחַת   pit (3 · 10) 809

פַּח   bird trap (3 · 25) 809

פַּחַד 18 dread (5 · 49) 808

פַּחַת   pit (3 · 10) 809

פַּח   bird trap (3 · 25) 809

אֲרֻבָּה   lattice, window (2 · 9) 70

רעש   to quake, shake (2 · 21 · 29) 950

מוֹסָד   foundation (3 · 13) 414

רֹעָה 19 breaking (1 · 1) 949   II רעע

התרעע   to be broken in pieces (1 · 2 · 5[?]) 949   II רעע

פרר   to split, divide (1 · 1 · 4) 830

התפורר   to be cracked through (1 · 1 · 4) 830   II פרר

מוט   to totter, shake (3 · 15 · 39) 556

התמוטט   to be shaken (1 · 1 · 39) 556 מוט

נוע 20 to tremble (6 · 22 · 38) 631

שִׁכּוֹר   drunken one, drunken (4 · 13) 1016

התנודד   to sway, totter (1 · 4 · 27) 626 נוד

מְלוּנָה   hut; frail, insecure structure (2 · 2) 534

אֲסֵפָה 22 gathering (1 · 1) 63

אַסִּיר   prisoners (4 · 17[?]) 64

מַסְגֵּר   dungeon (2 · 7) 689

חפר 23 to be abashed, ashamed (2 · 13 · 17) 344

לְבָנָה   moon [poet.] (2 · 3) 526

חַמָּה   sun, heat (3 · 6) 328

Chapter 25

פֶּלֶא 1 wonder (3 · 13) 810

מֵרָחֹק   long ago, of long standing (12 · 34) 935

אֹמֶן   faithfulness; אֱמוּנָה אֹמֶן = perfect faithfulness (1 · 1) 53

גַּל 2 heap (2 · 20) 164

קִרְיָה   town, city (10 · 30) 900

בָּצוּר   cut off, made inaccessible (5 · 25) 130 בצר

מַפֵּלָה   ruin (3 · 3) 658

אַרְמוֹן   palace, castle, citadel (5 · 33) 74

עַז 3 fierce, formidable, strong (4 · 22) 738

קִרְיָה   town, city (10 · 30) 900

עָרִיץ   awe inspiring; terror striking (7 · 20) 792

מָעוֹז 4 refuge (10 · 36) 731

דַּל   poor (5 · 48) 195

צַר   distress, straits (6 · 21[?]) 865 II צר

מַחְסֶה   shelter, refuge (4 · 20) 340

זֶרֶם   rain storm (7 · 9) 281

חֹרֶב   parching heat (5 · 16) 351

עָרִיץ   awe inspiring; terror striking (7 · 20) 792

חֹרֶב 5 parching heat (5 · 16) 351

צָיוֹן   dryness, parched ground (2 · 2) 851

שָׁאוֹן   roar, din (8 · 18) 981

הִכְנִיעַ   to humble (1 · 11 · 35) 488

עָב   dark cloud (7 · 30) 728

זָמִיר   song (2 · 6) 274

עָרִיץ   awe inspiring; terror striking (7 · 20) 792

מִשְׁתֶּה 6 feast (3 · 45) 1059

שֶׁמֶר   dregs (2 · 5) 1038

מחה   ptc. only = full of marrow (1 · 1 · 1) 526 IV מחה

זקק   to be refined; here = Pual. ptc. = refined (1 · 4 · 7) 279

בִּלַּע 7 to swallow up, engulf (3 · 20 · 41) 118

לוֹט envelope, covering (1 · 1) 532

לוֹט to cover, enwrap, envelop (1 · 3 · 4) 532

מַסֵּכָה woven stuff, web (2[?] · 2[?]) 651

נָסַךְ to weave (1 · 1 · 1) 651

בִּלַּע 8 to swallow up, engulf (3 · 20 · 41) 118

נֶצַח everlastingness; w. לְ = forever (7 · 43) 664

מָחָה to wipe, wipe out (3 · 22 · 34) 562   I

דִּמְעָה tears (3 · 23) 199

קִוָּה 9 to wait or look eagerly for (13 · 39 · 45) 875

גִּיל to rejoice (11 · 45 · 45) 162

נָדוֹשׁ 10 to be trampled down (2 · 2 · 16) 190

מַתְבֵּן straw heap (1 · 1) 1062

בְּמִי = בְּמוֹ poetic for בְּ (4 · 10) 91

מַדְמֵנָה dung place, dung pit (1 · 1) 198

שָׂחָה 11 to swim (2 · 2 · 3) 965

הִשְׁפִּיל to lay low (6 · 19 · 30) 1050

גַּאֲוָה pride, haughtiness (5 · 19) 144

אָרְבָּה tricks, artifice (1 · 1) 70

מִבְצָר 12 fortress, stronghold (3 · 37) 131

מִשְׂגָּב stronghold, secure height, retreat (2 · 17) 960

הֵשַׁח to prostrate, lay low (2 · 2 · 18[?]) 1005   שחח

הִשְׁפִּיל to lay low, humiliate (6 · 19 · 30) 1050

Chapter 26

חֵל 1 rampart, little wall, fortress (1 · 9) 298

יֵצֶר 3 purpose, device, imagination (2 · 9) 428

סָמַךְ to sustain, uphold (4 · 41 · 48) 701

בָּטוּחַ trusted, trusts (1 · 2[?]) 105 I בטח

עֲדֵי 4 as far as, until (poetic for עד) (1 · 12) 723 III עד

עַד forever, eternity (8 · 48) 723 I עד

עֲדֵי־עַד continuous existence, forever 723 [see above]

הֵשַׁח 5 to prostrate, lay low (2 · 2 · 18[?]) 1005

קִרְיָה town, city (10 · 30) 900

נִשְׂגָּב to be high (6 · 10 · 20) 960

הִשְׁפִּיל to lay low (6 · 19 · 30) 1050

רָמַס 6 to trample down (4 · 17 · 18) 942

דַּל reduced, weak, helpless (5 · 48) 195

מֵישָׁר 7 evenness, level (3 · 19) 449

מַעְגַּל track, course of action or life (2 · 13) 722

פִּלֵּס to make level, smooth (1 · 6 · 6) 814

קִוָּה 8 to wait or look eagerly for (13 · 39 · 45) 875

זֵכֶר memorial, memory (2 · 23) 271

תַּאֲוָה desire, wish (1 · 21) 16

אִוָּה 9 to desire (1 · 11 · 27) 16

שִׁחֵר to seek (2 · 12 · 13) 1007

תֵּבֵל world (9 · 36) 385

נָכֹחַ 10 true, honest, straight (4 · 8) 647

עִוֵּל to act wrongfully (1 · 2 · 2) 732

גֵּאוּת majesty (5 · 8) 145

רָם 11 high, exalted (7 · 31[?]) 926 רום

קִנְאָה [ardor of] anger (7 · 43) 888

שָׁפַת 12 to ordain, establish (1 · 5 · 5) 1046

בְּעָל 13 to rule over; to marry (4 · 10 · 12) 127

זוּלָה other than (4 · 16) 265

רְפָאִים 14 shades, ghosts (3 · 8) 952

זֵכֶר remembrance, memory (2 · 23) 271

קָצוּ 15 end, boundary (1 · 3) 892

צַר 16 straits, distress (5[?] · 20[?]) 865

צוּק to pour out (1 · 3 · 3) 848

לַחַשׁ whisper of prayer, whisper, charm (3 · 5) 538

מוּסָר chastening, chastisement (2 · 50) 416

הָרָה	17	pregnant (2 · 15) 247
חוּל		to twist, writhe (9 · 30 · 47) 296
חֵבֶל		pain, pang (3 · 7) 286
הָרָה	18	to conceive, become pregnant (4 · 38 · 40) 247
חוּל		to twist, writhe (9 · 30 · 47) 296
תֵּבֵל		world (9 · 36) 385
נְבֵלָה	19	corpse, carcass (2 · 48) 615
הֵקִיץ		to awake (3 · 22 · 23) 884 I קיץ
טַל		dew, night mist (3 · 31) 378
אוֹרָה		herb (1 · 2) 21
רְפָאִים		shades, ghosts; here of righteous (3 · 8) 952
הִפִּיל		[idiom] bring to life [drop one's young] (>50) 658 נפל 6.
חֶדֶר	20	chamber, room (1 · 37) 293
חבה		to withdraw, hide (1 · 1 · 4) 285
רֶגַע		moment (5 · 22) 921
זַעַם		indignation (5 · 22) 276

Chapter 27

קָשֶׁה	1	fierce, relentless, severe (6 · 36) 904
לִוְיָתָן		serpent, dragon, leviathon (2 · 6) 531
נָחָשׁ		serpent (4 · 31) 638
בָּרִחַ		fleeing (2 · 3) 138
עֲקַלָּתוֹן		crooked (1 · 1) 785
תַּנִּין		sea monster, serpent, dragon (2 · 15) 1072
חֶמֶר	2	wine (1 · 2) 330
ענה		to sing sweetly (1 · 3 · 16) 777
רֶגַע	3	moment; לְ + pl. = every moment (5 · 22) 921
שָׁמִיר	4	thorns, thorn bushes (8 · 11) 1038
שַׁיִת		thorn bushes (7 · 7) 1011
פשׂע		to step, march (1 · 1 · 1) 832
הִצִּית		to kindle, set on fire (1 · 1 · 1[?]) 428 יצת
יַחַד		altogether (7 · 44) 403

מָעוֹז	5	refuge (10 · 36) 731
הִשְׁרִישׁ	6	to take root (1 · 3 · 8)a 1057
צִיץ		to blossom (1 · 7 · 8) 847
פָּרַח		to bud, sprout (5 · 28 · 34) 827
תֵּבֵל		world (9 · 36) 385
תְּנוּבָה		fruit, produce (1 · 5) 626
מַכָּה		blow, wound, slaughter (5 · 48) 646
הֶרֶג		slaughter (2 · 5) 247
סאסא	8	to drive away (1 · 1 · 1) 684
הָגָה		to remove (1 · 3 · 3) 212
קָשֶׁה		severe, hard (6 · 36) 904
גִּר	9	chalk, lime (1 · 1) 162
נפץ		to be pulverized (1 · 1 · 21) 658
אֲשֵׁרָה		sacred trees or poles; symbol of Canaanitish goddess of fortune (2 · 40) 81
חַמָּן		sun pillar, used in idolatrous worship (2 · 8) 329
בצר	10	to cut off, make inaccessible; ptc. = cut off, made inaccessible; fortified (5 · 25 · 25) 130
בָּדָד		isolation, separation (1 · 11) 94
נָוֶה		habitation (6 · 45) 627
עֵגֶל		calf (2 · 35) 722
רָבַץ		to lie down (6 · 24 · 30) 918
סָעִיף		branches, boughs (2 · 2) 703
קָצִיר	11	boughs, branches (1 · 5) 894 II
הֵאִיר		to light [ignite] (2 · 24 · 40) 21 אור
בִּינָה		understanding (5 · 37) 108
רחם		to have compassion, be compassionate (12 · 42 · 47) 933
עֹשֶׂה		maker, creator (6 · 24) 793 I עשׂה
יָצַר		to form, fashion (22 · 41 · 44) 427
חבט	12	to beat out (1 · 4 · 5) 286
שִׁבֹּלֶת		flowing stream (3[?] · 20[?]) 987 I
לקט		to be picked up (1 · 1 · 37) 544
נִדָּח	13	banished one, outcast (5 · 11) 623 נדח

26

Chapter 28

עֲטָרָה	1	crown (4 · 23) 742
גֵּאוּת		majesty (5 · 8) 145
שִׁכּוֹר		drunken one, drunken (4 · 13) 1016
צִיץ		blossom, flower (4 · 15) 847
נָבֵל		to wither and fall, fade (11 · 21 · 25) 615
צְבִי		beauty, decoration (7 · 18) 840
תִּפְאָרָה		beauty, finery, glory (18 · 50) 802
גַּיְא		valley (5 · 47) 161
הלם		to smite down, strike down, hammer (3 · 8 · 8) 240
אַמִּיץ	2	mighty (2 · 6) 55
זֶרֶם		rain storm (7 · 9) 281
בָּרָד		hail (3 · 29) 135
שַׂעַר		storm (1 · 1) 973
קֶטֶב		destruction (1 · 4) 881
כַּבִּיר		great, mighty, much (3 · 10) 460
שָׁטַף		to overflow (9 · 28 · 31) 1009
נרמס	3	to be trampled (1 · 1 · 18) 942
עֲטָרָה		crown (4 · 23) 742
גֵּאוּת		majesty (5 · 8) 145
שִׁכּוֹר		drunken one, drunken (4 · 13) 1016
צִיצָה	4	blossom, flower (1 · 1[?]) 847
נָבֵל		to wither and fall, fade (11 · 21 · 25) 615
צְבִי		beauty, decoration (7 · 18) 840
תִּפְאָרָה		beauty, finery, glory (18 · 50) 802
גַּיְא		valley (5 · 47) 161
בִּכּוּרָה		first ripe fig, early fig (1 · 4) 114
בְּטֶרֶם		before (8 · 39) 382
קַיִץ		summer, summer fruit (2 · 20) 884
בְּעוֹד		while yet (3 · 20) 728 עוד 2.a.
בָּלַע		to swallow down (1 · 20 · 41) 118
עֲטָרָה	5	crown (4 · 23) 742
צְבִי		beauty, decoration (7 · 18) 840
צְפִירָה		diadem, coronet (1 · 3) 862
תִּפְאָרָה		beauty, finery, glory (18 · 50) 802
שְׁאָר		remnant (12 · 26) 984
שׁגה	7	to reel, roll [in drunkenness] (3 · 17 · 21) 993
שֵׁכָר		intoxicating drink, strong drink (8 · 23) 1016
תָּעָה		to wander about (8 · 27 · 50) 1073
נִבְלַע		to be swallowed up (1 · 1 · 6[?]) 118
רֹאֶה		seer (2 · 12) 909
פוק		to reel, totter (1 · 1 · 9) 807
פְּלִילִיָּה		the giving of a decision (1 · 1) 813
קִיא	8	vomit (2 · 3) 883
צֹאָה		filth (3 · 5) 844
בְּלִי		without (3 · 23) 115
הוֹרָה	9	to direct, teach (4[?] · 45[?] · 45[?]) 434 ירה
דֵּעָה		knowledge (2 · 6) 395
שְׁמוּעָה		report (4 · 27) 1035
גָּמַל		to wean (6 · 34 · 37) 168
חָלָב		milk (4 · 44) 316
עַתִּיק		removed (1 · 2) 801
שָׁד		breast (2 · 21) 994
צַו	10	command [dub.] (8 · 9) 846
קַו		mimicry of Isaiah's words (875), or line, measuring line (16 · [?] · 25[?]) 876
זְעֵיר		a little (4 · 5) 277
לָעֵג	11	mocking or לעג stammerings (1 [?] · 2[?]) 541
מְנוּחָה	12	rest, quietness (4 · 21) 629
עָיֵף		faint, weary (5 · 17) 746
מַרְגֵּעָה		rest, repose (1 · 1) 921
צַו	13	command [dub.] (8 · 9) 846
קַו		mimicry of Isaiah's words (875), or line, measuring line (16[?] · 25[?]) 876
זְעֵיר		a little (4 · 5) 277
אָחוֹר		backwards (9 · 41) 30
נוקש		to be caught by a bait, ensnared (2 · 4 · 8) 430 יקש
לָצוֹן	14	scorner, scorning (1 · 3) 539
מָשַׁל		ruler (1 · 2) 605 משל

חֹזֶה 15 vision (3 · 17) 304

שִׁיט scourge, whip (2 · 3[?]) 1002 שׁוֹט

שָׁטַף to overflow (9 · 28 · 31) 1009

כָּזָב lie, falsehood (2 · 31) 469

מַחְסֶה refuge (4 · 20) 340

יָסַד 16 to found, establish (2 · 10 · 41) 413

בֹּחַן tested, tried (1 · 1) 103

פִּנָּה corner, cornerstone (2 · 30) 819

מוּסָד foundation (1 · 2) 414

הוּסָד hoph. ptc. = founded (1 · 3 · 41) 413 יסד

הֵחִישׁ to hasten, come quickly (3 · 6 · 21) 301 חושׁ

קָו 17 line, measuring line (16[?] · 25[?]) 876

מִשְׁקֶלֶת leveling instrument, level (1 · 2) 1054

יָעָה to sweep together (1 · 1 · 1) 418

בָּרָד hail (3 · 29) 135

מַחְסֶה refuge (4 · 20) 340

כָּזָב lie, falsehood (2 · 31) 469

סֵתֶר hiding place (5 · 35) 712

שָׁטַף to overflow (9 · 28 · 31) 1009

חָזוּת 18 vision; perh. here = agreement (3 · 5) 303

שׁוֹט scourge, whip (2 · 3[?]) 1002

שָׁטַף to overflow (9 · 28 · 31) 1009

מִרְמָס trampling (4 · 7) 942

מִדֵּי 19 out of the abundance of, as often as (3 · 15) 191 דַּי 2.c

בַּבֹּקֶר בַּבֹּקֶר [idiom] morning by morning 133 בֹּקֶר 1.f.

זְוָעָה object of trembling, terror (1 · 1) 266

שְׁמוּעָה report (4 · 27) 1035

קָצַר 20 to be short (4 · 12 · 14) 894

מַצָּע couch, bed (1 · 1) 427

הִשְׂתָּרֵעַ to stretch oneself (1 · 1 · 3) 976

מַסֵּכָה covering, woven stuff (2[?] · 2[?]) 651

התכנס to gather oneself together (1 · 1 · 11) 488

רָגַז 21 to be excited, perturbed (6 · 30 · 41) 919

נָכְרִי strange; foreign, alien (2 · 45) 648

התלוצץ 22 to act as a scorner, show oneself a mocker (1 · 1 · 12) 539 ליץ

מוֹסֵר bond, band (2 · 12) 64

כָּלָה complete destruction; completion (2 · 22) 478

נחרץ Niph. ptc. = decisive (2 · 5 · 10) 358

הַאֲזִין 23 to give ear, hear (8 · 41 · 41) 24

הִקְשִׁיב to give attention (8 · 45 · 46) 904

אִמְרָה word, speech, utterance (5 · 30) 57

חָרַשׁ 24 to plough (2 · 23 · 26) 360

שָׂדַד to harrow (1 · 3 · 3) 961

שִׁוָּה 25 to level (2 · 5 · 16) 1000

קֶצַח black cumin, condiment (3 · 3) 892

כַּמֹּן cumin, condiment (3 · 3) 485

זָרַק to scatter, throw (1 · 32 · 34) 284

חִטָּה wheat (1 · 30) 334

שׂוֹרָה in rows [dub.] (1 · 1) 965

שְׂעֹרָה barley (1 · 34) 972

נסמן ptc. = an appointed place, or determined portion (1 · 1 · 1) 702

כֻּסֶּמֶת spelt (1 · 3) 493

גְּבוּלָה border, boundary (2 · 10) 148

יִסַּר 26 to discipline, correct (1 · 27 · 38) 415

הוֹרָה to teach, direct (4[?] · 45[?] · 45[?]) 435 ירה

חָרוּץ 27 sharp (2 · 4) 358

הוּדַשׁ to be threshed (1 · 1 · 15) 190 דושׁ

קֶצַח black cumin, condiment (3 · 3) 892

אוֹפַן wheel (1 · 34) 66

עֲגָלָה cart, wagon (3 · 25) 722

כַּמֹּן cumin, condiment (3 · 3) 485

נחבט to be beat out (1 · 1 · 5) 286

הוּדַק 28 to be crushed (1 · 1 · 13) 200 דקק

נֶצַח everlastingness; with ל = forever (7 · 43) 664

28

אדש	inf. only = to thresh (1 · 1 · 1) 12
הָמַם	to move noisily, make a noise (1 · 13 · 13) 243
גִּלְגָּל	wheel (1 · 1) 166
עֲגָלָה	cart, wagon (3 · 25) 722
דקק	to crush, pulverize (2 · 4 · 13) 200
הדק	to be crushed (1 · 1 · 13) 200
הִפְלִיא 29	to make wonderful, do wondrously (2 · 10 · 24) 810
תּוּשִׁיָּה	sound wisdom, abiding success (1 · 12) 444

Chapter 29

קִרְיָה 1	town, city (10 · 30) 900
נקף	to go around, to run the round of the year (1 · 1 · 17) 668
הֵצִיק 2	to bring into straits, press upon (2 · 11 · 11) 847
תַּאֲנִיָּה	mourning (1 · 2) 58
אֲנִיָּה	mourning (1 · 2) 58
דּוּר 3	circle (2 · 2) 189
צוּר	to shut in, besiege (3 · 31 · 31) 848
מֻצָּב	palisade, intrenchment (1 · 2[?]) 663
מְצוּרָה	siege works, rampart (1 · 8) 849
שָׁפֵל 4	to become low, be humiliated (10 · 11 · 30) 1050
נשחח	to proceed humbly; be humbled, reduced (3 · 34 · 18[?]) 1005
אִמְרָה	word, speech, utterance (5 · 30) 57
אוֹב	ghost [here only] (3 · 16) 15
צפצף	to chirp, peep (4 · 4 · 4) 861 צפף
אָבָק 5	dust (2 · 6) 7
דַּק	small, fine [dust] (2 · 14) 201
מֹץ	chaff (3 · 8) 558
עָרִיץ	awe inspiring; terror striking (7 · 20) 792
פֶּתַע	suddenness; w. פתאם = at an instant (2 · 7) 837
פִּתְאֹם	suddenly (4 · 25) 837

רַעַם 6	thunder (1 · 6) 947
רַעַשׁ	earthquake (2 · 17) 950
סוּפָה	storm wind (5 · 15) 693
סְעָרָה	tempest, storm wind (3 · 16) 704
לַהַב	flame (4 · 12) 529
חָזוֹן 7	vision (2 · 35) 302
צבא	to wage war (4 · 12 · 14) 838
מְצוֹדָה	fastness, stronghold (1 · 3) 845
הֵצִיק	to bring into straits, press upon (4 · 11 · 11) 847 I צוק
חָלַם 8	to dream (2 · 26 · 28) 321
רָעֵב	hungry, hungry one (5 · 19) 944
הֵקִיץ	to awake (3 · 22 · 23) 884 קיץ
רֵיק	empty, vain (1 · 14) 938
צָמֵא	thirsty one, thirsty (5 · 9) 854
עָיֵף	faint, weary (5 · 17) 746
שקק	to run, run about, rush (2 · 5 · 6) 1055
צבא	to wage war (4 · 12 · 14) 838
הִתְמַהְמַהּ 9	to linger, tarry, wait (1 · 9 · 9) 554 מהה
תמה	to be astounded (2 · 8 · 9) 1069
הִשְׁתַּעְשַׁע	to blind yourselves (1 · 1 · 3) 1044 I שעע
שׁעע	to be blind (1 · 1 · 3) 1044 I
שׁכר	to become drunken (2 · 9 · 18) 1016
נוע	to stagger (6 · 22 · 38) 631
שֵׁכָר	intoxicating drink, strong drink (8 · 23) 1016
נָסַךְ 10	to pour out (4 · 7 · 25) 650
תַּרְדֵּמָה	deep sleep (1 · 7) 922
עצם	to shut tightly (1 · 1 · 2) 783
חֹזֶה	seer (3 · 17) 302
חָזוּת 11	vision (3 · 5) 303
חתם	to seal up (3 · 23 · 27) 367
הִפְלִיא 14	to make wonderful, do wondrously (2 · 10 · 24) 810
פֶּלֶא	wonder (3 · 13) 810
בִּינָה	understanding (5 · 37) 108
נָבוֹן	intelligent, discerning (3 · 21) 106 בין

29

הֶעֱמִיק 15 to make deep (4 · 8 · 9) 770

מַחְשָׁךְ dark place (2 · 7) 365

הֶפֶךְ 16 perversity, contrariness; w. suffix = Oh, your perversity! (1 · 3) 246

חֹמֶר clay, mortar (5 · 17) 330

יוֹצֵר potter (3 · 17[?]) 427 יצר

עֹשֶׂה maker, creator (6 · 24[?]) 793 I עשׂה

יֵצֶר pottery (2 · 9) 428

יָצַר to form (22 · 41 · 44) 427

מִזְעָר 17 a little; מעט מזער = a very little while (4 · 4) 277

כַּרְמֶל garden land (8 · 14) 502

חֵרֵשׁ 18 deaf (5 · 9) 361

אֹפֶל darkness, gloom (1 · 9) 66

עִוֵּר blind (11 · 26) 734

עָנָו 19 poor and weak (3[?] · 21[?]) 776

גִּיל to rejoice (11 · 45 · 45) 162

אָפֵס 20 to cease, fail, come to an end (2 · 5 · 5) 67

עָרִיץ ruthless, terror-striking (7 · 20) 792

לֵץ scorner (1 · 16) 539 ליץ

שָׁקַד to keep watch, be wakeful over (1 · 11 · 17) 1052

קוֹשׁ 21 to lay bait or lure (1 · 1 · 1) 881

תֹּהוּ unreality, emptiness (11 · 20) 1062

חוּר 22 to be or grow white, pale (1 · 1 · 1) 301

הֶעֱרִיץ 23 to regard or treat with awe (2 · 2 · 14) 791

תָּעָה 24 to wander about (8 · 27 · 50) 1073

בִּינָה understanding (5 · 37) 108

רגן to murmur (1 · 1 · 3) 920

לֶקַח instruction, learning, teaching (1 · 9) 544

Chapter 30

סָרַר 1 to be stubborn, rebellious (3 · 17 · 17) 710

נָסַךְ to pour out (4 · 7 · 25) 650

מַסֵּכָה libation (in a covenant formation) (1[?] · 1[?]) 651

ספה to snatch away; sweep away (2 · 8 · 18) 705

עוז 2 to take or seek refuge (1 · 1 · 5) 781

מָעוֹז protection (10 · 36) 731

חָסָה to seek refuge (3 · 37 · 37) 340

מָעוֹז 3 protection (10 · 36) 731

בֹּשֶׁת shame (5 · 30) 102

חָסוּת refuge (1 · 1) 340

כְּלִמָּה ignominy, reproach (4 · 30) 484

הוֹעִיל 5 to profit, avail, benefit (8 · 23 · 23) 418

עֵזֶר help, succour (1 · 21) 740

בֹּשֶׁת shame (5 · 30) 102

מַשָּׂא 6 utterance, oracle (11 · 21) 672

צוּקָה pressure, distress (2 · 3) 848

לָבִיא lion, lioness (2 · 11) 522

לַיִשׁ lion (1 · 3) 539

אֶפְעֶה a kind of viper (2 · 3) 821

שָׂרָף fiery serpent (4 · 7[?]) 977

עוֹפֵף to fly about, to and fro (3 · 5 · 25) 733

עַיִר male ass (2 · 9) 747

דַּבֶּשֶׁת hump [of camel] (1 · 1) 185

הוֹעִיל to profit, avail, benefit (8 · 23 · 23) 418 יעל

רִיק 7 emptiness, vanity (3 · 12) 938

רַהַב storm, arrogance (2 · 7) 923

שֶׁבֶת cessation [dub.] (1 · 7[?]) 992

לוּחַ 8 tablet, plate (1 · 43) 531

הקק to cut in or on, inscribe (4 · 8 · 11) 349

עַד forever (8 · 48) 723 I עד

מְרִי 9 rebellion (1 · 22) 598

כֶּחָשׁ deceptive, false (1 · 1) 471

רֹאֶה seer (2 · 12) 909

נָכֹחַ true, honest (4 · 8) 647

חֹזֶה seer (3 · 17) 302

חָלָק smoothness = flattery (2[?] · 12[?]) 325

מַהֲתַלּוֹת 10 deceptions (1 · 1) 251, 1122

עֹשֶׁק 12 extortion, oppression (3 · 15) 799

נָלוֹז ptc. = devious, crooked (1 · 4 · 6) 531

נִשְׁעָן to lean, support oneself (5 · 22 · 22) 1043

פֶּרֶץ 13 broken wall, breach (2 · 19) 829

נִבְעֶה ptc. = swelling (1 · 2 · 4) 126

נִשְׂגָּב to be high (6 · 10 · 20) 960

פִּתְאֹם suddenly (4 · 25) 837

פֶּתַע suddenness; w. פתאם — at an instant, suddenly (2 · 7) 837

שֶׁבֶר shattering, breaking (9 · 45) 991

שֵׁבֶר 14 breaking (9 · 45) 991

נֵבֶל [earthen] jar, pitcher (2 · 11) 614

יוֹצֵר potter, activity of potter (3 · 17) 427 יצר

כָּתֹת to beat or crush fine (1 · 5 · 17) 510

חָמַל to spare, have compassion (2 · 40 · 40) 328

מְכִתָּת crushed fragments (1 · 1) 510

חֶרֶשׂ a fragment of earthenware, sherd (3 · 17) 360

חֲתָה to snatch up (1 · 3 · 3) 367

יָקוּד kindled, as subst. = what is kindled (1[?] · 1[?]) 428 יקד

חָשַׂף to draw, skim, take from the surface (3 · 10 · 10) 362

גֶּבֶא cistern, pool (1 · 2) 146

שׁוּבָה 15 retirement, withdrawal (1 · 1) 1000

נַחַת quietness, quiet attitude (1 · 7) 629

הַשְׁקֵט to show quietness, display quietness; inf. abs. = subst., quietness (4 · 10 · 41) 1052

בִּטְחָה trusting (1 · 1) 105

קַל 16 swift, light (4 · 13) 886

אֶלֶף 17 [pl. only] cattle (1 · 8) 48

גַּעֲרָה rebuke (6 · 15) 172

תֹּרֶן mast, flagstaff (2 · 3) 1076

נֵס standard, signal (10 · 21) 651

חָכָה 18 to wait (3 · 13 · 14) 314

רָחַם to have compassion, be compassionate (12 · 42 · 47) 933

אֶשֶׁר blessedness, happiness (3 · 45[?]) 80

חכה to wait for (1 · 1 · 14) 314

צַר 20 distress, straits (5[?] · 20[?]) 865

לַחַץ oppression, distress (1 · 12) 537

נִכְנַף to be thrust into a corner, cornered (1 · 1 · 1) 489

מוֹרֶה teacher (2 · 9) 435

תַּאֲמִינוּ 21 you go to the right (1 · 5 · 5) 412 ימן

הִשְׂמְאִיל to turn [aside] to the left [fr. true way] (1 · 5 · 5) 970 שמאל

צִפּוּי 22 plating (1 · 5) 860

פָּסִיל idol, image (4 · 23) 820

אֲפֻדָּה ephod [of sheathing of idol images] (1 · 3) 65

מַסֵּכָה molten metal, or image (2 · 25) 651

זרה to scatter (3 · 9 · 38) 279

דָּוֶה unwell, menstruous (1 · 5) 188

מָטָר 23 rain (3 · 38) 564

תְּבוּאָה product, yield (2 · 43) 100

דָּשֵׁן fat (1 · 3) 206

שָׁמֵן fat, rich (1 · 10) 1032

כַּר pasture (1 · 3) 499

נִרְחָב to be broad, roomy (1 · 1 · 25) 931

אֶלֶף 24 pl. only = cattle (1 · 8) 48

עַיִר male ass (2 · 9) 747

בְּלִיל fodder (1 · 3) 117

חָמִיץ seasoned; of provender for cattle (1 · 1) 330

זרה to scatter, winnow (3 · 9 · 38) 279

רַחַת winnowing shovel (1 · 1) 935

מִזְרֶה pitch fork (1 · 2) 280

גָּבֹהַּ 25 high (6 · 41) 147

פֶּלֶג channel, canal (2 · 10) 811

יָבָל watercourse, stream (2 · 2) 385

הֶרֶג slaughter (2 · 5) 247

מִגְדָּל tower (4 · 49) 153

לְבָנָה	26	moon [poet.] (2 · 3) 526
חַמָּה		sun; heat [poet.] (3 · 6) 328
חבש		to bind up (2 · 28 · 32) 289
שֶׁבֶר		fracture, breaking (9 · 45) 991
מַחַץ		severe wound (1 · 1) 563
מַכָּה		beating, scourging, wound (5 · 48) 646
מֶרְחָק	27	distant place, far country (7 · 18) 935
כֹּבֶד		vehemence, heaviness (2 · 4) 458
מַשָּׂאָה		the uplifted [cloud] (1[?] · 16[?]) 673
זַעַם		indignation (5 · 22) 276
שָׁטַף	28	to overflow (9 · 28 · 31) 1009
צַוָּאר		neck, back of neck (4 · 41) 848
חָצָה		to halve (1 · 11 · 15) 345
נָפָה		sieve, or other winnowing implement (1 · 1) 632
רֶסֶן		halter (1 · 4) 943
הִתְעָה		to cause to wander about (6 · 21 · 50) 1073
לְחִי		jaw, cheek (2 · 21) 534
חָלִיל	29	flute, pipe (2 · 6) 319
הוֹד	30	splendor, majesty (1 · 24) 217
נַחַת		descent (1 · 1) 639
זַעַף		rage (1 · 7) 277
לַהַב		flame (4 · 12) 529
נֶפֶץ		driving storm, bursting of clouds (1 · 1) 658
זֶרֶם		rain storm (7 · 9) 281
בָּרָד		hail (3 · 29) 135
מַעֲבָר	32	passing, sweep (1 · 3) 721
מוּסָדָה		appointment, foundation (1 · 2) 414
תֹּף		timbrel, tambourine (3 · 17) 1074
כִּנּוֹר		lyre (5 · 41) 490
תְּנוּפָה		a brandishing, waving (2 · 30) 632
אֶתְמוֹל	33	yesterday; w. מִן from yesterday = already (1 · 8) 1069
הֶעְמִיק		to make deep (4 · 8 · 9) 770
הִרְחִיב		to make large (5 · 21 · 25) 931
מְדוּרָה		pile, pyre (1 · 2) 190 .
נְשָׁמָה		breath; spirit (4 · 24) 675

גָּפְרִית		brimstone (2 · 7) 172

Chapter 31

עֶזְרָה	1	help, succour, assistance (4 · 26) 740
נִשְׁעַן		to lean, support oneself (5 · 22 · 22) 1043
עָצַם		to be numerous (1 · 16 · 18) 782
שָׁעָה		to regard, gaze at (5 · 12 · 15) 1043
מֵרַע	2	evildoer (4 · 18) 949 רעע vb. denom.
עֶזְרָה		help, succour, assistance (4 · 26) 740
הָגָה	4	to growl, moan (7 · 23 · 25) 211
אַרְיֵה		lion (6 · 45) 71
כְּפִיר		young lion (3 · 31) 498
טֶרֶף		prey, food (2 · 17) 383
מְלֹא		mass, fullness (5 · 38) 571
צבא		to wage war (4 · 12 · 14) 838
צִפּוֹר	5	[coll.] bird[s] (1 · 40) 861
עוף		to hover, fly (4 · 18 · 25) 733
גנן		to defend (4 · 8[?] · 8[?]) 170
פָּסַח		to pass or spring over (1 · 5 · 7[?]) 820
לַאֲשֶׁר	6	to whom (4 · 38) 82 אשר 4.c.
הֶעְמִיק		to make deep (4 · 8 · 9) 770
סָרָה		apostasy, withdrawal, defection (3 · 7) 694
אֱלִיל	7	worthless idols (10 · 20) 47
חֵטְא		sin (4 · 33) 307
בָּחוּר	8	young man (6 · 45) 104
מַס		labor bands, slave gangs (1 · 23) 587
מָגוֹר	9	fear, terror (1-8) 159
נֵס		standard, signal (10 · 21) 651
אוּר		fire (5 · 6) 22
תַּנּוּר		fire pot, portable stove (1 · 15) 1072

Chapter 32

שׂרר	1	to govern, rule, act as prince (1 · 5 · 8) 979
מַחֲבֵא	2	hiding place (1 · 1) 285

סֵ֫תֶר   hiding place (5 · 35) 712

זֶ֫רֶם   rain storm (7 · 9) 281

פֶּ֫לֶג   channel, canal (2 · 10) 811

צָיוֹן   dryness, parched ground (2 · 2) 851

כָּבֵד   heavy (3 · 40) 458

עָיֵף   faint, weary (5 · 17) 746

שָׁעָה   3   to be blinded (5 · 12 · 15) 1043 (1044 שׁעע)

קָשַׁב   to incline, attend (1 · 1 · 46) 904

עִלֵּג   4   speaking inarticulately (1 · 1) 748

צַח   clear, glowing (2 · 4) 850

נָבָל   5   fool, impious or presumptuous person (2 · 18) 614

נָדִיב   noble in mind, generous (3 · 27) 622

כִּילַי   knave (2 · 2) 647

שׁוֹעַ   noble (1 · 2) 447

נָבָל   6   fool, impious or presumptuous person (2 · 18) 614

נְבָלָה   disgraceful folly, senselessness (2 · 13) 615

חֹ֫נֶף   profaneness (1 · 1) 338

תּוֹעָה   error, wandering (1 · 2) 1073

הָרִיק   to empty, keep empty (1 · 17 · 19) 937

רָעֵב   hungry, hungry one (5 · 19) 944

מַשְׁקֶה   drink (1 · 19[?]) 1052

צָמֵא   thirsty one, thirsty (5 · 9) 854

הֶחְסִיר   to cause to be lacking, fail (1 · 2 · 23[?]) 341

כִּילַי   7   knave (2 · 2) 647

זִמָּה   evil device, plan (1 · 28[?]) 273

חִבֵּל   to ruin, destroy (3 · 6 · 10) 287

עָנָו   poor, weak (3 · 12) 776

אֹמֶר   speech, word (2 · 48[?]) 56

נָדִיב   8   noble in mind, generous (3 · 27) 622

נְדִיבָה   nobility, nobleness (2 · 3) 622

שַׁאֲנָן   9   at ease, carelessly at ease (5 · 11) 983

הַאֲזִין   to give ear, hear, listen (8 · 41 · 41) 24

אִמְרָה   word, speech, utterance (5 · 30) 57

רָגַז   10   to come quivering, quake (6 · 30 · 41) 919

בָּצִיר   vintage (2 · 7) 131

אֹסֶף   gathering (2 · 3) 63

בְּלִי   not; particle of negation (3 · 23) 115

חָרַד   11   to tremble, be terrified (4 · 23 · 39) 353

שַׁאֲנָן   at ease, carelessly at ease (5 · 11) 983

רְגַז   to come quivering, quake (6 · 30 · 41) 919

פָּשַׁט   to strip off, put off (1 · 24 · 43) 832

ערר   to strip oneself (1 · 1 · 4) 792

חגר   to gird on (3 · 44 · 44) 291

חֲלָץ   [dual] = loins (3 · 10) 323

שַׁד   12   breast (2 · 21) 994

ספד   to wail, lament (1 · 28 · 30) 704

חֶמֶד   desire, delight (1 · 5) 326

פרה   to bear fruit, be fruitful (4 · 22 · 29) 826

קוֹץ   13   thornbush (2 · 11) 881

שָׁמִיר   thorns, thornbushes (8 · 11) 1038

מָשׂוֹשׂ   exultation (10 · 17) 965

קִרְיָה   town, city (10 · 30) 900

עַלִּיז   exultant, jubilant (5 · 7) 759

אַרְמוֹן   14   palace, castle, citadel (5 · 33) 74

נֻטַּשׁ   to be abandoned, deserted (1 · 1 · 40) 643

עֹפֶל   mound, hill (1 · 8) 779

בַּחַן   watchtower (1 · 1) 103

בַּעַד   on behalf of = take the place of, serve as (>50) 126

מְעָרָה   den, cave (1[?] · 1[?]) 792

מָשׂוֹשׂ   exultation (10 · 17) 965

פֶּרֶא   wild ass (1 · 10) 825

מִרְעֶה   pasture (1 · 13) 945

עֵ֫דֶר   flock, herd (3 · 39) 727

נֵעָרֶה   15   to be poured out (1 · 1 · 15) 788

כַּרְמֶל   garden land (8 · 14) 502

כַּרְמֶל 16 garden land (8 · 14) 502

הַשְׁקֵט 17 to show quietness; inf. abs. =
subst. = quietness (4 · 10 · 41) 105

בֶּטַח security (3 · 43) 105

נָוֶה 18 habitation (6 · 45) 627

מִבְטָח confidence (1 · 15) 105

מְנוּחָה resting place, rest (4 · 21) 629

שַׁאֲנָן secure; at ease (5 · 11) 983

בָּרַד 19 to hail (1 · 1 · 1) 136

שִׁפְלָה humiliation (1 · 1) 1050

שָׁפֵל to be humiliated, brought low
(10 · 11 · 30) 1050

אֶשֶׁר 20 happiness, blessedness (3 · 45[?]) 80

Chapter 33

בָּגַד 1 to act treacherously (12 · 49 · 49) 93

כַּנְלֹתְךָ [dub.] when you cease, finish
(1 · 1) 649 נלה

קוה 2 to wait or look eagerly for
(13 · 39 · 45) 875

נדד 3 to retreat, flee (8 · 20 · 24) 622

רוֹמְמוּת uplifting, arising (1 · 1) 928

נָפֵץ to be scattered (1 · 5 · 21) 659 II

אֹסֶף 4 gathering (2 · 3) 63

חָסִיל [a kind of] locust (1 · 6) 340

מַשָּׁק running, rushing (1 · 1) 1055

גֵּב locust (1 · 1) 146

שָׁקַק to run, run about, rush (2 · 5 · 6) 1055

נִשְׂגָּב 5 to be exalted, high (6 · 10 · 20) 960

חֹסֶן 6 wealth, treasure (1 · 5) 340

יִרְאָה fear, reverence; terror (5 · 45) 432

אֶרְאֶלָּם 7 heroes [dub.] (1 · 1 · 1) 72 אראל

מַר bitter, bitterness; bitterly (6 · 38) 600

מְסִלָּה 8 highway, public road (9 · 27) 700

הֵפֵר to break, violate (4 · 42 · 45) 830 פרר

אֱנוֹשׁ men (8 · 42) 60

אָבַל 9 to mourn (5 · 18 · 38) 5

אֻמְלַל to be or grow feeble, languish
(6 · 15[?] · 15[?]) 51

הֶחְפִּיר to display shame (2 · 4 · 17) 344

קָמַל to be decayed (2 · 2 · 2) 888

נער to shake, shake out, shake off
(2 · 4 · 11) 654

הָרָה 11 to conceive, become pregnant
(4 · 38 · 40) 247

חֲשַׁשׁ chaff (2 · 2) 366

קַשׁ stubble, chaff (5 · 16) 905

מִשְׂרְפוֹת 12 burning (1 · 2) 977

שִׂיד lime (1 · 4) 966

קוֹץ thornbush (2 · 11) 881

כסח to cut off or away (1 · 2 · 2) 492

יצת to kindle, be kindled (2 · 4 · 27)
428

מֵרָחֹק 13 distant, at a distance (12 · 34) 935

פָּחַד 14 to be in dread (7 · 23 · 26) 808

חַטָּא sinners (3 · 19) 308

רְעָדָה trembling (1 · 4) 944

חָנֵף profane, godless (3 · 13) 338

מוֹקֵד a burning mass (1 · 3) 428

מֵישָׁר 15 uprightness, equity (3 · 19) 449

בֶּצַע unjust gain, gain made by violence
(3 · 23) 130

מַעֲשַׁקּוֹת extortionate act[s] (1 · 2) 799

נער to shake off, shake (2 · 4 · 11) 654

תמך to lay hold of, grasp (3 · 20 · 21)
1069

שֹׁחַד bribe, present (4 · 23) 1005

אטם to shut (1 · 8 · 8) 31

עצם to shut (1 · 1 · 2) 783 III

מְצָד 16 mountain fastness, stronghold
(1 · 11) 844

מִשְׂגָּב secure height, retreat (2 · 17) 960

יְפִי 17 beauty (2 · 19) 421

מֶרְחָק distant place, distance (7 · 18) 935

הָגָה 18 to meditate, muse, moan
(7 · 23 · 25) 211

אֵימָה terror, dread (1 · 16 · 17) 33

אַיֵּה where? (9 · 44) 32

שָׁקַל to weigh (4 · 19 · 22) 1053

מִגְדָּל tower (4 · 49) 153

נוֹעָז 19 ptc. = barbarous [dub.] (1 · 1 · 1) יעז 418

עָמֵק deep, unfathomable; עִמְקֵי שָׂפָה unintelligible of speech (1 · 3) 771

נִלְעַג to stammer, ptc. = stammering (1 · 1 · 18) 541

בִּינָה understanding (5 · 37) 108

קִרְיָה 20 town, city (10 · 30) 900

נָוֶה habitation (6 · 45) 627

שַׁאֲנָן secure, at ease (5 · 11) 983

צָעַן to travel, wander (1 · 1 · 1) 858

יָתֵד tent pin, peg (4 · 23) 450

נֶצַח everlastingness; with לְ = forever (7 · 43) 664

חֶבֶל cord, rope (3 · 49) 286

נָתַק to be torn apart, torn in two (2 · 10 · 27) 683

אַדִּיר 21 majestic (3 · 27) 12

רָחָב wide, broad (2 · 21) 932

רְחָב־יָדַיִם [idiom] wide in both directions 390 יָד 3.d.

אֳנִי ships, fleet (1 · 7) 58

שַׁיִט rowing (1[?] · 1[?]) 1002

צִי ship (1 · 4) 850

מְחֹקֵק 22 prescriber [of laws], commander (1 · 7) 349 חקק

נָטַשׁ 23 to be loosened, loose; let alone (2 · 6 · 40) 643

חֶבֶל cord, rope (3 · 49) 286

כֵּן base, pedestal (1 · 17) 487

תֹּרֶן mast, flagstaff (2 · 3) 1076

נֵס sail, ensign, standard (10 · 21) 651

עַד booty, prey (1 · 3) 723

מַרְבֶּה abundance, increase (2 · 2) 916

פִּסֵּחַ lame (2 · 14) 820

בָּזַז to plunder, dispoil (7 · 37 · 41) 102

בַּז spoil, booty, plunder (5 · 27) 103

שָׁכֵן 24 inhabitant (1 · 20) 1015

Chapter 34

לְאֹם 1 people (11 · 35) 522

הִקְשִׁיב to give attention (8 · 45 · 46) 904

מְלֹא fullness, entire contents (5 · 38) 571

תֵּבֵל world (9 · 36) 385

צֶאֱצָא produce, offspring (7 · 11) 425

קֶצֶף 2 wrath (3 · 28) 893

הֶחֱרִים to destroy, exterminate; to be devoted (3 · 46 · 49) 355

טֶבַח slaughter (4 · 12) 370

פֶּגֶר 3 corpse, carcass (4 · 22) 803

בְּאֹשׁ stench (1 · 3) 93

נָמַס to melt, dissolve (3 · 19 · 21) 587 מסס

נָמַק 4 to molder away, rot away (1 · 9 · 10) 596

נָגֹלל to roll (1 · 2 · 17) 164

נָבֵל to wither and fall, fade (11 · 21 · 25) 615

עָלֶה leaf, leafage (3 · 18) 750

תְּאֵנָה fig tree (3 · 39) 1061

רָוָה 5 to be intoxicated, drunk, saturated (3 · 6 · 14) 924

חֵרֶם devotion, ban involving destruction (2 · 29) 356

הִדַּשֵּׁן 6 hothp., to make oneself fat (1 · 1 · 11) 206

כַּר male lamb (2 · 11) 503

עַתּוּד male goat (3 · 29) 800

כִּלְיָה kidney (1 · 31) 480

טֶבַח slaughter (4 · 12) 370

רְאֵם 7 wild ox (1 · 9) 910

אַבִּיר mighty (3 · 17) 7

רָוָה to be intoxicated, drunk, saturated (3 · 6 · 14) 924

דָּשֵׁן to be made fat (1 · 4 · 11) 206

נָקָם 8 vengeance (6 · 17) 668

שִׁלּוּם requital, retribution, reward (1 · 3) 1024

זֶפֶת 9 pitch (2 · 3) 278

גָּפְרִית   brimstone, pitch, sulphur (2 · 7) 172

כבה   10 to be quenched, extinguished
(3 · 14 · 24) 459

עָשָׁן   smoke (7 · 25) 798

חרב   to be waste, desolate (6 · 17 · 37[?])
351

נֵצַח   everlastingness (7 · 43) 664

קָאַת   11 bird, usually a pelican (1 · 5) 886

קִפֹּד   porcupine (2 · 3) 891

יַנְשׁוֹף   bird, prob. a kind of owl (1 · 3) 676

עֹרֵב   raven (2 · 12) 788

קָו   line, measuring line (16[?] · 25[?]) 876

תֹהוּ   formlessness, primeval chaos
(11 · 20) 1062

בֹהוּ   emptiness, wasteness (1 · 3) 96

חֹר   12 noble (1 · 13) 359

מְלוּכָה   kingship, kingly office, royalty
(2 · 24) 574

אֶפֶס   nought; i.e., nothing (14 · 43) 67

אַרְמוֹן   13 palace, citadel, castle (5 · 33) 74

סִיר   thorn, hook (1 · 5) 696

קִמּוֹשׂ   thistles, nettles [coll.] (1 · 3) 888

חוֹחַ   brier, bramble (1 · 11) 296

מִבְצָר   fortress, stronghold (3 · 37) 131

נָוֶה   habitation (6 · 45) 627

תַּן   jackal (4 · 14) 1072

חָצִיר   green grass (8 · 18[?]) 348

יַעֲנָה   ostrich (3 · 8) 418

פגשׁ   14 to meet, encounter (1 · 10 · 14) 803

צִי   wild beast, desert dweller (3 · 6) 850

אִי   jackal (2 · 3) 17

שָׂעִיר   satyr [demon w. goat form] (2 · 4) 972

הרגיע   to rest, repose (2 · 8 · 13) 921 II

לִילִית   Lilith [female night demon] (1 · 1)
539

מָנוֹחַ   resting place (1 · 7) 629

קִנֵּן   15 to make a nest (1 · 4 · 5) 890

קִפּוֹז   arrow snake (1 · 1) 891

דגר   to gather together as a brood
(1 · 2 · 2) 186

דַּיָּה   bird of prey, possibly a kite (1 · 2)
178

רְעוּת   fellow [woman] (2 · 6) 946

נֶעְדָּר   16 to be lacking (3 · 6 · 7) 727

רְעוּת   fellow [woman] (2 · 6) 946

קָו   17 line, measuring line (16[?] · 25[?])
876

Chapter 35

שָׂשׂ   1 to exult, display joy (9 · 27 · 27) 965
שׂושׂ

צִיָּה   desert, dryness (3 · 16) 851

גִיל   to rejoice (11 · 45 · 45) 162

פָּרַח   to bud, sprout (5 · 28 · 34) 827

חֲבַצֶּלֶת   meadow saffron, or crocus (1 · 2)
287

פָּרַח   2 to bud, sprout (5 · 28 · 34) 827

גִיל   to rejoice (11 · 45 · 45) 162

גִּילָה   rejoicing (2 · 2) 162

הָדָר   splendor, majesty (7 · 30) 214

רָפֶה   3 slack (1 · 4) 952

בֶּרֶךְ   knee (3 · 25) 139

אמץ   to make firm, strengthen
(3 · 19 · 41)

נָקָם   4 vengeance (6 · 17) 668

גְּמוּל   dealing, recompense, benefit
(5 · 19) 168

נפקח   5 to be opened (1 · 3 · 20) 824

עִוֵּר   blind (11 · 26) 734

חֵרֵשׁ   deaf (5 · 9) 361

דלג   6 to leap, leap over (1 · 4 · 5) 194

אַיָּל   hart, stag, deer (1 · 11) 19

פִּסֵּחַ   lame (2 · 14) 820

אִלֵּם   dumb, unable to speak (2 · 6) 48

שָׁרָב   7 parched ground, burning heat (2 · 2)
1055

אֲגַם   troubled pool (4 · 8) 8

צִמָּאוֹן   thirsty ground (1 · 3) 855

מַבּוּעַ   spring of water (2 · 3) 616

36

נָוֶה habitation (6 · 45) 627

תַּן jackal (4 · 14) 1072

רֵבֶץ resting place, place of lying down (2 · 4) 918

חָצִיר an abode, home (2 · 3[?]) 347

גֹּמֶא rush, paper reeds (2 · 4) 167

מַסְלוּל 8 highway (1 · 1) 700

אֱוִיל foolish (2 · 26) 17

תָּעָה to wander about (8 · 27 · 50) 1073

אַרְיֵה 9 lion (6 · 45) 71

פָּרִיץ violent one (1 · 6) 829

רִנָּה 10 ringing cry [in joy] (9 · 33) 943

שָׂשׂוֹן exultation, joy (6 · 22) 965

הִשִּׂיג to reach, attain; to overtake (3 · 49 · 49) 673

יָגוֹן grief, sorrow (2 · 14) 387

אֲנָחָה sighing, groaning (3 · 11) 58

Chapter 36

בָּצוּר 1 cut off, made inaccessible (5 · 25) בצר 130

כָּבֵד 2 massive, abundant, numerous; heavy (3 · 40) 458

תְּעָלָה conduit, watercourse, trench (2 · 9) 752

בְּרֵכָה pool, pond (4 · 17) 140

מְסִלָּה highway, public road (9 · 27) 700

מַזְכִּיר 3 recorder, title of public officer (2 · 9) 271 גכר

בִּטָּחוֹן 4 trust (1 · 3) 105

מָרַד 5 to rebel, revolt (1 · 25 · 25) 597

מִשְׁעֶנֶת 6 staff (2 · 12) 1044

רצץ to crush, ptc. pass. = crushed (4 · 11 · 19) 954

נסמך to support oneself, brace oneself (2 · 6 · 48) 702

נקב to pierce, bore (2 · 13 · 19) 666

התערב 8 to exchange pledges; hence = make a bargain (1 · 2 · 17) 786

פֶּחָה 9 governor (1 · 28) 808

קָטָן small [with added idea of weakness] (2 · 47) 881

מִבַּלְעֲדֵי 10 apart from, without (5 · 12) 116 בלעדי b.

אֲרָמִית 11 Aramaic (1 · 4) 74

יְהוּדִית Jewish (2 · 6) 397

חֲרָאִים 12 dung (1 · 3) 351 חֲרֵא

[Q צֹאָה excrement, filth (3 · 5) 844]

שַׁיִן urine (1 · 2) 1010

יְהוּדִית 13 Jewish (2 · 6) 397

הִשִּׁיא 14 to beguile (2 · 15 · 16) 674 נשא

בְּרֵכָה 16 pond, pool (4 · 17) 140

תְּאֵנָה fig tree (3 · 39) 1061

דָּגָן 17 corn, grain (2 · 40) 186

תִּירוֹשׁ fresh or new wine (4 · 38) 440

הֵסִית 18 to instigate, allure, incite (1 · 18 · 18) 694

אַיֵּה 19 where? (9 · 44) 32

הֶחֱרִישׁ 21 to be silent (3 · 38 · 46) 361

מַזְכִּיר 22 recorder, title for public officer (2 · 9) 271 זכר

Chapter 37

שַׂק 1 sackcloth (8 · 48) 974

שַׂק 2 sackcloth (8 · 48) 974

תּוֹכֵחָה 3 rebuke, correction (1 · 4) 407

נְאָצָה contempt (1 · 2) 611

מַשְׁבֵּר breach, mouth of womb (1 · 3) 991

לֵדָה give birth (inf. cs.) (1 · 4[?]) 408 ילד

אוּלַי 4 perhaps (3 · 45) 19

חֵרֵף to reproach, say sharp things against, taunt (5 · 34 · 38) 357

גִּדֵּף 6 to blaspheme (2 · 7 · 7) 154

שְׁמוּעָה 7 report (4 · 27) 1035

הִשִּׁיא 10 to beguile (2 · 15 · 16) 674

הֶחֱרִים 11 to destroy, exterminate, be devoted (3 · 46 · 49) 355

אַיֵּה 13 where? (9 · 44) 32

37

פָּקַח 17 to open (3 · 17 · 20) 824

חָרַף to reproach, say sharp things against, taunt (5 · 34 · 38) 357

אָמְנָם 18 verily, truly (1 · 9) 53

הֶחֱרִיב to lay waste, make desolate (6 · 13 · 37[?]) 351

בָּז 22 to despise (1 · 13 · 13[?]) 100

לָעַג to mock or deride (1 · 12 · 18) 541

בְּתוּלָה virgin (5 · 50) 143

הֵנִיע to shake, wag (1 · 14 · 38) 631

חָרַף 23 to reproach, say sharp things against, taunt (5 · 34 · 38) 357

גִדֵּף to blaspheme (2 · 7 · 7) 154

חָרַף 24 to reproach, say sharp things against, taunt (5 · 34 · 38) 357

יַרְכָּה angle, recess, extreme part (3 · 28) 438

קוֹמָה height (2 · 45) 879

מִבְחַר choicest, best (2 · 12) 104

בְּרוֹשׁ cypress or fir (5 · 20) 141

כַּרְמֶל gardenlike; garden land; w. יַעַר = fertile forest (8 · 14) 502

קוּר 25 to bore, dig (1 · 2 · 2) 881

הֶחֱרִיב to dry up (6 · 13 · 37[?]) 351

לְמֵרָחוֹק 26 long ago; from afar (1 · 8) 935 רָחֹק 2.b.

יָצַר to form, fashion; fig. for to frame, preordain, plan (22 · 41 · 44) 427

הִשְׁאָה to cause to crash (1 · 2 · 6) 980

גַּל heap (2 · 20) 164

נָצָה to be ruined; ptc. = ruined (1 · 4 · 5) 663

בָּצוּר made inaccessible, cut off, fortified (5 · 25) 130 בצר

קְצַר 27 short (1 · 5) 894

עֵשֶׂב herb, herbage (2 · 33) 793

יָרָק herbs [coll.], herbage (2 · 8[?]) 438

דֶּשֶׁא grass (3 · 14) 206

חָצִיר green grass (8 · 18[?]) 348

גָּג roof (3 · 29) 150

שְׁדֵמָה field (2 · 6) 995

קָמָה standing grain (2 · 10) 879

הִתְרַגֵּז 28 to excite oneself (2 · 4 · 41) 919

הִתְרַגֵּז 29 to excite oneself (2 · 4 · 41) 919

שַׁאֲנָן as subst. = arrogance; at ease, carelessly at ease (5 · 11) 983

חָח hook, ring (1 · 7) 296

מֶתֶג bridle (1 · 5) 607

סָפִיח 30 growth from spilled kernels (1 · 4) 705

שָׁחִים grain that shoots up of itself in second year (1 · 2) 695 סחיש

קָצַר to reap (2 · 24 · 24) 984

פְּלֵיטָה 31 escaped remnant (5 · 28) 812

שֹׁרֶשׁ root (7 · 33) 1057

לְמַטָּה downward (1 · 10) 641 מטה 2.a.

לְמָעְלָה upward (3 · 34) 751 מעל 2.c.

פְּלֵיטָה 32 escaped remnant (5 · 28) 812

קִנְאָה zeal (7 · 43) 888

הוֹרָה 33 to shoot (1 · 11 · 25) 435

קִדֵּם to meet, confront (with hostility) (2 · 24 · 26) 869

סֹלְלָה mound (1 · 11) 700

גָּנַן 35 to defend (4 · 8[?] · 8[?]) 170

פֶּגֶר 36 corpse, carcass (4 · 22) 803

Chapter 38

אָנָּה 3 Ah, now!; I beseech thee! (1 · 6) 58 אנא

שָׁלֵם at peace, complete, perfect (1 · 28) 1023

בְּכִי weeping (8 · 32) 113

דִּמְעָה 5 tears (3 · 23) 199

גָּנַן 6 to defend (4 · 8[?] · 8[?]) 170

מַעֲלָה 8 step, stair, ascent (5 · 47) 752

אֲחֹרַנִּית backwards (1 · 7) 30

מִכְתָּב 9 writing, thing written (1 · 9) 508

חֳלִי sickness, disease (4 · 24) 318

דֳּמִי 10 quiet, peacefulness (1 · 1[?]) 198

38

חָדֵל 11 cessation, land of cessation = Sheol (1 · 1) 293

דּוֹר 12 dwelling place, habitation (1 · 1[?]) 189

רֹעִי m. pl. cs. of רעה (>50)

קפד to gather together, roll up (1 · 1 · 1) 891

אֹרֵג weaver (2 · 10[?]) 70 ארג

דַּלָּה hair, thrum; threads of warp hanging in loom (1 · 2) 195

בָּצַע to cut off (2 · 6 · 16) 130

שִׁוָּה 13 to make smooth, gain composure (2 · 5 · 16) 1000

אֲרִי lion (1 · 36) 71

סוּס 14 swallow, swift (a bird) (1 · 1) 692

עָגוּר a name of a bird, crane [dub.] (1 · 2) 723

צפצף to chirp, peep (4 · 4 · 4) 861

הָגָה to groan, moan (7 · 23 · 25) 211

יוֹנָה dove (3 · 33) 401

דלל to languish, be low; of eyes = look languishingly (3 · 8 · 8[?]) 195

עָשְׁקָה oppression, distress (1 · 1) 799

עָרַב to take on pledge; be surety for (1 · 15 · 17) 786

התדדה 15 to walk deliberately (1 · 2[?] · 2[?]) 186

מַר bitterness (6 · 38) 600

החלים 16 to restore to health (1 · 2 · 28) 321

מַר 17 bitter (6[?] · 38[?]) 600 מרר

חָשַׁק to be attached to, love (1 · 8 · 11) 365

שַׁחַת pit (2 · 23) 1001

בְּלִי destruction (1 · 1) 115

גֵו back (3 · 6) 156

חֵטְא sin (4 · 33) 307

שָׂבַר 18 to hope, wait (1 · 6 · 8) 960

נְגִינָה 20 music (1 · 14) 618

נגן to play a stringed instrument (2 · 13 · 14) 618

דְּבֵלָה 21 pressed fig cake (1 · 5) 179

תְּאֵנָה fig (3 · 39) 1061

מרח to rub (1 · 1 · 1) 598

שְׁחִין boil, eruption (1 · 13) 1006

Chapter 39

נְכֹת 2 treasure (1 · 2) 649

בֹּשֶׂם spice[s] (2 · 30) 141

טוֹב precious (1 · 3[?]) 373 II טוב 3.c.

מֶמְשָׁלָה realm, domain (2 · 17) 606

מֵאַיִן 3 whence? from where? (6 · 48[?]) 32 אין

אצר 6 to store up, treasure (1 · 3 · 5) 69

סָרִיס 7 eunuch, military official (3 · 45) 710

Chapter 40

נִרְצָה 2 to be accepted [as satisfactory] (1 · 1 · 7) 953

כֶּפֶל double, the double (1 · 3) 495

פִּנָּה דֶרֶךְ 3 [idiom] to make clear, free from obstacles 815 פנה, pi.

ישׁר to make smooth, straight (3 · 9 · 25) 448

מְסִלָּה highway, public road (9 · 27) 700

גַּיְא 4 valley (5 · 47) 161

שָׁפֵל to become low, be brought low (10 · 11 · 30) 1050

עָקֹב steep, hilly (1 · 3[?]) 784

מִישׁוֹר level country, plain (3 · 23) 449

רֶכֶס roughness; i.e., the impassable [dub.] (1 · 1) 940

בִּקְעָה valley (3 · 19) 132

חָצִיר 6 green grass]fig. for quickly perishing] (8 · 18[?]) 348

חֶסֶד only here = loveliness, lovely appearance (>50) 338

צִיץ blossom, flower (4 · 15) 847

חָצִיר 7 green grass [fig. for quickly perishing] (8 · 18[?]) 348

נָבֵל to wither and fall, fade (11 · 21 · 25) 615

צִיץ blossom, flower (4 · 15) 847

נשׁב to blow (1 · 1 · 3) 674

אָכֵן surely, truly (4 · 18) 38

חָצִיר 8 green grass [fig. for quickly perishing] (8 · 18[?]) 348

נָבֵל to wither and fall, fade (11 · 21 · 25) 615

צִיץ blossom, flower (4 · 15) 847

גָּבֹהַ 9 high, lofty, tall (6 · 41) 147

מְבַשֵּׂר preach, herald as glad tidings (4 · 9) 142 בשׂר Piel. 3.

שָׂכָר 10 reward, hire, wages (2 · 29) 969

פְּעֻלָּה reward, wages, recompense; work (5 · 14) 821

עֵדֶר 11 flock, herd (3 · 39) 727

טָלֶא lamb (2 · 3) 378 טלה

חֵיק bosom (3 · 38) 300

עול to give suck (1 · 5 · 5) 732

נהל to lead or guide to a watering place and cause to rest there (3 · 9 · 10) 625

שֹׁעַל 12 hollow hand, handful (1 · 3) 1043

זֶרֶת span (1 · 7) 284

תִּכֵּן to mete out, regulate (2 · 4 · 18) 1067

כּוּל to comprehend, contain (1 · 1 · 38) 465

שָׁלִשׁ third [part, = 13 ephah—dub.] (1 · 2) 1026

שָׁקַל to weigh (4 · 19 · 22) 1053

פֶּלֶס balance, scale (1 · 2) 813

מֹאזְנַיִם balances, scales (2 · 15) 24

תִּכֵּן 13 to mete out, regulate (2 · 4 · 18) 1067

תְּבוּנָה 14 the faculty of understanding, understanding (3 · 42) 108

מַר 15 drop (1 · 1) 601

דְּלִי bucket (1 · 2) 194

שַׁחַק fine dust, cloud (2 · 21) 1007

מֹאזְנַיִם balances, scales (2-15) 24

אִי coastlands, islands, coast (17 · 36) 15

דַּק small, fine [dust] (2 · 14) 201

נָטַל to life, bear (1 · 3 · 4) 642

דַּי 16 enough, sufficiency (2 · 12) 191

כְּאַיִן 17 as nothing (4 · 7) 34 אין, 1.

אֶפֶס nought; מאפס ותהו = as made of nought and worthlessness (14 · 43) 67

תֹּהוּ unreality, thing of nought (11 · 20) 1062

דָּמָה 18 to liken, compare (5 · 13 · 27) 197

דְּמוּת likeness, similitude (2 · 25) 198

פֶּסֶל 19 idol, image (9 · 31) 820

נָסַךְ to cast, pour out; w. פסל = to cast metal images (4 · 7 · 25) 650

חָרָשׁ graver, artificer [here in metal] (8 · 38) 360

צֹרֵף smelter, refiner (3 · 10[?]) 864 צרף

צָרַף to smelt, refine, test (3 · 19 · 22) 864

רקע to beat out; i.e., to overlay (1 · 3 · 11) 955

רְתֻקָה chain [dub.] (1 · 1) 958

סֻכָּן 20 ptc. pass. = poor, impoverished [dub.] (1 · 1 · 1) 698

רקב to rot (1 · 2 · 2) 955

חָרָשׁ graver, artificer (here, in wood) (8 · 38) 360

פֶּסֶל idol, image (9 · 31) 820

נמוט to be shaken, moved (2 · 22 · 39) 556

מוֹסָד 21 foundation (3 · 13) 414

חוּג 22 vault, horizon (1 · 3) 295

חָגָב locust, grasshopper (1 · 5) 290

דֹּק veil, curtain (1 · 1) 201

מתח to spread out (1 · 1 · 1) 607

רֹזֵן 23 ruler, potentate (1 · 6) 931 רזן

תֹּהוּ unreality, thing of nought (11 · 20) 1062

שֹׁרֵשׁ 24 to take root (1 · 1 · 8) 1057

גֵּזַע stock, stem (2 · 3) 160

נָשַׁף		to blow (1 · 2 · 2) 676
סְעָרָה		tempest, storm wind (3 · 16) 704
קַשׁ		stubble, chaff (5 · 16) 905
דָּמָה	25	to liken, compare (5 · 13 · 27) 197
שָׁוָה		to be like (1 · 8 · 16) 1000
בָּרָא	26	to shape, fashion, create (20 · 38 · 48) 135
אוֹן		strength (2 · 10) 20
אַמִּיץ		mighty (2 · 6) 55
נֶעְדָּר		to be lacking (3 · 6 · 7) 727
בָּרָא	28	to shape, fashion, create (20 · 38 · 48) 135
קָצֶה		end (3 · 28) 892
יָעֵף		to be weary, faint (4 · 8 · 9) 419
יגע		to grow or be weary (10 · 20 · 26) 388
חֵקֶר		thing [to be] searched out; אֵין ח׳ = it is unsearchable (1 · 12) 350
תְּבוּנָה		the object of knowledge; understanding, faculty of understanding (3 · 42) 108
יָעֵף	29	weary, faint (2 · 4) 419
לְאֵין		without (1 · 9) 34 אֵין, 6.c.
אוֹן		strength (2 · 10) 20
עָצְמָה		might (2 · 2[?]) 782
יָעֵף	30	to be weary, faint (4 · 8 · 9) 419
יגע		to grow or be weary (10 · 20 · 26) 388
בָּחוּר		young man (6 · 45) 104
קוה	31	to wait, look eagerly for (2 · 6 · 45) 875
הֶחֱלִף		to renew, change for the better (3 · 10 · 26) 322
אֵבֶר		pinions (1 · 3) 7
נֶשֶׁר		griffin vulture, eagle (1 · 26) 676
יגע		to grow or be weary (10 · 20 · 26) 388
יָעֵף		to be weary, faint (4 · 8 · 9) 419

Chapter 41

הַחֲרִישׁ	1	to keep silence, come silently (3 · 38 · 46) 361
אִי		coast (17 · 36) 15
לְאֹם		people (11 · 35) 522
הֶחֱלִף		to change, renew (3 · 10 · 26) 322
יַרְדְּ	2	read: יְרְדְּ subdues (1 · 1 · 23[?]) 921 רדד
קַשׁ		stubble, chaff (5 · 16) 905
נִדָּף		to be driven (2 · 6 · 9) 623
אִי	5	coast (17 · 36) 15
קָצֶה		end (3 · 28) 892
חָרַד		to tremble, quake (4 · 23 · 39) 353
אָתָה		to come (9 · 19 · 21) 87
חָרָשׁ	7	graver, artificer (8 · 38) 360
צֹרֵף		smelter, refiner (3 · 10[?]) 864 צרף
הֶחֱלִיק		to make smooth (1 · 7 · 9) 325
פַּטִּישׁ		forge hammer (1 · 3) 809
הלם		to strike (3 · 8 · 8) 240
פַּעַם		anvil (>50) 821 פעם 2.
דֶּבֶק		joining, soldering (1 · 3) 180
מַסְמֵר		nail (1 · 5) 702
נמוט		to be shaken, moved (2 · 22 · 39) 556
אֹהֵב	8	friend (2 · 36) 12 אָהֵב Qal 4.(b)
קָצֶה	9	end (3 · 28) 892
אָצִיל		sides [borders] (1 · 1) 69
הִשְׁתָּעָה	10	to gaze about [in anxiety] (2 · 2 · 15) 1043 שעה
אִמֵּץ		to make firm, strengthen (3 · 19 · 41) 54
תמך		to hold up, support (3 · 20 · 21) 1069
נכלם	11	to be put to shame (5 · 26 · 38) 483
כְּאַיִן		as nothing (4 · 7) 34 אַיִן 1.
מַצּוּת	12	strife, contention (1 · 1) 663
כְּאַיִן		as nothing (4 · 7) 34 אַיִן 1.
אֶפֶס		nought (13 · 27) 67
תּוֹלַעַת	14	worm, grub (3 · 41) 1069 תּוֹלֵעָה
מַת		man, male (3 · 21) 607
גֹּאֵל		redeemer (13 · 44[?]) 145 גָּאַל

מוֹרַג 15 threshing sledge (1 · 3[?]) 558

חָרוּץ sharp (2 · 4) 358

פִיפִיּוֹת־
בַּעַל [idiom] = double edged 127 I בַּעַל
5.a.

פִיפִיּוֹת edges [pl. form of פֶּה] (1 · 2) 804 פֶּה

דָּשׁ to thresh, tread (4 · 13 · 16) 190 דוֹשׁ

דַּק to crush (2 · 4 · 13) 200 דקק

מֹץ chaff (3 · 8) 558

זרה 16 to fan, winnow (3 · 9 · 38) 279

סְעָרָה tempest, storm wind (3 · 16) 704

גיל to rejoice (11 · 45 · 45) 162

צָמֵא 17 thirst (3 · 17) 854

נשׁת to be dry, parched (1 · 2 · 3) 677

שְׁפִי 18 bare place, height (2 · 10) 1046

בִּקְעָת valley (3 · 19) 132

מַעְיָן spring (2 · 23) 745

אֲגַם pool, pond; troubled pond (4 · 8) 8

צִיָּה land of drought, desert (3 · 16) 851

מוֹצָא spring, source, going forth (2 · 27) 425

שִׁטָּה 19 acacia tree (1 · 28) 1008

הֲדַס myrtle tree (2 · 6) 213

בְּרוֹשׁ cypress or fir (5 · 20) 141

תִּדְהָר name of tree, prob. elm or pine (2 · 2) 187

תְּאַשּׁוּר box tree, small evergreen tree (2 · 3) 81

שִׂים (לֵב) 20 [idiom] "to pay attention to" 962 שׂים Qal 2.b.

בָּרָא to transform, create (20 · 38 · 48) 135

עָצְמָה 21 defense, defensive argument (1 · 1) 783

קרה 22 to befall (1 · 13 · 28) 899

שִׂים (לֵב) [idiom] "to pay attention to" 962 שׂים Qal 2.b.

אָתָה 23 to come; here, ptc. pl. fem. as subst. = things to come (9 · 19 · 21) 87

אָחוֹר with ל = hereafter (9 · 41) 30

הִשְׁתָּעָה to gaze at one another [in rivalry] (2 · 2 · 15) 1043 שׁעה

מֵאַיִן 24 whence? from where? (6 · 48[?]) 32 אין

פֹּעַל deed, thing done (6 · 37) 821

מֵאֶפַע nought; nonexistence (1 · 1) 67 אֶפֶס 2.a.

אָתָה 25 to come (9 · 19 · 21) 87

סָגָן prefect, ruler (1 · 17) 688

חֹמֶר mire, clay, mortar (5 · 17) 330

יוֹצֵר potter (3 · 17) 427 יצר

רָמַס to trample (4 · 17 · 18) 942

טיט clay, mud (2 · 13) 376

אֹמֶר 26 utterance, word (2 · 48) 56

מְבַשֵּׂר 27 one bringing glad tidings (4 · 9) 142 בשׂר

יוֹעֵץ 28 counselor (5 · 22) 419

אֶפֶס 29 nought, nothing (13 · 27) 67

תֹּהוּ that which is empty, unreal; confusion, formlessness (11 · 20) 1062

נֶסֶךְ here = molten image (>50) 651

Chapter 42

תמך 1 to hold up, support (3 · 20 · 21) 1069

בָּחִיר chosen, elect (6 · 13) 104

רָצָה to be pleased with, favorable to (1 · 42 · 50) 953

רצץ 3 to crush, ptc. pass. = crushed (4 · 11 · 19) 954

פִּשְׁתָּה flax; i.e., wick (2 · 4) 834

כֵּהֶה dim, faint (2 · 7) 462

כבה to quench, extinguish (2 · 10 · 24) 459

כהה 4 to grow dim, faint (1 · 5 · 9) 462

רצץ to get crushed out (4 · 11 · 19) 954

אִי pl. = coastlands and islands (17 · 36) 15

יחל to wait for = hope for (2 · 25 · 42) 404

בָּרָא	5	to shape, fashion, create (20 · 38 · 48) 135
רקע		to spread out (2 · 6 · 11) 955
צֶאֱצָא		produce, offspring (7 · 11) 425
נְשָׁמָה		breath, spirit (4 · 24) 675
פָּקַח	7	to open (3 · 17 · 20) 824
עִוֵּר		blind (11 · 26) 734
מַסְגֵּר		dungeon (2 · 7) 689
אַסִּיר		[coll.] prisoner (4 · 17) 64
כֶּלֶא		confinement, imprisonment (2 · 10) 4/6
פָּסִיל	8	idol, image (4 · 23) 820
בְּטֶרֶם	9	before (8 · 39) 382
צָמַח		to sprout, spring up (4 · 15 · 33) 855
מְלֹא	10	fullness, entire contents (5 · 38) 571
אִי		pl. = coastlands and islands (17 · 36) 15
צוח	11	to cry aloud (1 · 1 · 1) 846
אִי	12	pl. = coastlands and islands (17 · 36) 15
קִנְאָה	13	zeal (7 · 43) 888
הֵרִיעַ		to shout a war cry, alarm of battle (3 · 40 · 44) 929 רוע
הִצְרִיחַ		to utter a roar (1 · 1 · 2) 863
הִתְגַּבֵּר		to show oneself mighty (1 · 3 · 25) 149
הֶחֱשָׁה	14	to be silent (2 · 9 · 16) 364
הֶחֱרִישׁ		to be silent (3 · 38 · 46) 361
הִתְאַפֵּק		to restrain oneself, refrain (3 · 7 · 7) 67
פעה		to groan (1 · 1 · 1) 821
נשם		to pant (1 · 1 · 1) 675
שָׁאַף		to gasp (1 · 14 · 14) 983
יַחַד		together (7 · 44) 403
הֶחֱרִיב	15	to lay waste, make desolate (6 · 13 · 37[?]) 351
עֵשֶׂב		herb, herbage (2 · 33) 793
אִי		coasts, banks (17 · 36) 15
אֲגַם		pool, pond (4 · 8) 8
עִוֵּר	16	blind (11 · 26) 734
נְתִיבָה		path, course of life (4 · 21) 677
מַחְשָׁךְ		dark region, dark place (2 · 7) 365
מַעֲקָשׁ		twisted, crooked place (1 · 1) 786
מִישׁוֹר		level country, plain (3 · 23) 449
נָסוֹג	17	to be turned, driven back (3 · 14 · 25) 690 סוג
אָחוֹר		with ל = hereafter (9 · 41) 30
בֹּשֶׁת		shame (5 · 30) 102
פֶּסֶל		idol, image (9 · 31) 820
מַסֵּכָה		molten metal, image (2 · 25) 651
חֵרֵשׁ	18	deaf (5 · 9) 361
עִוֵּר		blind (11 · 26) 734
עִוֵּר	19	blind (11 · 26) 734
חֵרֵשׁ		deaf (5 · 9) 361
מְשֻׁלָּם		ptc. = one in covenant of peace 1023 שלם
פָּקַח	20	to open (3 · 17 · 20) 824
הַאְדִּיר	21	to make glorious (1 · 1 · 3) 12
בָּזַז	22	to plunder, despoil (7 · 37 · 41) 102
שסה		to spoil, plunder (1 · 4 · 5) 1042
הֵפַח		to ensnare (1 · 1 · 1) 809 פחח
חוּר		hole (2 · 2) 359
כֶּלֶא		confinement, imprisonment (2 · 10) 476
הֶחְבָּא		to be hidden (1 · 1 · 34) 285
בַּז		spoil, booty, plunder (5 · 27) 103
מְשִׁסָּה		plunder, spoil, prey (2 · 6) 1042
הַאֲזִין	23	to give ear, listen (8 · 41 · 41) 24
הִקְשִׁיב		to give attention (8 · 45 · 46) 904
אָחוֹר		with ל = hereafter (9 · 41) 30
מְשִׁסָּה	24	K משוסה booty, plunder (2 · 6) 1042
בָּזַז		to plunder (7 · 37 · 41) 102
זוּ		which, who (2 · 14) 262
עֱזוּז	25	fierceness, might (1 · 3) 739
להט		to set ablaze (1 · 9 · 11) 529
מִסָּבִיב		on every side (1 · 42) 687

43

Chapter 43

בָּרָא 1 to shape, fashion, create
(20 · 38 · 48) 135

יָצַר to form, fashion (22 · 41 · 44)
427

שָׁטַף 2 to overflow (9 · 28 · 31) 1009

בְּמוֹ poet. for בְּ (4 · 10) 91

נכוה to be scorched (1 · 2 · 2) 464

לֶהָבָה flame (5 · 19) 529

מוֹשִׁיעַ 3 savior, deliverer (9 · 27) 446 ישׁע

כֹּפֶר ransom, the price of a life (1 · 13)
497

מֵאֲשֶׁר 4 from that, since (2 · 17) 84

יקר to be highly valued, esteemed, precious (1 · 9 · 11) 429

לְאֹם people (11 · 35) 522

מַעֲרָב 5 west, place of sunset (3 · 14) 788

תֵּימָן 6 south, southern quarter (1 · 24) 412

כלא to withhold (1 · 14 · 17) 476

מֵרָחוֹק from a distance (12 · 34) 935

בָּרָא 7 to shape, fashion, create
(20 · 38 · 48) 135

יָצַר to form, fashion (22 · 41 · 44) 427

עִוֵּר 8 blind (11 · 26) 734

חֵרֵשׁ deaf (5 · 9) 361

לְאֹם 9 people (11 · 35) 522

צדק to be justified (3 · 22 · 41) 842

נוֹצַר 10 to be formed (1 · 1 · 44) 428

מִבַּלְעֲדֵי 11 apart from, without (5 · 12) 116
בלעדי b.

מוֹשִׁיעַ savior, deliverer (9 · 27) 446
ישׁע

גָּאַל 14 redeemer (13 · 44) 145 גאל

בָּרִיחַ fugitive, fleeing one (2 · 3) 138

אֳנִיָּה ship (5 · 31) 58

רִנָּה ringing cry, exultation (9 · 33) 943

בָּרָא 15 to shape, fashion, create
(20 · 38 · 48) 135

עַז 16 strong, mighty, fierce (4 · 22) 738

נְתִיבָה path (4 · 21) 677

עִזּוּז 17 mighty, powerful (1 · 2) 739

דעך to go out, be extinguished (1 · 7 · 9)
200

פִּשְׁתָּה flax; i.e., wick (2 · 4) 834

כבה to be quenched, extinguished
(3 · 14 · 24) 459

קַדְמֹנִי 18 former things, former (1 · 10) 870

צָמַח 19 to sprout, spring up (4 · 15 · 33)
855

יְשִׁימֹן waste, wilderness (2 · 13) 445

תַּן 20 jackal (4 · 14) 1072

יַעֲנָה ostrich (3 · 8) 419

יְשִׁימֹן waste, wilderness (2 · 13) 445

בָּחִיר chosen, elect (6 · 13) 104

זוּ 21 who, which (2 · 14) 262

יָצַר to form, fashion (22 · 41 · 44)
427

יגע 22 to grow or be weary (10 · 20 · 26)
388

שֶׂה 23 a sheep, goat (4 · 45) 961

הוֹגִיעַ to make to toil, to weary (2 · 4 · 26)
388

לְבוֹנָה frankincense (3 · 21) 526

הִרְוָה 24 to cause to drink (2 · 5 · 14) 924

הוֹגִיעַ to make to toil, to weary (2 · 4 · 26)
388

מָחָה 25 to blot out, obliterate (3 · 22 · 34)
562

יַחַד 26 together (7 · 44) 403

צדק to be justified (3 · 22 · 41) 842

הֵלִיץ 27 *Hiph.* ptc. = interpreter, inter-
mediary; vb. = to deride
(1 · 9 · 12) 539

פָּשַׁע to transgress, rebel (9 · 40 · 41) 833

חֵרֶם 28 devotion, ban involving destruction
(2 · 29) 356

גִּדּוּפִים revilings, reviling words (2 · 2) 154

Chapter 44

עֹשֶׂה	2 maker, creator (6 · 24[?]) 793	I. עשה
יָצַר	to form, fashion (22 · 41 · 44) 427	
צָמֵא	3 thirsty place, thirsty (5 · 9) 854	
נֹזֵל	streams, flows (1 · 6) 633	נזל
יַבָּשָׁה	dry land, dry ground (1 · 14) 387	
צֶאֱצָא	offspring (7 · 11) 425	
צָמַח	4 to sprout, spring up (4 · 15 · 33) 855	
בְּבֵין	in the midst of, among (1 · 1) 107	
חָצִיר	green grass (2[?] · 3[?]) 348	
עֲרָבָה	poplar, Euphrates poplar (2 · 5) 788	
יָבָל	watercourse, stream (2 · 2) 385	
כנה	5 to title, give an epithet (2 · 4 · 4) 487	
גֹּאֵל	6 redeemer, kinsman (13 · 44) 145	גאל
מִבַּלְעֲדֵי	apart from, without (5 · 12) 116	
	בלעדי b.	
אתה	7 to come; ptc. pl. = things to come (9 · 19 · 21) 87	
פָּחַד	8 to be in dread (7 · 23 · 26) 808	
רהה	to fear [dub.] (1 · 1 · 1) 923	
מֵאָז	in time past = of old (8 · 18) 23	
מִבַּלְעֲדֵי	apart from, without (5 · 12) 116	
	בלעדי b.	
יָצַר	9 to form; ptc. = carver, graver (22 · 41 · 44) 427	
פֶּסֶל	idol, image (9 · 31) 820	
תֹּהוּ	what is empty, unreal (11 · 20) 1062	
חָמַד	to take pleasure in, desire (3 · 16 · 21) 326	
הוֹעִיל	to profit, avail, benefit (8 · 23 · 23) 418	
יָצַר	10 to form, fashion (22 · 41 · 44) 427	
פֶּסֶל	idol, image (9 · 31) 820	
נָסַךְ	to cast, pour out; with פסל, to cast metal images (4 · 7 · 25) 650	
הוֹעִיל	to profit, avail, benefit (8 · 23 · 23) 418	
חָבֵר	11 worshiping associate, worshiping companion (2 · 12) 288	

חָרָשׁ	graver, artificer, idol maker (8 · 38) 360	
פָּחַד	to be in dread (7 · 23 · 26) 808	
יַחַד	together, altogether (7 · 44) 403	
חָרָשׁ	12 graver, artificer (8 · 38) 360	
מַעֲצָד	axe (1 · 2) 781	
פֶּחָם	coal (2 · 3) 809	
מַקָּבֶת	hammer (1 · 4) 666	
יָצַר	to form, fashion (22 · 41 · 44) 427	
רָעֵב	to be hungry (5 · 12 · 14) 944	
יעף	to be weary, faint (4 · 8 · 9) 419	
חָרָשׁ	13 graver, artificer (8 · 38) 360	
קַו	measuring line, line (16[?] · 25[?]) 876	
תאר	to draw in outline, trace out (2 · 2 · 8[?]) 1061	
שֶׂרֶד	marking tool for wood, stylus (1 · 1) 975	
מַקְצוּעָה	scraping tool (1 · 1) 893	
מְחוּגָה	compass (1 · 1) 295	
תַּבְנִית	figure, image, pattern (1 · 20) 125	
תִּפְאֶרֶת	beauty, finery, glory (18 · 50) 802	
תִּרְזָה	14 tree, cypress [dub.] (1 · 1) 1076	
אַלּוֹן	oak (3 · 9) 47	
אמץ	to assure or secure for oneself; to make firm (3 · 19 · 41) 54	
אֹרֶן	fir or cedar (1 · 1) 75	
גֶּשֶׁם	rain, shower (2 · 35) 177	
חַם	15 to be or grow warm (5 · 23 · 26) 328	
	חמם	
הִשִּׂיק	to make a fire burn (1 · 2 · 3[?]) 969	
	שׂלק	
אָפָה	to bake (2 · 10 · 13) 66	
פֶּסֶל	idol, image (9 · 31) 820	
סגד	to prostrate oneself in worship (4 · 4 · 4) 688	
בְּמוֹ	16 poetic for ב (4 · 10) 91	
צלה	to roast (2 · 3 · 3) 852	
צָלִי	roast, roasted (1 · 3) 852	

חַם to be or grow warm (5 · 23 · 26) 328
חמם

הֶאָח Aha! interjection expressing joy (1 · 9) 210

פֶּסֶל 17 idol, image (9 · 31) 820

סגד to prostrate oneself in worship (4 · 4 · 4) 688

טַח 18 to be smeared (1 · 1 · 1) 377 טחח

תְּבוּנָה 19 the faculty of understanding, understanding (3 · 42) 108

בְּמוֹ poetic for בְּ (4 · 10) 91

אָפָה to bake (2 · 10 · 13) 66

גֶּחָלֶת coal (2 · 18) 160

צָלָה to roast (2 · 3 · 3) 852

בּוּל produce, outgrowth (1 · 2) 385

סגד to prostrate oneself in worship (4 · 4 · 4) 688

אֵפֶר 20 ashes (3 · 22) 68

הוּתַל to be deceived (1 · 1 · 9) 1068

יָצַר 21 to form, fashion (22 · 41 · 44) 427

נשה to be forgotten (1 · 1 · 5) 674

מָחָה 22 to blot out (3 · 22 · 34) 562

עָב dark cloud (7 · 30) 728

הָרִיעַ 23 to shout, cry out (3 · 40 · 44) 929

תַּחְתִּי lowest [place] (1 · 19) 1066

פָּצַח to break forth with (6 · 7 · 7) 822

רִנָּה ringing cry [in joy] (9 · 33) 943

הִתְפָּאֵר to get glory to oneself, be glorified by means of [בְּ] (5 · 7 · 13) 802

גֹּאֵל 24 redeemer, kinsman (13 · 44) 145

יָצַר to form, fashion (22 · 41 · 44) 427

רקע to spread out, beat out (2 · 6 · 11) 955

הֵפֵר 25 to frustrate, make ineffectual (4 · 42 · 45) 830 פרר

בַּד empty talker, prater (2 · 6) 95

קֹסֵם diviner (1 · 9[?]) 890 קסם

הוֹלֵל to make into a fool (1 · 4 · 14[?]) 239 הלל

אָחוֹר backwards; back part (9 · 41) 30

שָׂכַל to turn into foolishness (1 · 2 · 8) 698 סכל

חָרְבָּה 26 waste, ruin (9 · 42) 352

צוּלָה 27 ocean deep (1 · 1) 846

חרב to be waste, desolate (6 · 17 · 37[?]) 351

חֵפֶץ 28 good pleasure, delight (9 · 39) 343

נוּסַד to be founded (1 · 2 · 41) 413 יסד

Chapter 45

מָשִׁיחַ 1 anointed, commissioned one (1 · 39) 603

רדד to beat down (1 · 2 · 3) 921

מָתְנַיִם loins, place where sword (et al.) is attached (4 · 47) 608

הדר 2 to swell, honor; ptc. (1 · 1) = swells of land (1 · 4 · 6) 213

ישר to make smooth, strait (3 · 9 · 25) 448

נְחוּשָׁה copper, bronze (2 · 10) 639

בְּרִיחַ bar (2 · 41) 138

גָּדַע to hew off, [cut] down, [cut] in two (1 · 9 · 22) 154

מַטְמוֹן 3 hidden treasure, treasure (1 · 5) 380

מִסְתָּר secret place, hiding place (1 · 10) 712

בָּחִיר 4 chosen, elect (6 · 13) 104

כנה to title, give an epithet (2 · 4 · 4) 487

זוּלָה 5 except, besides (4 · 16) 265

אזר to gird (2 · 6 · 16) 25

מַעֲרָב 6 west, place of sunset (3 · 14) 788

אֶפֶס nonexistence; cessation of (13 · 27) 67

בִּלְעֲדֵי except, besides, apart from (1 · 4) 116

יָצַר 7 to form, fashion (22 · 41 · 44) 427

בָּרָא to create, shape, fashion (20 · 38 · 48) 135

הִרְעִיף 8 to trickle (1 · 1 · 5) 950

מִמַּעַל above (3 · 29) 751 מעל 1.

שַׁחַק   cloud, fine dust (2 · 21) 1007

נזל   to flow, stream (1 · 8 · 9) 633

פרה   to be fruitful, bear fruit (4 · 22 · 29) 826

יֶשַׁע   salvation, deliverance, rescue (5 · 36) 447

הצמיח   to cause to sprout, grow (4 · 14 · 33) 855

יַחַד   together (7 · 44) 403

בָּרָא   to create, shape, fashion (20 · 38 · 48) 135

יָצַר   9 to form, fashion; oft. ptc. = potter (22 · 41 · 44) 427

חֶרֶשׂ   earthen vessels (3 · 17) 360

חֹמֶר   clay, mortar, cement (5 · 17) 330

פֹּעַל   work, thing made (6 · 37) 821

חִיל   10 to twist, writhe [in childbirth] (9 · 30 · 47) 296 חול

יָצַר   11 to form, fashion; oft. ptc. = potter (22 · 41 · 44) 427

אתה   to come; ptc. pl. = things to come (9 · 19 · 21) 87

פֹּעַל   work, thing made (6 · 37) 821

בָּרָא   12 to shape, fashion, create (20 · 38 · 48) 135

ישׁר   13 to make smooth, strait (3 · 9 · 25) 448

גלות   [coll.] exiles (2 · 15) 163

מְחִיר   reward, gain, hire, price (2 · 15) 564

שֹׁחַד   bribe, present (4 · 23) 1005

יְגִיעַ   14 product, produce, acquired property (2 · 16) 388

סַחַר   traffic, gain (4 · 8) 695

זֵק   fetter; only זקים (1 · 4) 279

אֶפֶס   nonexistence, cessation of (13 · 27) 67

אָכֵן   15 surely, truly (4 · 18) 38

מוֹשִׁיעַ   savior, deliverer (9 · 27) 446 ישׁע

נכלם   16 to be put to shame, dishonored (5 · 26 · 38) 483

כְּלִימָה   reproach, ignominy (4 · 30) 484

חָרָשׁ   idol maker, graver, artificer (8 · 38) 360

צִיר   image (1 · 1) 849

תְּשׁוּעָה   17 deliverance, salvation (3 · 34) 448

נכלם   to be humiliated, ashamed (5 · 26 · 38) 483

עַד   forever (8 · 48) 723 I. עד

בָּרָא   18 to shape, fashion, create (20 · 38 · 48) 135

יָצַר   to form, fashion (22 · 41 · 44) 427

תֹּהוּ   formlessness, primeval chaos (11 · 20) 1062

סֵתֶר   19 secrecy; with ב = secretly (5 · 35) 712

תֹּהוּ   worthlessness, what is unreal (11 · 20) 1062

מֵישָׁר   uprightness, equity (3 · 19) 449

פָּלִיט   20 escaped one, fugitive (1 · 19) 812

פֶּסֶל   idol, image (9 · 31) 820

מֵאָז   21 in time past = of old (8 · 18) 23

מִבַּלְעֲדֵי   apart from, without (5 · 12) 116 בלעדי b.

מוֹשִׁיעַ   savior, deliverer (9 · 27) 446 ישׁע

זוּלָה   except, besides (4 · 16) 265

אֶפֶס   22 end, extremity (13 · 27) 67

כָּרַע   23 to bow, bow down (5 · 30 · 36) 502

בֶּרֶךְ   knee (3 · 25) 139

צדק   25 to be justified, be just (3 · 22 · 41) 842

Chapter 46

כָּרַע   1 to bow down, bow (5 · 30 · 36) 502

קרס   to bend down, stoop, crouch (2 · 2 · 2) 902

עָצָב   idol (2 · 17) 781

נְשׂוּאָה   things borne about (1 · 1[?]) 672

עמס   Qal pass. ptc. = being a load; i.e., burdensome (2 · 7 · 9) 770

מַשָּׂא   load, burden (3 · 42) 672

עָיֵף   faint, weary (5 · 17) 746

קרס   2 to bend down, stoop, crouch (2 · 2 · 2) 902

כָּרַע   to bow down, bow (5 · 30 · 36) 502

מַשָּׂא   load, burden (3 · 42) 672

שְׁבִי   captivity, captives (4 · 49) 985

עמס   3 *Qal* pass. ptc. = to be carried as a load (2 · 7 · 9) 770

רֶחֶם   womb (1 · 33) 933

זִקְנָה   4 old age (1 · 6) 279

שֵׂיבָה   gray hair, hoary head, old age (1 · 20[?]) 966

סבל   to bear a load, carry (5 · 7 · 9) 687

לְמִי   5 to whom (1 · 20) 566

דָּמָה   to liken to, consider to be like (5 · 13 · 26) 197

השׁוה   to make like (1 · 2 · 16) 1000

הַמְשִׁיל   to compare (1 · 1 · 15) 605

דָּמָה   to be like, resemble (2 · 13 · 27) 197

זול   6 to lavish (1 · 1 · 1) 266

כִּיס   bag, purse (1 · 5) 476

קָנֶה   beam [of scales]; here used idiomatically of scales (>50) 889 קנה 4.c.

שָׁקַל   to weigh (4 · 19 · 22) 1053

שָׂכַר   to hire (1 · 17 · 20) 968

צָרֵף   smelter, refiner (3 · 10) 864 צרף

סגד   to prostrate oneself in worship (4 · 4 · 4) 688

סבל   7 to carry, bear (5 · 7 · 9) 687

הָמִישׁ   to leave its place, depart (5 · 20 [?] · 20[?]) 559 מושׁ

התאשׁשׁ   8 to show oneself firm (1 · 1 · 1) 84

פָּשַׁע   to transgress, rebel (9 · 40 · 41) 833

אֶפֶס   9 end of, nonexistence of, cessation of (13 · 27) 67

חֵפֶץ   10 will, purpose, good pleasure, delight (9 · 39) 343

עַיִט   11 bird[s] of prey (3 · 8) 743

מֶרְחָק   distant place, far country (7 · 18) 935

יָצַר   to form, fashion; fig. for preordain, plan (22 · 41 · 44) 427

אַבִּיר   12 strong, the strong one (3 · 17) 7

תְּשׁוּעָה   13 deliverance, salvation (3 · 34) 448

אָחַר   to delay, tarry (2 · 15 · 17) 29

תִּפְאֶרֶת   glory, beauty (18 · 50) 802

Chapter 47

בְּתוּלָה   1 virgin (5 · 50) 143

רַךְ   tender, delicate, soft (1 · 16) 940

עָנֹג   dainty (1 · 3) 772

רֵחַיִם   2 [hand] mill (1 · 5) 932 רחה

טחן   to grind (2 · 7 · 7) 377

קֶמַח   flour, meal (1 · 14) 887

צַמָּה   woman's veil (1 · 4) 855

חָשַׂף   to strip off, make bare (3 · 10 · 10) 362

שֹׁבֶל   flowing skirt, train (1 · 1) 987

שׁוֹק   leg, lower leg, calf (1 · 19) 1003

נָקָם   3 vengeance (6 · 17) 668

פָּגַע   to meet (2 · 40 · 46) 803

גֹּאֵל   4 redeemer, kinsman (13 · 44) 145 גאל

דּוּמָם   5 in silence, silent; silence (1 · 3) 189

גְּבֶרֶת   lady, queen; mistress (3 · 15[?]) 150

קָצַף   6 to be angry (7 · 28 · 34) 893

רַחֲמִים   compassion (4 · 38) 933

עֹל   yoke (5 · 40) 760

גְּבֶרֶת   7 lady, queen; mistress (3 · 15[?]) 150

עַד   forever (8 · 48) 723 I. עד

עֲדִין   8 voluptuous (1 · 2) 726

בֶּטַח   security; w. לְ = securely (3 · 43) 105

אֶפֶס   nonexistence; w. עוד = none besides (13 · 27[?]) 67

שְׁכוֹל   bereavement, loss of children (2 · 3) 1013

רֶגַע   9 in a moment, suddenly (5 · 22) 921

שְׁכוֹל bereavement, loss of children (2 · 3) 1013

אַלְמֹן widowhood (1 · 1) 48

תֹם completeness, fullness, integrity (1-23) 1070

כֶּשֶׁף sorcery (2 · 6) 506

עָצְמָה might (2 · 2[?]) 782

חֶבֶר spell; association, company (2 · 7) 288

אֶפֶס 10 nonexistence; w. עוד = none besides (13 · 27[?]) 67

שַׁחַר 11 perh. dawn; i.e., origin (2 · 12 · 13 [?]) 1007 שחר

הֹוָה ruin, disaster (1 · 3) 217

פִּתְאֹם suddenly (4 · 25) 837

שׁוֹאָה devastation, ruin (2 · 13) 996

חֶבֶר 12 spell; association, company (2 · 7) 288

כֶּשֶׁף sorcery (2 · 6) 506

בַּאֲשֶׁר in [that] which (4 · 19) 84

יגע to toil, labor (10 · 20 · 26) 388

נְעוּרִים youth, early life (3 · 46) 655

אוּלַי perhaps (3 · 45) 19

הוֹעִיל to gain profit (8 · 23 · 23) 418

ערץ to cause to tremble = to inspire awe (3 · 11 · 14) 791

נִלְאָה 13 to be weary, weary oneself (3 · 10 · 19) 521

הבר to divide [dub.] (1 · 1 · 1) 211

כּוֹכָב star (3 · 37) 456

מֵאֲשֶׁר from [that] which (2 · 17) 84

קַשׁ 14 stubble, chaff (5 · 16) 905

לֶהָבָה flame [error in B.H.³ reads להבד] (5 · 19) 529

גַּחֶלֶת coal (2 · 18) 160

יגע 15 to toil, labor (10 · 20 · 26) 388

סֹחֵר trafficker, trader (3 · 16) 695 סחר

נְעוּרִים youth, early life (3 · 46) 655

תָּעָה to wander about, err (8 · 27 · 50) 1073

מוֹשִׁיעַ savior, deliverer (9 · 27[?]) 446 ישע

Chapter 48

נסמך 2 to support oneself (2 · 6 · 48) 701

מֵאָז 3 in time past = of old (8 · 18) 23

פִּתְאֹם suddenly (4 · 25) 837

קָשֶׁה 4 stubborn, hard (6 · 36) 904

גִּיד sinew (1 · 7) 161

עֹרֶף neck (1 · 33) 791

מֵצַח brow, forehead (1 · 13) 594

נְחוּשָׁה bronze (2 · 10) 639

מֵאָז 5 in time past = of old (8 · 18) 23

בְּטֶרֶם before (8 · 39) 382

עֹצֶב idol (1 · 1) 781

פֶּסֶל idol, image (9 · 31) 820

נברא 7 to be created (1 · 10 · 48) 135

מֵאָז in time past = of old (8 · 18) 23

מֵאָז 8 in time past = of old (8 · 18) 23

בגד to deal treacherously (12 · 49 · 49) 93

פָּשַׁע to transgress, rebel (9 · 40 · 41) 833

הַאֲרִיךְ 9 to postpone, prolong (4 · 31 · 34) 73

חטם to restrain, hold in (1 · 1 · 1) 310

צָרַף 10 to test, refine, smelt (3 · 19 · 22) 864

בחר to test, try (>50) 103 בחר Qal 8.

כּוּר smelting pot, furnace (1 · 9) 468

עֳנִי affliction (1 · 36) 777

יָסַד 13 to found, establish (5 · 20 · 41) 413

טפח to spread out (1 · 1 · 1[?]) 381

חֵפֶץ 14 will, purpose; good pleasure, delight (9 · 39) 343

סֵתֶר 16 secrecy, with בְּ = secretly (5 · 35) 712

גֹּאֵל 17 redeemer, kinsman (13 · 44) 145 גאל

הוֹעִיל to gain profit (8 · 23 · 23) 418

לוּא 18 if only! (2 · 3) 530

הִקְשִׁיב to give attention (8 · 45 · 46) 904

גַּל heap; pl., waves (2[?] · 16[?]) 164

חוֹל sand (2 · 22) 297

צֶאֱצָא 19 offspring, produce (7 · 11) 425

מֵעָה inward parts (4 · 32) 588

49

מֵעָה   grain [of sand] (1 · 1) 589

רִנָּה   20   ringing cry [in joy] (9 · 33) 943

צָמֵא   21   to be thirsty (3 · 10 · 10) 854

חָרְבָּה   desert, waste place, desolation
(9 · 42) 352

הִזִּיל   to cause to flow (1 · 1 · 9) 633

זוּב   to flow, gush (1 · 29 · 29) 264

Chapter 49

אִי   1   coast; אִיֵּי הַיָּם = coastlands and islands (17 · 36) 15

הִקְשִׁיב   to give attention (8 · 45 · 46) 904

לְאֹם   people (11 · 35) 522

מֵרָחוֹק   from a distance (12 · 134) 935

מֵעֶה   womb, internal organs (4 · 32) 588

חַד   2   sharp (1 · 4) 292

הֶחְבִּיא   to hide (1 · 6 · 34) 285

בָּרַר   to cleanse, polish (1 · 1 · 2) 140

אַשְׁפָּה   quiver (2 · 6) 80

הִתְפָּאֵר   3   to be glorified by means of [בְּ]
(5 · 7 · 13) 802

רִיק   4   emptiness, vanity; w. לְ = in vain
(3 · 12) 938

יָגַע   to toil, labor (10 · 20 · 26) 388

תֹּהוּ   worthlessness (11 · 20) 1062

אָכֵן   but indeed, but in fact (4 · 18) 38

פְּעֻלָּה   reward, wages (5 · 14) 821

יָצַר   5   to form, fashion (22 · 41 · 44) 427

גָּאַל   7   redeemer, kinsman (13 · 44) 145 גֹּאֵל

בָּזָה   to despise (1 · 31 · 42) 102

תִּעֵב   to cause to be an abomination
(1 · 15 · 22) 1073

מֹשֵׁל   ruler (4 · 24) 605 מָשַׁל

לַאֲשֶׁר   9   to him who, those who (4 · 38) 81
אֲשֶׁר 4.c.

שְׁפִי   bare place, height (2 · 10) 1046

מַרְעִית   pasturage (1 · 10) 945

רָעֵב   10   to be hungry (5 · 12 · 14) 944

צָמֵא   to be thirsty (3 · 10 · 10) 854

שָׁרָב   burning heat (2 · 2) 1055

רִחַם   to have compassion (12 · 42 · 47) 933

נָהַג   to lead on, guide (2 · 10 · 30) 624

מַבּוּעַ   spring of water (2 · 3) 616

נִהֵל   to lead to a watering place and
cause to rest there (3 · 9 · 10) 624

מְסִלָּה   11   raised way, highway (9 · 27) 700

מֵרָחוֹק   12   from a distance (12 · 34) 935

גִּיל   13   to rejoice (11 · 45 · 45) 162

פָּצַח   to break forth with (6 · 7 · 7) 822

רִנָּה   ringing cry (9 · 33) 943

רִחַם   to have compassion (12 · 42 · 47) 933

עוּל   15   suckling child (2 · 2) 732

רִחַם   to have compassion (12 · 42 · 47) 933

חָקַק   16   to engrave, inscribe (4 · 8 · 11) 349

הָרַס   17   to destroy, tear down (1 · 3 · 43) 248

הֶחֱרִיב   to lay waste, make desolate
(6 · 13 · 37[?]) 351

מִמֵּךְ   redupl. of מִן w. suffix 577

עֲדִי   18   ornaments (1 · 14) 725

קָשַׁר   to bind on (1 · 2 · 44) 905

כַּלָּה   bride, daughter-in-law (3 · 34) 483

חָרְבָּה   19   waste, ruin (9 · 42) 352

הֲרִסֻת   overthrow, destruction, ruin (1 · 1)
249

בִּלַּע   to swallow up, engulf (3 · 10 · 41)
118

שִׁכֻּלִים   20   bereavement, childlessness (1 · 1)
1014

צַר   narrow, tight (5[?] · 20[?]) 865

שָׁכוּל   21   childless (1 · 1) 1014

גַּלְמוּד   barren (1 · 4) 166

גּוֹלָה   exile, exiles (1 · 43) 163

סוּרָה   one made to depart, thrust away
(1 · 3) 693 סוּר Qal 2.

אֵיפֹה   where? (1 · 10) 33

נֵס   22   standard (10 · 21) 651

חֹצֶן   bosom (1 · 3) 346

אֹמֵן   23   foster father (1 · 7) 52 אָמַן Qal 2.

שָׂרָה   princess, noble lady (1 · 5) 979

מֵינֶקֶת nursing; אשה מ = a nursing woman, a nurse (1 · 5) 413 ינק

לחך to lick (1 · 5 · 6) 535

קוה to wait for; ptc. pl. = those waiting for (2 · 6 · 45) 875

מַלְקוֹחַ 24 booty, prey (2 · 6) 544

שְׁבִי [coll.] captives, captivity (4 · 49) 985

שְׁבִי 25 [coll.] captives, captivity (4 · 49) 985

מַלְקוֹחַ booty, prey (2 · 6) 544

עָרִיץ awe inspiring, terror striking (7 · 20) 792

יָרִיב opponent, adversary (1 · 3) 937

הוֹנָה 26 to oppress, maltreat (1 · 14 · 18) 413

עָסִיס sweet wine (1 · 5) 779

שׁכר to become drunken (2 · 9 · 18) 1016

מוֹשִׁיעַ savior, deliverer (9 · 27) 446 ישע Hiph. 1.b.

גֹּאֵל kinsman, redeemer (13 · 44) 145 גאל

אָבִיר strong, the Strong One (3 · 17) 7

Chapter 50

אֵי 1 where? (4 · 39) 32 אי

אֵי זֶה idiom = where, then? 261 זֶה 4.a.

כְּרִיתוּת divorcement (1 · 4) 504

נֹשֶׁא creditor (1 · 5) 674 נשה

קָצַר 2 to be short; short of hand = powerless (4 · 12 · 14) 894

פְּדוּת ransom (1 · 4) 804

גְּעָרָה rebuke (6 · 15) 172

הֶחֱרִיב to dry up (6 · 13 · 37[?]) 351

בָּאַשׁ to have a bad smell, stink (1 · 5 · 16) 92

דָּגָה fish [coll.] (1 · 15) 185

מֵאֵין from lack of (6 · 48[?]) 34 אין 6.d.

צָמָא thirst (3 · 17) 854

קַדְרוּת 3 darkness, gloom (1 · 1) 871

שַׂק sackcloth (8 · 48) 974

כְּסוּת clothing, covering (1 · 8) 492

לִמֻּד 4 taught [one]; i.e., a disciple (4 · 6) 541

עות to help [dub.] (1 · 1 · 1) 736

יָעֵף weary, faint (2 · 4) 419

בַּבֹּקֶר בַּבֹּקֶר idiom = morning by morning, every morning 134 בקר 1.f.

מָרָה 5 to be disobedient, rebellious (3 · 21 · 43) 598

אָחוֹר backwards; back part (9 · 41) 30

נָסוֹג to turn oneself away, turn back, prove faithless (3 · 14 · 25) 690

גֵּו 6 back (3 · 6) 156

לְחִי cheek, jaw (2 · 21) 534

מרט to make bare, bald, smooth (1 · 7 · 14) 598

כְּלִמָּה reproach, ignominy (4 · 30) 484

רֹק spittle (1 · 3) 956

נכלם 7 to be humiliated, ashamed (5 · 26 · 38) 483

חַלָּמִישׁ flint (1 · 5) 321

הַצְדִּיק 8 to justify, vindicate (3 · 12 · 41) 842

יַחַד together (7 · 44) 403

הַרְשִׁיעַ 9 to condemn as guilty (2 · 25 · 34) 957

בלה to wear out (2 · 11 · 16) 115

עָשׁ moth (2 · 7) 799

יָרֵא 10 fear, reverence, honor (1[?] · 45) 431 ירא

חֲשֵׁכָה darkness (2 · 6) 365

נֹגַהּ brightness (5 · 19) 618

נִשְׁעַן to lean, support oneself (5 · 22 · 22) 1043

קדח 11 to kindle (2 · 5 · 5) 869

אזר to gird (2 · 6 · 16) 25

זִיקוֹת sparks, brands (2 · 2) 278 זק

מַעֲצֵבָה place of pain (1 · 1) 781

51

Chapter 51

חָצֵב 1 to be hewn (1 · 1 · 17) 345

מַקֶּבֶת hole, excavation (1 · 1) 666

נקר to be dug (1 · 1 · 6) 669

חוֹלֵל 2 to writhe in travail with, bear, bring forth (1 · 7 · 47) 296

חָרְבָּה 3 waste place, ruin (9 · 42) 352

גַּן garden (2 · 42) 171

שָׂשׂוֹן exultation, joy (6 · 22) 965

תּוֹדָה thanksgiving in songs of liturgical worship, thanksgiving (1 · 32) 392

הִקְשִׁיב 4 to give attention (8 · 45 · 46) 904

לְאוֹם people (11 · 35) 522

הֶאֱזִין to hear, give ear (8 · 41 · 41) 24

הִרְגִּיעַ to give rest to [but use here idiomatic and uncertain] (2 · 8 · 13[?]) 921 II

יֶשַׁע 5 salvation, deliverance, rescue (5 · 36) 447

אִי coastlands, islands (17 · 36) 15

קוה to wait, look eagerly for (13 · 39 · 45) 875

יחל to wait for, hope for (2 · 25 · 42) 404

עָשָׁן 6 smoke (7 · 25) 798

נמלח to be dispersed in fragments, dissipated (1 · 1 · 1) 571

בלה to wear out (2 · 11 · 16) 115

כֵּן gnat, gnats, gnat swarm [dub.] (1 · 5) 48

אֱנוֹשׁ 7 men; man, mankind (8 · 42) 60

גִּדּוּפִים revilings, reviling words (2 · 3) 154

עָשׁ 8 moth (2 · 7) 799

צֶמֶר wool (2 · 16) 856

סָס moth (1 · 1) 703

הַחֲצִיב 9 to hew in pieces (1 · 1 · 17) 345

רַהַב storm, arrogance [here used for mythical sea monster] (2 · 7) 923

חוֹלֵל to pierce (2 · 3 · 7) 319

תַּנִּין sea monster, serpent, dragon (2 · 15) 1072

הֶחֱרִיב 10 to dry up (6 · 13 · 37[?]) 351

תְּהוֹם deep, sea, abyss (2 · 36) 1062

מַעֲמַקִּים depths (1 · 5) 771

רִנָּה 11 ringing cry [in joy] (9 · 33) 943

שָׂשׂוֹן exultation, joy (6 · 22) 965

הִשִּׂיג to reach, attain, overtake (3 · 49 · 49) 673

יָגוֹן grief, sorrow (2 · 14) 387

אֲנָחָה sighing, groaning (3 · 11) 58

אֱנוֹשׁ 12 man, mankind (8 · 42) 60

חָצִיר green grass, herbage (8 · 18[?]) 348

עֹשֶׂה 13 maker, creator (6 · 24) 793 I. עשה

יָסַד to found, establish (5 · 20 · 41) 413

פחד to be in great dread (1 · 2 · 26) 808

הֵצִיק to bring into straits; ptc. = oppressor (4 · 11 · 11) 847

אַיֵּה where? (9 · 44) 32

צעה 14 to stoop, bend, incline (2 · 4 · 5) 858

שַׁחַת pit (2 · 23) 1001

חָסֵר to be lacking (1 · 19 · 23) 341

רָגַע 15 to disturb (1 · 4 · 13) 920 I.

המה to roar, be boisterous, growl, murmur (5 · 33 · 33) 242

גַּל wave, billow, heap (2 · 16) 164

יָסַד 16 to found, establish (5 · 20 · 41) 413

כּוֹס 17 cup (4 · 31) 468

קֻבַּעַת cup (2 · 2) 867

תַּרְעֵלָה reeling (2 · 3) 947

מצה to drain, drain out (1 · 4 · 7) 594

נהל 18 to lead or guide (3 · 9 · 10) 624

נוד 19 to show grief; i.e., by shaking or nodding head (1 · 20 · 27) 626

שֹׁד devastation, ruin (6 · 25) 994

שֶׁבֶר shattering, crushing, breach (9 · 45) 991

עלף 20 to be covered [i.e., to have senses obscured]; to have fainted (1 · 2 · 5 [?]) 763

תּוֹא antelope (1 · 2) 1060

מִכְמָר net, snare (1 · 2) 485

גְּעָרָה rebuke (6 · 15) 172

שָׁכוּר 21 ptc. pass. = drunk (1 · 1) 1016 שכר

כּוֹס 22 cup (4 · 31) 468

תַּרְעֵלָה reeling (2 · 3) 947

קֻבַּעַת cup (2 · 2) 867

הוֹגֶה 23 to cause grief or sorrow (1 · 5 · 8) 387

שְׁחִי only *Qal* form of השתחוה; here = bow down! 1005

גֵּו back (3 · 6) 156

Chapter 52

תִּפְאֶרֶת 1 beauty, finery, glory (18 · 50) 802

עָרֵל uncircumcised (1 · 35) 790

הִתְנַעֵר 2 to shake oneself [free] (1 · 1 · 11) 654

מוֹסֵר bond [of captivity] (2 · 12) 64

צַוָּאר neck, back of neck (4 · 41) 848

שְׁבִי captive (1 · 1) 985

חִנָּם 3 for nothing, gratis; without cause (2 · 32) 336

אֶפֶס 4 nought, nonexistence (13 · 27) 67

עָשַׁק to oppress (1 · 36 · 37) 798

פֹּה 5 here (2 · 44) 805

מַה־לִּי־פֹה idiom = What have I here? 552 מָה 1.a. (d.)

חִנָּם for nothing, gratis; without cause (2 · 32) 336

מֹשֵׁל ruler (4 · 24) 605 III מָשַׁל

הֵילִל to howl (11 · 30 · 30) 410

מִנֹּאָץ = Hith. ptc. = contemned; to be contemned, spurned (1 · 1 · 24) 610 נאץ

נָאוָה 7 to be comely, fitting; *Pilel* form (1 · 3 · 3[?]) 610

מְבַשֵּׂר one bringing glad tidings (4 · 9) 142 בשר

בִּשַּׂר to herald as glad tidings (3 · 14 · 15) 142

צֹפֶה 8 watchman (2 · 19)[?]) 859

עַיִן בְּעַיִן idiom = eye to eye; eye for an eye 745 עין 5.

פָּצַח 9 to break forth with, burst forth (6 · 7 · 7) 822

חָרְבָּה waste, ruin (9 · 42) 352

חָשַׂף 10 to strip, lay bare (3 · 10 · 10) 362

אֶפֶס end, extreme limits, non-existence (13 · 27) 67

נִבְרַר 11 to purify oneself (1 · 3 · 15[?]) 140

חִפָּזוֹן 12 trepidation, hurried flight (1 · 3) 342

מְנוּסָה flight; i.e., escape (1 · 2) 631

גָּבַהּ 13 to be exalted, high (5 · 24 · 34) 146

מִשְׁחַת 14 disfigurement (1 · 1) 1008

תֹּאַר form, outline (2 · 15) 1061

הִזָּה 15 to cause to leap; i.e., startle; or to sprinkle (1 · 20 · 24[?]) 633 I & II נזה

קָפַץ to shut, draw together (1 · 5 · 7) 891

Chapter 53

שְׁמוּעָה 1 report (4 · 27) 1035

יוֹנֵק 2 young plant, sapling (2[?] · 11[?]) 413

שֹׁרֶשׁ root (7 · 33) 1057

צִיָּה land of drought, desert (3 · 16) 851

תֹּאַר form, outline (2 · 15) 1061

הָדָר splendor, majesty (7 · 30) 214

חָמַד to desire, take pleasure in (3 · 16 · 21) 326

נִבְזֶה 3 to be despised; ptc. = despised, vile, worthless (2 · 10 · 42) 102

חָדֵל lacking; here w. "men" = forsaken (1 · 3) 293

מַכְאוֹב pain, mental pain (2 · 16) 456

חֳלִי sickness, disease (4 · 24) 318

מַסְתֵּר hiding, act of hiding (1 · 1) 712

אָכֵן 4 surely, truly, but indeed (4 · 18) 38

חֳלִי sickness, disease (4 · 24) 318

מַכְאוֹב   pain, mental pain (2 · 16) 456

סֵבֶל   to carry, bear (5 · 7 · 9) 687

חוֹלָל   5 to be pierced, wounded (2 · 3 · 7) 319 I.

דֻּכָּא   to be crushed; ptc. crushed (2 · 4 · 18) 193

מוּסָר   chastisement (2 · 50) 416

חַבּוּרָה   stripe, blow, stroke (2 · 7) 289

תָּעָה   6 to wander about, err (8 · 27 · 50) 1073

הִפְגִּיעַ   to cause to light upon, cause one to entreat, interpose (3 · 6 · 46) 803

נִגַּשׂ   7 to be treated harshly (2 · 3 · 7) 620

שֶׂה   a sheep, goat (4 · 45) 961

טֶבַח   slaughtering, slaughter (4 · 12) 370

הוּבַל   to be led, conducted (3 · 11 · 18) 384

רָחֵל   ewe (1 · 4) 932

גָּזַז   to shear; ptc. = sheep-shearer (1 · 14 · 15) 159

נֶאֱלָם   to be dumb, unable to speak, bound (1 · 8 · 9) 47

עֹצֶר   8 coercion, restraint (1 · 3) 783

שׂוֹחֵחַ   to meditate, consider (1 · 2 · 20) 967

נִגְזַר   to be cut off, separated, excluded (1 · 6 · 12) 160

עָשִׁיר   9 rich (1 · 23) 799

מִרְמָה   deceit, treachery (1 · 39) 941

דִּכָּא   10 to crush (2 · 11 · 18) 193

אָשָׁם   trespass offering, substitute (1 · 46) 79

הֶאֱרִיךְ   to prolong (4 · 31 · 34) 73

חֵפֶץ   cause, purpose, good pleasure, delight (9 · 39) 343

הִצְדִּיק   11 to justify, vindicate the cause of, save (3 · 12 · 41) 842

סָבַל   to carry, bear (5 · 7 · 9) 687

עָצוּם   12 numerous, countless, many (3 · 31) 783

תַּחַת אֲשֶׁר   idiom = because that, instead of that 1066 תַּחַת II. 3.a.

הֶעֱרָה   to pour out; elsewhere = make naked (1 · 3 · 15) 788

פָּשַׁע   to transgress, rebel (9 · 40 · 41) 833

נִמְנָה   to be reckoned, assigned (1 · 6 · 28) 584

חֵטְא   punishment for sin, sin (4 · 33) 307

הִפְגִּיעַ   to interpose, make entreaty (3 · 6 · 46) 803

Chapter 54

עָקָר   1 barren (1 · 11) 785

פָּצַח   to break forth with, burst forth (6 · 7 · 7) 822

רִנָּה   ringing cry [in joy] (9 · 33) 943

צָהַל   to cry shrilly (3 · 7 · 8) 843

חוּל   to twist, writhe [in childbirth] (9 · 30 · 47) 296

בְּעוּלָה   married (2 · 4) 127 בעל

הִרְחִיב   2 to enlarge (5 · 21 · 25) 931

חָשַׂךְ   to refrain, keep back (3 · 26 · 28) 362

הַאֲרִיךְ   to make long (4 · 31 · 34) 73

מֵיתָר   cord, string (1 · 9) 452

יָתֵד   tent pin, peg (4 · 23) 450

פָּרַץ   3 to break over, increase (2 · 46 · 49) 829

נִכְלַם   4 to be humiliated, ashamed (5 · 26 · 38) 483

הֶחְפִּיר   to display shame (2 · 4 · 17) 344

בֹּשֶׁת   shame (5 · 30) 102

עֲלוּמִים   youth, youthful vigor (1 · 4) 761

אַלְמְנוּת   widowhood (1 · 4) 48

בָּעַל   5 to marry (4 · 10 · 12) 127

עֹשֶׂה   maker, creator (6 · 24) 793 I. עשה

גֹּאֵל   redeemer, kinsman (13 · 44) 145 גאל

עָצַב   6 to hurt, grieve; here ptc. pass. (1 · 3 · 15) 780

נְעוּרִים   youth, early life (3 · 46) 655

רֶגַע   7 a moment (5 · 22) 921

רַחֲמִים   compassion (4 · 38) 933

שֶׁצֶף   8 flood (1 · 1[?]) 1009 שטף

קֶצֶף   wrath (3 · 28) 893

רֶגַע   moment, one moment (5 · 22) 921

רָחַם   to have compassion, be compassionate (12 · 42 · 47) 933

גָּאַל   redeemer, kinsman (13 · 44) 145 גאל

קָצַף   9 to be angry (7 · 28 · 34) 893

גָּעַר   to rebuke (2 · 14 · 14) 172

מוּשׁ   10 to depart, be removed (5 · 20[?] · 20 [?]) 559

מוּט   to totter, shake (3 · 15 · 39) 556

רָחַם   to have compassion, be compassionate (12 · 42 · 47) 933

סָעַר   11 to storm, rage (1[?] · 1[?] · 7[?]) 704

הִרְבִּיץ   to lay, to cause to lie down (2 · 6 · 30) 918

פּוּךְ   antimony, stibium (1 · 4) 806

יָסַד   to found, establish (5 · 20 · 41) 413

סַפִּיר   sapphire, lapis lazuli (1 · 11) 705

כַּדְכֹד   12 a precious stone; perh. ruby (1 · 2) 461

אֶקְדָּח   fiery glow, sparkle (1 · 1) 869

חֵפֶץ   delight, good pleasure (9 · 39) 343

לִמֻּד   13 taught one; i.e., a disciple (4 · 6) 541

עֹשֶׁק   14 oppression (3 · 15) 799

מְחִתָּה   terror, destruction, ruin (1 · 11) 369

אֶפֶס   15 cessation of, nonexistence of, end of (13 · 27) 67

בָּרָא   16 to shape, fashion, create (20 · 38 · 48) 135

חָרָשׁ   graver, artificer (8 · 38) 360

נפח   to breathe, blow (1 · 9 · 12) 655

פֶּחָם   coal (2 · 3) 809

מַשְׁחִית   destroyer (1 · 19) 1007 שחת

חבל   to ruin, destroy (3 · 6 · 11) 287 II.

הוּצַר   17 to be formed (1 · 1 · 44) 427

הִרְשִׁיעַ   to condemn as guilty (2 · 25 · 34) 957

Chapter 55

צָמֵא   1 thirsty, thirsty one (5 · 9) 854

שׁבר   to buy grain (2 · 16 · 21) 991

בְּלוֹא   without (4 · 30) 518 לֹא 4.a.

מְחִיר   price (2 · 15) 564

חָלָב   milk (4 · 44) 316

שָׁקַל   2 to weigh out [a price] (4 · 19 · 22) 1053

בְּלוֹא   for what is not, for what does not (4 · 30) 518 לֹא 4.a.

יְגִיעַ   toil, produce, acquired property (2 · 16) 388

שָׂבְעָה   satiety (3 · 7[?]) 960

הִתְעַנֵּג   to take exquisite delight (4 · 9 · 10) 772

דֶּשֶׁן   fatness (1 · 15) 206

לְאֹם   4 people (11 · 35) 522

נָגִיד   ruler, prince (1 · 44) 617

פָּאַר   5 to beautify, glorify (4 · 6 · 13) 802

רָחַם   7 to have compassion (12 · 42 · 47) 933

סָלַח   to forgive, pardon (1 · 33 · 46) 699

גָּבַהּ   9 to be high (5 · 24 · 34) 146

גֶּשֶׁם   10 rain (2 · 35) 177

שֶׁלֶג   snow (2 · 20) 1017

הִרְוָה   to saturate, water (2 · 5 · 14) 924

הִצְמִיחַ   to cause to sprout, grow (4 · 14 · 33) 855

רֵיקָם   11 in vain (1 · 16) 938

הוּבַל   12 to be led, conducted (3 · 11 · 18) 384

פָּצַח   to break forth (6 · 7 · 7) 822

רִנָּה   ringing cry [in joy] (9 · 33) 943

מחא   to clap (1 · 2 · 3) 561

נַעֲצוּץ   13 thornbush (2 · 2) 654

בְּרוֹשׁ   cypress or fir (5 · 20) 141

סִרְפַּד   a desert plant (1 · 1) 710

הֲדַס   myrtle (2 · 6) 213

Chapter 56

אֲשֶׁר 2 happiness; אַשְׁרֵי = 0 the happiness of (3 · 45) 80

אֱנוֹשׁ man (8 · 42) 60

נֵכָר 3 foreignness, foreigner (5 · 36) 648

נִלְוָה to join oneself to, be joined (3 · 11 · 12) 530

הִבְדִּיל to separate (2 · 32 · 42) 95

סָרִיס eunuch (3 · 45) 710

יָבֵשׁ dry (1 · 9) 386

סָרִיס 4 eunuch (3 · 45) 710

בַּאֲשֶׁר in [that] which (4 · 19) 84

נֵכָר 6 foreignness, foreigner (5 · 36) 648

נִלְוָה to join oneself or be joined (3 · 11 · 12) 530

נִדָּח 8 banished ones[s], outcast[s] (5 · 11) 623 נדח

שָׂדַי 9 field (1 · 13) 961

אָתָה to come (9 · 19 · 21) 87

צֹפֶה 10 watchman (2 · 19[?]) 859 I. צפה

עִוֵּר blind (11 · 26) 734

כֶּלֶב dog (3 · 32) 476

אִלֵּם dumb (2 · 6) 48

נבח to bark (1 · 1 · 1) 613

הזה to dream, rave (1 · 1 · 1) 223

נום to be drowsy, slumber (2 · 6 · 6) 630

כֶּלֶב 11 dog (3 · 32) 476

עַז fierce, strong (4 · 22) 738

שָׂבְעָה satiety (3 · 7[?]) 960

בֶּצַע unjust gain (3 · 23) 130

אָתָה 12 to come (9 · 19 · 21) 87

סבא to imbibe (1 · 2 · 2) 684

שֵׁכָר strong drink (8-23) 1016

Chapter 57

בְּאֵין 1 in defect of, for want of, without (1 · 10) 35 II אין 6.a.

מִשְׁכָּב 2 couch, bed (4 · 46) 1012

נָכֹחַ straightness, straight, right (4 · 8) 647

הֵנָּה 3 hither (1 · 49) 244

עוֹנֵן to practice soothsaying; fem. ptc. = soothsaying woman (2 · 10 · 11) 778

נאף to commit adultery (1 · 14 · 31) 610

התענג 4 to make merry over, make sport of, take exquisite delight in (4 · 9 · 10) 772

הִרְחִיב to enlarge, open wide (5 · 21 · 25) 931

הֶאֱרִיךְ to make long, stretch out (4 · 31 · 34) 73

אַיִל 5 terebinth [deciduous tree] (3 · 4) 18

רַעֲנָן luxuriant (1 · 19) 947

סָעִיף cleft (2[?] · 4[?]) 703

חָלָק 6 smooth (2[?] · 12[?]) 325

גָּבֹהַּ 7 high, lofty, tall (6 · 41) 147

מִשְׁכָּב couch, bed (4 · 46) 1012

מְזוּזָה 8 doorpost, gatepost (1 · 20) 265

זִכָּרוֹן memorial, reminder (1 · 24) 272

הִרְחִיב to make wide, make large (5 · 21 · 25) 931

מִשְׁכָּב couch, bed (4 · 46) 1012

יָד idiomatic [dub.] phallus 388 יד 4.g.

שׁוּר 9 perh. to travel, journey (1 · 1 · 1[?]) 1003 I.

רִקֻּחַ perfumery, ointment (1 · 1) 955

צִיר envoy, messenger (2 · 6) 851

מֵרָחֹק to a distance, at a distance (12 · 34) 935

הִשְׁפִּיל to set in a lower place, to show abasement (6 · 19 · 30) 1050

יגע 10 to grow or be weary, toil (10 · 20 · 26) 388

נוֹאַשׁ to despair, be desperate, have no hope (1 · 5 · 6) 384

חַיָּה revival, renewal; w. יד = renewal of strength (1 · 12) 312

דָּאַג 11 to fear, dread, be anxious, concerned (1 · 7 · 7) 178

כָּזַב to lie (2 · 12 · 16) 469

הֶחֱשָׁה to be silent (2 · 9 · 16) 364

הוֹעִיל 12 to profit, avail, benefit (8 · 23 · 23) 418

קִבּוּץ 13 assemblage, masses (1 · 1) 868

חָסָה to seek refuge (3 · 37 · 37) 340

סָלַל 14 to cast up, lift up (4 · 10 · 12) 699

פִּנָּה דֶּרֶךְ [idiom] to make clear, free from obstacles 815

מִכְשׁוֹל means or occasion of stumbling, stumbling block (2 · 14) 506

רָם 15 high, exalted (7 · 31[?]) 926 רום

עַד forever (8 · 48) 723 עד I.

דַּכָּא contrite, crushed (1 · 1) 194

שָׁפָל lowly (2 · 18) 1050

נדכא ptc. = crushed (1 · 1 · 18) 193 דכא

נֶצַח 16 everlastingness; with ל = forever (7 · 43) 664

קָצַף to be angry (7 · 28 · 34) 893

עָטַף to be feeble, faint (1 · 3 · 11) 742

נְשָׁמָה breathing thing, breath, spirit (4 · 24) 675

בֶּצַע 17 unjust gain; gain made by violence (3 · 23) 130

קָצַף to be angry (7 · 28 · 34) 893

שׁוֹבָב back turning, apostate (1 · 3) 1000

הִנְחָה 18 to guide, lead (1 · 26 · 40) 634

נִחֻמִים comfort (1 · 3) 637 נחם

אָבֵל mourner, mourning (3 · 8) 5

בָּרָא 19 to shape, fashion, create (20 · 38 · 48) 135

נִיב fruit (1 · 2) 626

לָרָחוֹק distant (1 · 1) 935

לַקָּרוֹב near 898 קרב 2.b.

נִגְרָשׁ 20 to be driven, tossed (1 · 3 · 48) 176

הִשְׁקִיט to show quietness (4 · 10 · 41) 1052

גָּרַשׁ to cast out, thrust out (1 · 8 · 48) 176

רֶפֶשׁ mire (1 · 1) 952

טִיט mire, mud, clay (2 · 13) 376

Chapter 58

גָּרוֹן 1 throat (2 · 8) 173

חָשַׂךְ to refrain, keep back (3 · 26 · 28) 362

קִרְבָה 2 approach (1 · 2) 898

צוֹם 3 to abstain from food, fast (3 · 20 · 20) 847

צוֹם fasting, fast (4 · 26) 847

חֵפֶץ business, cause, good pleasure, delight (9 · 39) 343

עָצֵב toiler(1 · 1) 780

נָגַשׂ to press, drive (1 · 4 · 7) 620

מַצָּה 4 strife, contention (1 · 3) 663

צוֹם to abstain from food, fast (3 · 20 · 20) 847

אֶגְרֹף fist (1 · 2) 175

רֶשַׁע wickedness (2 · 30) 957

צוֹם 5 fast, fasting (4 · 26) 847

כָּפַף to bend, bend down (1 · 4 · 5) 496

אַגְמֹן rush, bulrush (3 · 5) 8

שַׂק sackcloth (8 · 48) 974

אֵפֶר ashes (3 · 22) 68

הִצִּיעַ to lay out, spread out (1 · 2 · 4) 426 יצע

צוֹם 6 fast, fasting (4 · 26) 847

חַרְצֻבּוֹת bond, fetter, pang (1 · 2) 359

רֶשַׁע wickedness (2 · 30) 957

הִתִּיר to unfasten, loosen (1 · 5 · 7) 684

אֲגֻדָּה band (1 · 4) 8

מוֹטָה bar of yoke (3 · 11) 557

רָצַץ crush; ptc. pass. = oppressed (4 · 11 · 19) 954

חָפְשִׁי free (1 · 17) 344

נִתַּק to tear apart, snap (1 · 11 · 27) 683

פָּרַס 7 to divide, break in two (1 · 2 · 14) 828

רָעֵב hungry, hungry one (5 · 19) 944

57

מָרוּד · restlessness, straying, wandering poor (1 · 3) 924

עָרֹם · naked (4 · 16) 736 עֲרוֹם

הִתְעַלֵּם · to hide oneself (1 · 6 · 29) 761

שַׁחַר · 8 dawn (3 · 23) 1007

אֲרֻכָה · healing, restoration (1 · 6) 74 אֲרוּכָה

מְהֵרָה · hastily, quickly; haste (2 · 20) 555

צָמַח · to sprout, spring up (4 · 15 · 33) 855

אָסַף · [idiom] bring up the rear of, be rear guard for 62 אסף Qal 3.

שִׁוַּע · 9 to cry for help (1 · 21 · 21[?]) 1002

מוֹטָה · bar of yoke (3 · 11) 557

אֶצְבַּע · finger, forefinger (4 · 31) 840

הֵפִיק · 10 וּתְפֵק to produce, furnish (1[?] · 8 [?] · 9[?]) 807 II. פוק

רָעֵב · hungry, hungry one (5 · 19) 944

זָרַח · to rise, come forth (3 · 18 · 18) 280

אֲפֵלָה · calamity, darkness, gloom (3 · 10) 66

צָהֳרַיִם · noon, midday (3 · 23) 843

נחה · 11 to lead, guide (2[?] · 14[?] · 40[?]) 634

צַחְצָחָה · scorched region (1 · 1) 850

הֶחֱלִיץ · to brace up, invigorate (1 · 1 · 27) 323

גַּן · garden (2 · 42) 171

רָוֶה · watered (1 · 3) 924

מוֹצָא · source, spring, going forth (2 · 27) 425

כָּזַב · to disappoint, fail (2 · 12 · 16) 469

חָרְבָּה · 12 waste, ruin (9 · 42) 352

מוֹסָד · foundation (3 · 13) 414

גָּדֵר · mason [wall builder] (1 · 3) 154 גדר

פֶּרֶץ · breach, bursting forth (2 · 19) 829

נְתִיבָה · path (4 · 21) 677

חֵפֶץ · 13 affairs, good pleasure, delight (9 · 39) 343

עֹנֶג · daintiness, exquisite delight (2 · 2) 772

הִתְעַנֵּג · 14 to take exquisite delight in (4 · 9 · 10) 772

Chapter 59

קָצַר · 1 to be short (4 · 12 · 14) 894

הִבְדִּיל · 2 to separate (3 · 32 · 42) 95

לְבֵין · and between (1 · 1) 107 בֵּין 1.d.

נִגְאָל · 3 to be defiled (1 · 3 · 11) 146

אֶצְבַּע · finger, forefinger (4 · 31) 840

עַוְלָה · injustice, wrong (1[?] · 32[?]) 732

הָגָה · to utter, groan, moan, growl (7 · 23 · 25) 211

תֹּהוּ · 4 [moral] unreality or falsehood (11 · 20) 1062

הָרָה · to conceive, become pregnant (4 · 38 · 40) 247

בֵּיצָה · 5 egg (3 · 6) 101

צִפְעוֹנִי · a poisonous serpent (3 · 5) 861

קוּר · thread (2 · 2) 881

עַכָּבִישׁ · spider (1 · 2) 747

ארג · to weave; [metaph.] weave a spider's web = intrigue (1 · 3 · 3) 70

זוּר · to press down (1 · 3 · 3) 266

אֶפְעֶה · a kind of viper (2 · 3) 821

קוּר · 6 thread (2 · 2) 881

פֹּעַל · dead, thing done (6 · 37) 821

נָקִי · 7 free from guilt, clean, innocent (1 · 43) 667

שֹׁד · violence, havoc, devastation (6 · 25) 994

שֶׁבֶר · shattering, crushing, breach (9 · 45) 991

מְסִלָּה · highway, public road (9 · 27) 700

מַעְגָּל · 8 track, course of action or life (2 · 13) 722

נְתִיבָה · path (4 · 21) 677

עִקֵּשׁ · to twist, make crooked (1 · 3 · 5) 786

הִשִּׂיג · 9 to overtake, reach, attain (3 · 49 · 49) 673

קוה · to wait or look eagerly for (13 · 39 · 45) 875

נְגֹהָה · brightness (1 · 1) 618

אֲפֵלָה calamity, darkness, gloom (3 · 10) 66

גָּשַׁשׁ 10 to grope, grope for, feel with the hand (2 · 2 · 2) 178

עִוֵּר blind (11 · 26) 734

כְּאֵין as no . . . (4 · 7) 34 אַיִן 6.b.

צָהֳרַיִם noon, midday (3 · 23) 843

נֶשֶׁף evening twilight, morning twilight (3 · 12) 676

אַשְׁמַנִּים stout, lusty [dub.] (1 · 1) 1032

הָמָה 11 to growl, groan, roar (5 · 33 · 33) 242

דֹּב bear (2 · 12) 179

יוֹנָה dove (3 · 33) 401

הָגָה to groan, moan, utter, growl (7 · 23 · 25) 211

קִוָּה to wait or look eagerly for (13 · 39 · 45) 875

רָבַב 12 to be [become] many (4 · 23 · 24) 912

פָּשַׁע 13 to transgress, rebel (9 · 40 · 41) 833

כַּחֵשׁ to act deceptively against, deceive (1 · 19 · 22) 471

נָסוֹג to turn oneself away, turn back, prove faithless (3 · 14 · 25) 690

עֹשֶׁק extortion, oppression (3 · 15) 799

סָרָה defection, apostasy, withdrawal (3 · 7) 694

הָרֹה to conceive, contrive, devise (1 · 1 · 40) 247

הוֹגֶה to moan, utter; here inf. abs. = uttering (1 · 1 · 25) 211 הגה

הֻסַּג 14 to be driven back (1 · 1 · 25) 690

אָחוֹר backwards; back part (9 · 41) 30

רָחוֹק distance; distant; מר' = at a distance (12 · 34) 935 2.a. (2)

רְחוֹב broad open place, plaza (2 · 43) 932

נְכֹחַ straightforwardness, honesty (4 · 8) 647

נֶעְדָּר 15 to be lacking (3 · 6 · 7) 727

הִשְׁתּוֹלֵל to be despoiled (1 · 2 · 15) 1021 II. שלל

הִפְגִּיעַ 16 to interpose, to make entreaty; ptc. = one interposing (3 · 6 · 46) 803

סָמַךְ to uphold, sustain (4 · 41 · 48) 701

שִׁרְיָן 17 body armor (1 · 8) 1056

כּוֹבַע helmet (1 · 6) 464

נָקָם vengeance (6 · 17) 668

תִּלְבֹּשֶׁת raiment, clothing (1 · 1) 528

עָטָה to wrap oneself, envelop oneself (1 · 11 · 14) 741

מְעִיל robe (2 · 28) 839

קִנְאָה zeal (7 · 43) 888

כְּעַל 18 according to, like (3 · 5) 758 עַל IV. 1.

גְּמוּלָה dealing, recompense (1 · 3) 168

גְּמוּל dealing, recompense (5 · 19) 168

אִי coastland, island (17 · 36) 15

מַעֲרָב 19 west, place of sunset (3 · 14) 788

צוּר to besiege, bind (3 · 31 · 31) 848; but perh. contracted; hence, swift [river] 865 I. צר

גֹּאֵל 20 redeemer, kinsman (13 · 44) 145 גאל

מוּשׁ 21 to depart, be removed (5 · 20[?] · 20 [?]) 559

Chapter 60

אוֹר 1 to shine (1 · 5 · 40) 21

זָרַח to rise, come forth (3 · 18 · 18) 280

עֲרָפֶל 2 cloud, heavy cloud (1 · 15) 791

לְאֹם people (11 · 35) 522

זָרַח to rise, come forth (3 · 18 · 18) 280

נֹגַהּ 3 brightness (5 · 19) 618

זֶרַח dawning, shining (1 · 1) 280

מֵרָחֹק 4 from a distance, at a distance (12 · 34) 935

צַד side, possibly hip (2 · 32) 841

נֶאֱמַן [idiom] to be carried 52

נָהַר 5 to shine, beam (1[?] · 3[?] · 3[?]) 626

59

פָּחַד	to be in awe, dread (7 · 23 · 26) 808	מָשׂושׂ	exultation (10 · 17) 965
רָחַב	to be widened, expanded [with joy] (1 · 3 · 25) 931	ינק 16	to suck (4 · 8 · 18) 413
		חָלָב	milk (4 · 44) 316
שִׁפְעָה 6	multitude, abundance, quantity (1 · 6) 1051	שַׁד	female breast (2 · 3) 994
		מוׁשִׁיעַ	savior, deliverer (9 · 27) 446 ישע
בִּכְרָה	young camel, dromedary (1 · 1) 114	גָּאַל	redeemer, kinsman (13 · 44) 145 גאל
לְבונָה	frankincense (3 · 21) 526	אָבִיר	strong, the Strong One, old name for God (3 · 6) 7
בָּשַׂר	to herald as good news (3 · 14 · 15) 142		
		פְּקֻדָּה 17	overseer, oversight, visitation (3 · 32) 824
תִּפְאָרֶת 7	glory (18 · 50) 802		
פָּאַר	to beautify, glorify (4 · 6 · 13) 802	נֹגֵשׂ	lord, ruler (5 · 15) 620 נגש
עָב 8	dark cloud (7 · 30) 728	שַׁד 18	violence, havoc, devastation (6 · 25) 994
עוּף	to fly (4 · 18 · 25) 733		
יונָה	dove (3 · 33) 401	שֶׁבֶר	shattering, crushing, breach (9 · 45) 991
אֲרֻבָּה	opening, lattice, window (2 · 9) 70		
אִי 9	coastland, island (17 · 36) 15	נֹגַהּ 19	brightness (5 · 19) 618
קוה	to wait or look eagerly for (13 · 39 · 45) 875	יָרֵחַ	moon (3 · 27) 437
		הֵאִיר	to give light (2 · 34 · 40) 21
אֳנִיָּה	ship (5 · 31) 58	תִּפְאֶרֶת	glory, beauty (18 · 50) 802
מֵרָחוק	from a distance, at a distance (12 · 34) 935	יָרֵחַ 20	moon (3 · 27) 437
		נאסף	[idiom] of moon = to withdraw itself (>50) 62
פָּאַר	to beautify, glorify (4 · 6 · 13) 802		
קֶצֶף 10	wrath (3 · 28) 893	אֵבֶל	mourning (2 · 24) 5
רָחַם	to have compassion, be compassionate (12 · 42 · 47) 933	נֵצֶר 21	sprout, shoot (3 · 4) 666
		מַטָּע	act of planting, place of planting (2 · 6) 642
נָהַג 11	to drive, conduct; ptc. pass. led (3 · 20 · 30) 624		
		הִתְפָּאַר	to be glorified (5 · 17 · 13) 802
חרב 12	to be waste, desolate (6 · 17 · 37) 351	אֶלֶף 22	thousand (1 · 12) 48
		צָעִיר	little, insignificant, young (1 · 22) 859
בְּרושׁ 13	cypress, fir (5 · 20) 141		
תִּדְהָר	tree, prob. elm or pine (2 · 2) 187	עָצוּם	mighty, numerous (3 · 31) 783
תְּאַשּׁוּר	box tree; a small evergreen (2 · 3) 81	הֵחִישׁ	to hasten, act quickly (3 · 6 · 21) 301
פָּאַר	to beautify, glorify (4 · 6 · 13) 802		
שָׁחַ 14	to bow [in homage] (3 · 12 · 18) 1005 שחח		Chapter 61
		בָּשַׂר 1	to herald as glad tidings (3 · 14 · 15) 142
נִאֵץ	to cause to spurn, blaspheme (3 · 15 · 24) 610		
		עָנָו	poor, weak, afflicted (3[?] · 21[?]) 776
גָּאון 15	excellency, majesty, pride (12 · 49) 144		
		חבשׁ	to bind up, bind on (2 · 28 · 32) 289

60

שָׁבָה — to take captive; ptc. = captive (1 · 30 · 38) 985

דְּרוֹר — liberty, free run (1 · 7) 204

פְּקַח־קוֹחַ — opening; fig. of freeing (1 · 1) 824

נָקָם — 2 vengeance (6 · 17) 668

אָבֵל — mourner, mourning (3 · 8) 5

אָבֵל — 3 mourner, mourning (3 · 8) 5

אֵבֶל — mourning (2 · 24) 5

פְּאֵר — headdress, turban (3 · 7) 802

אֵפֶר — ashes (3 · 22) 68

שָׂשׂוֹן — exultation, joy (6 · 22) 965

מַעֲטֶה — wrap, mantle (1 · 1) 742

כֵּהֶה — faint, dim, dull (2 · 7) 462

אַיִל — terebinth, a deciduous tree (3 · 4) 18

מַטָּע — plantation, place of planting, act of planting (2 · 6) 642

הִתְפָּאֵר — to be glorified (5 · 7 · 13) 802

חָרְבָּה — 4 waste place, ruin (9 · 42) 352

חדש — to repair, renew (1 · 9 · 10) 293

חֹרֶב — desolation (5 · 16) 351

נֵכָר — 5 foreigner (5 · 36) 648

אִכָּר — plowman, husband (1 · 7) 38

כֹּרֵם — vinedressers (1 · 5) 501 כרם

מְשָׁרֵת — 6 minister (1 · 20) 1058 שרת

תִּתְיַמָּרוּ — to boast (1 · 1 · 1[?]) 55 אמר *Hithp.*

בֹּשֶׁת — 7 shame (5 · 30) 102

מִשְׁנֶה — double portion, double, copy, second (2 · 36) 1041

כְּלִמָּה — reproach, ignominy (4 · 30) 484

גָּזֵל — 8 robbery, thing plundered (1 · 4) 160

עַוְלָה — violent deeds of injustice (1[?] · 32 [?]) 732

פְּעֻלָּה — reward, wages; work (5 · 14) 821

צֶאֱצָא — 9 offspring (7 · 11) 425

הִכִּיר — to be willing to recognize, acknowledge; to regard, observe (2 · 38 · 40) 647

שׂוּשׂ — 10 to exult, display joy (9 · 27 · 27) 965 שׂוּשׂ

גִּיל — to rejoice (11 · 45 · 45) 162

יֵשַׁע — salvation, deliverance, rescue (5 · 36) 447

מְעִיל — robe (2 · 28) 591

העטה — to wrap, envelop (1 · 3 · 14) 742

חָתָן — bridegroom; daughter's husband (2 · 20) 368

כֹּהֵן — to play the priest, to deck oneself out like a priest (1 · 23 · 23) 464

פְּאֵר — headdress, turban (3 · 7) 802

כַּלָּה — bride; daughter-in-law (3 · 34) 483

עדה — to deck oneself with ornaments (1 · 8 · 8) 725

צֶמַח — 11 sprout, growth (2 · 11) 855

גַּנָּה — garden (5 · 16) 171

זֵרוּעַ — sowing, thing sown (1 · 2) 283

הצמיח — to cause to sprout, grow (4 · 14 · 33) 855

Chapter 62

חשה — 1 to be silent, still (4 · 7 · 16) 364

שָׁקַט — to be quiet (3 · 31 · 41) 1052

נֹגַהּ — brightness (5 · 19) 618

לַפִּיד — torch (1 · 13) 542

נקב — 2 to prick off, designate, to pierce (2 · 13 · 19) 666

עֲטָרָה — 3 crown (4 · 23) 742

תְּפָאֶרֶת — glory, beauty (18 · 50) 802

צָנוּף — turban (2 · 5) 857 צניף

מְלוּכָה — kingship, kingly office, royalty (2 · 24) 574

חֵפֶץ — 4 delight, pleasure, good cause (9 · 39) 343

בְּעוּלָה — married (2 · 4) 127 בעל

נבעל — to be married (1 · 2 · 12) 127

בעל — 5 to marry (4 · 10 · 12) 127

בָּחוּר — young man (6 · 45) 104

בְּתוּלָה — virgin (5 · 50) 143

מָשׂוֹשׂ — exultation (10 · 17) 965

חָתָן — bridegroom; daughter's husband (2 · 20) 368

כַּלָּה — bride; daughter-in-law (3 · 34) 483

שָׂשׂ — to exult, display joy (9 · 27 · 27) שׂושׂ 965

חָשָׂה — 6 to be silent, still (4 · 7 · 16) 364

דֳּמִי — quiet, rest, pause (2 · 3) 198

דֳּמִי — 7 rest, quiet, pause (2 · 3) 198

דָּגָן — 8 corn, grain (2 · 40) 186

מַאֲכָל — food (1 · 30) 38

נֵכָר — foreigner (5 · 36) 645

תִּירוֹשׁ — fresh or new wine (4 · 38) 440

יגע — to toil, labor (10 · 20 · 26) 388

פַּנָּה דֶרֶךְ — 10 [idiom] to make clear, clear from obstacles 815 פנה Pi.

סלל — to cast up, lift up (4 · 10 · 12) 699

מְסִלָּה — highway, public road (9 · 27) 700

סקל — to free from stones; to pelt w. stones (2 · 4 · 22) 709

נֵס — standard, ensign, signal (10 · 21) 651

יֵשַׁע — 11 salvation, deliverance, rescue (5 · 36) 447

שָׂכָר — reward, hire, wages (2 · 29) 969

פְּעֻלָּה — reward, wages; work (5 · 14) 821

Chapter 63

חָמוּץ — 1 ptc. pass. = red (1 · 1) 330 II. חמץ

הדר — to adorn, honor, swell (1 · 4 · 6) 213

לְבוּשׁ — garment, clothing (3 · 47) 528

צעה — to bend, stoop, incline (2 · 4 · 5) 858

אָדֹם — 2 red (1 · 9) 10

לְבוּשׁ — garment, clothing (3 · 47) 528

גַּת — wine press (1 · 5) 387

פּוּרָה — 3 wine press (1 · 2) 807

רָמַס — to trample down (4 · 17 · 18) 942

נזה — to spurt, spatter (1 · 4 · 24[?]) 633

נֵצַח — juice of grapes; fig. of blood, gore (2 · 2) 664

מַלְבּוּשׁ — raiment, attire (1 · 8) 528

גאל — to pollute, stain (1 · 1 · 11) 146

נָקָם — 4 vengeance (6 · 17) 668

גְּאוּלִים — redemption (1 · 1) 145

עֹזֵר — 5 helper (1 · 19) 740 I. עזר

סָמַךְ — to uphold, support, sustain (4 · 41 · 48) 701

בוס — 6 to tread down, trample (2 · 7 · 12) 100

שׁכר — to make drunk (1 · 4 · 18) 1016

נֵצַח — juice of grapes; fig. of blood, gore (2 · 2) 664

כְּעַל — 7 according to (3 · 5) 758 על IV. 1.

גמל — to deal out to, deal fully with (6 · 34 · 37) 168

טוּב — goodness, goods, good things (3 · 32) 375

רַחֲמִים — compassion (4 · 38) 933

שׁקר — 8 to deal falsely (1 · 5 · 6) 1055

מוֹשִׁיעַ — savior, deliverer (9 · 27) 446 ישע

צַר — 9 distress (5[?] · 20[?]) 865

חֶמְלָה — compassion, mercy (1 · 2) 328

נטל — to bear, lift up (1 · 1 · 4) 642

מָרָה — 10 to be disobedient, rebellious (3 · 21 · 43) 598

עצב — to vex (1 · 2 · 15) 780

אַיֵּה — 11 where? (9 · 44) 32

תִּפְאֶרֶת — 12 glory, beauty (18 · 50) 802

תְּהוֹם — 13 abyss of sea, deep, sea (2 · 36) 1062

בִּקְעָה — 14 valley (3 · 19) 132

נהג — to lead on, guide (2 · 10 · 30) 624

תִּפְאֶרֶת — glory, beauty (18 · 50) 802

זְבֻל — 15 dwelling, lofty abode; elevation, height (1 · 5) 259

תִּפְאֶרֶת — glory, beauty (18 · 50) 802

אַיֵּה — where? (9 · 44) 32

קִנְאָה — zeal (7 · 43) 888

מֵעֶה — seat of emotions, inward parts, internal organs (4 · 32) 588

רַחֲמִים — compassion (4 · 38) 933

הִתְאַפֵּק — to restrain oneself (3 · 7 · 7) 67

הִכִּיר — 16 to be willing to recognize, acknowledge; to regard, observe (2 · 38 · 40) 647

גֹּאֵל   redeemer, kinsman (13 · 44) 145 גאל

הִתְעָה   17 to cause to err, mislead (6 · 21 · 50) 1073

הִקְשִׁיחַ   to make hard, stubborn (1 · 2 · 2) 905

יִרְאָה   fear, reverence, piety (5 · 45) 432

מִצְעָר   18 little while; small thing (1 · 6) 859

בּוֹסֵס   to tread down (1 · 2 · 12) 100

לוּא   19 O that!, if only . . . ! (2 · 3) 530

נָזֹלּ   to shake, quake (2 · 3 · 4) 272

Chapter 64

קָדַח   1 to kindle (2 · 5 · 5) 869

הֲמָסִים   brushwood (1 · 1) 243

בָּעָה   to cause to boil up; to inquire (2 · 2 · 4) 126

רָגַז   to quake (6 · 30 · 41) 919

נוֹרָא   2 wonderful thing; fearful, dreadful (4 · 44) 431

קִוָּה   to wait or look eagerly for (13 · 39 · 45) 875

נָזַל   shake, quake (2 · 3 · 4) 272

הֶאֱזִין   3 to hear, give ear (8 · 41 · 41) 24

זוּלָה   except, besides (4 · 16) 265

חִכָּה   to wait for, await (3 · 13 · 14) 314

פָּגַע   4 to meet (2 · 40 · 46) 803

שָׂשׂ   to exult, display joy (9 · 27 · 27) 965 שוש

קָצַף   to be angry (7 · 28 · 34) 893

עִדָּה   5 menstruation (1 · 1) 723

נָבֵל   to wither and fall, fade (11 · 21 · 25) 615

עָלֶה   leaf, leafage (3 · 18) 750

מוּג   6 to cause to melt (1 · 4 · 17) 556

חֹמֶר   7 clay, mortar, cement (5 · 7) 330

יָצַר   to form; ptc. = potter (22 · 41 · 44) 427

קָצַף   8 to be angry (7 · 28 · 34) 893

עַד־מְאֹד   to a great degree, exceedingly (2 · 16) 547 מאד 2.b.

עַד   forever (8 · 48) 723 עד I.

תִּפְאָרֶת   10 glory, beauty (18 · 50) 802

שְׂרֵפָה   burning (2 · 13) 977

מַחְמַד   desirable thing, precious thing (1 · 13) 326

חָרְבָּה   waste place, ruin (9 · 42) 352

הִתְאַפַּק   11 to restrain oneself, refrain (3 · 7 · 7) 67

חָשָׁה   to be silent, inactive (4 · 7 · 16) 364

עַד־מְאֹד   to a great degree, exceedingly (2 · 16) 547 מאד 2.b.

Chapter 65

לְלוֹא   1 without (2 · 11) 518 לא 4.e.

סָרַר   2 to be stubborn, rebellious (3 · 17 · 17) 710

גַּנָּה   3 garden (5 · 16) 171

לְבֵנָה   brick, tile (2 · 12) 527

נְצוּרִים   4 secret places (1 · 1) 665 נצר I. 4.

חֲזִיר   swine, boar (3 · 7) 306

פָּרָק   fragment (1 · 1) 830; Q מרק broth (1 · 3) 600

פִּגֻּל   foul thing, refuse (1 · 4) 803

קָרַב אֵלֶיךָ   5 [idiom] to keep to yourself 897

עָשָׁן   smoke (7 · 25) 798

יָקַד   to be kindled, burned (2 · 3 · 8) 428

חָשָׁה   6 to be silent, inactive, still (4 · 7 · 16) 364

חֵיק   bosom (3 · 38) 300

חֵרֵף   7 to reproach, say sharp things against, taunt (5 · 34 · 38) 357

פְּעֻלָּה   work; recompense (5 · 14) 821

חֵיק   bosom (3 · 38) 300

תִּירוֹשׁ   8 fresh or new wine (4 · 38) 440

אֶשְׁכּוֹל   cluster (1 · 9) 79

בָּחִיר   9 chosen, elect (6 · 13) 104

נָוֶה   10 abode of sheep, habitation (6 · 45) 627

רֵבֶץ   resting place, place of lying down (2 · 4) 918

שָׁכֵחַ 11 forgetting, forgetful (1 · 2) 1013

גַּד   fortune, god of fortune (1 · 2) 151

מְנִי   god of fate (1 · 1) 584

מִמְסָךְ   mixed drink, mixed wine (1 · 2) 587

מָנָה 12 to reckon, assign, appoint (1 · 12 · 28) 584

טֶבַח   slaughtering, slaughter (4 · 12) 370

כָּרַע   to bow down, bow (5 · 30 · 36) 502

בַּאֲשֶׁר   in [that] which (4 · 19) 84

רָעֵב 13 to be hungry (5 · 12 · 14) 944

צמא   to be thirsty (3 · 10 · 10) 854

טוּב 14 joy, fairness, beauty, good things (3 · 32) 375

כְּאֵב   pain (2 · 6) 456

שֵׁבֶר   breaking, crushing (9 · 45) 991

הֵילִל   to howl (11 · 30 · 30) 410

שְׁבוּעָה 15 curse, oath (1 · 30) 989

בָּחִיר   chosen, elect (6 · 13) 104

אָמֵן 16 verily, truly; amen (2 · 30) 53

בָּרָא 17 to shape, fashion, create (20 · 38 · 48) 135

שִׂישׂ 18 to exult, rejoice, display joy (9 · 27 · 27) 965 שׂושׂ

גִּיל   to rejoice (11 · 45 · 45) 162

גִּילָה   rejoicing (2 · 2) 162

עֲדֵי   as far as, until [poetic for עַד] (1 · 12) 723 III. עד

עַד   forever, eternity (8 · 48) 723 I. עד

עֲדֵי־עַד   continuous existence, forever

בָּרָא   to shape, fashion, create (20 · 38 · 48) 135

מָשׂושׂ   exultation (10 · 17) 965

גִּיל 19 to rejoice (11 · 45 · 45) 162

שִׂישׂ   to exult, rejoice, display joy (9 · 27 · 27) 965 שׂושׂ

בְּכִי   weeping (8 · 32) 113

זְעָקָה   cry of distress (3 · 19) 277

עוּל 20 suckling child; עוּל־יָמִים a short-lived

   child, suckling a few days old (2 · 2) 732

בלה 22 to wear out by use, use to the full (1 · 5 · 16) 115

בָּחִיר   chosen, elect (6 · 13) 104

יגע 23 to toil, labor (10 · 20 · 26) 388

רִיק   emptiness, vanity; w. ל = in vain (3 · 12) 938

בֶּהָלָה   sudden terror, ruin, dismay (1 · 4) 96

צֶאֱצָא   offspring (7 · 11) 425

טֶרֶם 24 before (1 · 16) 382

זְאֵב 25 wolf (2 · 8) 255

טָלֶה   lamb (2 · 3) 378

אַרְיֵה   lion (6 · 45) 71

תֶּבֶן   straw (2 · 17) 1061

נָחָשׁ   serpent (4 · 31) 638

Chapter 66

הֲדֹם 1 footstool (1 · 6) 213

אֵי   where? (4 · 39) 32 אי

מְנוּחָה   resting place, rest (4 · 21) 629

נָכֶה 2 contrite, smitten, stricken (1 · 3) 646

חָרֵד   trembling (2 · 6) 353

שֶׂה 3 a sheep, goat (4 · 45) 961

ערף   to break the neck (1 · 6 · 6) 791

כֶּלֶב   dog (3 · 32) 476

חֲזִיר   swine, boar (3 · 7) 306

לְבֹנָה   frankincense, incense (3 · 21) 526

שִׁקּוּץ   detested thing (1 · 28) 1055

תַּעֲלוּלִים 4 wantonness, wanton dealing, caprice (2 · 2) 760

מְגוֹרָה   fear, terror (1 · 3) 159

בַּאֲשֶׁר   in [that] which (4 · 19) 84

חָרֵד 5 trembling (2 · 6) 353

שֹׂנֵא   hating; enemy (1 · 41[?]) 971 שׂנא

נדה   to thrust away, exclude (1 · 2 · 2) 622

שָׁאוֹן 6 roar, din (8 · 18) 981

גְּמוּל   recompense, dealing (5 · 19) 168

בְּטֶרֶם   7 before (8 · 39) 382

חוּל   to twist, writhe [in labor]
(9 · 30 · 47) 296

חֵבֶל   pains of travail, pain (3 · 7) 286

הִמְלִיט   [idiom] to give birth 572 מלט

הוּחַל   8 to be born (1 · 1 · 47) 296

חוּל   to twist, writhe [in labor]
(9 · 30 · 47) 296

עָצַר   9 to restrain (1 · 36 · 46) 783

גִּיל   10 to rejoice (11 · 45 · 45) 162

אֹהֵב   one who loves; friend (2 · 36) 12

שׂוֹשׂ   to exult, rejoice, display joy
(9 · 27 · 27) 965 שׂושׂ

מָשׂוֹשׂ   exultation (10 · 17) 965

הִתְאַבֵּל   to mourn (1 · 19 · 38) 5

יָנַק   11 to suck (4 · 8 · 18) 413

שַׁד   female breast (2 · 3) 994

תַּנְחוּם   consolation (1 · 5) 637

מָצַץ   to drain out (1 · 1 · 1) 595

הִתְעַנַּג   to take exquisite delight in
(4 · 9 · 10) 772

זִיז   abundance, fullness; if cogn. to Ar.
= breast, teat (1 · 1) 265 II.

שָׁטַף   12 to overflow (9 · 28 · 31) 1009

יָנַק   to suck (4 · 8 · 18) 413

צַד   side, possibly hip (2 · 32) 841

בֶּרֶךְ   knee (3 · 25) 139

שָׁעֳשַׁע   to be fondled (1 · 1 · 6) 1044 II. שׁעע

שָׂשׂ   13 to exult, rejoice, display joy
(9 · 27 · 27) 965 שׂושׂ

דֶּשֶׁא   grass (3 · 14) 206

פָּרַח   to bud, sprout (5 · 28 · 34) 827

זָעַם   to be indignant (1 · 11 · 12) 276

סוּפָה   15 storm wind (5 · 15) 693

מֶרְכָּבָה   chariot (3 · 44) 939

גְּעָרָה   rebuke (6 · 15) 172

לַהַב   flame (4 · 12) 529

רבב   16 to be [become] many (4 · 23 · 24)
912

גַּנָּה   17 garden (5 · 16) 171

חֲזִיר   swine, boar (3 · 7) 306

שֶׁקֶץ   detestable thing (1 · 11) 1054

עַכְבָּר   mouse (1 · 6) 747

סוּף   to come to an end (1 · 4 · 8) 692

פָּלִיט   19 escaped one, fugitive (1 · 5) 812

מָשַׁךְ   to draw, draw out, draw off
(2 · 30 · 36) 604

אִי   coastland, island (17 · 36) 15

שֵׁמַע   report (3 · 17) 1034

צָב   20 pl. = litters (1 · 2) 839

פֶּרֶד   mule (1 · 14) 825

כִּרְכָּרָה   dromedary, camel (1 · 1) 503

מִדֵּי   23 as often as (3 · 15) 191 דֵי 2.c.

פֶּגֶר   24 corpse, carcass (4 · 22) 803

פָּשַׁע   to transgress, rebel (9 · 40 · 41)
833

תּוֹלֵעָה   worm, grub (3 · 41) 1069

כבה   to be quenched, extinguished
(3 · 14 · 24) 459

דֵּרָאוֹן   aversion, abhorrence, object of abhorrence (1 · 2) 201

JEREMIAH

Chapter 1

בְּטֶרֶם 5 before (6 · 39) 382

יָצַר to form, fashion (4 · 41 · 44[?]) 427

רֶחֶם womb (4 · 33) 933

אֲהָהּ 6 Alas! (4 · 15) 13

נָתַשׁ 10 to pull up, pluck up (11 · 16 · 21) 684

נָתַץ to pull down, break down (6 · 31 · 42) 683

הָרַס to tear down, throw down (5 · 30 · 43) 248

מַקֵּל 11 rod, stick, staff (2 · 18) 596

שָׁקֵד almond tree (1 · 4) 1052

שָׁקַד 12 to keep watch (5 · 11 · 17) 1052

סִיר 13 pot (3 · 29) 696 I

נפח to blow; ptc. = blown (i.e., well heated, boiling) (2 · 9 · 12) 655

אזר 17 to gird, gird on (1 · 6 · 16) 25

מָתְנַיִם loins (6 · 47) 608

מִבְצָר 18 fortification (7 · 37) 131

Chapter 2

נְעוּרִים 2 youth (7 · 46) 655

כְּלוּלָה betrothal, betrothal time (1 · 1) 483

תְּבוּאָה 3 product, yield (2 · 43) 100

אָשַׁם to be held guilty, be guilty (2 · 33 · 35) 79

עָוֶל 5 injustice, unrighteousness (1 · 21) 732

הבל to become vain, act emptily (1 · 4 · 5) 211

אַיֵּה 6 where? (6 · 44) 32

שׁוּחָה pit (3 · 5) 1001

צִיָּה drought (3 · 16) 851

צַלְמָוֶת deep shadow, darkness (2 · 18) 853

כַּרְמֶל 7 garden land (3 · 14) 502 I

טוֹב good things (3 · 32) 375

אַיֵּה 8 where? (6 · 44) 32

פָּשַׁע to transgress (4 · 40 · 41) 833

הוֹעִיל to profit, avail, benefit (7 · 23 · 23) 418

אִי 10 coast, border, region (4 · 36) 15

הֵמִיר 11 to exchange, change (2 · 13 · 14) 558

בְּלוֹא for not (4 · 30) 518 לֹא 4. a.(c)

הוֹעִיל to profit, avail, benefit (7 · 23 · 23) 418

שָׂעַר 12 to bristle [with horror] (1 · 3 · 3) 972

חרב to be waste, desolate (2 · 17 · 37) 351

מָקוֹר 13 spring, fountain, source (4 · 18) 881

חָצֵב to hew out, dig (1 · 14 · 17) 345

בֹּאר cistern, pit, well (2 · 5) 92

הכיל to contain, hold in (3 · 12 · 38) 465

יָלִיד 14 born; יְלִיד בַּיִת = born in [one's] house (1 · 13) 409

בַּז spoil, booty, plunder (5 · 27) 103

שָׁאַג 15 to roar (5 · 20 · 20) 980

כְּפִיר young lion (3 · 31) 498

נָתַן [idiom] with קוֹל = to lift up the voice 678 Qal 1.x.

שַׁמָּה waste (24 · 39) 1031

נצת to be kindled, burned (2 · 6 · 27) 428

מִבְּלִי so that there is no (4 · 25) 115 בְּלִי

יִרְעוּךְ 16 from רעה, to graze 944

קָדְקֹד hairy crown, scalp (2 · 11) 869

שִׁיחוֹר 18 Nile (1 · 4) 1009

יִסַּר 19 to chastise, chasten, correct (5 · 27 · 38) 415

מְשֻׁבָה turning back, apostacy (9 · 12) 1000 מְשׁוּבָה

מַר bitter (2 · 39) 600

פַּחְדָּה awe, dread (1 · 1) 808

עֹל 20 yoke (10 · 40) 760

נתק to tear apart, snap (3 · 11 · 27) 683

מוֹסֵר band or bond of restraint (4 · 12) 64

גָּבֹהַּ high, lofty, tall (4 · 41) 147

רַעֲנָן luxuriant, fresh (6 · 19) 947

צָעָה to stoop, bend (2 · 4 · 5) 858

שֹׂרֵק 21 vine [choice species] (1 · 2) 977

סוּר degenerate (2 · 3) 693 סור *Qal* 1.

נָכְרִי foreign, alien (1 · 45) 648

נֶתֶר 22 natron [carbonate of soda] (1 · 2) 684

בֹּרִית lye, alkali, soap (1 · 2) 141

נִכְתָּם to be stained; ptc. = stained (1 · 1 · 1) 508 I. כתם

גַּיְא 23 valley (4 · 48) 161

בִּכְרָה young camel, dromedary (1 · 1) 114

קַל swift, fleet (2 · 13) 886

שָׂרֵךְ to twist, ptc. = entangling (1 · 1 · 1) 976

פֶּרֶא 24 wild ass (2 · 10) 825

לִמֻּד taught, accustomed (2 · 6) 541

אַוָּה desire (1 · 7) 16

שָׁאַף to pant after (2 · 14 · 14) 983

תַּאֲנָה occasion or time of copulation (1 · 1) 58

יָעֵף to be weary, faint (3 · 8 · 9) 419

מָנַע 25 to withhold, hold back (5 · 25 · 29) 586

יָחֵף barefoot (1 · 5) 405

גָּרוֹן throat, neck (1 · 8) 173

צִמְאָה parched condition (1 · 1) 854

נוֹאָשׁ to despair (2 · 5 · 6) 384

בֹּשֶׁת 26 shame (6 · 30) 102

גַּנָּב thief (3 · 17) 170

עֹרֶף 27 back of neck (7 · 33) 791

אַיֵּה 28 where? (6 · 44) 32

פָּשַׁע 29 to transgress (4 · 40 · 41) 833

מוּסָר 30 chastisement, discipline (8 · 50) 416

אַרְיֵה lion (6 · 45) 71

מַאְפֵּלְיָה 31 deep darkness (1 · 1) 66

רוּד to wander restlessly, roam (1 · 2 · 4) 923

בְּתוּלָה 32 virgin (8 · 50) 143

עֲדִי ornaments (2 · 13) 725

כַּלָּה bride; daughter-in-law (5 · 34) 483

קִשֻּׁרִים bands, sashes (1 · 2) 905

נָקִי 34 innocent, free from guilt (6 · 43) 667

מַחְתֶּרֶת burglary, a breaking in (1 · 2) 369

נָקָה 35 to be clean, free from guilt, innocent (6 · 24 · 43) 667

אָזַל 36 to go about, go (1 · 5 · 5) 23

שָׁנָה to change, alter (2 · 9 · 26) 1040

מִבְטָח 37 object of confidence, confidence (3 · 15) 105

Chapter 3

חָנֵף 1 to be polluted (4 · 7 · 11) 337

שְׁפִי 2 bare place, height (6 · 10) 1046

אֵיפֹה where? (2 · 10) 33

שֻׁגַּל to be ravished (1 · 1 · 4) 993

הֶחֱנִיף to pollute (1 · 4 · 11) 337

זְנוּת fornication (3 · 9) 276

נִמְנַע 3 to be withheld (1 · 4 · 29) 586

רְבִיבִים copious showers; i.e., plentiful showers (2 · 6) 914

מַלְקוֹשׁ spring rain, latter rain (2 · 8) 545

מֵצַח brow, forehead (1 · 13) 594

זוֹנָה harlot (2 · 33[?]) 275 זָנָה

מֵאֵן to refuse (12 · 46) 549

נכלם to be humiliated, ashamed (4 · 26 · 38) 483

מֵעַתָּה 4 from now, henceforth (1 · 14) 773 עַתָּה 2.e.

אַלּוּף friend, intimate; tame (3 · 9) 48

נְעוּרִים youth (7 · 46) 655

נטר 5 to keep, maintain; i.e., keep anger (2 · 5 · 5) 643

נֶצַח everlastingness, ever; לָנֶצַח = forever (3 · 42) 664

יָכֹל to prevail, have one's way (>50) 407 2.a.

מְשֻׁבָה 6 turning back, apostasy (9 · 12) 1000 מְשׁוּבָה

גָּבֹהַּ high, lofty, tall (4 · 41) 147

רַעֲנָן	luxuriant, fresh (6 · 19) 947	
בָּגוֹדָה	7 treacherous (2 · 2) 93 בָּגוֹד	
אֹדֹת	8 cause; עַל־כָּל־א׳ = because of all (1 · 11) 15	
נאף	to commit adultery (5 · 17 · 31) 610	
מְשֻׁבָה	turning back, apostasy (9 · 12) 1000 מְשׁוּבָה	
כְּרִיתוּת	divorcement (1 · 4) 504	
בתד	to act or deal treacherously (8 · 49 · 49) 93	
קל	9 lightness, frivolity (1 · 1) 887	
זְנוּת	fornication (3 · 9) 276	
חנף	to be profane, godless; to be polluted (4 · 7 · 11) 337	
נאף	to commit adultery (5 · 17 · 31) 610	
בָּגוֹד	10 treacherous (2 · 2) 93	
צדק	11 to make to appear righteous (1 · 5 · 41) 842	
מְשֻׁבָה	turning back, apostasy (9 · 12) 1000 מְשׁוּבָה	
בגז	to act or deal treacherously (8 · 49 · 49) 93	
מְשֻׁבָה	12 turning back, apostasy (9 · 12) 1000 מְשׁוּבָה	
אַפִּיל פָּנַי	[idiom] to look displeased נָפַל 656 *Hiph.* 5	
חָסִיד	kind, pious (1 · 32) 339	
נטר	to keep, maintain; i.e., keep anger (2 · 5 · 5) 643	
פָּשַׁע	13 to transgress (4 · 40 · 41) 833	
פּזר	to scatter (1 · 7 · 10) 808	
רַעֲנָן	luxuriant, fresh (6 · 19) 947	
שׁוֹבֵב	14 recusant, apostate (2 · 3) 1000	
בָּעַל	to be lord [over], husband [of] (2 · 10 · 12[?]) 127	
דֵּעָה	15 knowledge (1 · 6) 395	
פרה	16 to be fruitful (2 · 22 · 29) 826	
פקד	to seek in vain, miss (>50) 823 *Qal* A.1.d.	
נקוה	17 to be collected (1 · 2 · 2) 876	

שְׁרִירוּת	stubbornness (8 · 10) 1057	
חֶמְדָּה	19 desire (3 · 16) 326	
צְבִי	decoration, beauty (pl. cstr. = צְבָאוֹת) (1 · 18) 840	
אָכֵן	20 surely, truly (5 · 18) 38	
בגז	to act or deal treacherously (8 · 49 · 49) 93	
שְׁפִי	21 bare place, height (6 · 10) 1046	
בְּכִי	weeping (8 · 30) 113	
תַּחֲנוּן	supplication for favor (2 · 18) 337	
הֶעֱוָה	to pervert (2 · 9 · 17[?]) 730	
שׁוֹבֵב	22 recusant, apostate (2 · 3) 1000	
מְשׁוּבָה	turning back, apostasy (9 · 12) 1000	
אָתָה	to come (1 · 19 · 21) 87	
אָכֵן	23 surely, truly (5 · 18) 38	
תְּשׁוּעָה	deliverance (1 · 34) 448	
בֹּשֶׁת	24 shameful thing, shame (6 · 30) 102	
יְגִיעַ	product, toil (2 · 16) 388	
נְעוּרִים	youth (7 · 46) 655	
בֹּשֶׁת	25 shame (6 · 30) 102	
כְּלִמָּה	reproach, ignominy, insult (3 · 30) 484	
נְעוּרִים	youth (7 · 46) 655	

Chapter 4

שִׁקּוּץ	1 detested thing (5 · 28) 1055	
נָד	to move to and fro, wander (8 · 19 · 26) 626 נוד	
ניר	3 to break up, freshly till (1 · 1 · 2) 644 I.	
נִיר	untilled, tillable (1 · 3) 644	
קוֹץ	thornbush (2 · 11) 881	
נִמֹּול	4 to circumcise yourself (1 · 17 · 29) 557	
עָרְלָה	foreskin (2 · 16) 790	
כבה	to quench, extinguish (2 · 10 · 24) 459	
רֹעַ	evil, badness (11 · 19) 947	
מַעֲלָל	practice, deed (17 · 41) 760	

מִבְצָר 5 fortification (7 · 37) 131

נֵס 6 standard, signal (5 · 21) 651

הֵעִיז to bring into safety (2 · 4 · 5) 731

שֶׁבֶר shattering (15 · 45) 991

אַרְיֵה 7 lion (6 · 45) 71

סְבֹךְ thicket (1 · 2) 687

שַׁמָּה waste (24 · 39) 1031

נצה to fall in ruins (1 · 1 · 5) 663 III.

מֵאֵין without (2 · 48[?]) 34 אֵין 6.d.

חגר 8 to gird on, bind on (3 · 44 · 44) 291

שַׂק sackcloth (4 · 48) 974

ספד to wail, lament (7 · 28 · 30) 704

הֵילִל to give a howl (8 · 30 · 30) 410

חָרוֹן [burning of] anger; ח׳ אף = burning anger (9 · 41) 354

תמה 9 to be astounded (1 · 8 · 9) 1069

אֲהָהּ 10 Alas! (4 · 15) 13

אָכֵן surely, truly (5 · 18) 38

הִשִּׁיא to beguile (5 · 15 · 16) 674

צַח 11 glowing, clear (1 · 4) 850

שְׁפִי bare place, height (6 · 10) 1046

זרה to fan, winnow (2 · 9 · 38) 279

הבריר to purify, cleanse (1 · 1 · 15) 140

סוּפָה 13 storm wind (1 · 15) 693

מֶרְכָּבָה war chariot, chariot (1 · 44) 939

נֶשֶׁר vulture, eagle (4 · 26) 676

אוֹי Woe! Alas! (8 · 25) 17

מָתַי 14 when? עד-מ׳ = how long? (7 · 42) 607

נצר to keep closed, blockade (>50) 665 Qal 5.

מֶרְחָק 16 distant place, far country (5 · 18) 935

שָׂדַי 17 land, field (2 · 13) 961

מָרָה to be disobedient, rebellious (2 · 21 · 43) 598

מַעֲלָל 18 practice, deed (17 · 41) 760

מַר bitter (2 · 39) 600

מֵעֶה 19 seat of emotions, internal organs (3 · 32) 589

הוֹחִיל [Q to wait, tarry (1 · 15 · 42) 403 יחל Hiph.]

חוּל to be in anguish, twist, writhe (5 · 30 · 47) 296

המה to murmur, growl (9 · 33 · 33) 242

הֶחֱרִישׁ to be silent (2 · 38 · 46) 361

תְּרוּעָה alarm, war cry (3 · 36) 929

שֶׁבֶר 20 shattering (15 · 45) 991

פִּתְאֹם suddenly (5 · 25) 837

רֶגַע moment (3 · 22) 921

מָתַי 21 when? עד-מ׳ = how long? (7 · 42) 607

נֵס standard, signal (5 · 21) 651

אֱוִיל 22 fool [always morally bad] (1 · 26) 17

סָכָל fool (2 · 7) 698

נָבוֹן discreet, discerning, intelligent (1 · 21) 106 בִּין Niph. ptc.

תֹּהוּ 23 formlessness, waste (1 · 20) 1062

בֹּהוּ emptiness (1 · 3) 96

רעשׁ 24 to quake, shake (5 · 21 · 29) 950

נדד 25 to retreat, flee (3 · 21 · 24) 622

כַּרְמֶל 26 garden land (3 · 14) 502

נתץ to be pulled down, broken down (1 · 3 · 42) 683

חָרוֹן [burning of] anger; ח׳אף burning anger (9 · 41) 354

כָּלָה 27 complete destruction (7 · 22) 478

אָבַל 28 to mourn (5 · 18 · 38) 5

קָדַר to be dark (3 · 13 · 17) 871

מִמַּעַל above, on the top of (4 · 29) 751

זָמַם to purpose, devise (2 · 13 · 13) 273

רָמָה 29 to shoot (1 · 4 · 4) 941

עָב thicket (1 · 1[?]) 728

כֵּף rock (1 · 2) 495

אַתִּי 30 you [fem.] (1 · 7) 61

שָׁנִי scarlet (1 · 42) 1040

עָדָה to deck oneself, ornament (2 · 8 · 8) 725

עֲדִי ornaments (2 · 13) 725

קָרַע to make wide, large (>50) 902 Qal 3.b.

פּוּךְ		antimony, stibium [a black mineral powder] (1 · 4) 806
הִתְיַפָּה		to beautify oneself (1 · 1 · 8) 421
עגב		to lust; ptc. = "paramour" (1 · 7 · 7) 721
חול	31	to twist, writhe [in child birth] (5 · 30 · 47) 296
הַבְּכִיר		ptc. = one bearing her first child (1 · 1 · 4) 114
הִתְיַפֵּחַ		to gasp for breath (1 · 1 · 1) 422
אוֹי		Woe! Alas! (8 · 25) 17
עיף		to be faint (1 · 5 · 5) 746

Chapter 5

שׁוֹטֵט	1	to go eagerly and quickly to and fro (1 · 5 · 13) 1001
רְחוֹב		broad open place (5 · 43) 932
סלח		to forgive, pardon (1 · 6 · 46) 699
הל	3	to be in severe pain, anguish; to twist, writhe (5 · 30 · 47) 296 חול
מֵאֵן		to refuse (12 · 46) 549
מוּסָר		chastisement, discipline (8 · 50) 416
דַּל	4	reduced, poor, low (2 · 48) 195
נואל		to show wicked folly, act foolishly (2 · 4 · 4) 383
עֹל	5	yoke (10 · 40) 760
נתק		to tear apart, snap (3 · 11 · 27) 683
מוֹסֵר		band or bond of restraint (4 · 12) 64
אַרְיֵה	6	lion (6 · 45) 71
זְאֵב		wolf (1 · 8) 255
נָמֵר		leopard (2 · 6) 649
שָׁקַד		to keep watch, to be wakeful (5 · 11 · 17) 1052
נטרף		to be torn (1 · 2 · 24) 382
רבב		to be, become, many (3 · 23 · 24) 912
עָצַם		to be numerous (4 · 16 · 18) 782
מְשֻׁבָה		turning back, apostasy (9 · 12) 1000 מְשׁוּבָה

אֵי	7	where?; אֵי־לָזֹאת = on what ground? how? (3 · 39) 32 אֵי 2.c.
סלח		to forgive, pardon (6 · 33 · 46) 699
בְּלוֹא		by no, by not (4 · 30) 518
נאף		to commit adultery (5 · 17 · 31) 610
זוֹנָה		ptc. = harlot; vb. to commit fornication (2 · 33) 275
הִתְגֹּדֵד		to gather in troops or bands, to go in troops or throngs (4 · 7 · 8) 151
מְיֻזָּנִים	8	[dub.] ruttish (1 · 1) 402
הַשְׁכֶּה		ptc. = lustful (1 · 1 · 1) 1013
צהל		to neigh (3 · 7 · 8) 843
הִתְנַקֵּם	9	to avenge oneself (3 · 5 · 35) 667
שׁוּרָה	10	row [of vines] (1 · 2) 1004
כָּלָה		complete destruction, annihilation (7 · 22) 478
נְטִישָׁה		twig, tendril (2 · 3) 644
בגד	11	to act or deal treacherously (8 · 49 · 49) 93
כָּחַשׁ	12	to act deceptively against, deceive (1 · 19 · 22) 471
דִּבֵּר	13	speaking (2 · 2) 184
מֶרְחָק	15	distant place, distance (5 · 18) 935
אֵיתָן		permanent, enduring, everflowing (3 · 14) 450
אַשְׁפָּה	16	quiver for arrows (1 · 6) 80
קָצִיר	17	harvest (5 · 49) 894
תְּאֵנָה		fig, fig tree (12 · 39) 1061
רשׁשׁ		to beat down, shatter (1 · 1 · 2) 958
מִבְצָר		fortification (7 · 37) 131
כָּלָה	18	complete destruction, annihilation (7 · 22) 478
נֵכָר	19	foreign (2 · 36) 648
סָכָל	21	fool (2 · 7) 698
חִיל	22	to be in severe pain or anguish; to twist, writhe (5 · 30 · 47) 296 חול
חוֹל		sand (3 · 22) 297
הִתְגָּעֵשׁ		to shake back and forth, reel to and fro (2 · 5 · 10) 172

הָמָה		to roar, murmur, growl (9 · 33 · 33) 242
גַּל		wave of water, roller, heap (4 · 16) 164
סָרַר	23	to be stubborn, rebellious (3 · 18 · 18) 710
מָרָה		to be disobedient, rebellious (2 · 21 · 43) 598
גֶּשֶׁם	24	shower, rain (2 · 35) 177
יוֹרֶה		early rain (1 · 2) 435
מַלְקוֹשׁ		latter rain, spring rain (2 · 8) 545
שָׁבֻעַ		week (1 · 20) 988
קָצִיר		harvest (5 · 49) 894
הִטּוּ		*Hiph.* perf. נטה; here = to turn (>50) 639 *Hiph.* 3.h.
מָנַע	25	to withhold, hold back (5 · 25 · 29) 586
שׁוּר	26	to lie in wait, watch (1 · 16 · 16) 1003
שׁכך		to bend, crouch (1 · 4 · 5) 1013
יָקוּשׁ		fowler, bait layer (1 · 4) 430
מַשְׁחִית		destroyer, ravager; fig. for snare, trap (4 · 19) 1008
כְּלוּב	27	basket, cage (1 · 3) 477
מִרְמָה		deceit, treachery (4 · 39) 941
הֶעֱשִׁיר		to cause to be [become] rich (1 · 14 · 17) 799
שָׁמֵן	28	to grow fat (1 · 3 · 5) 1031
עשׁת		[dub.] to be smooth, shiny (1 · 1 · 1) 799
דִּין		cause, plea, judgment (4 · 19) 192
דָּן		to plead the cause, administer judgment (4 · 23 · 24) 192 דין
יָתוֹם		orphan (4 · 42) 450
הִתְנַקֵּם	29	to avenge oneself (3 · 5 · 35) 667
שַׁמָּה	30	horror, an appalling thing (24 · 39) 1031
שַׁעֲרוּר		horrible thing (2 · 2) 1045
רָדָה	31	to rule, have dominion (1 · 3 · 3[?]) 921

Chapter 6

הָעִיז	1	to bring into safety (2 · 4 · 5) 731
מַשְׂאֵת		signal (2 · 16) 673 1.b.
נִשְׁקָף		to lean over, look down (1 · 10 · 22) 1054
שֶׁבֶר		shattering (15 · 45) 991
נָוֶה	2	comely, beautiful (1 · 2[?]) 610 נָאוֶה
עָנֹג		to be daintily bred (1 · 1 · 10) 772
דָּמָה		to cause to cease, cut off; cease (2 · 4 · 16) 198
עֵדֶר	3	flock (6 · 39) 727
תָּקַע		to pitch (>50) 1075 *Qal* 1.
צָהֳרַיִם	4	midday, noon (3 · 23) 843
אוֹי		Woe! Alas! (8 · 25) 17
אַרְמוֹן	5	citadel, castle (5 · 33) 74
עֵצָה	6	[coll.] trees (1 · 1) 782
סֹלְלָה		mound (3 · 11) 700
עֹשֶׁק		oppression, extortion (2 · 15) 799
הֵקַר	7	to make or keep cool (2 · 2 · 3) 903
בַּיִר		בּוֹר well (>50) 92
שֹׁד		violence, havoc (3 · 25) 994
חֳלִי		wound, sickness, disease (2 · 24) 318
מַכָּה		wound, blow (10 · 48) 646
נוֹסַר	8	to let oneself be corrected, chastened (2 · 5 · 38) 415
יָקַע		to be torn away, alienated (1 · 4 · 8) 429
עוֹלֵל	9	to glean (1 · 8 · 17) 760
בֹּצֵר		ptc. = grape-gatherer (2 · 7 · 7) 130
סַלְסִלָּה		shoot, branch (1 · 1) 700
הֵעִיד	10	to protest, warn (8 · 39 · 44) 729
עָרֵל		uncircumcised (3 · 35) 790
הִקְשִׁיב		to give attention (8 · 45 · 46) 904
נִלְאָה	11	to be weary, make oneself weary (4 · 10 · 19) 521
הֵכִיל		to contain, hold in (3 · 12 · 38) 465
עוֹלֵל		child (2 · 9) 760
סוֹד		circle, council (4 · 21) 691
בָּחוּר		young man (11 · 45) 104

קָטֹן 13 insignificant (3 · 47) 881

בצע to cut off, gain by violence; ptc.
= robber (2 · 10 · 16) 130

בֶּצַע unjust gain, gain made by violence
(4 · 23) 130

שֶׁבֶר 14 fracture, breaking (15 · 45) 991

נִקְלָה Niph. קלל to be trifling (>50) 886

הכלים 15 to exhibit shame, put to shame
(1 · 10 · 38) 483

נְתִיבָה 16 path (2 · 21) 677

אֵי where?; אֵי זֶה = where, then?
(3 · 39) 32 אֵי 1.b.

מַרְגּוֹעַ rest (1 · 1) 921

צֹפֶה 17 watchman (1 · 19[?]) 859

הִקְשִׁיב to give attention (8 · 45 · 46) 904

הִקְשִׁיב 19 to give attention (8 · 45 · 46) 904

לְבוֹנָה 20 frankincense (3 · 21) 526

טוֹב sweet-scented, fragrant (>50) 373
II. טוב 1.c.

מֶרְחָק distance, distant place (5 · 18) 935

ערב to be pleasing, sweet (2 · 8 · 8) 787

מִכְשׁוֹל 21 stumbling block, means or occasion
of stumbling (1 · 14) 506

שָׁכֵן neighbor (5 · 20) 1015

יַרְכָה 22 remote part, side (4 · 28) 438

כִּידוֹן 23 dart, javelin (2 · 9) 475

אַכְזָרִי cruel (3 · 8) 470

רחם to have compassion (9 · 41 · 46) 933

המה to roar, growl, murmur (9 · 33 · 33)
242

שֵׁמַע 24 report (1 · 4) 1035

רָפָה to sink, drop (3 · 14 · 45) 951

חִיל anguish, writhing (3 · 6) 297

מָגוֹר 25 terror, fear (6 · 8) 159

חגר 26 to gird on, bind on (3 · 44 · 44) 291

שַׂק sackcloth (4 · 48) 974

הִתְפַּלֵּשׁ to roll in (2 · 4 · 4) 814

אֵפֶר ashes (1 · 22) 68

אֵבֶל mourning (3 · 24) 5

יָחִיד only one (e.g., only son) (1 · 12) 402

מִסְפֵּד wailing (2 · 16) 704

תַּמְרוּרִים bitterness (2 · 3) 601

פִּתְאֹם suddenly (5 · 25) 837

בָּחוֹן 27 assayer, one who tries metals
(1 · 1) 103

מִבְצָר fortification [fortified city] (7 · 37)
131

בחן to prove, test, try (6 · 24 · 28) 103

סָרַר 28 to be stubborn, rebellious
(2 · 18 · 18) 710

רָכִיל slander; talebearer, informer (2 · 6)
940

נָחַר 29 to be scorched (1 · 5 · 9) 359 חרר

מַפֻּחַ bellows (1 · 1) 656

אֵשָׁה fire (1 · 1) 77

עֹפֶרֶת lead (1 · 9) 780

צָרַף to smelt, refine (2 · 18 · 26[?]) 864

נִתַּק to be separated (2 · 10 · 27) 683

Chapter 7

מַעֲלָל 3 practice, deed (17 · 41) 760

מַעֲלָל 5 practice, deed (17 · 41) 760

יָתוֹם 6 orphan (4 · 42) 450

עָשַׁק to oppress, wrong (3 · 36 · 37) 798

נָקִי innocent, free from guilt (6 · 43)
667

לְמִן 7 from (4 · 14) 577 מִן 9.b.(2)

הוֹעִיל 8 to profit, benefit (7 · 23 · 23) 418

גנב 9 to take by stealth, steal (1 · 30 · 39)
170

רָצַח to murder, slay (1 · 38 · 43) 953

נאף to commit adultery (5 · 17 · 31) 610

מְעָרָה 11 cave (1 · 40) 792

פָּרִיץ violent one (1 · 6) 829

רִנָּה 16 ringing cry (3 · 33) 943

פָּגַע to entreat (2 · 40 · 46) 803

לקט 18 to gather, gather up (1 · 21 · 37) 544

לוש to knead (1 · 5 · 5) 534

בָּצֵק dough (1 · 5) 130

72

כַּוָּן		cake, sacrificial cake (2 · 2) 467
מְלֶכֶת		queen (5 · 5) 573
הִסִּיךְ		to pour out libations (8 · 14 · 25) 650
		נסך
בֹּשֶׁת	19	shame (6 · 30) 102
נִתַּךְ	20	to be poured out (2 · 8 · 21) 677
כבה		to be quenched, extinguished (2 · 14 · 24) 459
הַטּוּ		*Hiph.* נטה (>50) 639
מוֹעֵצָה	24	counsel, plan, principle (1 · 7) 420
שְׁרִירוּת		stubbornness (8 · 10) 1057
אָחוֹר		with לְ = backwards (4 · 41) 30
לְמִן	25	from (4 · 14) 577 מִן 9.b.
הִקְשָׁה	26	to make stiff, stubborn (3 · 21 · 28) 904
עֹרֶף		back of neck (7 · 33) 791
מוּסָר	28	chastisement, discipline (8 · 50) 416
גָּזַז	29	to shear (1 · 14 · 15) 159
נֵזֶר		hair; consecration (1 · 25) 634
שְׁפִי		bare place, height (6 · 10) 1046
קִינָה		elegy, dirge (3 · 17) 884
נָטַשׁ		to abandon, forsake (5 · 33 · 40) 643
עֶבְרָה		overflowing rage, fury (2 · 34) 720
שִׁקּוּץ	30	detested thing (5 · 28) 1055
גַּיְא	32	valley (4 · 48) 161
הֲרֵגָה		slaughter (3 · 5) 247
מֵאֵין		from lack of (20 · 48[?]) 34 אַיִן 6.d.
נְבֵלָה		carcass, corpse (8 · 48) 615
מַאֲכָל		food (4 · 30) 38
הֶחֱרִיד		to terrify, drive in terror (3 · 16 · 39) 353
שָׂשׂוֹן	34	joy, exultation (7 · 22) 965
חָתָן		bridegroom (4 · 20) 368
כַּלָּה		bride; daughter-in-law (5 · 34) 483
חָרְבָּה		waste, desolation (10 · 42) 352

Chapter 8

שׁטח	2	to spread abroad (1 · 4 · 5) 1008

יָרֵחַ		moon (2 · 27) 437
דֹּמֶן		dung (4 · 6) 199
הִדִּיחַ	3	to thrust out, banish (13 · 27 · 43) 623
מְשֻׁבָה	5	turning back, apostasy (9 · 12) 1000
		מְשׁוּבָה
נצח		ptc. = enduring (1 · 1 · 8) 663
תַּרְמִית		deceitfulness (3 · 5) 941
מֵאֵן		to refuse (12 · 46) 549
הִקְשִׁיב	6	to give attention (8 · 45 · 46) 904
כֵּן		right, honest, true (4 · 24) 467
מְרוּצָה		course, running (2 · 4) 930
שָׁטַף		to overflow [fig. of dashing, rushing] (3 · 28 · 31) 1009
חֲסִידָה	7	stork (1 · 6) 339
תּוֹר		turtle dove (1 · 14) 1076
סוּס		swallow or swift (1 · 1) 692 סוס
עָגוּר		[dub.] crane (1 · 2) 723
אֵיכָה	8	in what manner? (2 · 18) 32
אָכֵן		surely, truly (5 · 18) 38
עֵט		stylus (2 · 4) 741
יוֹרֵשׁ	10	heir, inheritor (3 · 5) 439
בָּצַע		to gain by violence, ptc. = robber (2 · 10 · 16) 130
בֶּצַע		gain made by violence, unjust gain (4 · 23) 130
שֶׁבֶר	11	breaking (15 · 45) 991
נכלם	12	to be put to shame, dishonored, humiliated (4 · 26 · 38) 483
פְּקֻדָּה		visitation (9 · 32) 824
הֵסִיף	13	to make an end of (2 · 6 · 10) 692
עֵנָב		grape[s] (1 · 19) 772
תְּאֵנָה		fig, fig tree (12 · 39) 1061
עלה		leaf, leafage (2 · 17) 750
נָבֵל		to droop, wither and fall, fade (1 · 19 · 23) 615
מִבְצָר	14	fortification (7 · 37) 131
דמם		to perish; to be still, silent (3 · 23 · 30) 198

73

הַדְמִים	to silence = cause to perish (1 · 1 · 30) 198
רֹאשׁ	bitter, poisonous herb (3 · 12) 912
קוה 15	to wait, look eagerly for (5 · 39 · 45) 875
מַרְפֵּה	healing, cure (4 · 13) 951 מַרְפֵּא
בְּעָתָה	terror, dismay (2 · 2) 130
נַחְרָה 16	snorting (1 · 1) 637
מִצְהָלָה	neighing (2 · 2) 843
אַבִּיר	mighty, valiant (4 · 17) 7
רעשׁ	to quake, shake (5 · 21 · 29) 950
מְלוֹא	fullness, entire contents (2 · 38) 571
נָחָשׁ 17	serpent (2 · 31) 638 I.
צֶפַע	[dub.] venomous viper (1 · 5[?]) 861
לַחַשׁ	serpent-charming, whispering (1 · 5) 538
נשׁךְ	to bite fatally (1 · 2 · 12) 675
מַבְלִיגִית 18	smiling, cheerfulness, source of brightening (1 · 1) 114
יָגוֹן	grief, sorrow (4 · 14) 387
דַּוָּי	faint [adj.] (1 · 3) 188
שַׁוְעָה 19	cry for help (1 · 11) 1003
מֶרְחָק	distance, distant place (5 · 18) 935
פָּסִיל	idol, image (4 · 23) 820
נֵכָר	foreign (2 · 36) 648
קָצִיר 20	harvest (5 · 49) 894
קַיִץ	summer (4 · 20) 884
שֶׁבֶר 21	breaking (15 · 45) 991
קָדַר	to be dark; fig. of mourning (3 · 13 · 17) 871
שַׁמָּה	horror, an appalling thing (24 · 39) 1031
צֳרִי 22	a kind of balsam [for medication] (3 · 6) 863
רֹפֵא	physician (1 · 5[?]) 950
אֲרוּכָה	healing, restoration (3 · 6) 74
מִי יִתֵּן 23	here rhetorical = O that I had (>50) 678 נתן Qal 1.e.
מָקוֹר	spring, fountain, source (4 · 18) 881
דִּמְעָה	tears (5 · 23) 199

Chapter 9

מָלוֹן 1	lodging place, inn (1 · 8) 533
אֹרֵחַ	wayfarer, wanderer (2 · 4[?]) 72 אָרַח
נאף	to commit adultery (3 · 14 · 31) 610
עֲצֶרֶת	company, assemblage (1 · 11) 783
בגד	to act or deal treacherously (8 · 49 · 49) 93
הַדְרִיךְ 2	here = bending [the bow] (>50) 201 Hiph. 2.
גָּבַר	to prevail, be strong (1 · 17 · 25) 149
עָקַב 3	to overreach (1 · 3 · 3[?]) 784
רָכִיל	slander; tale bearer, informer (2 · 6) 940
חָתַל	to mock, trifle with (1 · 7 · 8) 1068
הֶעֱוָה	to commit iniquity (2 · 9 · 17[?]) 731
נִלְאָה	to be weary, make oneself weary (4 · 10 · 19) 521
שֶׁבֶת 5	dwelling (1 · 7[?]) 442 ישׁב
מִרְמָה	deceit, treachery (4 · 39) 941
מֵאֵן	to refuse (12 · 46) 549
צָרַף 6	to test (2 · 18 · 21) 864
בחן	to prove, test, try (6 · 24 · 28) 103
שׁחט 7	Qal pass. ptc. = hammered; i.e., sharpened (1 · 6 · 6[?]) 1006
מִרְמָה	deceit, treachery (4 · 39) 941
דִּבֵּר	speaking (2 · 2) 184
אֹרֵב	ambuscade, treachery (1 · 2) 70
הִתְנַקֵּם 8	to avenge oneself (3 · 5 · 35) 667
בְּכִי 9	weeping (8 · 30) 113
נְהִי	wailing, lamentation (4 · 7) 624
נְאוֹת	pasture, meadow (14 · 45[?]) 627 בָרָה
קִינָה	elegy, dirge (3 · 17) 884
נצת	to be kindled, burned (2 · 6 · 27) 428
מִבְּלִי	so that there is no (4 · 25) 115 בְּלִי
נדד	to retreat, flee (3 · 21 · 24) 622
גַּל	heap, pile (2 · 20) 164
מָעוֹן	lair, refuge, habitation (5 · 18) 732
תַּן	jackal (5 · 14) 1072

מִבְּלִי — so that there is no (4 · 25) 115 בְּלִי

נצה 11 to be desolated (2 · 4 · 5[?]) 428 יצת Niph.

מִבְּלִי — so that there is no (4 · 25) 115 בְּלִי

שְׁרִירוּת 13 stubbornness (8 · 10) 1057

לַעֲנָה 14 wormwood (2 · 8) 542

רֹאשׁ — bitter, poisonous herb (3 · 12) 912

קוֹנֵן 16 to chant (1 · 8 · 8) 884

חכם — skillful [here as mourners] (>50) 314

נְהִי 17 wailing, lamentation (4 · 7) 624

דִּמְעָה — tears (5 · 23) 199

עַפְעַף — eyelid (1 · 10) 733

נזל — to flow, trickle, drop (2 · 8 · 9) 633

נְהִי 18 wailing, lamentation (4 · 7) 624

נְהִי 19 mourning song, lamentation (4 · 7) 624

רְעוּת — fellow [woman] (1 · 6) 946

קִינָה — elegy, dirge (3 · 17) 884

חַלּוֹן 20 window (1 · 30) 319

אַרְמוֹן — castle, palace (5 · 33) 74

עוֹלָל — child (2 · 9) 760

בָּחוּר — young man (11 · 45) 104

רְחוֹב — broad open place (5 · 43) 932

נְבֵלָה 21 carcass, corpse (8 · 48) 615

דֹּמֶן — dung (4 · 6) 199

עָמִיר — swath, row of fallen grain (1 · 4) 771

קֹצֵר — reaper (1 · 10[?]) 894

עָשִׁיר 22 rich (1 · 23) 799

עֹשֶׁר — riches (2 · 37) 799

מול 24 to circumcise (1 · 12 · 29) 557

עָרְלָה — foreskin (2 · 16) 790

קצץ 25 to cut off (3 · 4 · 14) 893

עָרֵל — uncircumcised (3 · 35) 790

Chapter 10

חָרָשׁ 3 artificer, graver (4 · 38) 360

מַעֲצָד — axe (1 · 2) 781

יפה 4 to beautify (1 · 1 · 8) 421

מַסְמֵר — nail (1 · 5) 702

מַקֶּבֶת — hammer (1 · 4) 666

הפיק — to totter (1 · 8 · 9) 807

תֹּמֶר 5 palm tree, post (1 · 2) 1071

מִקְשָׁה — place or field of cucumbers (1 · 2) 903

צעד — to step, march (1 · 7 · 8) 857

מֵאִין 6 none at all or whence [is any] (28 · 48[?]) 34 אַיִן 6.d.

יאה 7 to be befitting (1 · 1 · 1) 383

מֵאִין — none at all or whence [is any] (20 · 48[?]) 34 אַיִן 6.d.

בער 8 to be stupid, dullhearted, unreceptive (1 · 3 · 7) 129

כסל — to be, become stupid (1 · 1 · 1) 492

מוּסָר — discipline, chastisement (8 · 50) 416

רקע 9 to be beaten (1 · 1 · 11) 955

חָרָשׁ — artificer, graver (4 · 38) 360

צֹרֵף — smelter; i.e., goldsmith (3 · 10[?]) 864

תְּכֵלֶה — violet stuff, fabric (1 · 49) 1067

אַרְגָּמָן — wool dyed with red purple, purple (1 · 39) 71

לְבוּשׁ — garment, clothing, raiment (1 · 31) 528

קֶצֶף 10 wrath (4 · 29) 893

רעשׁ — to quake, shake (5 · 21 · 29) 950

הכיל — to sustain, endure, contain, hold in (2 · 12 · 38) 465

זעם — indignation (3 · 22) 276

דְּנָה 11 [Aram.] this; כִּדְנָה = thus (1 · 43) 1088

אֲמַר — [Aram.] to say (1 · 1 · 72) 1081

לְהוֹם — [Aram.] to them, לְ + 3 mp. suffix

אֱלָהּ — [Aram.] god (1 · 92) 1080

דִּי — [Aram.] who, that (1 · 310) 1087

שְׁמַיָּא — [Aram.] heavens (2 · 38) 1116

אֲרַק — [Aram.] earth (1 · 21) 1083

לָא — [Aram.] not (1 · 80) 1098

עֲבַד — [Aram.] to make (1 · 19 · 28) 1104

אֲבַד   [Aram.] to perish (1 · 1 · 7) 1078

אֲרַע   [Aram.] earth (1 · 21) 1083

מִן   [Aram.] from (1 · 101) 1100

תְּחוֹת   [Aram.] under (1 · 5) 1117

אֵלֶּה   [Aram.] these (1 · 2) 1080

תֵּבֵל   12 world (2 · 36) 385

תְּבוּנָה   understanding (2 · 42) 108

נָשִׂיא   13 vapor (2 · 4) 672 II.

בָּרָק   lightning (2 · 21) 140

מָטָר   rain (2 · 38) 564

נִבְעַר   14 to be brutish, stupid (3 · 4 · 7) 129

צֹרֵף   smelter; i.e., goldsmith (3 · 10[?]) 864

תַּעְתֻּעִים   15 mockery (2 · 2) 1074

פְּקֻדָּה   visitation (9 · 32) 824

יָצַר   16 to form, fashion (4 · 41 · 44) 427

כִּנְעָה   17 bundle, pack (1 · 1) 488

מָצוֹר   siege; siegeworks (3 · 25) 848

קלע   18 to sling (1 · 2 · 4) 887

אוֹי   19 Woe! Alas! (8 · 25) 17

שֶׁבֶר   breaking (15 · 45) 991

נַחְלָה   serious, sore; diseased (3 · 5[?]) 317 חלה Niph.

מַכָּה   wound, blow (10 · 48) 646

חֳלִי   sickness, disease (2 · 24) 318

מֵיתָר   20 cord, string (1 · 9) 452

נְתַּק   to be torn apart or in two (2 · 10 · 27) 683

נִבְעַר   21 to be brutish, stupid, dull-hearted (3 · 4 · 7) 129

מַרְעִית   pasturage, pasturing; here = flock (3 · 10) 945

שְׁמוּעָה   22 report (6 · 27) 808

רַעַשׁ   quaking, shaking (2 · 17) 950

מָעוֹן   lair, refuge, habitation (5 · 18) 732

תַּן   jackal (5 · 14) 1072

צַעַד   23 step, steps (1 · 14) 857

יָסַר   24 to chasten, chastise (5 · 27 · 38) 415

המעיט   to make small or few, diminish (1 · 13 · 22) 589

נָוֶה   25 habitation (14 · 45[?]) 627

Chapter 11

כּוּר   4 furnace [for smelting metals] (1 · 9) 468

שְׁבוּעָה   5 oath (1 · 30) 989

זוב   to flow (3 · 29 · 29) 264

חָלָב   milk (2 · 44) 316

אָמֵן   verily, truly (2 · 30) 53

הֵעִיד   7 to admonish (8 · 39 · 44) 729

שְׁרִירוּת   8 stubbornness (8 · 10) 1057

קֶשֶׁר   9 conspiracy (1 · 14) 905

מֵאֵן   10 to refuse (12 · 46) 549

הֵפֵר   to break, frustrate (4 · 41 · 44[?]) 380

בֹּשֶׁת   13 shameful things, shame (6 · 30) 102

רִנָּה   14 ringing cry (3 · 33) 943

יָדִיד   15 beloved, lovely (1 · 8) 391

מְזִמָּה   wickedness; purpose, discretion (4 · 19) 273

עלז   to exult, triumph (4 · 16 · 16) 759

זַיִת   16 olive tree (1 · 38) 268

רַעֲנָן   luxuriant, fresh (6 · 19) 947

יָפֶה   fair, beautiful (1 · 41) 421

תֹּאַר   form, outline (1 · 15) 1061

הֲמוּלָה   rainstorm, rushing or roaring sound (1 · 2) 242

הִצִּית   to kindle, set on fire (8 · 17 · 27) 428

דָּלִית   branch, bough (1 · 8) 194

בִּגְלַל   17 on account of (2 · 10) 164 I. גָּלָל

מַעֲלָל   18 practice, deed (17 · 41) 760

אַלּוּף   19 docile, tame; friend (3 · 9) 48

הוּבַל   to be led, conducted, borne (1 · 11 · 18) 384

טבח   to slaughter, butcher (3 · 11 · 11) 370

בהן   20 to prove, test, try (6 · 24 · 28) 103

כִּלְיָה   (pl. only) kidneys, affections (4 · 31) 480

נְקָמָה   vengeance (11 · 27) 668

בָּחוּר   22 young man (11 · 45) 104

פְּקֻדָּה 23 visitation (9 · 32) 824

Chapter 12

שׁלה 1 to be at ease, prosper (1 · 5 · 7) 1017

בגד to act or deal treacherously (8 · 49 · 49) 93

בֶּגֶד treachery (1 · 2) 93

שׁרשׁ 2 to take root (1 · 1 · 8) 1057

הלך to grow (>50) 229 *Qal* I.3.

כִּלְיָה (pl. only) kidneys, affections (4 · 31) 480

בחן 3 to prove, test, try (6 · 24 · 28) 103

הִתִּיק to drag away (1 · 2 · 27) 683

טִבְחָה slaughter (1 · 4) 370

הֲרֵגָה slaughter (3 · 5) 247

מָתַי 4 when? (7 · 42) 607

אבל to mourn, lament (5 · 18 · 38) 5

עֵשֶׂב herb, herbage (2 · 33) 793

ספה to be snatched away (1 · 8 · 18) 705

רַגְלִי 5 on foot; as subst. = foot soldiery, infantry (1 · 12) 920

הלאה to weary, make weary, exhaust (1 · 6 · 19) 521

התחרה to contend hotly (>50) 354

גָּאוֹן majesty, exaltation, pride (7 · 49) 144

בגד 6 to act or deal treacherously (8 · 49 · 49) 93

נָטַשׁ 7 to abandon, forsake (5 · 33 · 40) 643

יְדִדוּת love, beloved one (1 · 1) 392

אַרְיֵה 8 lion (6 · 45) 71

עַיִט 9 bird[s] of prey (1 · 8) 743

צָבוּעַ colored, variegated (1 · 1) 840

הֵתָיוּ Bring! [impv.] (1 · 2 · 21) 87 אתה

אכלה food (1 · 18) 38; or to eat (>50) 37

בוסס 10 to tread down (1 · 2 · 12) 100

חֶלְקָה portion of ground (2 · 24) 324

חֶמְדָּה desire, desirable thing (3 · 16) 326

אָבַל 11 to mourn, lament (5 · 8 · 38) 5

שָׁמֵם devastated (1 · 3) 1031

שְׁפִי 12 bare place, height (6 · 10) 1046

חִטָּה 13 wheat (2 · 30) 334

קוֹץ thorn bush (2 · 11) 881

קצר to reap, harvest (1 · 24 · 24) 894

הוֹעִיל to gain profit, benefit (7 · 23 · 23) 418

תְּבוּאָה product (2 · 43) 100

חָרוֹן [burning of] anger; ח' אף = burning anger (9 · 41) 354

שָׁכֵן 14 neighbor (5 · 20) 1015

נָתַשׁ to pull up, pluck up (11 · 16 · 21) 684

נָתַשׁ 15 to pull up, pluck up (11 · 16 · 21) 684

רִחַם to have compassion (9 · 41 · 46) 933

נָתַשׁ 17 to pull up, pluck up (11 · 16 · 21) 684

Chapter 13

אֵזוֹר 1 waistcloth (8 · 14) 25

פֵּשֶׁת flax, linen (1 · 16) 833

מָתְנַיִם loins (6 · 47) 608

אֵזוֹר 2 waistcloth (8 · 14) 25

מָתְנַיִם loins (6 · 47) 608

אֵזוֹר 4 waistcloth (8 · 14) 25

מָתְנַיִם loins (6 · 47) 608

טָמַן to hide (7 · 28 · 31) 380

נָקִיק cleft (2 · 3) 669

טָמַן 5 to hide (7 · 28 · 31) 380

אֵזוֹר 6 waistcloth (8 · 14) 25

טָמַן to hide (7 · 28 · 31) 380

חָפַר 7 to dig, search for (1 · 23 · 23) 343

אֵזוֹר waistcloth (8 · 14) 25

טָמַן to hide (7 · 28 · 31) 380

צלח w. ל = to be good for (>50) 852 II.

כָּכָה 9 thus (5 · 34) 462

גָּאוֹן		majesty, excellence, pride (7 · 49) 144
מֵאֵן	10	to refuse (12 · 46) 549
שְׁרִירוּת		stubbornness (8 · 10) 1057
אֵזוֹר		waistcloth (8 · 14) 25
אֵזוֹר	11	waistcloth (8 · 14) 25
מָתְנַיִם		loins (6 · 47) 608
נֵבֶל	12	skin bottle, skin (3 · 11) 614
שִׁכָּרוֹן	13	drunkenness (1 · 3) 1016
נָפֵץ	14	to dash to pieces (11 · 15 · 21) 658
חָמַל		to spare, have compassion on (5 · 40 · 40) 328
חוּס		to pity, look with compassion (2 · 24 · 24) 299
רָחַם		to have compassion (9 · 41 · 46) 933
הֶאֱזִין	15	to give ear, hearken to = be obedient to (1 · 41 · 41) 24
גָּבַהּ		to be haughty, exalted, high (1 · 24 · 34) 146
בְּטֶרֶם	16	before (6 · 39) 382 טֶרֶם 2.
הֶחְשִׁיךְ		to cause darkness, make dark (1 · 6 · 17) 364
הִתְנַגֵּף		to stumble (1 · 1 · 48) 619
נֶשֶׁף		evening twilight (1 · 12) 676
קִרָּה		to wait, look eagerly for (5 · 39 · 45) 875
צַלְמָוֶת		deep shadow, darkness (2 · 18) 853
עֲרָפֶל		cloud, heavy cloud (1 · 15) 791
מִסְתָּר	17	secret place, hiding place (3 · 10) 712
גֵּוָה		pride, lifting up (1 · 3) 145
דָּמַע		to weep (2 · 2 · 2) 199
דִּמְעָה		tears (5 · 23) 199
נִשְׁבָּה		to be taken captive (1 · 8 · 37) 985
עֵדֶר		flock (6 · 39) 727
גְּבִירָה	18	queen mother, queen, lady (2 · 15) 150
הִשְׁפִּיל		to make low, sit down (1 · 18 · 29) 1050
מַרְאֲשׁוֹת		place at the head, head place (1 · 10) 912

עֲטָרָה		crown, [wreath] (1 · 23) 742
אַיֵּה	20	where? (6 · 44) 32
עֵדֶר		flock (6 · 39) 727
אַלּוּף	21	friend, intimate (3 · 9) 48
חֵבֶל		pains of travail (3 · 7) 286
לֵדָה		bringing forth (1 · 4) 408 יָלַד
שׁוּל	22	skirt (2 · 11) 1002
נֶחְמַס		to suffer violence (1 · 1 · 8) 329
עָקֵב		heel, foot print (1 · 14) 784
נָמֵר	23	leopard (2 · 6) 649
חֲבַרְבֻּרָה		(pl.) stripes, marks (1 · 1) 289
לִמֵּד		accustomed, taught (2 · 6) 541
קַשׁ	24	stubble, chaff (1 · 16) 905
מְנָת	25	portion (1 · 9) 584
מַד		measure (1 · 12) 551
חָשַׂף	26	to strip off, make bare (2 · 10 · 10) 362
שׁוּל		skirt (2 · 11) 1002
קָלוֹן		ignominy, dishonor (2 · 17) 885
נִאֻף	27	adultery (1 · 2) 610
מִצְהָלָה		neighing (2 · 2) 843
זִמָּה		wickedness, evil device (1 · 28) 273
זְנוּת		fornication (3 · 9) 276
שִׁקּוּץ		detested thing (5 · 28) 1055
אוֹי		Woe! Alas! (8 · 25) 17
מָתַי		when? (7 · 42) 607 אַחֲרֵי מ׳ עֹד = after how long yet? when? d.

Chapter 14

בַּצֹּרֶת	1	dearth, destitution (1 · 2) 131
אָבַל	2	to mourn, lament (5 · 18 · 38) 5
אֻמְלַל		to be or grow feeble, languish (2 · 15 · 15) 51
קָדַר		to be dark; fig. of mourning (3 · 13 · 17) 871
צְוָחָה		outcry (2 · 4) 846
אַדִּיר	3	subst. = majestic one [used of nobles, chieftains, etc.] (5 · 27) 12

צָעִיר insignificant, mean [as subst. here] (4 · 22) 859

גֵּב pit, ditch, cistern (1 · 3) 155

רֵיקָם in vain, without effect (2 · 16) 938

הכלם to be put to shame, dishonored; be humiliated (1 · 2 · 38) 484

חפה to cover (2 · 6 · 12) 341

בַּעֲבוּר 4 because of (1 · 45) 721   II. עֲבוּר

גֶּשֶׁם shower, rain (2 · 35) 177

אִכָּר plowman, husbandman (3 · 7) 38

חפה to cover (2 · 6 · 12) 341

אַיָּלָה 5 hind, doe (1 · 11) 19

דֶּשֶׁא grass (1 · 14) 206

פֶּרֶא 6 wild ass (2 · 10) 825

שְׁפִי bare place, height (6 · 10) 1046

שָׁאַף to pant after (2 · 14 · 14) 983

תַּן jackal (5 · 14) 1072

עֵשֶׂב herb, herbage (2 · 33) 793

רבב 7 to be, become many (3 · 23 · 24) 912

מְשׁוּבָה turning back, apostasy (9 · 12) 1000

מִקְוֶה 8 hope (3 · 5) 876

מוֹשִׁיע savior (1 · 27) 446   ישע Hiph. ptc.

אֹרֵחַ wanderer, traveler (2 · 4) 72

נדהם 9 to be astounded (1 · 1 · 1) 187

תַּנַּחֵנוּ fr. נוח to abandon (>50) 628   Hiph. B.4.

נוּעַ 10 to err, sin (1 · 22 · 38) 631

חָשַׂךְ to hold in check, withhold (1 · 26 · 28) 362

צום 12 to fast (1 · 20 · 20) 847

רִנָּה ringing cry (3 · 33) 943

דֶּבֶר plague (17 · 46) 184

אֲהָהּ 13 Alas! (4 · 15) 13

חָזוֹן 14 vision (2 · 35) 302

קֶסֶם divination (1 · 11) 890

אֱלִיל worthlessness (1 · 20) 47

תַּרְמִית deceitfulness (3 · 5) 941

דִּמְעָה 17 tears (5 · 23) 199

דמה to cease, cause to cease (2 · 4 · 16) 198

שֶׁבֶר breaking (15 · 45) 991

בְּתוּלָה virgin (8 · 50) 143

מַכָּה wound, blow (10 · 48) 646

נַחְלָה serious, sore; diseased (3 · 5[?]) חלה Niph.

תַּחֲלֻאִים 18 diseases (2 · 5) 316

סחר to go about; i.e., go about one's affairs (1 · 4 · 5[?]) 695

גּעל 19 to abhor, loathe (1 · 8 · 10) 171

מַרְפֵּא healing, cure (4 · 13) 951

קרה to wait, look eagerly for (5 · 39 · 45) 875

בְּעָתָה terror, dismay (2 · 2) 130

רֶשַׁע 20 wickedness (1 · 30) 957

נָאַץ 21 to contemn [treat with contempt] (2 · 8 · 24) 610

נבל to regard or treat as a foolish one [נָבֵל] (1 · 4 · 23[?]) 614   II. נָבֵל

חָפֵר to break, frustrate (4 · 41 · 44[?]) 830

הַגְשִׁים 22 to cause or send rain (1 · 1 · 1) 177

הֶבֶל here pl. = false gods (>50) 210

רְבִיבִים copious showers (2 · 6) 914

קוה to wait, look eagerly for (4 · 39 · 45) 875

Chapter 15

אָנָה 2 whither? where? (2 · 39) 33

שְׁבִי captivity (8 · 46) 985

מִשְׁפָּחָה 3 kind, species (>50) 1046   3.

כֶּלֶב dog (1 · 32) 476

סחב to drag (4 · 5 · 5) 694

זְוָעָה 4 object of trembling, terror (4 · 7) 266

בִּגְלַל on account of (2 · 10) 164   I. גלל

חָמַל 5 to spare, have compassion (5 · 40 · 40) 328

נָד to lament, show grief (8 · 19 · 26) 626

נָטַשׁ 6 to forsake, abandon (5 · 33 · 40) 643

אָחוֹר backwards (4 · 41) 30

79

אָט — *Hiph.* of נטה, to stretch out (>50) 639

נִלְאָה — to be weary, make oneself weary (4 · 10 · 19) 521

זרה — 7 to fan, winnow (2 · 9 · 38) 279

מִזְרֶה — pitchfork (1 · 2) 280

שִׁכֵּל — to make childless (1 · 18 · 24) 1013

עָצַם — 8 to be numerous (4 · 16 · 18) 782

חוֹל — sand (3 · 22) 297

בָּחוּר — [coll.] young men; young man (11 · 45) 104

צׇהֳרַיִם — midday, noon (3 · 23) 843

פִּתְאֹם — suddenly (5 · 25) 837

עִיר — agitation [of terror] (1 · 2) 735

בֶּהָלָה — sudden terror, dismay (1 · 4) 96

אֻמְלַל — 9 to be or grow feeble, languish (2 · 15 · 15) 51

נפח — to breathe; here = breathe out (2 · 9 · 12) 655

בְּעֹד — while, so long as (3 · 20) 728   2.a.

חפר — to be abashed, ashamed (2 · 17 · 17) 344

אוֹי — 10 Woe! Alas! (8 · 25) 17

מָדוֹן — contention, strife (1 · 12) 193

נשה — to lend (4 · 12 · 14[?]) 674   I. נשׁה

שׁרה — 11 [dub.] to set free (1 · 1 · 2) 1056

הִפְגִּיעַ — to cause one to entreat (2 · 6 · 46) 803

רעע — 12 to break (1 · 3 · 5[?]) 949

בַּז — 13 spoil, booty, plunder (5 · 27) 103

מְחִיר — price, hire (1 · 15) 564

קדח — 14 to be kindled (2 · 5 · 5) 869

הוּקַד — to be burning, burn (2 · 5 · 8) 428   יקד

נקם — 15 to avenge oneself (3 · 12 · 35) 667

אָרֵךְ — long; w. אף = slow to anger (1 · 15) 74

שָׂשׂוֹן — 16 joy, exultation (7 · 22) 965

סוֹד — 17 intimate circle, council (4 · 21) 691

שׂחק — to play (3 · 17 · 36) 965

עלז — to exult, triumph (4 · 16 · 16) 759

בָּדָד — isolation, separation (2 · 11) 94

זַעַם — indignation (3 · 22) 276

כְּאֵב — 18 pain (1 · 6) 456

נֶצַח — everlastingness, ever (3 · 42) 664

מַכָּה — wound, blow (10 · 48) 646

אָנוּשׁ — incurable (5 · 8) 60   אנשׁ

מֵאֵן — to refuse (12 · 46) 549

אַכְזָב — deceptive, disappointing (1 · 2) 469

יָקָר — 19 precious, highly valued (1 · 35) 429

זוֹלֵל — worthless, insignificant (1 · 6) 272   זלל

כְּפִי — according to my mouth, as my mouth (1 · 16) 804   פֶּה 6.b.

בָּצוּר — 20 made inaccessible, fortified (2 · 25) 130   בצר

עָרִיץ — 21 awe inspiring, terror striking (2 · 20) 792

Chapter 16

יִלּוֹד — 3 born (1 · 5) 409

מָמוֹת — 4 death [of painful death] (1 · 2) 560

תַּחֲלֻאִים — diseases (2 · 5) 316

נספד — to be bewailed (2 · 2 · 30) 704

דֹּמֶן — dung (4 · 6) 199

נְבֵלָה — carcass, corpse (8 · 48) 615

מַאֲכָל — food (4 · 30) 38

מַרְזֵחַ — 5 mourning cry (1 · 2) 931

ספד — to wail, lament (7 · 28 · 30) 704

נָד — to lament, show grief (8 · 19 · 26) 626

רַחֲמִים — compassion (2 · 38) 933

קָטֹן — 6 young (3 · 47) 881

ספד — to wail, lament (7 · 28 · 30) 704

התגדד — to cut oneself [as relig. practice]; to gather in troops or bands (4 · 7 · 8) 151

נקרח — to make themselves bald (1 · 1 · 5) 901

80

פָּרַס 7 to break (1 · 2 · 14) 828

אֵבֶל mourning (3 · 24) 5

כּוֹס cup (7 · 31) 468

תַּנְחוּם consolation (1 · 5) 637

מִשְׁתֶּה 8 feast, banquet, drink (2 · 46) 1059

שָׂשׂוֹן 9 joy, exultation (7 · 22) 965

חָתָן bridegroom (4 · 20) 368

כַּלָּה bride; daughter-in-law (5 · 34) 483

שְׁרִירוּת 12 stubbornness (8 · 10) 1057

הֵטִיל 13 to hurl, cast, cast out (2 · 9 · 14) 376

חֲנִינָה favor (1 · 1) 337

הִדִּיחַ 15 to thrust out, banish (13 · 27 · 43) 623

דַּוָּג 16 fisherman (1 · 2) 186

דִּיג to fish for, catch (1 · 1 · 1) 185

צַיָּד hunter (1 · 1) 844

צוד to hunt (1 · 12 · 16) 844

נָקִיק cleft (2 · 3) 669

נִצְפַּן 17 to be hidden (1 · 3 · 28) 860

מִנֶּגֶד from before (1 · 26) 617 נֶגֶד 2.c.

מִשְׁנֶה 18 double, copy (3 · 36) 1041

נְבֵלָה carcass, corpse (8 · 48) 615

שִׁקּוּץ detested thing (5 · 28) 1055

מָעוֹז 19 refuge, place of safety (1 · 36) 731

מָנוֹס place of escape, refuge; flight (3 · 8) 631

אֶפֶס end, extremity (1 · 27) 67

הוֹעִיל to profit, benefit (7 · 23 · 23) 418

Chapter 17

עֵט 1 stylus (2 · 4) 741

צִפֹּרֶן point (1 · 2) 862

שָׁמִיר adamant, flint (1 · 11) 1038

חרשׁ to cut in, engrave (1 · 23 · 26) 360

לוּחַ tablet, board, plank (1 · 43) 531

אֲשֵׁרָה 2 sacred tree or pole as symbol of Canaanitish goddess (1 · 40) 81

רַעֲנָן luxuriant, fresh (6 · 19) 947

גָּבֹהַּ high, lofty, tall (4 · 41) 147

בַּז 3 spoil, booty, plunder (5 · 27) 103

שׁמט 4 to let fall, drop (1 · 7 · 9) 1030

קדה to be kindled (2 · 5 · 5) 869

הוּקַד to be burning, burn (2 · 5 · 8) 428 יקד

עַרְעָר 6 tree or bush (1 · 2) 792 עֲרוֹעֵר

חֲרֵרִים parched places (1 · 1) 359

מְלֵחָה saltiness, barrenness (1 · 2) 572

מִבְטָח 7 object of confidence, confidence (3 · 15) 105

שָׁתַל 8 to transplant (1 · 10 · 10) 1060

יוּבַל stream (1 · 1) 385

שֹׁרֶשׁ root (1 · 33) 1057

חֹם heat (1 · 4) 328

עָלֶה leaf, leafage (2 · 17) 750

רַעֲנָן luxuriant, fresh (6 · 19) 947

בַּצֹּרֶת dearth (2 · 2) 131

דאג to be anxious, concerned (3 · 7 · 7) 178

הֵמִישׁ to cease from, depart (2 · 20 · 20) 559 מושׁ I.

עָקֹב 9 deceitful, insidious (1 · 3[?]) 784

אָנֻשׁ incurable, sick (5 · 8) 60

חקר 10 to search (1 · 22 · 27) 350

בחן to prove, test, try (6 · 24 · 28) 103

כִּלְיָה pl. only, kidneys, affections (4 · 31) 480

מַעֲלָל practice, deed (17 · 41) 760

קֹרֵא 11 partridge (1 · 2) 896

דָּגַר to gather together as a brood (1 · 22) 186

עֹשֶׁר riches (2 · 37) 799

נָבָל foolish, senseless (1 · 18) 614

מִקְוֵה 13 hope (3 · 5) 876

יְסוּרַי read: those revolting from Me [with Q] (2 · 3) 693 סור Qal 1.

מָקוֹר spring, fountain, source (4 · 18) 881

אַיֵּה 15 where[?] (6 · 44) 32

אָץ 16 to hasten, make haste (1 · 8 · 10) 21 אוץ

אָנוּשׁ incurable (5 · 8) 60 אנשׁ

הַתַּאֲוָה — to desire, long for, lust after (1·16·27) 16

מוֹצָא — utterance, that which goes forth (1·27) 425

נֹכַח — before (1·22) 647

מְחִתָּה 17 — terror, destruction, ruin (2·11) 369

מַחְסֶה — refuge, shelter (1·20) 340

מִשְׁנֶה 18 — double, copy, second (3·36) 1041

שִׁבָּרוֹן — breaking, crushing (1·2) 991

מַשָּׂא 21 — load, burden (12·45) 672 III.

מַשָּׂא 22 — load, burden (12·45) 672 III.

הִקְשָׁה 23 — to make stiff, stubborn (3·21·28) 904

עֹרֶף — back of neck (7·33) 791

מוּסָר — discipline, correction; chastisement (8·50) 416

מַשָּׂא 24 — load, burden (12·45) 672 III.

שְׁפֵלָה 26 — lowland (3·20) 1050

לְבוֹנָה — frankincense (3·21) 526

תוֹדָה — sacrifice of thanksgiving (3·32) 392

מַשָּׂא 27 — load, burden (12·45) 672 III.

הִצִּית — to kindle, set on fire (8·17·27) 428

אַרְמוֹן — palace, citadel (5·33) 74

כבה — to be quenched, extinguished (2·14·24) 459

Chapter 18

יוֹצֵר 2 — ptc. = potter, former (8·17) 427
יצר

יוֹצֵר 3 — ptc. = potter, former (8·17) 427
יצר

אֹבֶן — potter's wheel, disc (1·2) 7

חֹמֶר 4 — clay (2·17) 330

יוֹצֵר — ptc. = potter, former (8·17) 427
יצר

יָשַׁר — to be pleasing, right, straight (2·13·25) 448

יוֹצֵר 6 — ptc. = potter, former (8·17) 427
יצר

חֹמֶר — clay (2·17) 330

רֶגַע 7 — moment (3·22) 921

נָתַשׁ — to pull up, pluck up (11·16·21) 684

נָתַץ — to pull down, break down (6·31·42) 683

רֶגַע 9 — moment (3·22) 921

יָצַר 11 — to form, fashion (4·41·44) 427

מַעֲלָל — practice, deed (17·41) 760

נוֹאָשׁ 12 — to despair (2·5·6) 384

שְׁרִירוּת — stubbornness (8·10) 1057

שַׁעֲרוּרִי 13 — horrible thing (1·2) 1045

בְּתוּלָה — virgin (8·50) 143

שָׂדַי 14 — land, field (2·13) 961

שֶׁלֶג — snow (1·20) 1017

נתש — to be rooted up (2·4·21) 684; to be dried up 677 נשת

קַר — cool (1·3) 903

נזל — to flow (2·8·9) 633

שְׁבִיל 15 — way, path (1·2) 987

נְתִיבָה — path, bypath (2·21) 677

סלל — to cast up (2·10·12) 699

שַׁמָּה 16 — waste (24·39) 1031

שְׁרִיקֹת — hissing (1·2) 1057 שְׁרִיקָה

הָנוּד — to wag (1·3·26) 626

עֹרֶף 17 — neck (7·33) 791

אֵיד — distress, calamity (5·24) 15

הִקְשִׁיב 18 — to give attention (8·45·46) 904

הִקְשִׁיב 19 — to give attention (8·45·46) 904

יָרִיב — opponent, adversary (1·3) 937

כָּרָה 20 — to dig (2·13·14) 500

שׁוּחָה — pit (3·5) 1001

הִגִּיר 21 — to deliver over to (1·5·10) 620

שַׁכּוּל — bereaved, robbed of offspring (1·6) 1014

בָּחוּר — young man (11·45) 104

זְעָקָה 22 — cry of distress (6·18) 277

גְּדוּד — marauding band, troop (1·33) 151

פִּתְאֹם — suddenly (5·25) 837

כָּרָה — to dig (2·13·14) 500

שִׁיחָה	pit (3 · 5) 1001 שׁוּחָה	עֹרֶף	neck, back of neck (7 · 33) 791
פַּח	bird trap (3 · 25) 809		
טָמַן	to hide, conceal (7 · 28 · 31) 380		
הַמְחֵה	23 to blot out (1 · 3 · 34) 562		**Chapter 20**

Chapter 19

בַּקְבֻּק	1 flask (2 · 3) 132
יוֹצֵר	potter, former (8 · 17) 427 יצר
חֶרֶשׂ	earthenware, earthen vessel (2 · 17) 360
גַּיְא	2 valley (4 · 48) 161
חַרְסוּת	potsherd (1 · 1) 360
צלל	3 to tingle (1 · 4 · 4) 852
נכר	4 to treat as foreign (1 · 4 · 8) 649
נָקִי	innocent, free from guilt, clean (6 · 43) 667
גַּיְא	6 valley (4 · 48) 161
הֲרֵגָה	slaughter (3 · 5) 247
בקק	7 to make void, lay waste (1 · 4 · 7) 132
נְבֵלָה	carcass, corpse (8 · 48) 615
מַאֲכָל	food (4 · 30) 38
שַׁמָּה	8 waste (24 · 39) 1031
שְׁרֵקָה	hissing (5 · 7) 1056
שָׁרַק	to hiss (3 · 12 · 12) 1056
מַכָּה	wound, blow (10 · 48) 646
מָצוֹר	9 siege, siege works (3 · 25) 848
מָצוֹק	stress, straits (1 · 6) 848
הֵצִיק	to bring into straits, constrain, press upon (1 · 11 · 11) 847
בַּקְבֻּק	10 flask (2 · 3) 132
כָּכָה	11 thus (5 · 34) 462
יוֹצֵר	potter, former (8 · 17) 427 יצר
מֵאֵין	without (20 · 48[?]) 34 אֵין 6.d.
גַּג	13 roof, top (3 · 29) 150
הִסִּיךְ	to pour out libations (8 · 14 · 25) 650
מֵבִי	K, מֵבִיא Q Hiph. ptc. (>50) 97
עֹרֶף	15 to make stiff, stubborn (3 · 21 · 28) 904

Chapter 20

פָּקִיד	1 commissioner, deputy, overseer (3 · 13) 824
נָגִיד	prince, leader (1 · 44) 617
מַהְפֶּכֶת	2 stocks [or similar instrument of punishment] (3 · 4) 246
מָחֳרָת	3 with מִן = on the morrow (1 · 32) 564
מַהְפֶּכֶת	stocks, cf. vs. 2. (3 · 4) 246
מָגוֹר	terror, fear (6 · 8) 159
מָגוֹר	4 terror, fear (6 · 8) 159
אֹהֵב	friend, lover (2 · 36) 12 אָהֵב
חֹסֶן	5 wealth, treasure (1 · 5) 340
יְגִיעַ	product, toil (2 · 16) 388
יְקָר	precious things; preciousness, price, honor (1 · 17) 430
בָּזַז	to spoil, plunder (2 · 37 · 41) 102
שְׁבִי	6 captivity (8 · 46) 985
אֹהֵב	friend, lover (2 · 36) 12 אָהֵב
פתה	7 to deceive (1 · 17 · 27) 834
נִפְתָּה	to be deceived (1 · 2 · 27) 834
שְׂחוֹק	derision (4 · 15) 966
לעג	to mock, have in derision (1 · 12 · 18) 541
מִדֵּי	8 as often as (3 · 15) 191 דַּי 2.c.
שֹׁד	violence, havoc (3 · 25) 994
קֶלֶס	derision (1 · 3) 887
עָצַר	9 to shut up (4 · 36 · 46) 783
נִלְאָה	to be weary, make oneself weary (4 · 10 · 19) 521
כִּלְכֵּל	to contain, hold in, restrain; sustain (1 · 24 · 38) 465
דִּבָּה	whispering, evil report (1 · 9) 179
מָגוֹר	terror, fear (6 · 8) 159
הִגִּיד	to inform of (>50) 616 נגד Hiph. 3.
אֱנוֹשׁ	man, mankind (1 · 42) 60

צֶלַע   limping, stumbling (1 · 4) 854

אוּלַי   perhaps (6 · 45) 19

פתה   to be deceived (1 · 3 · 27) 834

נְקָמָה   vengeance (11 · 27) 668

עָרִיץ   11 awe inspiring, terror striking (2 · 20) 792

כְּלִמָּה   ignominy, reproach, insult (3 · 30) 484

בחן   12 to prove, test, try (6 · 24 · 28) 103

כִּלְיָה   pl. only = kidneys, affection (4 · 31) 480

נְקָמָה   vengeance (11 · 27) 668

מֵרַע   13 evildoer (2 · 18) 949   מרע *Hiph.*

בִּשַּׂר   15 to gladden with good tidings (1 · 14 · 15) 142

זְעָקָה   16 cry of distress (6 · 18) 277

תְּרוּעָה   alarm, war cry (3 · 36) 929

צָהֳרִים   midday, noon (3 · 23) 843

רֶחֶם   17 womb (4 · 33) 933

הָרָה   pregnant, woman with child (2 · 15) 248

רֶחֶם   18 womb (4 · 33) 933

יָגוֹן   grief, sorrow (4 · 14) 387

בֹּשֶׁת   shame (6 · 30) 102

Chapter 21

אוּלַי   2 perhaps (6 · 45) 19

נִפְלָאוֹת   wonderful acts (1 · 44[?]) 810   פלא *Niph.* 4.

צוּר   4 to besiege, shut in (5 · 31 · 31) 848

קֶצֶף   5 wrath (4 · 29) 893

דֶּבֶר   6 plague, pestilence (17 · 46) 184

דֶּבֶר   7 plague, pestilence (17 · 46) 184

חוס   to pity, look upon with compassion (2 · 24 · 24) 299

חמל   to spare, have compassion (5 · 40 · 40) 328

רֶחֶם   to have compassion (9 · 41 · 46) 933

דֶּבֶר   9 plague, pestilence (17 · 46) 184

צוּר   to shut in, besiege (5 · 31 · 31) 848

דִּין   12 to execute judgment, plead the cause, judge (4 · 23 · 24) 192

גָּזַל   to tear away, seize, plunder (2 · 29 · 30) 159

עָשַׁק   to oppress (3 · 36 · 37) 798

כבה   to quench, extinguish (2 · 10 · 24) 459

רַע   evil, badness (11 · 19) 947

מַעֲלָל   practice, deed (17 · 41) 760

מִישׁוֹר   13 tableland, level country (3 · 23) 449

נחת   to go down, descend (1 · 3 · 8) 639

מְעֹנָה   den, lair, habitation (1 · 9) 733

מַעֲלָל   14 practice, deed (17 · 41) 760

הִצִּית   to kindle, set on fire (8 · 17 · 27) 428

Chapter 22

גָּזַל   3 to tear away, seize, plunder (2 · 29 · 30) 159

עָשׁוֹק   oppressor, extortioner (1 · 1) 799

יָתוֹם   orphan (4 · 42) 450

הוֹנָה   to oppress, maltreat (1 · 14 · 18) 413

חמס   to treat violently, wrong (2 · 8 · 8) 329

נָקִי   innocent, free from guilt, clean (6 · 43) 667

הָרְבָּה   5 waste, ruin (10 · 42) 352

מַשְׁחִית   7 destroyer (4 · 19) 1008

מִבְחָר   choicest, best (2 · 12) 104

כָּכָה   8 thus (5 · 34) 462

נוד   10 to lament, show grief (8 · 19 · 26) 626

מוֹלֶדֶת   kindred, birth, offspring (2 · 22) 409

בְּלֹא   13 without (4 · 30) 518

עֲלִיָּה   roof chamber (2 · 20) 751

חִנָּם   for naught (1 · 32) 336

פֹּעַל   wages (3 · 37) 821

מִדָּה   size (>50) 551

עֲלִיָּה   14 roof chamber (2 · 20) 751

רָוַח *Pual* ptc. = spacious (1 · 1 · 14[?]) 926

חַלּוֹן window (1 · 1[?]) 319

ספן to cover in, panel (1 · 6 · 6) 706

שָׁשֵׁר red color, vermilion (1 · 2) 1059

התחרה 15 to strive eagerly [dub.] (>50) 354

דָּן 16 to plead the cause, minister judgment, judge (4 · 23 · 24) 192 דין

דִּין cause, plea; judgment (4 · 19) 192

בֶּצַע 17 unjust gain, gain made by violence (4 · 23) 130

נָקִי innocent, free from guilt, clean (6 · 43) 667

עֹשֶׁק oppression, extortion (2 · 15) 799

מְרוּצָה crushing, oppression (1 · 1) 954

ספד 18 to wail, lament (7 · 28 · 30) 704

הוֹד splendor, majesty (1 · 24) 217

קְבוּרָה 19 burial (1 · 14) 869

סחב to drag (4 · 5 · 5) 694

מֵהָלְאָה beyond (1 · 3) 229 הָלְאָה

חִנִי 20 lift up! (>50) 678 נחן *Qal* 1. x.

מְאַהֵב lover, friend (3 · 16) 12

שַׁלְוָה 21 prosperity (1 · 8) 1017

נְעוּרִים youth (7 · 46) 655

מְאַהֵב 22 lover, friend (3 · 16) 12

שְׁבִי captivity (8 · 46) 985

נכלם to be put to shame, dishonored, humiliated (4 · 26 · 38) 483

קנן 23 to be nested (1 · 4 · 5) 890

נֵחַנְתְּ to be pitied (>50) 335 חנן *Niph.*

חֵבֶל pains of travail (3 · 7) 286

חִיל anguish, writhing (3 · 6) 297

חוֹתָם 24 seal, signet ring (1 · 14) 368

נתק to draw off, pull off (1 · 3 · 27) 683

יָגוֹר 25 fearing (2 · 2) 388

הֵטִיל 26 to hurl, cast out (2 · 9 · 14) 376

עֶצֶב 28 vessel (1 · 1) 781

נבזה ptc. = despised (1 · 10 · 42) 102

נפץ to shatter (1 · 5 · 21) 658

חֵפֶץ pleasure, delight (2 · 39) 343

הוּטַל to be hurled, hurled down (1 · 4 · 14) 376

עֲרִירִי 30 childless (1 · 4) 792

Chapter 23

מַרְעִית 1 pasturing, pasturage (3 · 10) 945

הִדִּיחַ 2 to thrust out, banish (13 · 27 · 43) 623

רֹעַ evil, badness (11 · 19) 947

מַעֲלָל practice, deed (17 · 41) 760

הִדִּיחַ 3 to thrust out, banish (13 · 27 · 43) 623

נָוֶה abode, habitation (14 · 45[?]) 627

פרה to be fruitful (2 · 22 · 29) 826

צֶמַח 5 growth, sprout (2 · 12) 855

בֶּטַח 6 security, as adv. = securely (5 · 43) 105

הִדִּיחַ 8 to thrust out, banish (13 · 27 · 43) 623

רחף 9 to grow soft, relax (1 · 1 · 3[?]) 934

שָׁכּוֹר drunken (1 · 13) 1016

נאף 10 to commit adultery (3 · 14 · 31) 610

אלה curse, oath (4 · 36) 46

אבל to mourn, lament (5 · 18 · 38) 5

נוה cs. נְאוֹת, pasture, meadow (14 · 45 [?]) 627

מְרוּצָה course, running (2 · 4) 930

כֵּן right, honest, true (4 · 24) 467

חנף 11 to be profane, godless (4 · 7 · 11) 337

חֲלַקְלַקּוֹת 12 slipperiness (1 · 4) 325

אֲפֵלָה darkness, gloominess (2 · 12) 66

נדחח to push, push violently (1 · 2 · 2) 190 דחח

פְּקֻדָּה visitation (9 · 32) 824

תִּפְלָה 13 unseemliness (1 · 3) 1074

הִתְעָה to cause to err, mislead (4 · 21 · 50) 1073

שַׁעֲרוּר 14 horrible thing (2 · 2) 1045

85

נָאַף to commit adultery (5 · 17 · 31) 610

מֵרַע evildoer (2 · 18) 949 רעע *Hiph.* 2.

לַעֲנָה 15 wormwood (2 · 8) 542

רֹאשׁ bitter, poisonous herb (3 · 12) 912

חֲנֻפָּה profaneness, pollution (1 · 1) 338

הַהְבִּיל 16 to cause to become vain (1 · 1 · 5)
211

חָזוֹן vision (2 · 35) 302

נָאַץ 17 to contemn, spurn (1 · 15 · 24) 610

שְׁרִירוּת stubbornness (8 · 10) 1057

סוֹד 18 intimate circle, council (4 · 21) 691

הִקְשִׁית to give attention (8 · 45 · 46) 904

סְעָרָה 19 tempest, storm wind (2 · 16) 704

סַעַר tempest (3 · 8) 704

הִתְחוֹלֵל ptc. = whirling (1 · 1 · 9) 296 I. חול

חוּל to whirl (2 · 6 · 9) 296 I.

מְזִמָּה 20 purpose, device (4 · 19) 273

בִּינָה the act of understanding; understanding (1 · 37) 108

סוֹד 22 intimate circle, council (4 · 21) 691

רַע evil, badness (11 · 19) 947

מַעֲלָל practice, deed (17 · 41) 760

מִסְתָּר 24 hiding place, secret place (3 · 10)
712

חָלַם 25 to dream (2 · 27 · 29) 321

מָתַי 26 when? (2 · 42) 607

תַּרְמִית deceitfulness (3 · 5) 941

תֶּבֶן 28 straw (1 · 17) 1061

בַּר grain, corn (1 · 14) 141

פַּטִּישׁ 29 forge hammer (2 · 3) 809

פָּצַץ to shatter (1 · 1 · 3) 823

גָּנַב 30 to steal away [transitive] (1 · 2 · 40)
170

נָאַם 31 utter a prophecy, speak as a
prophet (1 · 1) 610

הִתְעָה 32 to cause to err, mislead (4 · 21 · 50)
1073

פַּחֲזוּת recklessness, extravagance (1 · 1)
808

הוֹעִיל to profit, benefit (7 · 23 · 23) 418

מַשָּׂא 33 utterance, oracle (12 · 45) 672 III.

נָטַשׁ to abandon, forsake (5 · 33 · 40) 643

מַשָּׂא 34 utterance, oracle (12 · 45) 672 III.

מַשָּׂא 36 utterance, oracle (12 · 45) 672 III.

מַשָּׂא 38 utterance, oracle (12 · 45) 672 III.

נשה 39 to forget (4 · 12 · 14[?]) 674 II. נשה

נָטַשׁ to abandon, forsake (5 · 33 · 40) 643

כְּלִמּוּת 40 ignominy (1 · 1) 484

Chapter 24

דּוּד 1 basket, pot, jar (1 · 1) 188

תְּאֵנָה fig, fig tree (12 · 39) 1061

הוּעַד ptc. = set, placed (1 · 2 · 28) 416
יָעַד

חָרָשׁ artificer, graver (4 · 38) 360

מַסְגֵּר [coll.] smiths, locksmiths (2 · 7) 689

דּוּד 2 basket, pot, jar (2 · 7) 188

תְּאֵנָה fig, fig tree (12 · 39) 1061

בְּכוּרָה first ripe fig (1 · 4) 114

רַע badness, bad quality (11 · 19) 947

תְּאֵנָה 3 fig, fig tree (12 · 39) 1061

רַע badness, bad quality (11 · 19) 947

תְּאֵנָה 5 fig, fig tree (12 · 39) 1061

הִכִּיר to regard (1 · 37 · 40) 647

גָּלוּת exile; [coll.] exiles (5 · 15) 163

הָרַס 6 to tear, throw down (5 · 30 · 43) 248

נָתַשׁ to pull up, pluck up (11 · 16 · 21)
684

תְּאֵנָה 8 fig, fig tree (12 · 39) 1061

רַע badness, bad quality (11 · 19) 947

זְוָעָה 9 object of trembling, terror (K 4 · 4)
(Q 4 · 7) 266

מָשָׁל byword, proverb, parable (1 · 39)
605

שְׁנִינָה sharp word, taunt (1 · 4) 1042

קְלָלָה curse (9 · 33) 887

הִדִּיחַ to thrust out, banish (13 · 27 · 43)
623

דֶּבֶר 10 plague, pestilence (17 · 46) 184

Chapter 25

רֵאשֵׁנִי	1	first (1 · 1) 912
רֹעַ	5	evil, badness (11 · 19) 947
מַעֲלָל		practice, deed (17 · 41) 760
לְמִן		from (4 · 14) 577 מִן 9.b.
הֶחֱרִים	9	to destroy, devote to destruction (5 · 46 · 49) 355
שַׁמָּה		horror, an appalling thing (24 · 39) 1031
שְׁרֵקָה		hissing (5 · 7) 1056
חָרְבָּה		waste, ruin (10 · 42) 352
שָׂשׂוֹן	10	joy, exultation (7 · 22) 965
חָתָן		bridegroom (4 · 20) 368
כַּלָּה		bride; daughter-in-law (5 · 34) 483
רֵחַיִם		hand mill (1 · 5) 932
נֵר		lamp (1 · 44) 632
חָרְבָּה	11	waste, ruin (10 · 42) 352
שַׁמָּה		horror, an appalling thing (24 · 39) 1031
פֹּעַל	14	deed, thing done (3 · 37) 821
כּוֹס	15	cup (7 · 31) 468
הִתְגָּעֲשׁ	16	to reel to and fro (2 · 2 · 10) 172
הִתְהֹלֵל		to act like a madman (4 · 6 · 14) 237 II. הלל *Hithpo.*
כּוֹס	17	cup (7 · 31) 468
חָרְבָּה	18	waste, ruin (10 · 42) 352
שַׁמָּה		horror, an appalling thing (24 · 39) 1031
שְׁרֵקָה		hissing (5 · 7) 1056
קְלָלָה		curse (9 · 33) 887
עֶרֶב	20	mixture, mixed company (2 · 5) 786
אִי	22	coast, border, region (4 · 36) 15
קָצַץ	23	to cut off (3 · 4 · 14) 893
עֶרֶב	24	mixture, mixed company (2 · 5) 786
שָׁכַר	27	to be, become drunk (1 · 9 · 20) 1016
קיה		to vomit (1 · 1 · 1) 883
מֵאֵן	28	to refuse (12 · 46) 549
כּוֹס		cup (7 · 31) 468
נָקָה	29	to be free, exempt from punish-

		ment (6 · 24 · 43) 667
שָׁאַג	30	to roar (5 · 20 · 20) 980
מָעוֹן		dwelling, refuge, lair (5 · 18) 732
נָוֶה		habitation (14 · 45[?]) 627
הֵידָד		shout, shouting, cheer (5 · 7) 212
ענה		to sing (2 · 13 · 16) 777
שָׁאוֹן	31	roar, din (4 · 17) 981
סַעַר	32	tempest (3 · 8) 704
יַרְכָּה		remote part, side (4 · 28) 438
נספד	33	to be bewailed (2 · 2 · 30) 704
דֹּמֶן		dung (4 · 6) 199
הֵילִיל	34	to give a howl (8 · 30 · 30) 410
הִתְפַּלֵּשׁ		to roll in (2 · 4 · 4) 814
אַדִּיר		[subst.] majestic one [used of nobles, chieftains, etc.] (5 · 27) 12
טבח		to slaughter, butcher (3 · 11 · 11) 370
תְּפוּצָה		dispersion (1 · 1) 807
חֶמְדָּה		desire (3 · 16) 326
מָנוֹס	35	place of escape, refuge; flight (3 · 8) 631
פְּלֵיטָה		escape, deliverance (2 · 28) 812
אַדִּיר		[subst.] majestic one [used of nobles, chieftains, etc.] (5 · 27) 12
צְעָקָה	36	cry of distress (4 · 21) 858
יְלָלָה		howling (1 · 5) 410
אַדִּיר		[subst.] majestic one [used of nobles, chieftains, etc.] (5 · 27) 12
מַרְעִית		pasturage, pasturing (3 · 10) 945
נדמם	37	to be made silent (4 · 5 · 30) 198
נָוֶה		cstr. נְאוֹת, meadow, pasture (14 · 45[?]) 627 II.
חָרוֹן		[burning of] anger; ח׳ אף = burning anger (9 · 41) 354
כְּפִיר	38	young lion (3 · 31) 498
סֹךְ		lair (1 · 4) 697
שַׁמָּה		horror, an appalling thing (24 · 39) 1031
חָרוֹן		[burning of] anger (9 · 41) 354
ינה		ptc. = oppressor (3 · 4 · 18) 413

Chapter 26

מַמְלָכוּת 1 dominion, kingdom (1 · 9) 575

גָּרַע 2 to diminish (2 · 14 · 22) 175

אוּלַי 3 perhaps (6 · 45) 19

רַע evil, badness (11 · 19) 947

מַעֲלָל practice, deed (17 · 41) 760

קְלָלָה 6 curse (9 · 33) 887

חָרֵב 9 to be waste, desolate (2 · 17 · 37) 351

מֵאֵין without (20 · 48[?]) 34 אַיִן 6.d.

נִקְהַל to assemble (1 · 19 · 39)

מַעֲלָל 13 practice, deed (17 · 41) 760

נָקִי 15 free from guilt, clean, innocent (6 · 43) 667

נֶחֱרַשׁ 18 to be plowed (1 · 2 · 26) 360

עִי ruin, heap of ruins (1 · 5) 730

נְבֵלָה 23 carcass, corpse (8 · 48) 615

Chapter 27

מוֹסֵר 2 band or bond of restraint (4 · 12) 64

מוֹטָה bar of yoke (5 · 11) 557

צַוָּאר neck, back of neck (9 · 41) 848

לַאֲשֶׁר 5 to him who (3 · 38) 81 אֲשֶׁר

יָשַׁר to be pleasing, agreeable, right (2 · 13 · 25) 448

צַוָּאר 8 neck (9 · 41) 848

עֹל yoke (10 · 40) 760

דֶּבֶר plague, pestilence (17 · 46) 184

קֹסֵם 9 false prophet, diviners (2 · 9[?]) 890

עוֹנֵן to practice soothsaying (1 · 10 · 11) 778

כַּשָּׁף sorcerer (1 · 1) 506

הִדִּיחַ 10 to thrust out, banish (13 · 27 · 43) 623

צַוָּאר 11 neck, back of neck (9 · 41) 848

עֹל yoke (10 · 40) 760

צַוָּאר 12 neck, back of neck (9 · 41) 848

עֹל yoke (10 · 40) 760

דֶּבֶר 13 plague, pestilence (17 · 46) 184

הִדִּיחַ 15 to thrust out, banish (13 · 27 · 43) 623

מְהֵרָה 16 hastily, quickly (1 · 20) 555

חָרְבָּה 17 waste, ruin (10 · 42) 352

פָּגַע 18 to entreat (2 · 40 · 46) 803

מְכוֹנָה 19 base, stand (3 · 25) 467

חֹר 20 noble (2 · 13) 359

Chapter 28

עֹל 2 yoke (10 · 40) 760

בְּעוֹד 3 within yet (3 · 20) 728 עוֹד 2.a.

יָמִים time; שְׁנָתַיִם יָמִ׳ = two years' time (>50) 398 יוֹם 6.b.

גָּלוּת 4 exile; [coll.] exiles (5 · 15) 163

עֹל yoke (10 · 40) 760

אָמֵן 6 verily, truly (2 · 30) 53

גּוֹלָה exile; [coll.] exiles (10 · 42) 163

דֶּבֶר 8 plague, pestilence (17 · 46) 184

מוֹטָה 10 bar of yoke (5 · 11) 557

צַוָּאר neck, back of neck (9 · 41) 848

כָּכָה 11 thus (5 · 34) 462

עֹל yoke (10 · 40) 760

בְּעוֹד within yet (3 · 20) 728 עוֹד 2.a.

יָמִים time; שְׁנָתַיִם יָמִ׳ = two years' time (>50) 398 יוֹם 6.b.

צַוָּאר neck, back of neck (9 · 41) 848

מוֹטָה 12 bar of yoke (5 · 11) 557

צַוָּאר neck, back of neck (9 · 41) 848

מוֹטָה 13 bar of yoke (5 · 11) 557

עֹל 14 yoke (10 · 40) 760

צַוָּאר neck, back of neck (9 · 41) 848

סָרָה 16 apostasy (2 · 7) 694

Chapter 29

גּוֹלָה 1 exile; [coll.] exiles (10 · 42) 163

צֵאת 2 *Qal* inf. cstr. of יצא (>50) 422

גְּבִירָה queen mother; queen, lady (2 · 15) 150

סָרִיס		eunuch (7 · 45) 710
חָרָשׁ		artificer, graver (4 · 38) 360
מַסְגֵּר		[coll.] smiths, locksmith; dungeon (2 · 7) 689
גּוֹלָה	4	exile; [coll.] exiles (10 · 42) 163
גַּנָּה	5	garden, orchard (2 · 16) 171
מעט	6	to be, become small, few (2 · 8 · 22) 589
הִשִּׁיא	8	to beguile (5 · 15 · 16) 674
קֹסֵם		false prophet, diviner (2 · 9) 890
החלים		to dream (1 · 2 · 29) 321
תִּקְוָה	11	hope (2 · 32) 876
שְׁבִית	14	captivity (12 · 26) 986
הִדִּיחַ		to thrust out, banish (13 · 27 · 43) 623
גּוֹלָה	16	exile; [coll.] exiles (10 · 42) 163
דֶּבֶר	17	plague, pestilence (17 · 46) 184
תְּאֵנָה		fig, fig tree (12 · 39) 1061
שֹׁעָר		horrid, disgusting (1 · 1) 1045
רֹעַ		badness, bad quality (11 · 19) 947
דֶּבֶר	18	plague, pestilence (17 · 46) 184
זַוְעָה		object of trembling, terror (K. 4 · 4) (Q. 4 · 7) 266
אלה		execration, curse, oath (4 · 36) 46
שַׁמָּה		horror, an appalling thing (24 · 39) 1031
שְׁרֵקָה		hissing (5 · 7) 1056
הִדִּיחַ		to thrust out, banish (13 · 27 · 43) 623
גּוֹלָה	20	exile; [coll.] exiles (10 · 42) 163
קְלָלָה	22	curse (9 · 33) 887
גָּלוּת		exile; [coll.] exiles (5 · 15) 163
קלה		to roast, parch (1 · 3 · 4) 885
נְבָלָה	23	disgraceful folly, senselessness (1 · 13) 615
נאף		to commit adultery (3 · 14 · 31) 610
פָּקִיד	26	commissioner, deputy, overseer (3 · 13) 824
שׁגע		to be maddened (1 · 5 · 7) 993

מַהְפֶּכֶת		stocks [or similar instrument of punishment] (3 · 4) 246
צִינֹק		pillory (1 · 1) 857
גָּעַר	27	to rebuke (1 · 14 · 14) 172
אָרֹךְ	28	long (1 · 3) 74
גַּנָּה		garden, orchard (2 · 16) 170
גּוֹלָה	31	exile; [coll.] exiles (10 · 42) 163
סָרָה	32	apostasy (2 · 7) 694

Chapter 30

שְׁבוּת	3	captivity (12 · 26) 986
חֲרָדָה	5	trembling, fear (1 · 9) 353
פַּחַד		dread (4 · 49) 808
חָלָץ	6	[dual only] loins (1 · 10) 323
יֵרָקוֹן		paleness, mildew, lividness (1 · 6) 439
עֹל	8	yoke (10 · 40) 760
צַוָּאר		neck, back of neck (9 · 41) 848
מוֹסֵר		band or bond of restraint (4 · 12) 64
נתק		to tear apart, snap (3 · 11 · 27) 683
שְׁבִי	10	captivity (8 · 46) 985
שָׁקַט		to be undisturbed, quiet (5 · 31 · 41) 1052
שַׁאֲנַן		to be at ease, secure (3 · 5 · 5) 983
הֶחֱרִיד		to terrify, drive in terror (3 · 16 · 39) 353
כָּלָה	11	complete destruction, annihilation (7 · 27) 478
יִסַּר		to chasten, chastise (5 · 27 · 38) 415
נקה		to leave unpunished (4 · 18 · 43) 667
אָנוּשׁ	12	incurable, sick (5 · 8) 60 I. אנשׁ
שֶׁבֶר		breaking (15 · 45) 991
נַחְלָה		serious, sore, diseased (3 · 5[?]) 317 חלה Niph.
מַכָּה		wound, blow (10 · 48) 646
דָּן	13	to plead the cause, minister judgment, judge (4 · 23 · 24) 192 דין
דִּין		plea, cause; judgment (4 · 19) 192
מָזוֹר		wound (1 · 3) 267
רְפָאָה		remedy, medicine (2 · 3) 951

תְּעָלָה	healing (2 · 2) 752
מְאַהֵב	14 lover, friend (3 · 16) 12 אהב
מַכָּה	wound, blow (10 · 48) 646
מוּסָר	chastisement, discipline, correction (8 · 50) 416
אַכְזָרִי	cruel (3 · 8) 470
עצם	to be numerous (4 · 16 · 18) 782
שֶׁבֶר	15 breaking (15 · 45) 991
אָנוּשׁ	incurable, sick (5 · 8) 60
מַכְאוֹב	pain (3 · 16) 456
עֶצֶם	to be numerous (4 · 16 · 18) 782
שְׁבִי	16 captivity (8 · 46) 985
שֹׁאסַיִךְ	ptc. = those who plunder you (2 · 7[?]) 1042 שסס
מְשִׁסָּה	plunder, spoil, prey (1 · 6) 1042
בָּזַז	to spoil, plunder (2 · 37 · 41) 102
בַּז	spoil, booty, plunder (5 · 27) 103
אֲרוּכָה	17 healing, restoration (3 · 6) 74
מַכָּה	wound, blow (10 · 48) 646
נדח	to be banished, thrust out; here ptc. = outcast (4 · 13 · 43) 623
רָחַם	18 to have compassion (9 · 41 · 46) 933
תֵּל	mound (2 · 5) 1068
אַרְמוֹן	citadel, palace (5 · 33) 74
תּוֹדָה	19 thanksgiving, praise (3 · 32) 392
שׂחק	to play (17 · 36) 965
מעט	to be, become small, few (2 · 8 · 22) 589
צער	to be or grow insignificant (1 · 3 · 3) 858
לֹחֵץ	20 oppressing, oppressor (1 · 4) 537 לחץ
אַדִּיר	21 [subst.] majestic one [used of nobles, chieftains, etc.] (5 · 27) 12
מֹשֵׁל	ruling, ruler (4 · 24) 605 III. מָשַׁל
עָרַב	to give in pledge (1 · 15 · 17) 786
סְעָרָה	23 tempest, storm wind (2 · 16) 704
סַעַר	tempest (3 · 8) 704
הִתְגּוֹרֵר	sweeping, roaring (1 · 1 · 5) 176 גרר
חול	to whirl, whirl about (2 · 6 · 9) 297

חָרוֹן	24 [burning of] anger; ח׳ אף = burning anger (9 · 41) 354
מְזִמָּה	purpose, devise (4 · 19) 273

Chapter 31

שָׂרִיד	2 survivor (4 · 28) 975
הִרְגִּיעַ	to give rest (4 · 8 · 13[?]) 921 II.
מָשַׁךְ	3 to draw out, prolong; draw (2 · 30 · 36) 604
בְּתוּלָה	4 virgin (8 · 50) 143
עָדָה	to deck oneself, ornament (2 · 8 · 8) 725
תֹּף	timbrel, tambourine (1 · 17) 1074
מָחוֹל	dance (2 · 6) 298
שׂחק	to play (3 · 17 · 36) 965
חלל	5 i.e., to begin to use the fruit (>50) 320 Piel 4.
צהל	7 to cry shrilly (3 · 7 · 8) 843
יַרְכָה	8 remote part, side (4 · 28) 438
עִוֵּר	blind (1 · 25) 734
פִּסֵּחַ	lame (1 · 14) 820
הָרָה	pregnant, woman with child (2 · 15) 248 II.
הֵנָּה	hither (4 · 49) 244
בְּכִי	weeping (8 · 30) 113
תַּחֲנוּן	supplication (2 · 18) 337
הוֹבִיל	to lead, conduct; bear along (1 · 7 · 18) 384
אִי	10 coast, border, region, island (4 · 36)
מֶרְחָק	distance, distant place (5 · 18) 935
זרה	to scatter, disperse (4 · 25 · 38) 279
עֵדֶר	flock (6 · 39) 727
נהר	12 to flow, stream (1 · 3 · 3[?]) 625
טוֹב	good things (3 · 32) 375
דָּגָן	corn, grain (1 · 40) 186
תִּירוֹשׁ	fresh or new wine (1 · 38) 440
יִצְהָר	fresh oil (1 · 23) 844
גַּן	garden (3 · 42) 171
רָוֶה	watered (1 · 3) 924

דאב	to become faint, languish (2 · 3 · 3) 178			ternal organs (3 · 32) 589

דאב — to become faint, languish (2 · 3 · 3) 178

בְּתוּלָה — 13 virgin (8 · 50) 143

מָחוֹל — dance (2 · 6) 298

בָּחוּר — young man (11 · 45) 104

אֵבֶל — mourning (3 · 24) 5

שָׂשׂוֹן — joy, exultation (7 · 22) 965

יָגוֹן — grief, sorrow (4 · 14) 387

רוה — 14 to water abundantly, drench (1 · 6 · 14) 924

דֶּשֶׁן — fatness, abundance; ashes mixed w fat (2 · 15) 206

טוּב — good things (3 · 32) 375

נְהִי — 15 lamentation, wailing (5 · 8) 624

בְּכִי — weeping (8 · 30) 113

תַּמְרוּרִים — bitterness (2 · 3) 601

מֵאֵן — to refuse (12 · 46) 549

מָנַע — 16 to withhold, hold back (5 · 25 · 29) 586

בְּכִי — weeping (8 · 30) 113

דִּמְעָה — tears (5 · 23) 199

שָׂכָר — hire, wages (1 · 29) 969

פְּעֻלָּה — work (1 · 14) 821

תִּקְוָה — 17 hope (2 · 32) 876

הִתְנוֹדֵד — 18 to bemoan oneself (2 · 4 · 26) 626

יִסַּר — to chasten, chastise (5 · 27 · 38) 415

נוסר — to let oneself be chastened, admonished (2 · 5 · 38) 415

עֵגֶל — calf (4 · 35) 722

סָפַק — 19 to slap (1 · 6 · 6) 706

יָרֵךְ — thigh, loin, side (1 · 34) 437

נכלם — to be put to shame, dishonored, humiliated (4 · 26 · 38) 483

נְעוּרִים — youth (7 · 46) 655

יַקִּיר — 20 very precious, dear (1 · 1) 430

שַׁעֲשׁוּעַ — delight (1 · 9) 1044

מִדֵּי — as often as (3 · 15) 191   דֵּי 2.c.

המה — to murmur, growl, roar (9 · 33 · 33) 242

מעה — inward parts; i.e., compassion; in-

רחם — to have compassion (9 · 41 · 46) 933

צִיּוּן — 21 signpost, monument (1 · 3) 846

תַּמְרוּרִים — signposts (1 · 1) 1071

מְסִלָּה — highway (1 · 27) 700

בְּתוּלָה — virgin (8 · 50) 143

מָתַי — 22 when? (7 · 42) 607

התחמק — to turn here and there (1 · 1 · 2) 330

שׁוֹבֵב — backturning, apostate (2 · 3) 1000

בָּרָא — to shape, fashion, create (1 · 38 · 48) 135

נְקֵבָה — woman (1 · 22) 666

שְׁבוּה — 23 captivity (12 · 26) 986

נָוֶה — habitation (14 · 45[?]) 627

אִכָּר — 24 plowman, husbandman (3 · 7) 38

עֵדֶר — flock (6 · 39) 727

הִרְוָה — 25 to cause to drink (1 · 5 · 14) 924

עָיֵף — weary, faint (1 · 17) 746

דאב — to become faint, languish (2 · 3 · 3) 178

הֵקִיץ — 26 to awake (3 · 22 · 23) 884

שֵׁנָה — sleep (3 · 23) 446

ערב — to be pleasing, sweet (2 · 8 · 8) 787

שָׁקַד — 28 to keep watch, to be wakeful (5 · 11 · 17) 1052

נָתַשׁ — to pull up, pluck up (11 · 16 · 21) 684

נָתַץ — to pull down, break down (6 · 31 · 42) 683

חָרַס — to tear down, throw down (5 · 30 · 43) 248

בֹּסֶר — 29 unripe or sour grapes (2 · 5) 126

קהה — to be blunt, dull (2 · 3 · 4) 874

בֹּסֶר — 30 unripe or sour grapes (2 · 5) 126

קהה — to be blunt, dull (2 · 3 · 4) 874

הֵפֵר — 32 to break, frustrate (4 · 41 · 44[?]) bd 830

בָּעַל — to be lord [over], husband [of] (2 · 10 · 12) 127

קָטָן — 34 insignificant (3 · 47) 881

סלח to forgive, pardon (6 · 33 · 46) 699

יָרֵחַ 35 moon (2 · 27) 437

כּוֹכָב star (1 · 37) 456

רָגַע to disturb (1 · 4 · 13[?]) 920

המה to roar, murmur, growl (9 · 33 · 33) 242

גַּל wave [of water], billow; heap (4 · 16) 164

מוש 36 to depart, be removed (2 · 20 · 20) 559

מִלְמַעְלָה 37 above (1 · 24) 751 מַעַל 2.d.

נֶחְקַר to be searched out, found (2 · 4 · 27) 350

מוֹסָד foundation (2 · 13) 414

לְמַטָּה downward (1 · 10) 641 מַטֶּה 2.

מִגְדָּל 38 tower (1 · 49) 153

פִּנָּה corner (3 · 30) 819

קָוֶה 39 line (1 · 17) 876 קַו

פֶּגֶר 40 corpse, carcass (3 · 22) 803

דֶּשֶׁן ashes mixed with fat; fatness, abundance (2 · 15) 206

שְׁרֵמָה field (1 · 6) 995 שְׁדֵמָה

פִּנָּה corner (3 · 30) 819

נתש to be rooted up (2 · 4 · 21) 684

נהרס to be thrown or torn down (2 · 10 · 43) 248

Chapter 32

צור 2 to shut in, besiege (5 · 31 · 31) 848

כלא to shut up, restrain (2 · 14 · 17) 476

מַטָּרָה guard, ward, prison (11 · 16) 643

כלא 3 to shut up, restrain (2 · 14 · 17) 476

גְּאֻלָּה 7 right of redemption, redemption (2 · 14) 145

מַטָּרָה 8 guard, ward, prison (11 · 16) 643

יְרֻשָּׁה possession, inheritance (1 · 14) 440

גְּאֻלָּה right of redemption, redemption (2 · 14) 145

שָׁקַל 9 to weigh out (2 · 19 · 22) 1053

חתם 10 to seal up, fasten up by sealing (4 · 23 · 27) 367

הֵעִיד to cause to testify (8 · 39 · 44) 729

שָׁקַל to weigh out (2 · 19 · 22) 1053

מֹאזְנַיִם balances, scales (1 · 15) 24

מִקְנָה 11 purchase; w. ספר = document of purchase (5 · 15) 889

חתם to seal up, fasten up by sealing (4 · 23 · 27) 367

מִקְנָה 12 purchase; cf. vs. 11 (5 · 15) 889

מַטָּרָה guard, ward, prison (11 · 16) 643

מִקְנָה 14 purchase; cf. vs. 11 (5 · 15) 889

חתם to seal up, fasten up by sealing (4 · 23 · 27) 367

חֶרֶשׂ earthenware, earthen vessel (2 · 17) 360

מִקְנָה 16 purchase; cf. vs. 11 (5 · 15) 889

אֲהָהּ 17 Alas! (4 · 15) 13

נפלא to be too difficult for (2 · 13 · 24) 810

חֵיק 18 bosom, fold of garment at breast (1 · 38) 300

עֲלִילִיָּה 19 deed (1 · 1) 760

פָּקַח to open (1 · 17 · 20) 824

מַעֲלָל practice, deed (17 · 41) 760

מוֹפֵת 20 wonder, sign, token (2 · 36) 68

מוֹפֵת 21 wonder, sign, token (2 · 36) 68

אֶזְרוֹעַ arm (1 · 2) 284

מוֹרָא awe-inspiring spectacle or deed (1 · 12) 432

זוב 22 to flow (3 · 29 · 29) 264

חלב milk (2 · 44) 316

סֹלְלָה 24 mound (3 · 11) 700

דֶּבֶר plague, pestilence (17 · 46) 184

הֵעִיר 25 to cause to testify (8 · 39 · 44) 729

נפלא 27 to be too difficult for (2 · 13 · 24) 810

הִצִּית 29 to kindle, set on fire (8 · 17 · 27) 428

גָּג roof, top (3 · 29) 150

הִסִּיךְ to pour out libations (8 · 14 · 25) 650 נסך

נְעוּרִים 30 youth (8 · 46) 655

לְמִן 31 from (4 · 14) 577 מִן 9.b.

עֹרֶף 33 neck (7 · 33) 791

מוּסָר discipline, correction, chastisement (8 · 50) 416

שִׁקּוּץ 34 detested thing (5 · 28) 1055

דֶּבֶר 36 plague, pestilence (17 · 46) 184

הִדִּיחַ 37 to thrust out, banish (13 · 27 · 43) 623

קֶצֶף wrath (4 · 29) 893

בֶּטַח security, as adv. = securely (5 · 43) 105

יִרְאָה 40 reverence, fear (1 · 45) 432

שׂוֹשׂ 41 to exult, rejoice (1 · 26 · 26) 965

מֵאֵין 43 without (20 · 48[?]) 34 אֵין 6.d.

חתם 44 to seal up, fasten up by sealing (4 · 23 · 27) 367

הֵעִיד to cause to testify (8 · 39 · 44) 729

שְׁפֵלָה lowland (3 · 20) 1050

שְׁבוּת captivity (12 · 26) 986

Chapter 33

עָצַר 1 to shut up (4 · 36 · 46) 783

מַטָּרָה guard, prison, ward (11 · 16) 643

יָצַר 2 to devise, plan; to form (4 · 41 · 44) 427

בָּצוּר 3 secret things; elsewhere = cut off, made inaccessible (2 · 25) 130 בצר

נתץ 4 to pull down, break down (6 · 31 · 42) 683

סֹלְלָה mound (3 · 11) 700

פֶּגֶר 5 corpse, carcass (3 · 22) 803

מַרְפֵּא 6 healing, cure (4 · 13) 951

אֲרוּכָה healing, restoration (3 · 6) 74

עֲתֶרֶת abundance (1 · 1) 801

שְׁבוּת 7 captivity (12 · 26) 986

סלח 8 to forgive, pardon (6 · 33 · 46) 699

פָּשַׁע to transgress (4 · 40 · 41) 833

שָׂשׂוֹן 9 joy, exultation (7 · 22) 965

פָּחַד to be in dread (3 · 23 · 26) 808

רגז to quake (1 · 30 · 41) 919

חָרֵב 10 waste, desolate (2 · 10) 351

מֵאֵין without (20 · 48[?]) 34 אֵין 6.d.

שָׂשׂוֹן 11 joy, exultation (7 · 22) 965

חָתָן bridegroom (4 · 20) 368

כַּלָּה bride; daughter-in-law (5 · 34) 483

תּוֹדָה sacrifice of thanksgiving (3 · 32) 392

שְׁבוּת captivity (12 · 26) 986

חָרֵב 12 waste, desolate (2 · 10) 351

מֵאֵין without (20 · 48[?]) 34 אֵין 6.d.

נָוֶה abode of shepherds (14 · 45[?]) 627

הרביץ to cause to lie down (1 · 6 · 30) 918

שְׁפֵלָה 13 lowland (3 · 20) 1050

מָנָה to count, number (1 · 12 · 28) 584

הַצְמִיחַ 15 to cause to grow (1 · 14 · 33) 855

צמח growth, sprout (2 · 12) 855

בֶּטַח 16 security; as adv. = securely (5 · 43) 105

הֵפֵר 20 to break, frustrate (4 · 41 · 44[?]) 830

הפר 21 to be broken (1 · 3 · 44[?]) 830

מְשָׁרֵת minister, ministering (1 · 20) 1058 שרת

חוֹל 22 sand (3 · 22) 297

נאץ 24 to contemn, spurn (2 · 8 · 24) 610

מֹשֵׁל 26 ruling, ruler (4 · 24) 605 III. מָשַׁל

שְׁבוּת captivity (12 · 26) 986

רחם to have compassion (9 · 41 · 46) 933

Chapter 34

מֶמְשָׁלָה 1 dominion, rule (2 · 17) 606

מַשְׂרֵפָה 5 burning (1 · 2) 977

ספד to wail, lament (7 · 28 · 30) 704

מבצר 7 fortification (7 · 37) 131

דְּרוֹר 8 liberty; w. קרא, to proclaim liberty (4 · 7) 204

חָפְשִׁי 9 free [from slavery] (5 · 17) 344

חָפְשִׁי 10 free [from slavery] (5 · 17) 344

חָפְשִׁי 11 free [from slavery] (5 · 17) 344

כבש to bring into bondage (2 · 8 · 14) 461

חָפְשִׁי 14 free [from slavery] (5 · 17) 344

דְּרוֹר 15 liberty; w. קרא, to proclaim liberty (4 · 7) 204

חָפְשִׁי 16 free [from slavery] (5 · 17) 344

כבש to bring into bondage (2 · 8 · 14) 461

דְּרוֹר 17 liberty; w. קְ, = to proclaim liberty (4 · 7) 204

דֶּבֶר plague, pestilence (17 · 46) 184

זְוָעָה object of trembling, terror (K 4 · 4) (Q 4 · 7) 266

עֵגֶל 18 calf (4 · 35) 722

בֶּתֶר part, piece (2 · 3) 144

סָרִיס 19 eunuch (7 · 45) 710

בֶּתֶר part, piece (2 · 3) 144

עֵגֶל calf (4 · 35) 722

נְבֵלָה 20 carcass, corpse (8 · 48) 615

מַאֲכָל food (4 · 30) 38

מֵאֵין 22 without (20 · 48[?]) 34 אֵין 6.d.

Chapter 35

לִשְׁכָה 2 chamber, room (8 · 47) 545

לִשְׁכָה 4 chamber, room (8 · 47) 545

מִמַּעַל above, on the top of (4 · 29) 751 II. מַעַל

סַף threshold; שֹׁמֵר הַסַּף = doorkeeper (2 · 25) 706 II.

גָּבִיעַ 5 bowl, cup (1 · 14) 149

כּוֹס cup (7 · 31) 468

מוּסָר 13 discipline, correction, chastisement (8 · 50) 416

מַעֲלָל 15 practice, deed (17 · 41) 760

Chapter 36

מְגִלָּה 2 roll (14 · 21) 166

אוּלַי 3 perhaps (6 · 45) 19

סלח to forgive, pardon (6 · 33 · 46) 699

מְגִלָּה 4 roll (14 · 21) 166

עָצַר 5 to shut up (4 · 36 · 46) 783

מְגִלָּה 6 roll (14 · 21) 166

צוֹם fast, fasting (2 · 25) 847

אוּלַי 7 perhaps (6 · 45) 19

תְּחִנָּה supplication for favor (5 · 25) 337

צוֹם 9 fast, fasting (2 · 25) 847

לִשְׁכָה 10 chamber, room (8 · 47) 545

לִשְׁכָה 12 chamber, room (8 · 47) 545

מְגִלָּה 14 roll (14 · 21) 166

פָּחַד 16 to be in dread (3 · 23 · 26) 808

דְּיוֹ 18 ink (1 · 1) 188

אֵיפֹה 19 where? (2 · 10) 33

מְגִלָּה 20 roll (14 · 21) 166

לִשְׁכָה chamber, room (8 · 47) 545

מְגִלָּה 21 roll (14 · 21) 166

לִשְׁכָה chamber, room (8 · 47) 545

חֹרֶף 22 autumn; w. בֵית = autumn house, palace (1 · 7) 358

אָח brazier, firepot (3 · 3) 28

דֶּלֶת fig. for column of MS (>50) 195 4.

תַּעַר 23 razor (2 · 13) 789

אָח brazier, firepot (3 · 3) 28

מְגִלָּה roll (14 · 21) 166

פָּחַד 24 to be in dread; w. אֶל = to turn in dread (3 · 23 · 26) 808

הִפְגִּיעַ 25 to make entreaty (2 · 6 · 46)

מְגִלָּה roll (14 · 21) 166

מְגִלָּה 27 roll (14 · 21) 166

מְגִלָּה 28 roll (14 · 21) 166

מְגִלָּה 29 roll (14 · 21) 166

נְבֵלָה 30 carcass, corpse (8 · 48) 615

חֹרֶב parching heat (3 · 16) 351

קֶרַח frost (1 · 7) 901

מְגִלָּה 32 roll (14 · 21) 166

Chapter 37

כְּלִיא 4 confinement, imprisonment (2 · 2) 476 כלוא

צוּר 5 to shut in, besiege (5 · 31 · 31) 848

שֵׁמַע report, hearing (2 · 17) 1034

עֶזְרָה 7 help (1 · 26) 740

הִשִּׁיא 9 to beguile (5 · 15 · 16) 674

דקר 10 ptc. = pierced, riddled (2 · 3 · 11) 201

עַם 12 kinsman (1 · 34) 769

פְּקִדֻת 13 sentinel, oversight (1 · 1) 824

קָצַף 15 to be wroth (1 · 28 · 34) 893

אָסוּר band, bond; w. בֵּית = prison (1 · 3) 64

כֶּלֶא confinement, restraint, imprisonment (3 · 10) 476

חָנוּת 16 cell (1 · 1) 333

סֵתֶר 17 secretly; בַּסּ׳ = in secrecy (3 · 35) 712

כֶּלֶא 18 confinement, restraint, imprisonment (3 · 10) 476

אַיֵּו 19 where? (6 · 44) 32 אַיֵּה

תְּחִנָּה 20 supplication for favor (5 · 23) 337

מַטָּרָה 21 guard, ward, prison (11 · 16) 643

אֹפֶה baker (1 · 12) 66 אָפָה

Chapter 38

דֶּבֶר 2 plague, pestilence (17 · 46) 184

רִפָּה 4 to enfeeble, dishearten (1 · 5 · 45) 951

מַטָּרָה 6 guard, ward, prison (11 · 16) 643

חֶבֶל cord, rope (4 · 49) 286

טִיט mud, mire (2 · 13) 376

טָבַע to sink down (1 · 6 · 10) 371

סָרִיס 7 eunuch (7 · 45) 710

בְּטֶרֶם 10 before (6 · 39) 382 טֶרֶם

בְּלוֹא 11 worn out thing, rag; pl. cs. בְּלוֹיֵ (3 · 3) 115

סְחָבָה rag, clout (2 · 2) 695

מֶלַח rag (2 · 2) 571

חֶבֶל cord, rope (4 · 49) 286

בְּלוֹא 12 worn out thing, rag (3 · 3) 115

סְחָבָה rag, clout (2 · 2) 695

מֶלַח rag (2 · 2) 571

אַצִּיל joint, joining (1 · 3) 69

חֶבֶל cord, rope (4 · 49) 286

מָשַׁךְ 13 to draw, drag (2 · 30 · 36) 604

חֶבֶל cord, rope (4 · 49) 286

מַטָּרָה guard, ward, prison (11 · 16) 643

מָבוֹא 14 entrance, a coming in (1 · 23) 99

כָּחַד to hide, conceal (3 · 15 · 32) 470

סֵתֶר 16 secretly; בַּסּ׳ = in secrecy (3 · 35) 712

דָּאַג 19 to fear, dread, be anxious (3 · 7 · 7) 178

הִתְעַלֵּל to deal wantonly, ruthlessly (1 · 7 · 17) 759

לַאֲשֶׁר 20 in what (3 · 38) 81 אֲשֶׁר

מֵאֵן 21 to refuse (12 · 46) 549

הִסִּית 22 to instigate, incite, allure (2 · 18 · 18) 694 סות

הָטְבַּע to be sunk (1 · 3 · 10) 371

בֹּץ mire (1 · 1) 130

נָסוֹג to turn oneself away, turn back; fig. = prove faithless (2 · 14 · 25) 690

אָחוֹר backwards (4 · 41) 30

כָּחַד 25 to hide, conceal (3 · 15 · 32) 470

תְּחִנָּה 26 supplication for favor (5 · 25) 337

הֶחֱרִישׁ 27 to cease to speak (2 · 38 · 46) 361

מַטָּרָה 28 guard, ward, prison (11 · 16) 643

Chapter 39

צוּר 1 to shut in, besiege (5 · 31 · 31) 848

סָרִיס 3 eunuch (7 · 45) 710

רַב־מָג chief soothsayer (2 · 2) 913 II. רַב

גַּן 4 garden (3 · 42) 171

95

הִשִּׂיג 5 to overtake (3 · 49 · 49) 673

חֹר 6 noble (2 · 13) 359

עִוֵּר 7 to blind (2 · 5 · 5) 734

נָתַץ 8 to pull down, break down (6 · 31 · 42) 683

טַבָּח 9 bodyguard (17 · 32) 371

דַּל 10 reduced, poor, low (2 · 48) 195

מְאוּמָה anything (2 · 32) 548

טַבָּח bodyguard (17 · 32) 371

יָגֵב field (1 · 1) 387

טַבָּח 11 bodyguard (10 · 32) 371

מְאוּמָה 12 anything (2 · 32) 548

טַבָּח 13 bodyguard (17 · 32) 371

סָרִיס eunuch (7 · 45) 710

רַב־מָג chief soothsayer (2 · 2) 913 II. רב

מַטָּרָה 14 guard, ward, prison (11 · 16) 643

עָצַר 15 to shut up (4 · 36 · 46) 783

מַטָּרָה guard, ward, prison (11 · 16) 643

מֵבִי 16 K. for מֵבִיא 97 בוא Hiph.

יָגוֹר 17 fearing (2 · 2) 388

Chapter 40

טַבָּח 1 bodyguard (17 · 32) 371

אֵזֵק manacle [fetter] (2 · 2) 279

גָּלוּת exile; [coll.] exiles (5 · 15) 163

טַבָּח 2 bodyguard (17 · 32) 371

אֵזֵק 4 manacle [fetter] (2 · 2) 279

טַבָּח 5 bodyguard (17 · 32) 371

אֲרֻחָה meal, allowance [of food] (3 · 7) 73

מַשְׂאֵת present, portion, uplifting (2 · 16) 673

טַף 7 children, little ones (3 · 42) 381

דַּלָּה the poor (3 · 5) 195

מֵאֲשֶׁר who (1 · 17) 84

קַיִץ 10 summer fruit (4 · 20) 884

נדח 12 to be thrust out, banished (4 · 13 · 43) 623

קַיִץ summer fruit (4 · 20) 884

סֵתֶר 15 secretly; בַּסֵּ׳ = in secrecy (3 · 35) 712

Chapter 41

מְלוּכָה 1 kingship, royalty (1 · 24) 574

גָּלַח 5 to be shaven (1 · 3 · 23) 164

זָקָן beard (2 · 19) 278

התגדד to cut oneself [in relig. practice]; to gather in troops or bands (4 · 7 · 8) 151

לְבוֹנָה frankincense (3 · 21) 526

פגש 6 to meet, encounter (1 · 10 · 14) 803

מַטְמוֹן 8 hidden treasure, treasure (1 · 5) 380

חִטָּה wheat (2 · 30) 334

שְׂעֹרָה barley (1 · 34) 972

פֶּגֶר 9 corpse, carcass (3 · 22) 803

שָׁבָה 10 to take captive (4 · 29 · 37) 985

טַבָּח bodyguard (17 · 32) 371

שָׁבָה to take captive (4 · 29 · 37) 985

שָׁבָה 14 to take captive (4 · 29 · 37) 985

טַף 16 children, little ones (3 · 42) 381

סָרִיס eunuch (7 · 45) 710

גֵּרוּת 17 lodging place, inn (1 · 1) 158

Chapter 42

תְּחִנָּה 2 supplication for favor (5 · 25) 337

מָנַע 4 to withhold, hold back (5 · 25 · 29) 586

תְּחִנָּה 9 supplication for favor (5 · 25) 337

הָרַס 10 to tear, throw down (5 · 30 · 43) 248

נָתַשׁ to pull up, pluck up (11 · 16 · 21) 684

רַחֲמִים 12 compassion (2 · 38) 933

רִחַם to have compassion (9 · 41 · 46) 933

רָעֵב 14 to be hungry (1 · 12 · 14) 944

הִשִּׂיג 16 to overtake (3 · 49 · 49) 673

דאג to be anxious, concerned (3 · 7 · 7) 178

דֶּבֶר 17 plague, pestilence (17 · 46) 184

שָׂרִיד		survivor (4 · 28) 975
פָּלִיט		fugitive (3 · 19) 812
נִתַּךְ	18	to be poured out (2 · 8 · 21) 677
נתך		to pour forth (2 · 7 · 21) 677
אָלָה		execration, curse, oath (4 · 36) 46
שַׁמָּה		horror, an appalling thing (24 · 39) 1031
קְלָלָה		curse (9 · 33) 887
הֵעִיד	19	to protest, warn (8 · 39 · 44) 729 עוד
הִתְעָה	20	w. בּ = to err at cost of (4 · 21 · 50) 1073
דֶּבֶר	22	plague, pestilence (17 · 46) 184

Chapter 43

זֵד	2	insolent, presumptuous (1 · 13) 267
הֵסִית	3	to instigate (2 · 18 · 18) 694
נדח	5	to be thrust out, banished (4 · 13 · 43) 623
טַף	6	children, little ones (3 · 42) 381
טַבָּח		bodyguard (17 · 32) 371
טָמַן	9	to hide, conceal (7 · 28 · 31) 380
מֶלֶט		mortar, cement (1 · 1) 572
מַלְבֵּן		quadrangle; brick mold (1 · 3) 527
מִמַּעַל	10	above, on the top of (4 · 29) 751 II. מַעַל
טָמַן		to hide, conceal (7 · 28 · 31) 380
שַׁפְרִיר		[dub.] carpet, splendor; pavilion, canopy (1 · 1) 1051
שְׁבִי	11	captivity (8 · 46) 985
הִצִּית	12	to kindle, set on fire (8 · 17 · 27) 428
שָׁבָה		to take captive (4 · 29 · 37) 985
עטה		to grasp (2 · 44) 742
מַצֵּבָה	13	pillar, sacred pillar, stump (1 · 36) 663

Chapter 44

חָרְבָּה	2	waste, ruin (10 · 42) 352
נתך	6	to pour forth (2 · 7 · 21) 677

חָרְבָּה		waste, ruin (10 · 42) 352
עוֹלֵל	7	child (1 · 11) 760
יוֹנֵק		suckling, babe (1 · 11) 413 ינק
קְלָלָה	8	curse (9 · 33) 887
דכא	10	to be crushed; to be made humble, contrite (1 · 4 · 18) 193
אָלָה	12	execration, curse, oath (4 · 36) 46
שַׁמָּה		horror, an appalling thing (24 · 39) 1031
קְלָלָה		curse (9 · 33) 887
דֶּבֶר	13	plague, pestilence (17 · 46) 184
פָּלִיט	14	fugitive (3 · 19) 812
שָׂרִיד		survivor (4 · 28) 975
פָּלִיט		escaped one, fugitive (3 · 5) 812
מְלֶכֶת	17	queen (5 · 5) 573
הִסִּיךְ		to pour out (8 · 14 · 25) 650 I. נסך
מְלֶכֶת	18	queen (5 · 5) 573
הִסִּיךְ		to pour out (8 · 14 · 25) 650 I. נסך
חָסֵר		to lack, need (1 · 19 · 23) 341
מְלֶכֶת	19	queen (5 · 5) 573
הִסִּיךְ		to pour out (8 · 14 · 25) 650 I. נסך
מִבַּלְעֲדֵי		without, apart from (1 · 12) 116 בִּלְעֲדֵי
כַּוָּן		cake, sacrificial cake (2 · 2) 467
הֶעֱצִיב		to shape, fashion (1 · 1 · 2) 781
קִטֵּר	21	incense (1 · 1) 883
רֹעַ	22	evil, badness (11 · 19) 947
מַעֲלָל		practice, deed (17 · 41) 760
חָרְבָּה		waste, desolation (10 · 42) 352
שַׁמָּה		appalling waste (24 · 39) 1031
קְלָלָה		curse (9 · 33) 887
מֵאֵין		without (20 · 48[?]) 34 אֵין 6.d.
נָדַר	25	to vow (1 · 30) 623
מְלֶכֶת		queen (5 · 5) 573
הִסִּיךְ		to pour out (8 · 14 · 25) 650 I. נסך
שָׁקַד	27	to keep watch, be wakeful (5 · 11 · 16) 1052
פָּלִיט	28	fugitive (3 · 19) 812
מַת		male, man (1 · 22) 607

Chapter 45

אוֹי	3	Woe! Alas! (8 · 25) 17
יָגוֹן		grief, sorrow (4 · 14) 387
מַכְאוֹב		pain (3 · 16) 456
יגע		to grow or be weary (2 · 20 · 26) 388
אנחה		sighing, groaning (1 · 11) 58
מְנוּחָה		rest, resting-place (2 · 21) 629
הָרַס	4	to tear down, throw down (5 · 30 · 43) 248
נָתַשׁ		to pull up, pluck up (11 · 16 · 21) 684

Chapter 46

צִנָּה	3	large shield (1 · 20) 857
התיצב	4	to station oneself, take one's stand (2 · 48 · 48) 426
כּוֹבַע		helmet (1 · 6) 464
מרק		to polish, scour (1 · 2 · 4) 599
רֹמַח		spear, lance (1 · 15) 942
סִרְיֹן		armor (2 · 2) 710
חַת	5	dismayed (1 · 4) 369
נָסוֹג		to be turned or driven back, be repulsed (2 · 14 · 25) 690
אָחוֹר		backwards (4 · 41) 30
הכתת		*Hoph.* to be crushed (1 · 4 · 17) 510
מָנוֹס		flight; refuge, place of escape (3 · 8) 631
מָגוֹר		fear, terror (6 · 8) 159
קַל	6	swift, fleet (2 · 13) 886
התגעש	7	to shake back and forth, toss or reel to and fro (2 · 5 · 10) 172
התגעש	8	to shake back and forth, toss or reel to and fro (2 · 2 · 10) 172
התהלל	9	to act like a madman (4 · 6 · 14) 237 II.
נְקָמָה	10	vengeance (11 · 27) 668
נקם		to avenge oneself (3 · 12 · 35) 667

רוה		to be saturated, take one's fill (1 · 3 · 14) 924
צֳרִי	11	a kind of balsam [used as medicine] (3 · 6) 863
בְּתוּלָה		virgin (8 · 50) 143
רְפֻאָה		remedy, medicine (2 · 3) 951
תְּעָלָה		healing (2 · 2) 752
קָלוֹן	12	ignominy, dishonor (2 · 17) 885
צְוָחָה		outcry (2 · 4) 846
התיצב	14	to station oneself, take one's stand (2 · 48 · 48) 426
נסחף	15	to be prostrate, (1 · 1 · 2) 695
אַבִּיר		mighty, valiant (4 · 17) 7
הדף		to thrust out, drive out, push (1 · 11 · 11) 213
מוֹלֶדֶת	16	kindred, birth, offspring (2 · 22) 409
ינה		ptc. = oppressor (3 · 4 · 18) 413
שָׁאוֹן	17	roar, din (4 · 17) 981
גּוֹלָה	19	exile; [coll.] exiles (10 · 42) 163
שַׁמָּה		waste (24 · 39) 1031
נצת		to be desolated, burned (2 · 4 · 5[?]) 428 יצת *Niph.*
מֵאֵין		without (20 · 48[?]) 34 אֵין 6.d.
עֶגְלָה	20	heifer (2 · 12) 722
יְפֵה־פִיָּה		pretty (1 · 1) 421
קֶרֶץ		[dub.] gadfly (1 · 1) 903
שָׂכִיר	21	hireling, hired laborer (1 · 18) 969
עֵגֶל		calf (4 · 35) 722
מַרְבֵּק		stall; w. עגל = fatted [stall-fed] calf (1 · 4) 918
אֵיד		distress, calamity (5 · 24) 15
פְּקֻדָּה		visitation (9 · 32) 824
נָחָשׁ	22	serpent (2 · 31) 638 I.
קַרְדֹּם		axe (1 · 5) 899
חֹטֵב		cutter; w. עֵץ = wood cutter (1 · 6) 310 I. חטב
נֶחְקַר	23	to be searched out, found out, ascertained (2 · 4 · 27) 350
רבב		to be, become many (3 · 23 · 24) 912

אַרְבֶּה locust (1 · 24) 916

שְׁבִי 27 captivity (8 · 46) 985

שָׁקַט to be undisturbed, quiet (5 · 31 · 41) 1052

שַׁאֲנָן to be at ease, secure (3 · 5) 983

הֶחֱרִיד to terrify, drive in terror (3 · 16 · 39) 353

כָּלָה 28 complete destruction, annihilation (7 · 22) 478

הִדִּיחַ to thrust out, banish (13 · 27 · 43) 623

יִסֵּר to chasten, chastise (5 · 27 · 38) 415

נקה to leave unpunished (4 · 18 · 43) 667

Chapter 47

בְּטֶרֶם 1 before (6 · 39) 382   טֶרֶם

שָׁטַף 2 to overflow, rinse or wash off (3 · 28 · 31) 1009

מְלוֹא that which fills, entire contents (2 · 38) 571

הֵילִיל to give a howl (8 · 30 · 30) 410

שַׁעֲטָה 3 stamping (1 · 1) 1043

פַּרְסָה hoof (1 · 21) 828

אַבִּיר mighty, valiant [here of horses] (4 · 17) 7

רַעַשׁ earthquake (2 · 17) 950

גַּלְגַּל wheel (1 · 11) 165

רִפָּיוֹן sinking (1 · 1) 952

שָׂרִיד 4 survivor (4 · 28) 975

עֹזֵר helper (1 · 19[?]) 740   I. עזר

אִי coast, border, region (4 · 36) 15

קָרְחָה 5 baldness (2 · 11) 901

נִדְמָה to be cut off, destroyed, ruined (1 · 12 · 16) 198

מָתַי when[?] עד מ׳ = how long[?] (7 · 42) 607

הִתְגֹּדֵד to cut oneself [as relig. practice]; to gather in troops or bands (4 · 7 · 8) 151

אָנָה 6 where? עד א׳ = how long? (2 · 39)

אוֹ 33

שָׁקַט to be quiet, inactive (5 · 31 · 41) 1052

תַּעַר sheath (2 · 13) 789

נרגע to repose, be at rest (1 · 1 · 13[?]) 921

דמם to be still, motionless, stand still (3 · 23 · 30) 198

שָׁקַט 7 to be quiet, inactive (5 · 31 · 41) 1052

חוֹף shore, coast (1 · 7) 342

יָעַד to appoint (1 · 5 · 28) 416

Chapter 48

מִשְׂגָּב 1 stronghold, refuge (1 · 17) 960   I. & II.

דמם 2 to be still, silent (3 · 23 · 30) 198

צְעָקָה 3 cry of distress (4 · 21) 858

שֹׁד devastation, ruin (3 · 25) 994

שֶׁבֶר shattering (15 · 45) 991

זְעָקָה 4 cry of distress (6 · 18) 277

צָעִיר young (4 · 22) 859

מַעֲלֶה 5 ascent, stairs (1 · 19) 751

בְּכִי weeping (8 · 30) 113

מוֹרָד descent, slope (1 · 5) 434

צְעָקָה cry of distress (4 · 21) 858

שֶׁבֶר shattering (15 · 45) 991

עֲרוֹעֵר 6 tree, bush; perh. juniper (1 · 1) 792

בֶּטַח 7 security (5 · 43) 105

גּוֹלָה exile; [coll.] exiles (10 · 42) 163

יַחַד together, altogether (1 · 44) 403   יַחְדָּו

מִישׁוֹר 8 tableland, level country (3 · 23) 449

צִיץ 9 [dub.] [coll.] wings (1 · 15) 851   II.

נצא to fly (1 · 1 · 1) 661

שַׁמָּה waste (24 · 39) 1031

מֵאֵין without (20 · 48[?]) 34   אַיִן 6.d.

רְמִיָּה 10 deceit, treachery (1 · 15) 941

מָנַע to withhold, hold back (5 · 25 · 29) 586

שַׁאֲנָן 11 at ease, secure (3 · 5) 983

נְעוּרִים youth (7 · 46) 655

שָׁקַט to be undisturbed, quiet (5 · 31 · 41) 1052

שֶׁמֶר lees, dregs (1 · 5) 1038

הוּרַק to be emptied out (1 · 2 · 19) 937

גּוֹלָה exile; [coll.] exiles (10 · 42) 163

טַעַם taste, discernment (1 · 13) 381

נָמָר to be changed (1 · 1 · 14) 558 מור

צעה 12 ptc. pl. = tippers (2 · 4 · 5) 858

צעה to tip over (1 · 1 · 5) 858

הֵרִיק to empty (1 · 17 · 19) 937

נֶבֶל jar, pitcher (3 · 11) 614

נָפֵץ to dash to pieces (11 · 15 · 21) 658

מִבְטָח 13 confidence, object of confidence (3 · 15) 105

מִבְחָר 15 choicest, best (2 · 12) 104

בָּחוּר young man (11 · 45) 104

טֶבַח a slaughter, slaughtering (2 · 12) 370

אֵיד 16 distress, calamity (5 · 24) 15

נָד 17 to lament, show grief (8 · 19 · 26) 626 נוד

אֵיכָה how! (2 · 18) 32

מַקֵּל rod, stick, staff (2 · 18) 596

צָמָא 18 thirst (1 · 17) 854

מִבְצָר fortress, stronghold (7 · 37) 131

צפה 19 to watch, look (1 · 9 · 18) 859

הֵילִיל 20 to give a howl (8 · 30 · 30) 410

מִישׁוֹר 21 tableland, level country (3 · 23) 449

נִגְדַּע 25 to be hewn off (2 · 7 · 22) 154

הִשְׁכִּיר 26 to make drunken (5 · 6 · 20) 1016

סָפַק to splash; i.e., to fall with a splash (1 · 1 · 1[?]) 706

קִיא vomit (1 · 3) 883

שְׂחֹק derision (4 · 15) 966

שְׂחֹק 27 derision (4 · 15) 966

גַּנָּב thief (3 · 17) 170

מְדֵי as often as (3 · 15) 191 דֵּי 2.c.

הִתְנוֹדֵד to shake oneself (2 · 4 · 26) 626

יוֹנָה 28 dove (1 · 33) 401

קִנֵּן to make a nest (1 · 4 · 5) 890

פַּחַת pit (4 · 10) 809

גָּאוֹן 29 pride, majesty, excellence (7 · 49) 144

גֵּאֶה proud (1 · 8) 144

גֹּבַהּ haughtiness, height (1 · 17) 147

גַּאֲוָה majesty, pride (1 · 19) 144

רֻם height, loftiness (1 · 6) 927

עֶבְרָה 30 arrogance (2 · 34) 720

בַּד empty talker, prater; empty talk (2 · 6) 95

כֵּן veritable, true, honest, right (4 · 24) 467

הֵילִיל 31 to give a howl (8 · 30 · 30) 410

הֶגָה to groan, moan (1 · 23 · 25) 211

בְּכִי 32 weeping (8 · 30) 113

נְטִישָׁה twig, tendril (2 · 3) 644

קַיִץ summer fruit (4 · 20) 884

בָּצִיר vintage (1 · 7) 131

גִּיל 33 rejoicing (1 · 8) 162

כַּרְמֶל garden land (3 · 14) 502

יֶקֶב winepress, wine vat (1 · 16) 428

הֵידָד shout, shouting, cheer (5 · 7) 212

זְעָקָה 34 cry of distress (6 · 18) 277

מְשַׁמָּה devastation, waste (1 · 7) 1031

חָלִיל 36 flute, pipe (2 · 6) 319

המה to murmur, roar, growl (9 · 33 · 33) 242

יִתְרָה abundance, riches (1 · 2) 452

קָרְחָה 37 baldness, bald spot (2 · 11) 901

זָקָן beard (2 · 19) 278

גרע to diminish, clip (2 · 14 · 22) 175

גְּדֻדָה cutting; furrow (1[?] · 1[?]) 151

מָתְנַיִם loins (6 · 47) 608

שַׂק sackcloth (4 · 48) 974

גָּג 38 roof, top (3 · 29) 150

רְחוֹב broad open place (5 · 43) 932

מִסְפֵּד wailing (2 · 16) 704

חֵפֶץ pleasure, delight (2 · 39) 343

הֵילֵל 39 to give a howl (8 · 30 · 30) 410

עֹרֶף neck (7 · 33) 791

שְׂחֹק derision (4 · 15) 966

מְחִתָּה terror, object of terror; ruin (2 · 11) 369

נֶשֶׁר 40 eagle, vulture (4 · 26) 676

דָּאָה to fly swiftly, dart (2 · 4 · 4) 178

קִרְיָה 41 town, city (2 · 30) 900

מְצָד stronghold, mountain fastness (2 · 11) 844

מְצֵרָה Hiph. ptc. of צרר (>50) 864

פַּחַד 43 dread (4 · 49) 808

פַּחַת pit (4 · 10) 809

פַּח bird trap (3 · 25) 809

הַנִּיס 44 Q הֵנַס (>50) 630 נוס

פַּחַד dread (4 · 49) 808

פַּחַת pit (4 · 10) 809

פַּח bird trap (3 · 25) 809

פְּקֻדָּה visitation (9 · 32) 824

לֶחָבָה 45 flame (1 · 19) 529

מִבֵּין from the midst (1 · 21) 107 בֵּין 2.d.

פֵּאָה temples [of lead] (>50) 802

קָדְקֹד hairy crown, scalp (2 · 11) 869

שָׁאוֹן roar, din (4 · 17) 981

אוֹי 46 Woe! Alas! (8 · 25) 17

שְׁבִי captivity (8 · 46) 985

שִׁבְיָה captivity (1 · 9) 986

שְׁבוּת 47 captivity (12 · 26) 986

הֵנָּה hither; עד ה׳ = to this point (4 · 49) 244

Chapter 49

יוֹרֵשׁ 1 heir, inheritor (3 · 5) 439 יָרֵשׁ

תְּרוּעָה 2 alarm, war cry (3 · 36) 929

תֵּל mound (2 · 5) 1068

בָּנוֹת villages (>50) 123 בַּת I.

יצת to be kindled (2 · 4 · 27) 428

יוֹרֵשׁ heir, inheritor, possessor (3 · 5) 439 יָרֵשׁ

הֵילֵל 3 to give a howl (8 · 30 · 30) 410

חגר to gird on, bind on (3 · 44 · 44) 291

שַׂק sackcloth (4 · 48) 974

ספד to wail, lament (7 · 28 · 30) 704

הִתְשׁוֹטֵט to run to and fro (1 · 5 · 13) 1001

גְּדֵרָה wall, hedge (1 · 8) 155

גּוֹלָה exile; [coll.] exiles (10 · 42) 163

זוב 4 to flow (3 · 29 · 29) 264

שׁוֹבֵב backturning; apostate (2 · 3) 1000

פַּחַד 5 dread (4 · 49) 808

נדח to be thrust out, banished (4 · 13 · 43) 623

נדד to retreat, flee (3 · 21 · 24) 622

שְׁבוּת 6 captivity (12 · 26) 986

נסרח 7 to be let loose (1 · 1 · 4) 710

הֶעְמִיק 8 to make deep (2 · 8 · 9) 770

אֵיד distress, calamity (5 · 24) 15

בצר 9 to cut off, gather grapes (2 · 7 · 7) 130

עֹלֵלוֹת gleaning (1 · 6) 760

גַּנָּב thief (3 · 17) 170

דַּי sufficiency, enough (1 · 12) 191

חָשַׂף 10 to strip off, make bare (2 · 10 · 10) 362

מִסְתָּר hiding place, secret place (3 · 10) 712

נֶחְבָּה to withdraw, hide oneself (1 · 3 · 4) 285

שָׁכֵן neighbor (5 · 20) 1015

יָתוֹם 11 orphan (4 · 42) 450

כּוֹס 12 cup (7 · 31) 468

נקה to be empty, clean (1 · 1 · 43) 667

נִקָּה to be free, exempt from punishment (6 · 24 · 43) 667

שַׁמָּה 13 horror, an appalling thing (24 · 39) 1031

חֹרֶב desolation (3 · 16) 351

קְלָלָה curse (9 · 33) 887

חָרְבָּה ruin, desolation (10 · 42) 352

שְׁמוּעָה 14 report (6 · 27) 1035

צִיר   envoy (1 · 6) 851

בָּזָה   15 to despise, regard with contempt (1 · 31 · 42) 102

תִּפְלֶצֶת   16 shuddering, horror (1 · 1) 814

הִשִּׁיא   to beguile (5 · 15 · 16) 674

זָדוֹן   insolence, presumptuousness (3 · 10) 268

חֲגוּ   retreat, place of concealment (1 · 3) 291

הגבה   to make high, exalt (1 · 10 · 34) 146

נֶשֶׁר   vulture, eagle (4 · 26) 676

קֵן   nest (1 · 13) 890

שַׁמָּה   17 horror, an appalling thing (24 · 39) 1031

שָׁרַק   to hiss (3 · 12 · 12) 1056

מַכָּה   wound, blow (10 · 48) 646

מַהְפֵּכָה   18 overthrow (2 · 6) 246

שָׁכֵן   neighbor (5 · 20) 1015

אַרְיֵה   19 lion (6 · 45) 71

גָּאוֹן   majesty, excellence, pride (7 · 49) 144

נָוֶה   habitation (14 · 45[?]) 627

אֵיתָן   permanent, enduring, everflowing (3 · 14) 450

הרגיע   to make a twinkling, to twinkle (4 · 8 · 13) 920

בָּחוּר   chosen (2 · 19) 103   בָּחַר

הוֹעִיד   to summon, arraign (2 · 3 · 28) 416

סָחַב   20 to drag (4 · 5 · 5) 694

צָעִיר   young (4 · 22) 859

נָוֶה   abode (14 · 45[?]) 627

רַעַשׁ   21 to quake, shake (5 · 21 · 29) 950

צְעָקָה   cry of distress (4 · 21) 858

נֶשֶׁר   22 vulture, eagle (4 · 26) 676

דָּאָה   to fly swiftly, dart (2 · 4 · 4) 178

מְצֵרָה   *Hiph.* ptc. of צרר (>50) 864

שְׁמוּעָה   23 report (6 · 27) 1035

נָמוֹג   to melt away (1 · 8 · 17) 556

דְּאָגָה   anxious care (1 · 6) 178

השקיט   to show quietness (1 · 10 · 41) 1052

רָפָה   24 to sink, drop (3 · 14 · 45) 951

רֶטֶט   trembling panic (1 · 1) 936

חֵבֶל   pains of travail (3 · 7) 286

קִרְיָה   25 city, town (2 · 30) 900

מָשׂוֹשׂ   exultation, joy (1 · 17) 965

בָּחוּר   26 young man (11 · 45) 104

רְחוֹב   broad open place (5 · 43) 932

נדמם   to be made silent, quiet (4 · 5 · 30) 198

הִצִּית   27 to kindle, set on fire (8 · 17 · 27) 428

אַרְמוֹן   palace, citadel (5 · 33) 74

מָגוֹר   29 fear, terror (6 · 8) 159

נָד   30 to take flight (8 · 19 · 26) 626   נוד

הֶעְמִיק   to make deep (2 · 8 · 9) 770

שָׁלֵי   31 at ease (1 · 8) 1017

בֶּטַח   security; as adv. = securely (5 · 43) 105

בָּרִיחַ   bar (2 · 41) 138

בָּדָד   alone; isolation, separation (2 · 11) 94

בַּז   32 spoil, booty, plunder (5 · 27) 103

זרה   to scatter, disperse (4 · 25 · 38) 279

קצץ   to cut off (3 · 4 · 14) 893

אֵיד   distress, calamity (5 · 24) 15

מָעוֹן   33 lair, refuge, habitation (5 · 18) 732

תַּן   jackal (5 · 14) 1072

קצה   36 end (1 · 28[?]) 892

זרה   to scatter, disperse (4 · 25 · 38) 279

נִדָּח   banished one, outcast (1 · 11[?]) 623 נדח

חָרוֹן   37 [burning of] anger; ח׳ אף = fierce anger (9 · 41) 354, 60   I. אף 3.

שְׁבִית   39 captivity (12 · 26) 986   שְׁבוּת

Chapter 50

נֵס   2 standard, signal (5 · 21) 651

כָּחֵד   to hide, conceal from (3 · 15 · 32) 470

עָצָב   idol (1 · 17) 781

גִּלּוּל idol (1 · 48) 165

שַׁמָּה 3 waste (24 · 39) 1031

נָד to wander, take flight (8 · 19 · 26) נוד 626

הֵנָּה 5 hither (4 · 49) 244

נִלְוָה to join oneself, be joined to (1 · 11 · 12) 530

אָבַד to be lost (>50) 1

הִתְעָה 6 to cause to wander about (4 · 21 · 50) 1073

רֵבֶץ resting place, dwelling place (1 · 4) 918

אָשֵׁם 7 to be or become guilty (2 · 33 · 35) 79

נָוֶה habitation (14 · 45[?]) 627

מִקְוֶה hope (3 · 5) 876

נָד 8 to wander, take flight (8 · 19 · 26) נוד 626

עַתּוּד he-goat (2 · 29) 800

הִשְׁכִּיל 9 to make childless (1 · 2 · 24) 1013

רֵיקָם in vain, without effect (2 · 16) 938

שָׁלַל 10 to spoil, plunder (1 · 12 · 14) 1021

עָלַז 11 to exalt, triumph (4 · 16 · 16) 759

שֹׁסֶה spoiler, plunderer (2 · 7[?]) 1042 שסה

פּוּשׁ to spring about (1 · 3 · 3) 807

עֶגְלָה heifer (2 · 12) 722

דּוּשׁ to tread on, trample on (1 · 13 · 16) 190

צָהַל to neigh (3 · 7 · 8) 843

אַבִּיר mighty, valiant [of horses] (4 · 17) 7

חָפֵר 12 to be abashed, ashamed (2 · 17 · 17) 344

צִיָּה drought (3 · 16) 851

קֶצֶף 13 wrath (4 · 29) 893

שָׁרַק to hiss (3 · 12 · 12) 1056

מַכָּה wound, blow (10 · 48) 646

ידה 14 to shoot (1 · 1 · 3) 392

חָמַל to spare, have compassion (5 · 40 · 40) 328

הֵרִיעַ 15 to shout in triumph (1 · 40 · 44) 929

אָשְׁיָה buttress, support (1 · 1) 78

נֶהֱרַס to be thrown down, torn down (2 · 10 · 43) 248

נְקָמָה vengeance (11 · 27) 668

נָקַם to avenge oneself (3 · 12 · 35) 667

מַגָּל 16 sickle (1 · 2) 618

קָצִיר harvest (5 · 49) 894

יוֹנָה oppressor (3 · 4 · 18) 413 ינה

שֶׂה 17 flock (1 · 45) 961

פָּזַר Qal. ptc. pass. = scattered (1 · 1 · 10) 808

אֲרִי lion (2 · 35) 71

חִדִּיחַ to thrust out, banish (13 · 27 · 43) 623

עִצֵּם to break the bones (1 · 1 · 1) 782

נָוֶה 19 abode, habitation (14 · 45[?]) 627

סָלַח 20 to forgive, pardon (6 · 33 · 46) 699

לַאֲשֶׁר those whom (3 · 38) 81 אֲשֶׁר

חָרַב 21 to attack, smite down (2 · 2 · 3) 352

הֶחֱרִים to destroy, exterminate, ban (5 · 46 · 49) 355

שֶׁבֶר 22 crashing, breaking (15 · 45) 991 I.

נִגְדַּע 23 to be hewn off (2 · 7 · 22) 154

פַּטִּישׁ forge hammer (2 · 3) 809

שַׁמָּה horror, an appalling thing (24 · 39) 1031

יָקַשׁ 24 to lay snares, bait (1 · 3 · 8) 430

הִתְגָּרָה to excite oneself, engage in strife (1 · 11 · 14) 173

זַעַם 25 indignation (3 · 22) 276

מַאֲבוּס 26 granary (1 · 1) 7

סָלַל to cast up (2 · 10 · 12) 699

עֲרֵמָה heap (1 · 10) 790

הֶחֱרִים to destroy, exterminate, ban (5 · 46 · 49) 355

חָרַב 27 to attack, smite down (2 · 2 · 3) 352

טֶבַח a slaughtering, slaughter (2 · 12) 370

פְּקֻדָּה visitation (9 · 32) 824

פָּלִיט 28 escaped one, fugitive (3 · 5) 812

נְקָמָה vengeance (11 · 27) 668

רַב 29 archer (1 · 2) 914 III.

פְּלֵיטָה escaped remnant (2 · 28) 812

פֹּעַל deed, thing done (3 · 37) 821

זִיד to act presumptuously, rebelliously (1 · 2 · 10) 267

בָּחוּר 30 young man (11 · 45) 104

רְחוֹב broad open place (5 · 43) 932

נדמם to be made silent, quiet (4 · 5 · 30) 198

זָדוֹן 31 presumption, insolence (3 · 10) 268

זָדוֹן 32 presumption, insolence (3 · 10) 268

הִצִּית to kindle, set on fire (8 · 17 · 27) 428

עָשַׁק 33 to oppress; ptc. pass. = oppressed one (3 · 35 · 37) 798

שִׁבְיָה captives (1 · 9) 985

מֵאֵן to refuse (12 · 46) 549

גֹּאֵל 34 redeemer, kinsman (1 · 44) 145 גָּאַל

הִרְגִּיעַ to give rest to (4 · 8 · 13[?]) 921

הִרְגִּיז to cause disquiet (1 · 7 · 41) 919

בַּד 36 empty, idle talk, imaginary claim (2 · 6) 95

נוֹאַל to become fools, show wicked folly (2 · 4 · 4) 383

עֶרֶב 37 mixture, mixed company (2 · 5) 786

בֹּזַז to be taken as spoil (1 · 1 · 41) 102

חֹרֶב 38 dryness, drought, heat (3 · 16) 351

פָּסִיל idol, image (4 · 23) 820

אֵימָה terror, dread (1 · 17) 33

הִתְהֹלֵל to act like a madman (4 · 6 · 14) 237

צִי 39 wild beast (1 · 6) 850

אִי jackal (1 · 3) 17

יַעֲנָה ostrich (1 · 8) 419

נֶצַח evelastingness, ever; לָנֶצַח = forever (3 · 42) 664

מַהְפֵּכָה 40 overthrow (2 · 6) 246

שָׁכֵן neighbor (5 · 20) 1015

יַרְכָה 41 remote part, side (4 · 28) 438

כִּידוֹן 42 dart, javelin (2 · 9) 475

אַכְזָרִי cruel (3 · 8) 470

רִחַם to have compassion (9 · 41 · 46) 933

הָמָה to roar, murmur, growl (9 · 33 · 33) 242

שֵׁמַע 43 hearing report (2 · 17) 1034

רָפָה to sink, drop (3 · 14 · 45) 951

חִיל anguish, writhing (3 · 6) 297

אַרְיֵה 44 lion (6 · 45) 71

גָּאוֹן majesty, excellence, pride (7 · 49) 144

נָוֶד habitation (14 · 45[?]) 627

אֵיתָן permanent, enduring, ever-flowing (3 · 14) 450

הִרְגִּיעַ to make a twinkling, to twinkle (4 · 8 · 13[?]) 920

בָּחוּר chosen (2 · 19) 103 בָּחַר

הוֹעִיד to summon, arraign (2 · 3 · 28) 416

סָחַב 45 to drag (4 · 5 · 5) 694

צָעִיר young (4 · 22) 859

נָוֶה abode (14 · 45[?]) 627

נִרְעַשׁ 46 to be made to quake (1 · 1 · 29) 950

זְעָקָה cry of distress (6 · 18) 277

Chapter 51

קָם 1 adversary (1 · 12) 878 קוּם

מַשְׁחִית destroyer (4 · 19) 1007 שָׁחַת Hiph. ptc.

זָרָה 2 to scatter, disperse (4 · 25 · 38) 279

בָּקַק to empty out, devastate (1 · 1 · 7) 132

סִרְיוֹ 3 armor (2 · 2) 710

חָמַל to spare, have compassion (5 · 40 · 40) 328

בָּחוּר young man (11 · 45) 104

הֶחֱרִים to destroy, exterminate; ban (5 · 46 · 49) 355

דָּקַר 4 ptc. = pierced, riddled (2 · 3 · 11) 201

אַלְמָן 5 widowed (1 · 1) 48

אָשָׁם guilt, guilt offering (1 · 47) 79

נדמם	6 to be made silent, quiet (4 · 5 · 30) 198
נִקְמָם	vengeance (11 · 27) 668
גְּמוּל	recompense, what is gained from dealing; dealing (1 · 19) 168
כּוֹס	7 cup (7 · 31) 468
שִׁכֵּר	to make drunken (1 · 4 · 20) 1016
הִתְהֹלֵל	to act like a madman (4 · 6 · 14[?]) 237 Hithpo.
פִּתְאֹם	8 suddenly (5 · 25) 837
הֵילִל	to give a howl (8 · 30 · 30) 410
צֳרִי	a kind of balsam (3 · 6) 863
מַכְאוֹב	pain (3 · 16) 456
אוּלַי	perhaps (6 · 45) 19
שַׁחַק	9 cloud (1 · 21) 1007
הברִיר	11 to polish (1 · 1 · 2) 140
שֶׁלֶט	perh. shield; quiver, equipment (1 · 7) 1020
מְזִמָּה	purpose, device (4 · 19) 273
נְקָמָה	vengeance (11 · 27) 668
נֵס	12 standard, signal (5 · 21) 651
מִשְׁמָר	guard, prison (1 · 22) 1038
אֹרֵב	licr-in-wait = ambusher (1 · 18) 70 ארב
זָמַם	to purpose, devise (2 · 13 · 13) 273
בֶּצַע	13 unjust gain, gain made by violence (4 · 23) 130
יֶלֶק	14 [a kind of] locust (2 · 9) 410
ענה	to sing (2 · 13 · 16) 777
הֵידָד	shout, shouting, cheer (5 · 7) 212
תֵּבֵל	15 world (2 · 36) 385
תְּבוּנָה	understanding (2 · 42) 108
נָשִׂיא	16 vapor (2 · 4) 672 II.
בָּרָק	lightning (2 · 21) 140
מָטָר	rain (2 · 38) 564
נִבְעַר	17 to be dull hearted, brutish, stupid (3 · 4 · 7) 129
צֹרֵף	smelter; i.e., goldsmith (3 · 10[?]) 864
פֶּסֶל	idol, image (2 · 31) 820

תַּעְתֻּעִים	18 mockery (2 · 2) 1074
פְּקֻדָּה	visitation (9 · 32) 824
יָצַר	19 to form, fashion (4 · 41 · 44) 427
מַפֵּץ	20 war club (1 · 1) 659
נִפֵּץ	to dash to pieces (11 · 15 · 21) 658
נִפֵּץ	21 to dash to pieces (11 · 15 · 21) 658
נִפֵּץ	22 to dash to pieces (11 · 15 · 21) 658
בָּחוּר	[coll.] young men, young man (11 · 45) 104
בְּתוּלָה	virgin (8 · 50) 143
נִפֵּץ	23 to dash to pieces (11 · 15 · 21) 658
עֵדֶר	flock (6 · 39) 727
אִכָּר	plowman, husbandman (3 · 7) 38
צֶמֶד	span; couple, pair (1 · 15) 855
פֶּחָה	governor (3 · 28) 802
סָגָן	perfect, ruler (3 · 17) 688
מַשְׁחִית	25 destroyer, destruction (4 · 19) 1008
גלגל	to roll down (1 · 1 · 17) 164
שְׂרֵפָה	burning (1 · 13) 977
פִּנָּה	26 corner (3 · 30) 819
מוֹסָד	foundation (2 · 13) 414
נֵס	27 standard, signal (5 · 21) 651
טִפְסָר	marshal, scribe (1 · 2) 381
יֶלֶק	[a kind of] locust (2 · 9) 410
סָמָר	bristling, rough (1 · 1) 702
פֶּחָה	28 governor (3 · 28) 808
סָגָן	perfect, ruler (3 · 17) 688
מֶמְשָׁלָה	dominion, rule (2 · 17) 606
רעש	29 to quake, shake (5 · 21 · 29) 950
חוּל	to be in severe pain, or anguish, twist, writhe (5 · 30 · 47) 296
שַׁמָּה	waste (24 · 39) 1031
מֵאֵין	without (20 · 48[?]) 34 אֵין 6.d.
מְצָד	30 stronghold, mountain fastness (2 · 11) 844
נשת	to be dry (1 · 2 · 3) 677
הִצִּית	to kindle, set on fire (8 · 17 · 27) 428
בְּרִיחַ	bar (2 · 41) 138
נָץ	31 runner·(2 · 25) 930
מַעְבָּרָה	32 passage, ford, pass (1 · 8) 721

אֲגַם swamp reed, rush; troubled pool (1 [?] · 1[?]) 8

נִבְהַל to be disturbed, dismayed, terrified (1 · 24 · 39) 96

גֹּרֶן 33 threshing floor (1 · 34) 175

קָצִיר harvest (5 · 49) 894

הָמַם 34 to confuse, discomfit; to make a noise (1 · 13 · 13) 243

הִצִּיג to set, place (1 · 16 · 16) 426 יצג

רִיק vanity, emptiness (2 · 12) 938

בָּלַע to swallow up, engulf (1 · 20 · 41) 118

תַּנִּין dragon (1 · 15) 1072

כָּרֵשׂ belly (1 · 1) 503

עֵדֶן dainties (1 · 3) 726

הֵדִיחַ to rinse, cleanse (1 · 4 · 4) 188

שְׁאָר 35 flesh (1 · 16) 984

נקם 36 to take vengeance (1 · 2 · 35) 667

נְקָמָה vengeance (11 · 27) 668

הֶחֱרִיב to dry up (1 · 13 · 37) 351

מָקוֹר spring, fountain (4 · 18) 881

גַּל 37 heap, pile (2 · 20) 164

מָעוֹן lair, refuge, habitation (5 · 18) 732

תַּן jackal (5 · 14) 1072

שַׁמָּה horror, an appalling thing (24 · 39) 1031

שְׁרֵקָה hissing (5 · 7) 1056

מֵאֵין without (20 · 48[?]) 34 אֵין 6.d.

כְּפִיר 38 young lion (3 · 31) 498

שָׁאַג to roar (5 · 20 · 20) 980

נָעַר to growl (1 · 1 · 1) 654

גּוּר whelp, young of an animal (1 · 2) 158

אֲרִי lion (2 · 35) 71

חמם 39 to be or grow warm (1 · 23 · 26) 328

מִשְׁתֶּה feast, banquet, drink (2 · 46) 1059

הִשְׁכִּיר to make drunken (5 · 6 · 20) 1016

עלז to exult, triumph (4 · 16 · 16) 759

ישׁן to sleep, go to sleep (2 · 15 · 16) 445

שֵׁנָה sleep (3 · 23) 446

הֵקִיץ to awake (3 · 22 · 23) 884

כַּר 40 he-lamb; battering ram (1 · 12) 503

טבח to slaughter (3 · 11 · 11) 370

עַתּוּד he-goat (2 · 29) 800

שַׁמָּה 41 horror, an appalling thing (24 · 39) 1031

גַּל 42 wave [of water], roller; heap (4 · 16) 164

שַׁמָּה 43 waste (24 · 39) 1031

צִיָּה draught (3 · 16) 851

בֶּלַע 44 thing swallowed (1 · 1) 118

נהר to flow, stream (1 · 3 · 3[?]) 625

חָרוֹן 45 [burning of] anger; ח׳ אף = fierce anger (9 · 41) 354, 60 אַף 3.

רכך 46 to be timid, fearful (1 · 6 · 8) 939

שְׁמוּעָה report (6 · 27) 1035

מֹשֵׁל ruler (4 · 24) 605 מָשַׁל III.

פָּסִיל 47 idol, image (4 · 23) 820

פָּלִיט 50 escaped one, fugitive (6 · 24) 812

כְּלִמָּה 51 ignominy, reproach, insult (3 · 30) 484

פָּסִיל 52 idol, image (4 · 23) 820

אנק to cry, groan (1 · 2 · 4) 60

בצר 53 to fortify (1 · 2 · 4) 130

זְעָקָה 54 cry of distress (6 · 18) 277

שֶׁבֶר crashing (15 · 45) 991

המה 55 to roar, murmur, growl (9 · 33 · 33) 242

גַּל wave [of water], roller; (4 · 16) 164

שָׁאוֹן roar, din (4 · 17) 981

גְּמוּלָה 56 recompense, dealing (1 · 3) 168

הִשְׁכִּיר 57 to make drunken (5 · 6 · 20) 1016

פֶּחָה governor (3 · 28) 808

סָגָן prefect, ruler (3 · 17) 688

ישׁן to sleep, go to sleep (2 · 15 · 16) 445

שֵׁנָה sleep (3 · 23) 446

הֵקִיץ to awake (3 · 22 · 23) 884

רָחָב 58 thick (1 · 21) 932

ערער to lay bare (1 · 1 · 4) 792

הִתְעַרְעַר to be laid bare (1 · 1 · 4) 792

גָּבֹהַּ high, lofty, tall (4 · 41) 147

יצח to be burned, to kindle (2 · 4 · 27) 428

יָגַע   to toil, labor, be or grow weary (2 · 20 · 26) 388

בְּדֵי   for what suffices for, for (2 · 6) 191 דַי 2.a.

רִיק   vanity, emptiness (2 · 12) 938

לְאֹם   people (1 · 35) 522

יָעֵף   to be weary, faint (3 · 8 · 9) 419

מְנוּחָה   59 resting place, rest (2 · 21) 629

קָשַׁר   63 to bind (1 · 36 · 44) 905

כָּכָה   64 thus (5 · 34) 462

שָׁקַע   to sink down (1 · 3 · 6) 1054

יָעֵף   to be weary, faint (3 · 8 · 9) 419

הֵנָּה   hither (4 · 49) 244

Chapter 52

מרד   3 to rebel, revolt (1 · 25 · 25) 597

עָשׂוֹר   4 tenth day (1 · 15) 797

דָּיֵק   bulwark, siege wall (1 · 6) 189

מָצוֹר   5 siege, siege works (3 · 25) 848

גַּן   7 garden (3 · 42) 171

הִשִּׂיג   8 to overtake (3 · 49 · 49) 673

עִוֵּר   11 to blind (2 · 5 · 5) 734

פְּקֻדָּה   visitation (9 · 32) 824

עָשׂוֹר   12 tenth day (1 · 15) 797

טַבָּח   bodyguard (17 · 32) 371

נָתַץ   14 to pull down, break down (6 · 31 · 42) 683

טַבָּח   bodyguard (17 · 32) 371

דַּלָּה   15 the poor (3 · 5) 195

אָמוֹן   master workman, architect (1 · 2) 54 II.

טַבָּח   bodyguard (17 · 32) 371

דַּלָּה   16 the poor (3 · 5) 195

טַבָּח   bodyguard (17 · 32) 371

כֹּרֵם   vine dresser (1 · 5) 501 כרם

יגב   to till, be husbandman (1 · 2 · 2) 387

מְכוֹנָה   17 base, stand (3 · 25) 467

סִיר   18 pot (3 · 29) 696 I.

יָע   shovels (1 · 9) 418

מְזַמֶּרֶת   snuffers (1 · 5) 275

מִזְרָק   bowl, basin (2 · 32) 284

סַף   19 basin, goblet (1 · 6) 706 I.

מַחְתָּה   fire pan, censer (1 · 22) 367

מִזְרָק   bowl, basin (2 · 32) 284

סִיר   pot (3 · 29) 696 I.

מְנוֹרָה   lampstand (1 · 40) 633

מְנַקִּית   sacrificial bowl (1 · 4) 667

טַבָּח   bodyguard (17 · 32) 371

מְכוֹנָה   20 base, stand (3 · 25) 467

מִשְׁקָל   weight (1 · 49) 1054

קוֹמָה   21 height (2 · 45) 879

חוּט   measuring line, cord (1 · 7) 296

עֳבִי   thickness (1 · 5) 716

אֶצְבַּע   finger (1 · 31) 840

נבב   to hollow out (1 · 4 · 4) 612

כֹּתֶרֶת   22 capital [of pillar] (3 · 24) 509

קוֹמָה   height (2 · 45) 879

שְׂבָכָה   lattice work, network (2 · 16) 959

רִמּוֹן   pomegranate (4 · 32) 941

רִמּוֹן   23 pomegranate (4 · 32) 941

שְׂבָכָה   lattice work, network (2 · 16) 959

טַבָּח   24 bodyguard (17 · 32) 371

מִשְׁנֶה   second in rank; double, copy (3 · 36) 1041

סַף   threshold; שֹׁמֵר הַסַּף = doorkeeper (2 · 25) 706 II.

סָרִיס   25 eunuch (7 · 45) 710

פָּקִיד   commissioner, deputy, overseer (3 · 13) 824

הצביא   to muster (1 · 2 · 14) 838

טַבָּח   26 bodyguard (17 · 32) 371

טַבָּח   30 bodyguard (17 · 32) 371

גָּלוּת   31 exile; [coll.] exiles (5 · 15) 163

כְּלִיא   confinement, imprisonment (2 · 2) כלוא 476

מִמַּעַל   32 above, on the top of (4 · 29) 751 מַעַל

שָׁנָה   33 to change, alter (2 · 9 · 26) 1040

כֶּלֶא   imprisonment, confinement (3 · 10) 476

אֲרֻחָה   34 meal, allowance [of food] (3 · 7) 73

107

EZEKIEL

Chapter 1

גּוֹלָה 1 [coll.] exiles (11 · 42) 163
מַרְאָה vision (4 · 12) 909 I.
גָּלוּת 2 exile (3 · 15) 163
סְעָרָה 4 tempest, storm (3 · 16) 704
נֹגַהּ brightness (5 · 19) 618
עֵין gleam, sparkle (so in ch. 1.) (>50) 744 עַיִן 4.c.
חַשְׁמַל [dub.] amber (3 · 3) 365
דְּמוּת 5 likeness, similitude (16 · 25) 198
עֵגֶל 7 calf (1 · 35) 722
נצץ to shine, sparkle (1 · 1 · 4) 665 I.
קָלָל burnished (1 · 2) 887
רֶבַע 8 pl. = four sides (5 · 7) 917
חבר 9 to unite, be joined (2 · 11) 287
דְּמוּת 10 likeness, similitude (16 · 25) 198
אַרְיֵה lion (2 · 45) 71
נֶשֶׁר vulture, eagle (4 · 26) 676
פרד 11 ptc. pass. = divided; i.e., spread (1 · 1 · 26) 825
מִלְמָעְלָה above (6 · 24) 751 II. מַעַל 2.d.
חבר to unite, be joined (2 · 11 · 28) 287
גּוִיָּה body (2 · 13) 156
דְּמוּת 13 likeness, similitude (16 · 25) 198
גַּחֶלֶת cool (3 · 18) 160
לַפִּיד torch (1 · 13) 542
נֹגַהּ brightness (5 · 19) 618
בָּרָק lightning (4 · 21) 140
רצא 14 to run (1 · 1 · 1) 952
בָּזָק lightning flash [dub.] (1 · 1) 103
אוֹפַן 15 wheel (25 · 35) 66
אוֹפַן 16 wheel (25 · 35) 66
תַּרְשִׁישׁ [perh.] yellow jasper (3 · 7) 1076
דְּמוּת likeness, similitude (16 · 25) 198
רֶבַע 17 pl. = four sides (5 · 7) 917
גַּב 18 rim (7 · 13) 146
גֹּבַהּ height (6 · 17) 147

יִרְאָה a terror = obj. of terror (2 · 45) 432
אוֹפַן 19 wheel (25 · 35) 66
אוֹפַן 20 wheel (25 · 35) 66
לְעֻמָּה side by side with (15 · 31) 769 I. עֻמָּה
אוֹפַן 21 wheel (25 · 35) 66
לְעֻמָּה side by side with (15 · 31) 769 I. עֻמָּה
דְּמוּת 22 likeness, similitude (16 · 25) 198
רָקִיעַ expanse (5 · 17) 956
קֶרַח ice (1 · 7) 901
נוֹרָא awe inspiring, awful (1 · 44) 431 יָרֵא
Niph.
מִלְמָעְלָה above (6 · 24) 751 II. מַעַל 2.d.
רָקִיעַ 23 expanse (5 · 17) 956
גּוִיָּה body (2 · 13) 156
שַׁדַּי 24 name of God (2 · 48) 994
הֲמֻלָּה rushing or roaring sound [dub.] (1 · 2) 242
רָפָה to let drop (2 · 5 · 45) 951
רָקִיעַ 25 expanse (5 · 17) 956
רָפָה to let drop (2 · 5 · 45) 951
מִמַּעַל 26 above, on the top (1 · 29) 751 II. מַעַל 1.
רָקִיעַ expanse (5 · 17) 956
סַפִּיר sapphire (3 · 11) 705
דְּמוּת likeness, similitude (16 · 25) 198
מִלְמָעְלָה above (6 · 24) 751 II מַעַל 2.d.
חַשְׁמַל 27 [dub.] amber (3 · 3) 365
מָתְנַיִם loins (12 · 47) 608
לְמַעְלָה upward (8 · 34) 751 מַעַל 2.c.
לְמַטָּה downward (2 · 10) 641 מַטָּה 2.
נֹגַהּ brightness (5 · 19) 618
גֶּשֶׁם 28 rain, shower (6 · 35) 177
נֹגַהּ brightness (5 · 19) 618
דְּמוּת likeness, similitude (16 · 25) 198

Chapter 2

מָרַד 3 to rebel, revolt (4 · 25 · 25) 597
פֶּשַׁע to transgress (3 · 40 · 41) 833
קְשִׁי 4 stiff, stubborn (2 · 36) 904 קָשֶׁה

מְרִי 5 rebellion (15 · 22) 598

סָרָב 6 rebel; resistance; briers (1 · 1) 709

סַלּוֹן brier (2 · 2) 699

עַקְרָב scorpion (1 · 9) 785

מְרִי rebellion (15 · 22) 598

מְרִי 7 rebellion (15 · 22) 598

מְרִי 8 rebellion (15 · 22) 598

פצה to part, open (1 · 15 · 15) 822

מְגִלָּה 9 roll [writing, book] (4 · 21) 166

אָחוֹר 10 behind (2 · 41) 30

קִינָה elegy, dirge (9 · 17) 884

הֶגֶה a moaning (1 · 3) 211

הִי lamentation, wailing (1 · 1) 223

Chapter 3

מְגִלָּה 1 roll [writing, book] (4 · 21) 166

מְגִלָּה 2 roll [writing, book] (4 · 21) 166

מֵעֶה 3 stomach, belly (2 · 32) 588

מְגִלָּה roll [writing, book] (4 · 21) 166

מָתוֹק sweetness (1 · 12) 608

עָמֵק 5 deep, unfathomable (2 · 3) 771

כָּבֵד burdensome, heavy (2 · 39) 458

עָמֵק 6 deep, unfathomable (2 · 3) 771

כָּבֵד burdensome, heavy (2 · 39) 458

מֵצַח 7 forehead (5 · 13) 594

קָשֵׁי stiff, stubborn (2 · 36) 904

לְעֻמָּה 8 side by side with (15 · 31) 769 I. עמה

מֵצַח forehead (5 · 13) 594

שָׁמִיר 9 adamant, thorns (1 · 11) 1038

צֹר flint (1 · 6) 866

מֵצַח forehead (5 · 13) 594

מְרִי rebellion (15 · 22) 598

גּוֹלָה 11 [coll.] exiles (11 · 42) 163

רַעַשׁ 12 earthquake (5 · 17) 950

מַשִּׁיקוֹת 13 ptc. = gently touching (1 · 1 · 32) 676 I. נשׁק Hiph.

אוֹפַן wheel (25 · 35) 66

לְעֻמָּה side by side with (15 · 31) 769 I. עמה

רַעַשׁ earthquake (5 · 17) 950

מַר 14 bitterly; bitter (3 · 38) 600 I.

גּוֹלָה 15 [coll.] exiles (11 · 42) 163

צֹפֶה 17 watchman (5 · 19[?]) 859 I. צפה

הִזְהִיר to warn, give a warning (10 · 13 · 21) 264 II.

הִזְהִיר 18 to warn, give a warning (10 · 13 · 21) 264 II.

הִזְהִיר 19 to warn, give a warning (10 · 13 · 21) 264 II.

רֶשַׁע wickedness (4 · 30) 957

עָוֶל 20 injustice, unrighteousness (10 · 21) 732

מִכְשׁוֹל stumbling block, means or occasion of stumbling (8 · 14) 506

הִזְהִיר to warn, give a warning (10 · 13 · 21) 264 II.

הִזְהִיר 21 to warn, give a warning (10 · 13 · 21) 264 II.

נִזְהָר to take warning (5 · 8 · 21) 264 II.

בִּקְעָה 22 plain (5 · 19) 132

בִּקְעָה 23 plain (5 · 19) 132

עֲבֹת 25 cord, rope (6 · 24) 721

חֵךְ 26 palate, roof of mouth (1 · 18) 335

נאלם to be dumb (3 · 8 · 9) 47

מְרִי rebellion (15 · 25) 598

מְרִי 27 rebellion (15 · 25) 598

חָדֵל forbearing, lacking (1 · 3) 293

Chapter 4

לְבֵנָה 1 tile, brick (1 · 12) 527

חקק to engrave, inscribe (2 · 8 · 11) 349

מָצוֹר 2 siege, entrenchment (5 · 25) 848 I.

דָּיֵק bulwark, siege wall (4 · 6) 189

סֹלְלָה mound (4 · 11) 700

כַּר battering ram (5 · 12) 305 III.

מַחֲבַת 3 plate (1 · 5) 290

מָצוֹר siege (5 · 25) 848 I.

צוּר to besiege (2 · 31 · 31) 848

צַד 4 side (6 · 32) 841

שְׂמָאלִי   left, on the left (1 · 9) 970

צַד   6 side (6 · 32) 841

יְמָנִי   right, right hand (3 · 33) 412

מָצוֹר   7 siege (5 · 25) 848 I.

חָשַׂף   to strip, lay bare (1 · 10 · 10) 362

עֲבֹת   8 cord, rope (6 · 24) 721

צַד   side (6 · 32) 841

מָצוֹר   siege (5 · 25) 848 I.

חִטִּין   9 wheat (3 · 30) 334 חטה

שְׂעֹרָה   barley (4 · 34) 972

פּוֹל   bean[s] (1 · 2) 806

עֲדָשָׁה   lentil (1 · 4) 727

דֹּחַן   millet (1 · 1) 191

כֻּסֶּמֶת   spelt (1 · 3) 493

צַד   side (6 · 32) 841

מַאֲכָל   10 food (3 · 30) 38

מִשְׁקוֹל   weight, heaviness (1 · 1) 1054

מְשׂוּרָה   11 measure [of liquids] (2 · 4) 601

הִין   hin [liquid measure] (6 · 22) 228

עֻגָה   12 cake of bread (1 · 7) 728

שְׂעֹרָה   barley (4 · 34) 972

גֵּל   dung; pl. cstr. גֶּלְלֵי (2 · 3) 165

צֵאָה   filth, human excrement (1 · 2) 844

עוּג   to bake (1 · 1 · 1) 728

כָּכָה   13 thus (2 · 34) 462

אדיח   to thrust out, banish (1 · 27 · 43) הִדִּיחַ 623

אֲהָהּ   14 Alas! (4 · 15) 13

נְבֵלָה   carcass, corpse (2 · 48) 615

טְרֵפָה   animal torn [by wild beasts] (2 · 9) 383

נְעוּרִים   youth (9 · 46) 655

פִּגּוּל   foul thing, refuse (1 · 4) 803

צפוע   15 Q., dung (1 · 1) 861 צְפִיעַ

גֵּל   dung; pl. cstr. גֶּלְלֵי (2 · 3) 165

מִשְׁקָל   16 weight (2 · 49) 1054

דְּאָגָה   anxiety, anxious care (3 · 6) 178

מְשׂוּרָה   measure [of liquids] (2 · 4) 601

שִׁמָּמוֹן   horror, an appalling thing (2 · 2) 1031

חָסֵר   17 to lack, need, be lacking (1 · 19 · 23) 341

נמוק   to pine away (3 · 9 · 10) 596 מקק

Chapter 5

חַד   1 sharp (1 · 4) 292

תַּעַר   razor (5 · 13) 789

גַּלָּב   barber (1 · 1) 162

זָקָן   chin; beard (1 · 19) 278

מֹאזְנַיִם   balances, scales (2 · 15) 24 מאזן

מִשְׁקָל   weight (2 · 49) 1054

אוּר   2 flame (1 · 6) 22

מָצוֹר   siege (5 · 25) 848 I.

זרה   to scatter (1 · 9 · 38) 279

הריק   to empty out (5 · 17 · 19) 937

צור   3 to secure (2 · 31 · 31) 848

תֶּמֶר   6 Hiph. impf. 2fs, to show disobedience, rebelliousness (4 · 22 · 43) 598 מרה

רִשְׁעָה   wickedness (5 · 15) 958

הֲמָנְכֶם   7 inf. of המן to rage, be turbulent (1 · 1) 243

שֶׁפֶט   10 judgment (10 · 16) 1048

זרה   to scatter, disperse (10 · 25 · 38) 279

שִׁקּוּץ   11 detested thing (8 · 28) 1055

גרע   to withdraw (2 · 14 · 22) 175

חוס   to pity, look upon with compassion (9 · 24 · 24) 299

חָמַל   to spare, have compassion (7 · 40 · 40) 328

דֶּבֶר   12 plague, pestilence (12 · 46) 184

זרה   to scatter, disperse (10 · 25 · 38) 279

הריק   to empty out (5 · 17 · 19) 937

קִנְאָה   13 anger (10 · 43) 888

חָרְבָּה   14 waste, ruin (14 · 42) 352

גְּדוּפָה   15 taunt (1 · 1) 154

מוּסָר   discipline; i.e., warning (1 · 50) 416

מְשַׁמָּה   horror (5 · 7) 1031

שֶׁפֶט   judgment (10 · 16) 1048

תּוֹכַחַת correction, rebuke (2 · 24) 407
מַשְׁחִית 16 ruin, destruction (4 · 19) 1008
שָׁכֹל 17 to make childless (5 · 18 · 24) 1013
דֶּבֶר plague, pestilence (12 · 46) 184

Chapter 6

אָפִיק 3 channel (7 · 18) 67
גַּיְא valley (10 · 47) 161
חַמָּן 4 sun pillar [for idolatrous worship] (2 · 8) 329
גִּלּוּל idol (39 · 48) 165
פֶּגֶר 5 a corpse, carcass (3 · 22) 803
גִּלּוּל idol (39 · 48) 165
זרה to scatter, disperse (10 · 25 · 38) 279
מוֹשָׁב 6 dwelling, habitable place (7 · 44) 444
חרב to waste, desolate (3 · 17 · 37) 351 II.
אשם to be held guilty, bear punishment (4 · 33 · 35) 79
גִּלּוּל idol (39 · 48) 165
נִגְדַּע to be hewn off (1 · 5 · 22) 154
חַמָּן sun pillar [for idolatrous worship] (2 · 8) 329
נמחה to be exterminated (1 · 9 · 34) 562 I.
פָּלִיט 8 fugitive (7 · 19) 812
נזרה to be scattered, dispersed (2 · 2 · 38) 279
פָּלִיט 9 fugitive (7 · 19) 812
נשבה to be taken captive (1 · 8 · 37) 985
גִּלּוּל idol (39 · 48) 165
נקט to feel loathing (3 · 4 · 7) 876
בִּפְנֵי against (4 · 17) 816 פָּנֶה II.3.
חִנָּם 10 for no purpose, in vain (2 · 32) 336
רקע 11 to stomp down (2 · 6 · 11) 955
אָח Ah! Alas! (2 · 2) 25 III.
דֶּבֶר plague, pestilence (12 · 46) 184
דֶּבֶר 12 plague, pestilence (12 · 46) 184
גִּלּוּל 13 idol (39 · 48) 165
רָם high (5 · 31[?]) 926 רום

רַעֲנָן luxuriant, fresh (1 · 19) 947
אֵלָה terebinth [a deciduous tree] (1 · 17) 18 I.
עָבוֹת leafy (2 · 4) 721
נִיחֹחַ a soothing, tranquilizing (4 · 43) 629
מְשַׁמָּה 14 devastation, waste (5 · 7) 1031
מוֹשָׁב dwelling place (7 · 44) 44

Chapter 7

חוס 4 to pity, look upon with compassion (9 · 24 · 24) 299
חָמַל to spare, have compassion (7 · 40 · 40) 328
הֵקִיץ 6 to awake (1 · 22 · 23) 884
צְפִירָה 7 [dub.] plait, chaplet (2 · 3) 862
מְהוּמָה tumult, confusion, panic (2 · 12) 223
הֵד shout, shouting, cheer (1 · 1) 212
חוס 9 to pity, look upon with compassion (9 · 24 · 24) 299
חָמַל to spare, have compassion (7 · 40 · 40) 328
צְפִירָה 10 [dub.] plait, chaplet (2 · 3) 862
צָץ to blossom (1 · 7 · 8) 847 I. צוץ
פֶּרַח to bud, sprout (1 · 29 · 34) 827
זָדוֹן insolence (1 · 10) 268
רֶשַׁע 11 wickedness (4 · 30) 957
מֵהֲמֵהֶם [dub.] wealth (1 · 1) 241 הָם[?]
נֹהַּ eminency, distinction (1 · 1) 627
קֹנֶה 12 owner (1 · 7[?]) 888 קָנָה
הִתְאַבֵּל to mourn (2 · 19 · 38) 5 I.
חָרוֹן [burning of] anger (2 · 41) 354
מִמְכָּר 13 ware, thing sold, merchandise (1 · 10) 569
חַיָּה life (2 · 12) 312 I. חַיָּה 2.
חָזוֹן vision (7 · 35) 302
תָּקוֹעַ 14 blast instrument (1 · 1) 1075
חָרוֹן [burning of] anger (2 · 41) 354
דֶּבֶר 15 plague, pestilence (12 · 46) 184
פלט 16 to escape (1 · 1 · 27) 812

פָּלִיט	fugitive (7 · 19) 812
יוֹנָה	dove (1 · 33) 401
גְּיְא	valley (10 · 47) 161
המה	to groan, murmur (1 · 33 · 33) 242
רָפָה	17 to lose heart (2 · 14 · 45) 951
בֶּרֶךְ	knee (3 · 25) 139
חגר	18 to gird on, bind on (3 · 44 · 44) 291
שַׂק	sackcloth (2 · 48) 974
פַּלָּצוּת	shuddering (1 · 4) 814
בּוּשָׁה	shame (1 · 4) 102
קָרְחָה	baldness, bald spot (2 · 11) 901
נִדָּה	19 impure thing (5 · 30) 622
עֶבְרָה	rage, fury (5 · 34) 720
מֵעֶה	stomach, belly (2 · 32) 588
מִכְשׁוֹל	stumbling block (8 · 14) 506
צְבִי	20 beauty, decoration (5 · 18) 840
עֲדִי	[coll.] ornaments (5 · 14) 725
גָּאוֹן	pride (9 · 49) 144
צֶלֶם	image (3 · 17) 853
שִׁקּוּץ	detested thing (8 · 28) 1055
נִדָּה	impure thing (5 · 30) 622
בַּז	21 spoiling, robbery (12 · 27) 103
צָפוּן	22 treasured, cherished place (1 · 3[?]) 860 צָפַן
פָּרִיץ	violent one (2 · 6) 829
רַתּוֹק	23 chain (1 · 2) 958
גָּאוֹן	24 pride, exaltation (9 · 49) 144
עַז	strong, mighty, fierce (1 · 22) 738
קְפָדָה	25 shuddering (1 · 1) 891
הֹוָה	26 ruin, disaster (2 · 3) 217
שְׁמוּעָה	report (4 · 27) 1035
חָזוֹן	vision (7 · 35) 302
הִתְאַבֵּל	27 to mourn (2 · 19 · 38) 5 I.
נִבְהַל	to be disturbed, dismayed, terrified (2 · 24 · 39) 96

Chapter 8

דְּמוּת	2 likeness, similitude (16 · 25) 198
מָתְנַיִם	loins (12 · 47) 608
לְמַטָּה	downward (2 · 10) 641 מַטָּה
לְמַעְלָה	upward (8 · 34) 751 מַעַל 2.c.
זֹהַר	shining, brightness (1 · 2) 264
חַשְׁמַל	[dub.] amber (3 · 3) 365
תַּבְנִית	3 figure, image (3 · 20) 125
צִיצת	lock (1 · 4) 851
מַרְאָה	vision (4 · 12) 909 I.
פְּנִימִי	inner (24 · 33) 819
מוֹשָׁב	location, dwelling (7 · 44) 444
סֵמֶל	statue (2 · 5) 702
קִנְאָה	anger (10 · 43) 888
הקנא	to provoke to jealous anger (1 · 4 · 34) 888
בִּקְעָה	4 plain (5 · 19) 132
סֵמֶל	5 image, figure (2 · 5) 702
קִנְאָה	anger (10 · 43) 888
בָּאָה	entrance, entry (1 · 1) 99
פֹּה	6 here, hither (3 · 44) 805
חֹר	7 hole (1 · 7) 359 III.
חָתַר	8 to dig (5 · 8 · 8) 369
פֹּה	9 here, hither (3 · 44) 805
תַּבְנִית	10 figure, image (3 · 20) 125
רֶמֶשׂ	creeping things (2 · 16) 943
שֶׁקֶץ	detestable (1 · 11) 1054
גִּלּוּל	idol (39 · 48) 165
מחקה	*Pual* ptc. = carved (2 · 3 · 4) 348
מְקַטֶּרֶת	11 censer (1 · 2) 883
עָתָר	odor (1 · 1) 801
חֶדֶר	12 chamber, room (1 · 37) 293
מַשְׂכִּית	showpiece, figure (1 · 6) 967
פְּנִימִי	16 inner (24 · 33) 819
אוּלָם	porch (32 · 49) 17 I.
אָחוֹר	pl. cs. אֲחֹרֵי = hinder part (2 · 41) 30
קֶדֶם	קָדְמָה = eastward (3 · 26) 870
פֹּה	17 here, hither (3 · 44) 805
זְמוֹרָה	branch, twig (2 · 5) 274
חוס	18 to pity, look upon with compassion (9 · 24 · 24) 299

חָמַל	to spare, have compassion (7 · 40 · 40) 328

קֶסֶת	pot, ink horn (3 · 3) 903
מָתְנַיִם	loins (12 · 47) 608

Chapter 9

פְּקֻדָּה	1 visitation (2 · 32) 824
מַשְׁחֵת	destruction, ruin (1 · 1) 1008
מַפָּץ	2 shattering (1 · 1) 658
לָבוּשׁ	clothed with (9 · 16[?]) 527 לבשׁ
בַּד	white linen (6 · 23) 94 I.
קֶסֶת	pot, ink horn (3 · 3) 903
מָתְנַיִם	loins (12 · 47) 608
מִפְתָּן	3 threshold (5 · 8) 837
לָבוּשׁ	clothed with (9 · 16[?]) 527 לבשׁ
בַּד	white linen (6 · 23) 94 I.
קֶסֶת	pot, ink horn (3 · 3) 903
מָתְנַיִם	loins (12 · 47) 608
הִתְוָה	4 to make a mark (1 · 1 · 2) 1063
תָּו	mark (2 · 3) 1063
מֵצַח	forehead (5 · 13) 594
נֶאֱנָח	to sigh (4 · 12 · 12) 58
נֶאֱנָק	to cry, groan (2 · 4 · 4) 60
חוּס	5 to pity, look upon with compassion (9 · 24 · 24) 299
חָמַל	to spare, have compassion (7 · 40 · 40) 328
בָּחוּר	6 young man (5 · 45) 104
בְּתוּלָה	virgin (1 · 50) 143
טַף	[coll.] children (1 · 42) 381
מַשְׁחִית	destruction, ruin (4 · 19) 1008
תָּו	mark (2 · 3) 1063
אֲהָהּ	8 Alas! (4 · 15) 13
מֶטֶה	9 perverseness, perversion (1 · 1) 642
חוּס	10 to pity, look upon with compassion (9 · 24 · 24) 299
חָמַל	to spare, have compassion (7 · 40 · 40) 328
לָבוּשׁ	11 clothed with (9 · 16) 527 לבשׁ
בַּד	white linen (6 · 23) 94 I.

Chapter 10

רָקִיעַ	1 expanse (5 · 17) 956
סַפִּיר	sapphire (3 · 11) 705
דְּמוּת	likeness, similitude (16 · 25) 198
לָבוּשׁ	2 clothed with (9 · 16) 527 לבשׁ
בַּד	white linen (6 · 23) 94 I.
גַּלְגַּל	wheel, whirling (5 · 11) 165
חֹפֶן	hollow of hand (2 · 6) 342
גַּחֶלֶת	coal (3 · 18) 160
מִבֵּין	from between (9 · 21) 107 בֵּין 2.a.
זָרַק	to toss, throw (3 · 32 · 34) 284
פְּנִימִי	3 inner (24 · 33) 819
מִפְתָּן	4 threshold (5 · 8) 837
נֹגַהּ	brightness (5 · 19) 618
חִיצוֹן	5 outer (18 · 25) 300
שַׁדַּי	name of God (2 · 48) 994
לָבוּשׁ	6 clothed with (9 · 16) 527 לבשׁ
בַּד	white linen (6 · 23) 94 I.
מִבֵּין	from between (9 · 21) 107 בֵּין 2.a.
גַּלְגַּל	wheel, whirling (5 · 11) 165
אוֹפָן	wheel (25 · 35) 66
מִבֵּין	7 from between (9 · 21) 107 בֵּין 2.a.
חֹפֶן	hollow of hand (2 · 6) 342
לָבוּשׁ	clothed with (9 · 16) 527 לבשׁ
בַּד	white linen (6 · 23) 94 I.
תַּבְנִית	8 figure, image (3 · 20) 125
אוֹפָן	9 wheel (25 · 35) 66
תַּרְשִׁישׁ	[perh.] yellow jasper (3 · 7) 1076
דְּמוּת	10 likeness, similitude (16 · 25) 198
אוֹפָן	wheel (25 · 35) 66
רֶבַע	11 pl. = four sides (5 · 7) 917 I.
גַּב	12 back (7 · 13) 146
אוֹפָן	wheel (25 · 35) 66
אוֹפָן	13 wheel (25 · 35) 66
גַּלְגַּל	wheel, whirling (5 · 11) 165
אַרְיֵה	14 lion (2 · 45) 71

נֶשֶׁר		vulture, eagle (4 · 26) 676
נרמם	15	to rise up (3 · 4 · 5) 942
אוֹפָן	16	wheel (25 · 35) 66
מֵאֵצֶל		beside (2 · 6) 69 I. אֵצֶל
נרמם	17	to rise up (3 · 4 · 5) 942
מִפְתָּן	18	threshold (5 · 8) 837
נרמם	19	to rise up (3 · 4 · 5) 942
אוֹפָן		wheel (25 · 35) 66
לְעֻמָּה		side by side with (15 · 31) 769 עֻמָּה
קַדְמֹנִי		eastern (4 · 10) 870
מִלְמָעְלָה		above (6 · 24) 751 II. מַעַל 2.d.
דְּמוּת	21	likeness, similitude (16 · 25) 198
דְּמוּת	22	likeness, similitude (16 · 25) 198

Chapter 11

קַדְמֹנִי	1	eastern (4 · 10) 870
סִיר	3	pot (5 · 29) 696
מַעֲלָה	5	ascent, step, stair (9 · 47) 752
סִיר	7	pot (5 · 29) 696
שֶׁפֶט	9	judgment (10 · 16) 1048
סִיר	11	pot (5 · 29) 696
אֲהָהּ	13	Alas! (4 · 15) 13
כָּלָה		complete destruction, annihilation (3 · 22) 478
גְאֻלָּה	15	kin, kindred (1 · 14) 145
מוֹרָשָׁה		a possession (7 · 9) 440
שִׁקּוּץ	18	detested thing (8 · 28) 1055
שִׁקּוּץ	21	detested thing (8 · 28) 1055
אוֹפָן	22	wheel (25 · 35) 66
לְעֻמָּה		side by side with (15 · 31) 769 עֻמָּה
מִלְמָעְלָה		above (6 · 24) 751 מַעַל 2.d.
גּוֹלָה	24	[coll.] exiles (11 · 42) 163
גּוֹלָה	25	[coll.] exiles (11 · 42) 163

Chapter 12

מְרִי	2	rebellion (15 · 22) 598
גּוֹלָה	3	exile (11 · 42) 163
אוּלַי		perhaps (1 · 45) 19

מְרִי		rebellion (15 · 22) 598
גּוֹלָה	4	exile (11 · 42) 163
מוֹצָא		a going forth (4 · 27) 425 I.
חָתַר	5	to dig (5 · 8 · 8) 369
עֲלָטָה	6	thick darkness (3 · 4) 759
מוֹפֵת		sign, wonder (4 · 36) 68
גּוֹלָה	7	exile (11 · 42) 163
חָתַר		to dig (5 · 8 · 8) 369
עֲלָטָה		thick darkness (3 · 4) 759
מְרִי	9	rebellion (15 · 22) 598
מַשָּׂא	10	utterance (2 · 45) 672 III.
מוֹפֵת	11	sign, wonder (4 · 36) 68
גּוֹלָה		exile (11 · 42) 163
שְׁבִי		captivity (3 · 46) 985
עֲלָטָה	12	thick darkness (3 · 4) 759
חָתַר		to dig (5 · 8 · 8) 369
רֶשֶׁת	13	net (4 · 22) 440
מְצוּדָה		net (3 · 3) 845
עֵזֶר	14	help (1 · 21) 740
אֲגַף		bands, armies (7 · 7) 8
זרה		to scatter, disperse (10 · 25 · 38) 279
הריק		to empty out; i.e., draw (5 · 17 · 19) 937
זרה	15	to scatter, disperse (10 · 25 · 38) 279
דֶּבֶר	16	plague, pestilence (12 · 46) 184
רַעַשׁ	18	quaking, trembling (5 · 17) 950
רְגְזָה		quivering, shaking (1 · 1) 919
דְּאָגָה		anxiety, anxious care (3 · 6) 178
דְּאָגָה	19	anxiety, anxious care (3 · 6) 178
שִׁמָּמוֹן		horror, an appalling thing (2 · 2) 1031
מְלֹא		fullness (5 · 38) 571
חרב	20	to be waste, desolate (3 · 17 · 37) 351 II.
מָשָׁל	22	proverbial saying (8 · 39) 605 III.
ארך		to be long (2 · 3 · 34) 73
חָזוֹן		vision (7 · 35) 302
מָשָׁל	23	proverbial saying (8 · 39) 605 II.
משל		to use a proverb (6 · 7 · 15) 605 II.
חָזוֹן		vision (7 · 35) 302

114

חָזוֹן 24 vision (7 · 35) 302

מִקְסָם divination (2 · 2) 890

חָלָק flattery (1 · 12) 325

נִמְשַׁךְ 25 to be postponed (2 · 3 · 36) 604

מְרִי rebellion (15 · 22) 598

חָזוֹן 27 vision (7 · 35) 302

נִמְשַׁךְ 28 to be postponed (2 · 3 · 36) 604

Chapter 13

נָבָל 3 senseless (1 · 18) 614 I.

שׁוּעָל 4 fox (1 · 7) 1043

חָרְבָּה waste, ruin (14 · 42) 352

פֶּרֶץ 5 breach (2 · 18) 829

גָּדַר to wall up, shut off (2 · 7 · 7) 154

גָּדֵר wall, fence (4 · 14) 154

קֶסֶם 6 divination (4 · 11) 890

כָּזָב lie, falsehood (7 · 31) 469

יַחֵל to wait for = hope for (1 · 25 · 42) 403

מַחֲזֶה 7 vision (1 · 4) 303

מִקְסָם divination (2 · 2) 890

כָּזָב lie, falsehood (7 · 31) 469

כָּזָב 8 lie, falsehood (7 · 31) 469

קֹסֵם 9 to practice divination (6 · 11 · 11) 890

כָּזָב lie, falsehood (7 · 31) 469

סוֹד assembly, company (1 · 21) 691

כְּתָב register, enrollment (1 · 17) 508

בְּיַעַן 10 by the cause (2 · 3) 774

הִטְעָה to lead astray (1 · 1 · 1) 380

חַיִץ thin or party wall (1 · 1) 300

טוּחַ to coat, overlay (7 · 9 · 11) 376

תָּפֵל whitewash (5 · 6[?]) 1074

טוּחַ 11 to coat, overlay (7 · 9 · 11) 376

תָּפֵל whitewash (5 · 6[?]) 1074

גֶּשֶׁם rain, shower (6 · 35) 177

שָׁטַף to overflow, rinse or wash off (4 · 28 · 31) 1009

אֶלְגָּבִישׁ hail (3 · 3) 38

סְעָרָה tempest, storm wind (3 · 16) 704

אַיֵּה 12 where? (1 · 44) 32

טִיחַ a coating (1 · 1) 376

טוּחַ to coat, overlay (7 · 9 · 11) 376

סְעָרָה 13 tempest, storm wind (3 · 16) 704

גֶּשֶׁם rain, shower (6 · 35) 177

שָׁטַף to overflow, rinse or wash off (4 · 28 · 31) 1009

אֶלְגָּבִישׁ hail (3 · 3) 38

כָּלָה complete destruction, annihilation (3 · 22) 478

הָרַס 14 to throw down, tear down (4 · 30 · 33) 248

טוּחַ to coat, overlay (7 · 9 · 11) 376

תָּפֵל whitewash (5 · 6[?]) 1074

יְסוֹד foundation, base (2 · 19) 414

טוּחַ 15 to coat, overlay (7 · 9 · 11) 376

תָּפֵל whitewash (5 · 6[?]) 1074

חָזוֹן 16 vision (7 · 35) 302

תָּפַר 18 to keep sewing (1 · 1 · 4) 1074

כֶּסֶת band, fillets (2 · 2) 492

אַצִּיל joint; i.e., elbow (2 · 3) 69

מִסְפָּחָה long veil (2 · 2) 705

קוֹמָה height (8 · 45) 879

צוֹדֵד to hunt (4 · 4 · 16) 844

שֹׁעַל 19 handful (1 · 3) 1043

שְׂעֹרָה barley (4 · 34) 972

פְּתוֹת fragment, bit, morsel (1 · 1) 837

כַּזֵּב to lie (1 · 12 · 16) 469

כָּזָב lie, falsehood (7 · 31) 469

כֶּסֶת 20 band, fillet (2 · 2) 492

צוֹתֵת to hunt (4 · 4 · 16) 844

פָּרַח to fly (2 · 2 · 2) 827

מִסְפָּחָה 21 long veil (2 · 2) 705

מְצוּדָה prey, net (3 · 3) 845

הַכְאָה 22 to cause to be disheartened (1 · 1 · 3) 456

הִכְאִיב to pain, mar (2 · 4 · 8) 456

קֶסֶם 23 divination (4 · 11) 890

קֹסֵם to practice divination (6 · 11 · 11) 890

Chapter 14

גִּלּוּג	3	idol (39 · 48) 165
מִכְשׁוֹל		stumbling block (8 · 14) 506
נֹכַח		before (5 · 22) 647
גִּלּוּג	4	idol (39 · 48) 165
מִכְשׁוֹל		stumbling block (8 · 14) 506
נֹכַח		before (5 · 22) 647
נזור	5	to be estranged (1 · 2 · 6) 266 I. זור
גִּלּוּל		idol (39 · 48) 165
גִּלּוּל	6	idol (39 · 48) 165
נזר	7	to devote oneself, dedicate oneself (1 · 4 · 10) 634
גִּלּוּל		idol (39 · 48) 165
מִכְשׁוֹל		stumbling block (8 · 14) 506
נֹכַח		before (5 · 22) 647
מָשָׁל	8	byword (8 · 39) 605 II.
פתה	9	to be deceived (1 · 3 · 27) 834
פתה		to deceive (1 · 17 · 27) 834
תָּעָה	11	to err (7 · 27 · 50) 1073
מָעַל	13	to act unfaithfully, treacherously (7 · 35 · 35) 591
מַעַל		unfaithful, treacherous act (6 · 29) 591
לוּ	15	if (1 · 19) 530
שׁכל		to make childless (5 · 18 · 24) 1013
מִבְּלִי		so that there is no (2 · 25) 115
דֶּבֶר	19	plague, pestilence (12 · 46) 184
שֶׁפֶט	21	judgment (10 · 16) 1048
דֶּבֶר		plague, pestilence (12 · 46) 184
פְּלֵיטָה	22	escaped remnant (1 · 28) 812
עֲלִילָה		deed (8 · 24) 760
עֲלִילָה	23	deed (8 · 24) 760
חִנָּם		without cause, undeservedly (2 · 32) 336

Chapter 15

זְמוֹרָה	2	branch, twig (2 · 5) 274
יָתֵד	3	peg, pin (1 · 24) 450
תָּלָה		to hang up (1 · 23 · 27) 1067
אָכְלָה	4	consuming, eating (10 · 18) 38
נחר		to be scorched, charred (3 · 5 · 9) 359 I. חרר
נחר	5	to be scorched, charred (3 · 5 · 9) 359 I. חרר
אָכְלָה	6	consuming, eating (10 · 18) 38
מָעַל	8	to act unfaithfully, treacherously (7 · 35 · 35) 591
מַעַל		unfaithful, treacherous act (6 · 29) 591

Chapter 16

מְכֹרָה	3	origin (3 · 3) 468
מוֹלֶדֶת		circumstances of birth, birth (3 · 22) 409
מוֹלֶדֶת	4	circumstances of birth, birth (3 · 22) 409
שֹׁר		navel cord (1 · 3) 1057
מִשְׁעִי		cleansing (1 · 1) 606
המלח		המלח לא המלחת = not at all were you rubbed, washed, with salt (2 · 2 · 4) 572 III.
החתיל		החתל לא חתלת = not at all were you swaddled (1 · 1 · 2) 367
חוס	5	to pity, look upon with compassion (9 · 24 · 24) 299
חֶמְלָה		compassion (1 · 1) 328 חמל
גֹּעַל		loathing (1 · 1) 172
מִתְבּוֹסֶסֶת	6	ptc. = kick out (2 · 2 · 12) 100
רְבָבָה	7	myriad (1 · 16) 914
צֶמַח		growth, sprout (3 · 12) 855
עֲדִי		ornament (5 · 14) 725
שַׁד		breast (4 · 21) 994
שֵׂעָר		hair (1 · 28) 972

צָמַח	to grow abundantly (1 · 4 · 33) 855
עֵירֹם	nakedness (6 · 10) 735
עֶרְיָה	nakedness (4 · 6) 789
שָׁטַף 9	to overflow, rinse or wash off (4 · 28 · 31) 1009
סוּךְ	to anoint (1 · 7 · 9) 691 I.
רִקְמָה 10	variegated stuff (8 · 12) 955
נָעַל	to shoe (1 · 7 · 8) 653
תַּחַשׁ	a kind of leather or skin (1 · 14) 1065
חָבַשׁ	to bind, bind on (6 · 28 · 32) 289
שֵׁשׁ	linen (3 · 38) 1058
מֶשִׁי	[dub.] silk (2 · 2) 603
עָדָה 11	to ornament, deck (3 · 8 · 8) 725
עֲדִי	ornament (5 · 14) 725
צָמִיד	bracelet (2 · 6) 855
רָבִיד	chain (1 · 2) 914
גָּרוֹן	neck, throat (1 · 8) 173
נֶזֶם 12	ring (1 · 17) 633
עָגִיל	hoop, ring (1 · 2) 722
עֲטָרָה	crown (3 · 23) 742
עָדָה 13	to ornament, deck oneself (3 · 8 · 8) 725
מַלְבּוּשׁ	raiment, attire (1 · 8) 528
שֵׁשׁ	linen (3 · 38) 1058
מֶשִׁי	[dub.] silk (2 · 2) 603
רִקְמָה	variegated stuff (8 · 12) 955
יפה	to be beautiful (2 · 6 · 8) 421
מְלוּכָה	kingship, royalty (2 · 24) 574
יְפִי 14	beauty (10 · 19) 421
כָּלִיל	entire, whole (3 · 15) 483
הָדָר	ornament, honor (2 · 30) 214
יְפִי 15	beauty (10 · 19) 421
תַּזְנוּת	fornication (20 · 20) 276
טָלוּא 16	variegated (1 · 7[?]) 378 טלא
צֶלֶם 17	image (3 · 17) 853
רִקְמָה 18	variegated stuff (8 · 12) 955
נִיחֹחַ 19	a soothing, tranquilizing (4 · 43) 629
תַּזְנוּת 20	fornication (20 · 20) 276
תַּזְנוּת 22	fornication (20 · 20) 276

נְעוּרִים	youth (9 · 46) 655
עֵירֹם	nakedness (6 · 10) 735
עֶרְיָה	nakedness (4 · 6) 789
מִתְבּוֹסֶסֶת	ptc. = kick out (2 · 2 · 12) 100
אוֹי 23	Woe! Alas! (4 · 25) 17
גַּב 24	mound (7 · 13) 146
רָמָה	high place (4 · 5) 928
רְחוֹב	broad open place, plaza (2 · 43) 93
רָמָה 25	high place (4 · 5) 928
תעב	to cause to be an abomination (1 · 14 · 21) 107
יֳפִי	beauty (10 · 19) 421
פשׂק	to part, open wide (1 · 1 · 2) 832
תַּזְנוּת	fornication (20 · 20) 276
שָׁכֵן 26	neighbor (1 · 20) 1015
גָּדֵל	great (1 · 4) 152
תַּזְנוּת	fornication (20 · 20) 276
גרע 27	to diminish (2 · 14 · 22) 175
שֹׂנֵא	enemy (1 · 41[?]) 971
נכלם	to be humiliated, ashamed (6 · 26 · 38) 483
זִמָּה	wickedness (14 · 28) 273 I.
מִבַּלְתִּי 28	on account of, not (1 · 2) 116 בְּלֵת 4.b.
שָׂבְעָה	satiety (3 · 7[?]) 960
תַּזְנוּת 29	fornication (20 · 20) 276
כְּנַעַן	merchant[s] (2 · 4) 488
אֲמֻלָה 30	weak (1 · 1[?]) 51 עמל Qal.
לִבָּה	anger (1 · 1) 525
זוֹנָה	harlot (6 · 33) 275 זנה Qal. 1.
שַׁלֶּטֶת	domineering, imperious (1 · 1[?]) 1020
גַּב 31	mound (7 · 13) 146
רָמָה	high place (4 · 5) 928
רְחוֹב	broad open place, plaza (2 · 43) 932
זוֹנָה	harlot (6 · 33) 275 זנה Qal. 1.
קלס	to scoff, mock (1 · 1 · 4) 887
אֶתְנַן	hire [a harlot's earnings] (4 · 11) 1072
נאף 32	to commit adultery (3 · 14 · 31) 610

117

זוֹנָה 33 harlot (6 · 33) 275 זנה *Qal*. 1.

נֵדֶה gift (1 · 1) 622

נָדָן gift (1 · 1) 623 I.

מְאַהֵב lover (6 · 16) 12 אהב *Piel*

שׁחד to bribe (1 · 2) 1005

תַּזְנוּת fornication (20 · 20) 276

הֵפֶךְ 34 the contrary, opposite thing (2 · 3) 246

תַּזְנוּת fornication (20 · 20) 276

זוֹנָה לֹא ז׳ fornication was not done (>50) 275 *Pual*

אֶתְנַן hire [a harlot's earnings] (4 · 11) 1072

זוֹנָה 35 harlot (6 · 33) 275 זנה *Qal*. 3.

נְחֹשֶׁת 36 lust, harlotry (1 · 1) 639

תַּזְנוּת fornication (20 · 20) 276

מְאַהֵב lover (6 · 16) 12 אהב *Piel*

גִּלּוּל idol (39 · 48) 165

מְאַהֵב 37 lover (6 · 16) 12 אהב *Piel*

ערב to be sweet, pleasing (1 · 8 · 8) 787

נאף 38 to commit adultery (3 · 17 · 31) 610

קִנְאָה anger (10 · 43) 888

הָרַס 39 to throw down, tear down (4 · 30 · 43) 248

גַּב mound (7 · 13) 146

נתץ to tear down (1 · 3 · 42) 683

רָמָה high place (4 · 5) 928

הִפְשִׁיט to strip (2 · 15 · 43) 833

הִנִּיחוּךְ I will leave you (>50) 628 נוח *Hiph.* B. 2.

עֵירֹם nakedness (6 · 10) 735

עֶרְיָה nakedness (4 · 6) 789

רגם 40 to kill by stoning (2 · 15 · 15) 920

בתק to cut, cut down (1 · 1 · 1) 144

שֶׁפֶט 41 judgment (10 · 15) 1048

זוֹנָה harlot (6 · 33) 275 זנה *Qal*. 3.

אֶתְנַן hire [a harlot's earnings] (4 · 11) 1072

קִנְאָה 42 anger (10 · 43) 888

שָׁקַט to be quiet, inactive (2 · 31 · 41) 1052

נְעוּרִים 43 youth (9 · 46) 655

רָגַז to be excited, perturbed (1 · 30 · 41) 919

הֵא Lo! Behold! (1 · 2) 210

זִמָּה wickedness (14 · 28) 273 I.

משׁל 44 to use a proverb (6 · 7 · 15) 605 II.

גּעל 45 to abhor, loathe (2 · 8 · 10) 171

קָטָן 46 small (3 · 47) 881

קָט 47 [dub.] only (1 · 1) 881

גָּאוֹן 49 exaltation, majesty, excellency (9 · 49) 144

שִׂבְעָה satiety (3 · 7[?]) 960 שָׂבְעָה

שַׁלְוָה ease, careless security (1 · 8) 1017

הִשְׁקִיט to show quietness (1 · 10 · 41) 1052

גָּבַהּ 50 to be haughty (8 · 24 · 34) 146

צדק 51 to justify (2 · 5 · 41) 842

כְּלִמָּה 52 reproach, ignominy (13 · 30) 484

פלל to mediate (1 · 4 · 5) 813

הִתְעִיב to do abominably (1 · 4 · 21) 1073

צדק to be justified (1 · 22 · 41) 842

צדק to justify (2 · 5 · 41) 842

שְׁבִית 53 captivity (2 · 6) 986

שְׁבִית captivity (5 · 26) 986

כְּלִמָּה 54 reproach, ignominy (13 · 30) 484

נכלם to be humiliated, ashamed (6 · 26 · 38) 483

קַדְמָה 55 former state (4 · 6) 870

שְׁמוּעָה 56 mention (4 · 27) 1035

גָּאוֹן exaltation, majesty, excellence (9 · 49) 144

בְּטֶרֶם 57 before (1 · 39) 382 טֶרֶם

שָׁאטוֹת ptc. = one who despises (3 · 3 · 3) 1002 II. שׁוט

זִמָּת 58 wickedness (14 · 28) 273 I.

בָּזָה 59 to despise, regard with contempt (5 · 31 · 42) 102

אָלָה oath (5 · 36) 46

הֵפֵר to break, frustrate (5 · 41 · 44[?]) 830

נְעוּרִים 60 youth (9 · 46) 655

נכלם 61 to be humiliated, ashamed (6 · 26 · 38) 483
קָטֹן small (3 · 47) 881
פְּתָחוֹן 63 opening (2 · 2) 836
כְּלִמָּה reproach, ignominy (13 · 30) 484

Chapter 17

חוד 2 to propound a riddle (1 · 4 · 4) 295
חִידָה riddle (1 · 17) 295
מָשַׁל to use a parable (6 · 7 · 15) 605 II.
מָשָׁל similitude, parable (8 · 39) 605 II
נֶשֶׁר 3 vulture, eagle (4 · 26) 676
אָרֵךְ long (1 · 15) 74
אֵבֶר pinions (1 · 3) 7
נוֹצָה plumage (2 · 3) 663
רִקְמָה variegated work (8 · 12) 955
צַמֶּרֶת treetop (5 · 5) 856
יְנִיקָה 4 shoot, twig (1 · 1) 413
קָטַף to pluck off (2 · 4 · 5) 882
כְּנַעַן merchant[s] (2 · 4) 484 II.
רֹכֵל trader (11 · 17[?]) 940 רכל
צַפְצָפָה 5 [a kind of] willow (1 · 1) 861
צָמַח 6 to sprout, spring up (1 · 15 · 33) 855
סרח ptc. = overrunning, spreading (1 · 3 · 4) 710
שָׁפָל low (6 · 18) 1050
קוֹמָה height (8 · 45) 879
דָּלִיּוֹת branches, boughs (7 · 8) 194
שֹׁרֶשׁ root (5 · 33) 1057
בַּד rods or shoots (2 · 41) 94 II. בַּד 3.(b)
פֹּארָה bough (6 · 6) 802
נֶשֶׁר 7 vulture, eagle (4 · 26) 676
נוֹצָה plumage (2 · 3) 663
כפן to stretch hungrily (1 · 1 · 1) 495
שֹׁרֶשׁ root (5 · 33) 1057
דָּלִיּוֹת branches, boughs (7 · 8) 194
עֲרוּגָה garden terrace, bed (2 · 4) 788
מַטָּע planting place; עֲרֻגֹת מ׳ = beds

where it was planted (3 · 6) 642
שׁתל 8 to transplant (6 · 10 · 10) 1060
עָנָף branch[es], bough[s] (4 · 7) 778
אַדֶּרֶת glory, magnificence (1 · 12) 12
שֹׁרֶשׁ 9 root (5 · 33) 1057
נתק to tear out, up (2 · 11 · 27) 683
קוסס to strip off (1 · 1 · 1) 890
טָרָף fresh-plucked (1 · 2) 383
צֶמַח growth, sprout (3 · 12) 855
שׁתל 10 to transplant (6 · 10 · 10) 1060
עֲרוּגָה garden terrace or bed (2 · 4) 788
צֶמַח growth, sprout (3 · 12) 855
מְרִי 12 rebellion (15 · 22) 598
מְלוּכָה 13 royalty, kingship (2 · 24) 574
אָלָה oath (5 · 36) 46
אֵילֵי mighty (>50) 42 אל
שָׁפָל 14 low (6 · 18) 1050
מרד 15 to rebel, revolt (4 · 25 · 25) 597
הפר to break, frustrate (5 · 41 · 44) 830
בָּזָה 16 to despise, regard with contempt (5 · 31 · 42) 102
אָלָה oath (5 · 36) 46
הֵפֵר to break, frustrate (5 · 41 · 44) 830
סֹלְלָה 17 mound (4 · 11) 700
דָּיֵק bulwark, siege wall (4 · 6) 189
בָּזָה 18 to despise, regard with contempt (5 · 31 · 42) 102
אָלָה oath (5 · 36) 46
הֵפֵר to break, frustrate (5 · 41 · 44) 830
אָלָה 19 oath (5 · 36) 46
בָּזָה to despise, regard with contempt (5 · 31 · 42) 102
הֵפִיר to break, violate (1 · 3 · 3[?]) 830
רֶשֶׁת 20 net (4 · 22) 440
מְצוּדָה net (3 · 3) 845
מַעַל unfaithful, treacherous act (6 · 29) 591
מָעַל to act unfaithfully, treacherously (7 · 35 · 35) 591
מִבְרָח 21 fugitive (1 · 1) 138

אֲגַף   bands, armies (7 · 7) 8

צַמֶּרֶת 22 treetop (5 · 5) 856

רָם   high (5 · 31[?]) 926 רום

יוֹנֶקֶת   shoot, twig (1 · 6) 413

רַךְ   tender, delicate, soft (1 · 16) 940

קָטַף   to pluck off (2 · 4 · 5) 882

שָׁתַל   to transplant (6 · 10 · 10) 1060

גָּבֹהַּ   high, exalted (6 · 41) 147

תָּלוּל   exalted, lofty (1 · 1) 1068

שָׁתַל 23 to transplant (6 · 10 · 10) 1060

עָנָף   branch[es], bough[s] (4 · 7) 778

אַדִּיר   majestic (2 · 27) 12

צִפּוֹר   bird [coll.] (3 · 40) 861

דָּלִיּוֹת   branches, boughs (7 · 8) 194

הִשְׁפִּיל 24 to lay low, humiliate (2 · 9 · 30) 1050

גָּבֹהַּ   high, exalted (6 · 41) 147

הגביה   to make high, exalt (2 · 10 · 34) 146

שָׁפָל   low (6 · 18) 1050

לַח   moist, fresh (2 · 6) 535

הפריח   to cause to bud, sprout (1 · 5 · 34) 827

יָבֵשׁ   dry (4 · 9) 386

Chapter 18

מָשַׁל 2 to use a proverb (6 · 7 · 15) 605 II.

מָשָׁל   proverbial saying (8 · 39) 605 II.

בֹּסֶר   [coll.] unripe or sour grapes (1 · 5) 126

קָהָה   to be dull, blunt (1 · 3 · 4) 874

מָשַׁל 3 to use a proverb (6 · 7 · 15) 605 II.

מָשָׁל   proverbial saying (8 · 39) 605 II.

גִּלּוּל 6 idol (39 · 48) 165

נִדָּה   impurity (5 · 30) 622

הוֹנָה 7 to oppress, maltreat (7 · 14 · 18) 413 ינה

חֲבֹלָה   pledge (5 · 6[?]) 287

חוֹב   debt (1 · 1) 295

גְּזֵלָה   plunder, spoil (4 · 6) 160

גָּזַל   to seize, plunder (5 · 29 · 30) 159

רָעֵב   hungry (2 · 19) 944

עֵירֹם   naked (6 · 10) 735

נֶשֶׁךְ 8 interest, usury (4 · 12) 675

תַּרְבִּית   increment, interest, usury (4 · 6) 916

עָוֶל   injustice, unrighteousness (10 · 21) 732

פָּרִיץ 10 violent one (2 · 6) 829

הוֹנָה 12 to oppress, maltreat (7 · 14 · 18) 413 ינה

גְּזֵלָה   plunder, spoil (4 · 6) 160

גָּזַל   to seize, plunder (5 · 29 · 30) 159

חָבַל   pledge (3 · 3) 287

גִּלּוּל   idol (39 · 48) 165

נֶשֶׁךְ 13 interest, usury (4 · 12) 675

תַּרְבִּית   increment, interest, usury (4 · 6) 916

גִּלּוּל 15 idol (39 · 48) 165

הוֹנָה 16 to oppress, maltreat (7 · 14 · 18) 413 ינה

חָבַל   pledge (3 · 3) 287

חבל   to bind, pledge (2 · 13 · 14) 286

גְּזֵלָה   plunder, spoil (4 · 6) 160

גָּזַל   to seize, plunder (5 · 29 · 30) 159

רָעֵב   hungry (2 · 19) 944

עֵירֹם   naked (6 · 10) 735

נֶשֶׁךְ 17 interest, usury (4 · 12) 675

תַּרְבִּית   increment, interest, usury (4 · 6) 916

עָשַׁק 18 to practice extortion (3 · 36 · 37) 798

עֹשֶׁק   oppression, extortion (4 · 15) 799

גָּזַל   to seize, plunder (5 · 29 · 30) 159

גֵּזֶל   robbery; here as acc. cogn. = thing plundered, plunder (1 · 2) 160 גזל

עַם   kinsman (1 · 34) 769

מַדֻּעַ 19 defective for מַדּוּעַ wherefore? 396

רִשְׁעָה 20 wickedness (5 · 15) 958

עָוֶל 24 injustice, unrighteousness (10 · 21) 732

מַעַל   unfaithful, treacherous act (6 · 29) 591

מָעַל   to act unfaithfully, treacherously (7 · 35 · 35) 591

נתכן 25 to be adjusted to standard (9 · 10 · 18) 1067

עָוֶל 26 injustice, unrighteousness (10 · 21) 1067

רִשְׁעָה 27 wickedness (5 · 15) 958

נתכן 29 to be adjusted to standard (9 · 10 · 18) 1067

מִכְשׁוֹל 30 stumbling block (8 · 14) 506

פָּשַׁע 31 to transgress (3 · 40 · 41) 833

Chapter 19

קִינָה 1 elegy, dirge (9 · 17) 884

לְבִיָּא 2 lioness (1 · 1) 522

אֲרִי lion (3 · 35) 71

רָבַץ to lie down, lie (3 · 24 · 30) 918

כְּפִיר young lion (7 · 31) 498

גּוּר whelp, young (3 · 7) 158 II.

גּוּר 3 whelp, young (3 · 7) 158 II.

כְּפִיר young lion (7 · 31) 498

טָרַף to tear, rend (4 · 19 · 24) 382

טֶרֶף prey (4 · 18) 383

שַׁחַת 4 pit (3 · 23) 1001

חָח hook, ring (4 · 7) 296

נוחל 5 to wait, tarry (1 · 2 · 42) 403

תִּקְוָה things hoped for, outcome (2 · 32) 876

גּוּר whelp, young (3 · 7) 158 II.

כְּפִיר young lion (7 · 31) 498

אֲרִי 6 lion (3 · 35) 71

כְּפִיר young lion (7 · 31) 498

טָרַף to tear, rend (4 · 19 · 24) 382

טֶרֶף prey (4 · 18) 383

הֶחֱרִיב 7 to lay waste, make desolate (1 · 13 · 37) 351 II.

מְלֹא fullness (5 · 38) 571

שְׁאָגָה roaring (1 · 7) 980

מְדִינָה 8 province (1 · 44) 193

רֶשֶׁת net (4 · 22) 440

שַׁחַת pit (3 · 23) 1001

סוּגַר 9 prison, cage (1 · 1) 689

חָח hook, ring (4 · 7) 296

מְצוֹדָה net (1 · 3) 845

שָׁתַל 10 to transplant (6 · 10 · 10) 1060

פָּרָה to be fruitful, bear fruit (2 · 22 · 29) 826

עָנֵף full of branches (1 · 1) 778

משׁל 11 ruler (1 · 24) 605 III. מָשָׁל

גָּבַהּ to be high, lofty, tall (8 · 24 · 34) 146

קוֹמָה height (8 · 45) 879

עָבֹת interwoven foliage (6 · 24) 721

גֹּבַהּ height (6 · 17) 147

דָּלִיּוֹת branches, boughs (7 · 8) 194

התשׁ 12 to be rooted up (1 · 1 · 21) 684

התפרק to be broken off (1 · 3 · 10) 830

שָׁתַל 13 to transplant (6 · 10 · 10) 1060

צִיָּה drought (1 · 16) 851

צָמָא thirst (1 · 17) 854

בַּד 14 rods or shoots (2 · 41) 93 II. בַּד 3. (b)

קִינָה elegy, dirge (9 · 17) 884

Chapter 20

עָשׂוֹר 1 tenth day (3 · 15) 797

תּוּר 6 to seek out, select (1 · 19 · 22) 1064

זוב ptc. = flowing (2 · 29 · 29) 264

חָלָב milk (3 · 44) 316

צְבִי beauty, decoration (5 · 18) 840

שִׁקּוּץ 7 detested thing (8 · 28) 1055

גִּלּוּל idol (39 · 48) 165

המרה 8 to show disobedience, rebelliousness (4 · 22 · 43) 598

שִׁקּוּץ detested thing (8 · 28) 1055

גִּלּוּל idol (39 · 48) 165

המרה 13 to show disobedience, rebelliousness (4 · 22 · 43) 598

זוב 15 ptc. = flowing (2 · 29 · 29) 264

חָלָב milk (3 · 44) 316

צְבִי beauty, decoration (5 · 18) 840

גִּלּוּל 16 idol (39 · 48) 165

חוּס 17 to pity, look upon with compassion (9 · 24 · 24) 299

כָּלָה complete destruction, annihilation (3 · 22) 478

גִּלּוּל 18 idol (39 · 48) 165

הִמְרָה 21 to show disobedience, rebelliousness (4 · 22 · 43) 598

זָרָה 23 to scatter, disperse (10 · 25 · 38) 279

גִּלּוּל 24 idol (39 · 48) 165

מַתָּנָה 26 gift (5 · 17) 682

פֶּטֶר firstborn (1 · 11) 809

רֶחֶם womb (1 · 33) 933

גָּדַף 27 to blaspheme (1 · 7 · 7) 154

מַעַל unfaithful, treacherous act (6 · 29) 591

מָעַל to act unfaithfully, treacherously (7 · 35 · 35) 591

רָם 28 high (5 · 31[?]) 926 רוּם

עָבוֹת leafy (2 · 4) 721

כַּעַס vexation, anger (1 · 25) 429

נִיחֹחַ a soothing, tranquilizing (4 · 43) 629

הִסִּיךְ to pour out libations (1 · 14 · 25) 650 I.

שִׁקּוּץ 30 detested thing (8 · 28) 1055

מַתָּנָה 31 gift (5 · 17) 682

גִּלּוּל idol (39 · 48) 165

מָסֹרֶת 37 bond (1 · 1) 64

בָּרַר 38 to purge out, purify (1 · 7 · 15) 140

מָרַד to rebel, revolt (4 · 25 · 25) 597

פָּשַׁע to transgress (3 · 40 · 41) 833

מְגוּרִים sojourning (place) (1 · 11) 158 I. מָגוֹר

מַתָּנָה 39 gift (5 · 17) 682

גִּלּוּל idol (39 · 48) 165

מַשְׂאֵת 40 offering, portion (1 · 16) 673

נִיחֹחַ 41 a soothing, tranquilizing (4 · 43) 629

עֲלִילָה 43 deed (8 · 24) 760

נָקֹט to feel loathing (3 · 4 · 7) 876

בִּפְנֵי against (4 · 17) 815 פָּנֶה II. 3.

עֲלִילָה 44 deed (8 · 24) 76

Chapter 21

תֵּימָן 2 south (4 · 24) 412

הִטִּיף to discourse; to drip (2 · 9 · 18) 643

דָּרוֹם south (13 · 17) 204

הִצִּית 3 to kindle, set on fire (1 · 17 · 27) 428

לַח moist, fresh (2 · 6) 525

יָבֵשׁ dry (4 · 9) 386

כבה to be quenched, extinguished (2 · 14 · 24) 459

לֶהָבָה flame (1 · 19) 529

שַׁלְהֶבֶת flame (1 · 2[?]) 529

נִצְרַב to be scorched (1 · 1 · 1) 863

כבה 4 to be quenched, extinguished (2 · 14 · 24) 459

אֲהָהּ 5 Alas! (4 · 15) 13

משׁל to make a parable (1 · 1 · 15) 605 II.

מָשָׁל similitude, parable (8 · 39) 605 II.

הִטִּיף 7 to discourse, drip (2 · 9 · 18) 643

תַּעַר 8 sheath (5 · 13) 789

תַּעַר 9 sheath (5 · 13) 789

תַּעַר 10 sheath (5 · 13) 789

נֶאֱנַח 11 to sigh (4 · 12 · 12) 58

שִׁבָּרוֹן breaking, crushing (1 · 2) 991

מָתְנַיִם loins (12 · 47) 608

מְרִירוּת bitterness (1 · 1) 601

נֶאֱנַח 12 to sigh (4 · 12 · 12) 58

שְׁמוּעָה report (4 · 27) 1035

נָמֵס to faint, grow fearful (1 · 19 · 21) 587

רָפָה to lose heart (2 · 14 · 45) 951

כהה to grow faint (1 · 4 · 10) 462 I.

בֶּרֶךְ knee (3 · 25) 139

הוּחַד 14 to be sharpened (3 · 3 · 6) 292 חדד

מרט to polish, scour (4 · 7 · 14) 598

טבח 15 to slay, kill ruthlessly (1 · 11 · 11) 370

122

טֶבַח slaughtering, slaughter (3 · 12) 370

הוחד to be sharpened (3 · 3 · 6) 292 חדד

בָּרָק lightning (4 · 21) 140

מרט to be polished, scoured (2 · 5 · 14) 598

שָׂשׂ to exult (1 · 26 · 26) 965

מרט 16 to polish, scour (4 · 7 · 14) 598

הוחד to be sharpened (3 · 3 · 6) 292 חדד

מרט to be polished, scoured (2 · 5 · 14) 598

הילל 17 to utter, make a howling, give a howl (2 · 30 · 30) 410

מגר ptc. pass. = thrown (1 · 1 · 2) 550

ספק to slap (1 · 6 · 6) 706

יָרֵךְ thigh (2 · 34) 437

בֹּחַן 18 the trial has been made (1 · 1 · 29) 103 בֹּחַן Pual

נכפל 19 [dub.] to be doubled (1 · 1 · 5) 495

חדר to surround, enclose (1 · 1 · 1) 293

מוג 20 to melt; inf. = faint (1 · 4 · 17) 556

מִכְשׁוֹל a stumbling (8 · 14) 506

אִבְחָה slaughter (1 · 4) 5 Lis. טִבְחָה

אָח Ah! Alas! (2 · 2) 25

בָּרָק lightning (4 · 21) 140

מְעֻטָּה read מְרֻטָּה, ptc. pass. of מרט, to scour, polish (1 · 1) 598 מרט Qal 2.

טֶבַח slaughtering, slaughter (3 · 12) 370

התאחד 21 to show oneself sharp; unite oneself (1 · 1 · 1[?]) 25 אחד

הימין to go to the right (1 · 5 · 5) 412

השמיל to go to the left (1 · 5 · 5) 970 שמאל

אָנָה whence? whither? (1 · 39) 33

מֻעָדוֹת Hoph. ptc. = to be set (1 · 2 · 28) 416 יעד

ברא 24 to cut down (3 · 5 · 5) 135 I. ברא Piel

בָּצוּר 25 cut off, made inaccessible (2 · 25) 130 בצר

קסם 26 to practice divination (6 · 11 · 11) 890

קֶסֶם divination (4 · 11) 890

תְּרָפִים idol (1 · 15) 1076

כָּבֵד liver (1 · 14) 458

קֶסֶם 27 divination (4 · 11) 890

כַּר battering ram (5 · 12) 305 III

רֶצַח slaughter (1 · 2) 954

תְּרוּעָה alarm, war cry (1 · 36) 929

סֹלְלָה mound (4 · 11) 700

דָּיֵק bulwark, siege wall (4 · 6) 189

קסם 28 to practice divination (6 · 11 · 11) 890

שְׁבֻעֵי Qal pass. ptc. שבע 989

שְׁבוּעָה oath, curse (1 · 30) 989

עֲלִילָה 29 deed (8 · 24) 760

מִצְנֶפֶת 31 turban (1 · 12) 857

עֲטָרָה crown (3 · 23) 742

שָׁפָל low (6 · 18) 1050

הגביה to make high, exalt (2 · 10 · 34) 146

גָּבֹהַּ exalted, high (6 · 41) 147

השפיל to lay low, humiliate (2 · 9 · 30) 1050

עַוָּה 32 distortion, ruin (3 · 3) 730

טֶבַח 33 slaughtering (3 · 12) 370

מרט to polish, scour (4 · 7 · 14) 598

הכיל to contain, hold, hold in, endure (2 · 12 · 38) 465

בָּרָק lightning (4 · 21) 140

קסם 34 to practice divination (6 · 11 · 11) 890

כָּזָב lie, falsehood (7 · 31) 469

צַוָּאר neck, back of neck (1 · 41) 848

תַּעַר 35 sheath (5 · 31) 789

נברא to be created (3 · 10 · 48) 135 I.

מְכוּרָה origin (3 · 3) 468 מְכֹרָה

זַעַם 36 indignation (3 · 22) 276

עֶבְרָה rage, fury (5 · 35) 720

הפיח to blow (1 · 12 · 14) 806

בער ptc. = inhuman, cruel, barbarous (1 · 3 · 7) 129 II.

חָרָשׁ graver, artificer (1 · 38) 360

מַשְׁחִית destruction, ruin (4 · 19) 1008

אָכְלָה 37 consuming, eating (10 · 18) 38

Chapter 22

גִּלּוּל 3 idol (39 · 48) 165

אָשֵׁם 4 to be [become] guilty (4 · 33 · 35) 79

גִּלּוּל idol (39 · 48) 165

קַלָּסָה derision (1 · 1) 887

הִתְקַלֵּס 5 to scoff, mock, deride (1 · 3 · 4) 887

מְהוּמָה disturbance, turmoil (2 · 12) 223

עֹשֶׁק 7 oppression, extortion (4 · 15) 799

יָתוֹם orphan (1 · 42) 450

הוֹנָה to oppress, maltreat (7 · 14 · 18) 413
ינה

בָּזָה 8 to despise, regard with contempt (5 · 31 · 42) 102

רָכִיל 9 slander (1 · 6) 940

זִמָּה wickedness (14 · 28) 273 I.

נִדָּה 10 impurity (5 · 30) 622

כַּלָּה 11 daughter-in-law (1 · 34) 483

זִמָּה wickedness (14 · 28) 273 I.

שֹׁחַד 12 bribe (1 · 23) 1005

נֶשֶׁךְ interest, usury (4 · 12) 675

תַּרְבִּית increment, interest, usury (4 · 6) 916

בָּצַע to violently make gain of (1 · 6 · 16) 130

עֹשֶׁק oppression, extortion (4 · 15) 799

בֶּצַע 13 unjust gain (3 · 23) 130

זרה 15 to scatter, disperse (10 · 25 · 38) 279

טֻמְאָה uncleanness (8 · 37) 380

סוּג 18 dross (3 · 8) 691 סיג

בְּדִיל tin (3 · 5) 95

עֹפֶרֶת lead [metal] (3 · 9) 780

כּוּר smelting pot, furnace (3 · 9) 468

סרג 19 dross (3 · 8) 691 סיג

קְבֻצָה 20 gathering (1 · 1) 868

עֹפֶרֶת lead [metal] (3 · 9) 780

בְּדִיל tin (3 · 5) 95

כּוּר smelting pot, furnace (3 · 9) 468

לָפַחַת inf. = to breathe, blow (3 · 9 · 12) נפה 655

הַנְתִּיךְ inf. cs. to melt (2 · 5 · 21) 677

הִתִּיךְ to melt (2 · 5 · 21) 677 נתך

כּנס 21 to gather (2 · 3 · 11) 488

נפח to breathe, blow; inf. = פַּחַת (3 · 9 · 12) 655

עֶבְרָה rage, fury (5 · 34) 720

נִתַּךְ to be poured forth (2 · 8 · 21) 677

הִתּוּךְ 22 a melting (1 · 1) 678

כּוּר smelting pot, furnace (3 · 9) 468

הֻתַּךְ to be melted (1 · 1 · 21) 677

גֶּשֶׁם 24 rain (1 · 1) 177

זַעַם indignation (3 · 22) 276

קֶשֶׁר 25 conspiracy (1 · 16) 905

אֲרִי lion (3 · 35) 71

שָׁאַג to roar (1 · 20 · 20) 980

טָרַף to tear, rend (4 · 19 · 24) 382

טֶרֶף prey (4 · 18) 383

חֹסֶן wealth, treasure (1 · 5) 340

יְקָר precious things [coll.] (1 · 17) 430

חמס 26 to treat violently, wrong (1 · 7 · 7) 329

חֹל profaneness, commonness (4 · 11) 320

הִבְדִּיל to make a distinction, separate (3 · 32 · 42) 95

הֶעְלִים to conceal, hide (1 · 11 · 29) 761

זְאֵב 27 wolf (1 · 8) 255

טָרַף to tear, rend (4 · 19 · 24) 382

טֶרֶף prey (4 · 18) 383

בֶּצַע unjust gain (3 · 23) 130

בָּצַע to gain by violence or wrongfully (1 · 10 · 16) 130

טוח 28 to coat, overlay (7 · 9 · 11) 376

תָּפֵל whitewash (5 · 6[?]) 1074

קסם to practice divination (6 · 11 · 11) 890

כָּזָב lie, falsehood (7 · 31) 469

עָשַׁק 29 to practice extortion (3 · 36 · 37) 798

עָשַׁק oppression, extortion (4 · 15) 799

גָּזַל to seize, plunder (5 · 29 · 30) 159

גָּזֵל robbery; here as acc. cogn. = thing plundered, plunder (1 · 4) 160

הוֹנָה to oppress, maltreat (7 · 14 · 18) 413 ינה

בְּלֹא without (1 · 30) 518 לא, 4.a.

גָּדַר 30 to wall up, shut off (2 · 7 · 7) 154

גָּדֵר wall, fence (4 · 14) 154

פֶּרֶץ breach (2 · 18) 829

זַעַם 31 indignation (3 · 22) 276

עֶבְרָה rage, fury (5 · 34) 720

Chapter 23

נְעוּרִים 3 youth (9 · 46) 655

מָעַךְ to press, squeeze (1 · 1 · 3) 590

שַׁד breast (4 · 21) 994

עִשָּׂה to press, squeeze (2 · 2 · 3[?]) 796

דַּד teat, nipple, breast (3 · 4) 186

בְּתוּלִים virginity (2 · 10) 144

עגב 5 to lust (6 · 7 · 7) 721

מְאַהֵב lover (6 · 16) 12 אהב Piel

לָבוּשׁ 6 clothed with (9 · 16) 527 לבשׁ

תְּכֵלֶת violet fabric (3 · 49) 1067

פֶּחָה governor (3 · 28) 808

סָגָן perfect (3 · 17) 688

בָּחוּר young man (5 · 45) 104

חֶמֶד desirable = fine, attractive (3 · 5) 326

תַּזְנוּת 7 fornication (20 · 20) 276

מִבְחָר choicest, best (4 · 12) 104 I.

עגב to lust (6 · 7 · 7) 721

גִּלּוּל idol (39 · 48) 165

תַּזְנוּת 8 fornication (20 · 20) 276

נְעוּרִים youth (9 · 46) 655

עִשָּׂה to press, squeeze (2 · 2 · 3[?]) 796

דַּד teat, nipple, breast (3 · 4) 186

בְּתוּלִים virginity (2 · 10) 144

מְאַהֵב 9 lover (6 · 16) 12 אהב Piel

עגב to lust (6 · 7 · 7) 721

שְׁפוֹט 10 judgment, act of judgment (1 · 2) 1048

עֶגְבָה 11 lustfulness (1 · 1) 721

תַּזְנוּת fornication (20 · 20) 276

זְנוּנִים fornication (2 · 12) 276

עגב 12 to lust (6 · 7 · 7) 721

פֶּחָה governor (3 · 28) 808

סָגָן perfect (3 · 17) 688

לָבוּשׁ clothed with (9 · 16) 527 לבשׁ

מִכְלוֹל perfection (2 · 2) 483

בָּחוּר young man (5 · 45) 104

חֶמֶר desirable = fine, attractive (3 · 5) 326

לִשְׁתֵּיהֶן 13 הן + שׁתים + ל to both of them 1040 שְׁנַיִם 1.a.

תַּזְנוּת 14 fornication (20 · 20) 276

מְחֻקֶּה Pual ptc. = carved (2 · 3 · 4) 348 חקה

צֶלֶם image (3 · 17) 853

חקק to engrave, inscribe (2 · 8 · 11) 349

שָׁשֵׁר red color, vermilion (1 · 2) 1059

חָגוֹר 15 girt, girded (1 · 1) 292

אֵזוֹר waistcloth (1 · 14) 25

מָתְנַיִם loins (12 · 47) 608

סָרוּחַ overhung (1 · 3[?]) 710 סרח

טְבוּל turban (1 · 1) 371

שָׁלִישׁ adjutant, officer (2 · 16) 1026

דְּמוּת likeness, similitude (16 · 25) 198

מוֹלֶדֶת kindred (3 · 22) 409

עגב 16 to lust (6 · 7 · 7) 721

מִשְׁכָּב 17 lying down, couch (2 · 46) 1012

תַּזְנוּת fornication (20 · 20) 276

יקע to be torn away, alienated (2 · 4 · 8) 429

תַּזְנוּת 18 fornication (20 · 20) 276

נקע to be estranged, alienated (3 · 3 · 3) 668

יקע to be torn away, alienated (2 · 4 · 8) 429

תַזְנוּת 19 fornication (20 · 20) 276

נְעוּרִים youth (9 · 46) 655

עגב 20 to lust (6 · 7 · 7) 271

פִּלֶגֶשׁ concubine (1 · 37) 811

זִרְמָה issue (2 · 2) 281

זִמָּה 21 wickedness (14 · 28) 273 I.

נְעוּרִים youth (9 · 46) 655

עשה to press, squeeze (1 · 1 · 3[?]) 796

דַּד teat, nipple, breast (3 · 4) 186

שַׁד breast (4 · 21) 994

מְאַהֵב 22 lover (6 · 16) 12 אָהֵב *Piel*

נקע to be estranged, alienated (3 · 3 · 3) 668

בָּחוּר 23 young man (5 · 45) 104

חֶמֶד desirable, fine, attractive (3 · 5) 326

פֶּחָה governor (3 · 28) 808

סָגָן perfect (3 · 17) 688

שָׁלִישׁ adjutant, officer (2 · 16) 1026

הֹצֶן 24 [dub.] multitude; shoulder, arms (1 · 1) 246

גַּלְגַּל [coll.] wheel (5 · 11) 165

צִנָּה large shield (4 · 20) 857

קוֹבַע helmet (1 · 2) 875

קִנְאָה 25 anger (10 · 43) 888

הִפְשִׁיט 26 to strip (2 · 15 · 43) 844

זִמָּה 27 wickedness (14 · 28) 273 I.

זְנוּת fornication (3 · 9) 276

נקע 28 to be estranged, alienated (3 · 3 · 3) 668

שָׂנֵא 29 hating, hatred (2 · 17) 971

יְגִיעַ toil, product (1 · 16) 388

עֵירֹם nakedness (6 · 10) 735

עֶרְיָה nakedness (4 · 6) 789

זְנוּנִים fornication (2 · 12) 276

זִמָּה wickedness (14 · 28) 273 I.

תַזְנוּת fornication (20 · 20) 276

גִּלּוּל 30 idol (39 · 48) 165

כּוֹס 31 cup (4 · 31) 468

כּוֹס 32 cup (4 · 31) 468

עָמֹק deep (1 · 17) 771

רָחָב wide, broad (1 · 21) 932

צְחֹק laughter (1 · 2) 850

לַעַג mocking, derision (2 · 7) 541

הכיל to contain, hold (2 · 12 · 38) 465

שִׁכָּרוֹן 33 drunkenness (2 · 3) 1016

יָגוֹן sorrow, grief (1 · 14) 387

כּוֹס cup (4 · 31) 468

שַׁמָּה waste (1 · 39) 1031

מצה 34 to drain, drain out (1 · 4 · 7) 594

חֶרֶשׂ sherd, a fragment of earthenware (1 · 17) 360

גרם to break bones, break (1 · 2 · 3) 175 II.

שַׁד breast (4 · 21) 994

נתק to tear out, away (2 · 11 · 27) 683

גַּו 35 back (1 · 3) 156

זִמָּה wickedness (14 · 28) 273 I.

תַזְנוּת fornication (20 · 20) 276

נאף 37 to commit adultery (3 · 14 · 31) 610

גִּלּוּל idol (39 · 48) 165

אָכְלָה consuming, eating (10 · 18) 38

גִּלּוּל 39 idol (39 · 48) 165

מֶרְחָק 40 distance; ממ׳ = from afar (1 · 18) 935

לַאֲשֶׁר for whom (1 · 38) 81 אֲשֶׁר

כחל to paint (1 · 1 · 1) 471

עָדָה to ornament, deck oneself (3 · 8 · 8) 725

עֲדִי ornament (5 · 14) 725

מִטָּה 41 couch, bed (1 · 29) 641

כְּבוּדָה glorious (1 · 3) 458 I. כָּבוֹד

שָׁלֵו 42 at ease, carefree (1 · 8) 1017

סוֹבָאִים drunkards (1 · 1) 685 סָבָא

צָמִיד bracelet (2 · 6) 855

עֲטָרָה crown (3 · 23) 742

בָּלֶה 43 worn out (1 · 5) 115

נִאֻפִים adulteries (1 · 2) 610 נאף

תַזְנוּת fornication (20 · 20) 276

זוֹנָה 44 harlot (6 · 33) 275 זנה *Qal* 2.

זִמָּה wickedness (14 · 28) 273 I.

נָאַף 45 to commit adultery (3 · 17 · 31) 610

זַעֲוָה 46 terror, object of trembling (1 · 7) 266
    זועה

בַּז   spoiling, robbery (12 · 27) 103

רָגַם 47 to kill by stoning (2 · 15 · 15) 920

בָּרָא   to cut down (3 · 5 · 5) 135 I. ברא
    Piel

זִמָּה 48 wickedness (14 · 28) 273 I.

נִוַּסְּרוּ   [3 c.p.] to be disciplined, corrected
    (1 · 1 · 41) 415 יסר *Niph.*

זִמָּה 49 wickedness (14 · 28) 273 I.

חֵטְא   sin (1 · 33) 308

גִּלּוּל   idol (39 · 48) 165

Chapter 24

עָשׂוֹר 1 tenth day (3 · 15) 797

סָמַךְ 2 to lean, rest (2 · 41 · 48) 701

מָשַׁל 3 to use a proverb (6 · 7 · 15) 605 II.

מְרִי   rebellion (15 · 22) 598

מָשָׁל   similitude, parable (8 · 39) 605 II.

שְׁפֹת   to set (2 · 5 · 5) 1046

סִיר   pot (5 · 29) 696

נֵתַח 4 piece (3 · 12) 677

יָרֵךְ   thigh, loin (2 · 34) 437

מִבְחָר   choicest, best (4 · 12) 104 I.

מִבְחָר 5 choicest, best (4 · 12) 104 I.

דּוּר   to heap up (1 · 2 · 2) 189

רָתַח   to cause to boil (1 · 1 · 3) 958

רֶתַח   boiling (1 · 1) 958

בָּשַׁל   to boil, cook (1 · 2 · 28) 143

אוֹי 6 Woe! Alas! (4 · 25) 17

סִיר   pot (5 · 29) 696

חֶלְאָה   rust (5 · 5) 316 I.

נֵתַח   piece (3 · 12) 677

צָחִיחַ 7 shining, glaring surface (4 · 5) 850

נָקַם 8 to avenge, take vengeance
    (2 · 13 · 35) 667

נָקָם   vengeance (3 · 17) 667

צְחִיחַ   shining, glaring surface (4 · 5) 850

אוֹי 9 Woe! Alas! (4 · 25) 17

מְדוּרָה   pile (1 · 2) 190

הִדְלִיק 10 to kindle, inflame (1 · 2 · 9) 196

הִרְקִיחַ   to spice (1 · 1 · 8) 955

מֶרְקָחָה   [dub.] spice seasoning (1 · 2) 955
    רקח *Hiph.*

נָחוּר   to be scorched, charred (3 · 5 · 9)
    359 I. חרר

גַּחֶלֶת 11 coal (3 · 18) 160

רֵיק   empty (1 · 14) 938

חַם   to be or grow warm (1 · 23 · 26)
    328 חמם

חָרַר   to be hot, scorched (1 · 3 · 9) 359 I.

נִתַּךְ   to be poured forth (2 · 8 · 21) 677

טֻמְאָה   uncleanness (8 · 37) 380

חֶלְאָה   rust (5 · 5) 316 I.

תְּאֻנִים 12 toil (1 · 1) 20

הֶלְאָה   to weary, make weary, exhaust
    (1 · 6 · 19) 521

חֶלְאָה   rust (5 · 5) 316 I.

זִמָּה 13 wickedness (14 · 28) 273 I.

טֻמְאָה   uncleanness (8 · 37) 380

פָּרַע 14 to refrain (1 · 13 · 16) 828

חוּס   to pity, look upon with compassion
    (9 · 24 · 24) 299

עֲלִילָה   deed (8 · 24) 760

מַחְמַד 16 desire (3 · 13) 362

מַגֵּפָה   blow; slaughter (1 · 26) 620

סָפַד   to wail, lament (2 · 28 · 30) 704

דִּמְעָה   [coll.] tears (1 · 23) 199

נֵאָנֵק 17 to cry, groan (2 · 2 · 4) 60

דֹּם   to be silent (1 · 23 · 30) 198 I. דמם

אֵבֶל   mourning (1 · 24) 5

פְּאֵר   headdress, turban (3 · 7) 802

חָבַשׁ   to bind, bind on; ptc. pass. =
    bound, twisted (6 · 28 · 32) 289

נַעַל   sandal, shoe (2 · 22) 653

עָטָה   to wrap, envelope [oneself]
    (2 · 11 · 14) 741

שָׂפָם   moustache (2 · 5) 974

גָּאוֹן 21 pride, exaltation (9 · 49) 144

מַחְמָד desire (3 · 13) 326

מַחְמָל compassion (1 · 1) 328

שָׂפָם 22 moustache (2 · 5) 974

עָטָה to wrap, envelope [oneself] (2 · 11 · 14) 741

פְּאֵר 23 headdress, turban (3 · 7) 802

נַעַל sandal, shoe (2 · 22) 653

ספד to wail, lament (2 · 28 · 30) 704

נמוק to pine away (3 · 9 · 10) 596 מקק

נהם to groan, growl (1 · 5 · 5) 625

מוֹפֵת 24 sign, wonder (4 · 36) 68

מָעוֹז 25 fastness, place of safety (2 · 36) 731

מָשׂוֹשׂ exultation (1 · 17) 965

מַחְמָד desire (3 · 13) 326

מַשָּׂא lifting, uplifting (2 · 45) 672 II.

פָּלִיט 26 fugitive (7 · 19) 812

הַשְׁמָעוּת a causing to hear (1 · 1) 1036

פָּלִיט 27 fugitive (7 · 19) 812

נאלם to be dumb (3 · 8 · 9) 47

מוֹפֵת sign, wonder (4 · 36) 68

Chapter 25

הָאָח 3 Aha! (3 · 9) 210

גּוֹלָה exile (11 · 42) 163

מוֹרָשָׁה 4 a possession (7 · 9) 440

טִירָה encampment (2 · 7) 377

חָלָב milk (3 · 44) 316

נָוֶה 5 abode (3 · 45) 627

מִרְבָּץ resting place, dwelling place (1 · 2) 918 מַרְבֵּץ

מחא 6 to clap (1 · 3 · 3) 561

רקע to stomp down (2 · 6 · 11) 955

שְׁאָט despite, contempt (3 · 3) 1002

בג 7 spoil, booty, plunder (12 · 27) 103 בַּז

צְבִי 9 beauty, decoration (5 · 18) 840

מוֹרָשָׁה 10 a possession (7 · 9) 440

שֶׁפֶט 11 judgment (10 · 16) 1048

נקם 12 to avenge, take vengeance

(2 · 13 · 35) 667

נָקָם vengeance (3 · 17) 667

אָשַׁם to commit an offense, do a wrong; here w. inf. = to commit lasting [irreparable] wrong (4 · 33 · 35) 79

נקם to avenge oneself (2 · 12 · 35) 667

חָרְבָּה 13 waste, ruin (14 · 42) 352

נְקָמָה 14 vengeance (5 · 27) 668

נְקָמָה 15 vengeance (5 · 27) 668

נקם to avenge oneself (2 · 12 · 35) 667

נָקָם vengeance (3 · 17) 667

שְׁאָט despite, contempt (3 · 3) 1002

מַשְׁחִית destruction, ruin (4 · 19) 1008

אֵיבָה enmity (2 · 5) 33

חוֹף 16 shore, coast (1 · 7) 342

נְקָמָה 17 vengeance (5 · 27) 668

תּוֹכַחַת correction, rebuke (2 · 24) 407

Chapter 26

הָאָח 2 Aha! (3 · 9) 210

החרב to be laid waste (2 · 3 · 7) 351 II. Hoph.

גַּל 3 wave, billow; heap (1 · 16) 164

הָרַס 4 to throw down, tear down (4 · 30 · 43) 248

מִגְדָּל tower (3 · 49) 153

סחה to scrape clean, scour (1 · 1 · 1) 695

צָחִיחַ shining, glaring surface (4 · 5) 850

מִשְׁטָח 5 spreading place (3 · 3) 1009

חֵרֶם net (4 · 9) 357 II.

בַּז spoil, booty, plunder (12 · 27) 103

דָּיֵק 8 bulwark, siege wall (4 · 6) 189

סֹלְלָה mound (4 · 11) 700

צִנָּה large shield (4 · 20) 857

מְחִי 9 stroke (1 · 1) 562

קְבָל attacking engine (1 · 1) 867

מִגְדָּל tower (3 · 49) 153

נָתַץ to pull down (2 · 31 · 42) 683

שִׁפְעָה 10 abundance, quantity (1 · 6) 1051

אָבָק   dust (1 · 6) 7

גַּלְגַּל   [coll.] wheel (5 · 11) 165

רָעַשׁ   to quake, shake (4 · 21 · 29) 950

מָבוֹא   entering (5 · 23) 99

פַּרְסָה 11 hoof (2 · 21) 828

רָמַס   to trample (2 · 17 · 18) 942

מַצֵּבָה   pillar (1 · 36) 663

שָׁלַל 12 to spoil, plunder (7 · 13 · 15) 1021

בָּזַז   to spoil, plunder (5 · 38 · 42) 102

רְכֻלָּה   merchandise (4 · 4) 940

הָרַס   to throw down, tear down (4 · 30 · 43) 248

חֶמְדָּה   desire (1 · 16) 326

נָתַץ   to pull down (2 · 31 · 42) 683

כִּנּוֹר 13 lyre (1 · 41) 490

צְחִיחַ 14 shining, glaring surface (4 · 5) 850

מִשְׁטָח   spreading place (3 · 3) 1009

חֵרֶם   net (4 · 9) 357 II.

מַפֶּלֶת 15 overthrow, ruin (6 · 8) 658

אנק   to cry, groan (1 · 2 · 4) 60

הֶרֶג   slaughter (1 · 5) 247

רָעַשׁ   to quake, shake (4 · 21 · 29) 950

אִי   coast, border, region (9 · 36) 15 I.

מְעִיל 16 robe (1 · 28) 591

רִקְמָה   variegated stuff (8 · 12) 955

פָּשַׁט   to strip off, put off (2 · 24 · 43) 833

חֲרָדָה   trembling, fear (1 · 9) 353

חָרַד   to tremble (3 · 23 · 39) 353

רֶגַע   moment (2 · 22) 921

קִינָה 17 elegy, dirge (9 · 17) 884

חַתִּית   terror (8 · 8) 369

חָרַד 18 to tremble, quake (3 · 23 · 39) 353

אִי   coast, border, region (9 · 36) 15 I.

מַפֶּלֶת   overthrow, ruin (6 · 8) 658

נִבְהָל   to be disturbed, dismayed, terrified (2 · 24 · 39) 96

נחרב 19 ptc. = desolate (2 · 2 · 37) 351 II.

תְּהוֹם   deep, sea, abyss (3 · 36) 1062

תַּחְתִּי 20 lower, lowest (6 · 19) 1066

חָרְבָּה   waste, ruin (14 · 42) 352

צְבִי   honor (5 · 18) 840

בַּלָּהָה 21 calamity, destruction (3 · 10) 117

Chapter 27

קִינָה 2 elegy, dirge (9 · 17) 884

מָבוֹא 3 entrance (5 · 23) 99

רֹכֵל   trader (11 · 17[?]) 940 רכל

אִי   coasts, border, region (9 · 36) 15 I.

יָפִי   beauty (10 · 19) 421

כָּלִיל   entire, perfect, whole (3 · 15) 483

בֹּנֶה 4 builder (1 · 9) 124 בָּנָה Qal 1.c.

כלל   to perfect (2 · 2 · 2) 480

יָפִי   beauty (10 · 19) 421

בְּרוֹשׁ 5 cypress or fir (2 · 20) 141

לוּחַ   planks, boards (1 · 43) 531

תֹּרֶן   mast (1 · 3) 1076

אַלּוֹן 6 oak (1 · 9) 47

מָשׁוֹט   oar (2 · 2) 1002

אֲשֻׁרִים   read בִּתְאַשֻּׁרִים = with boxwood (1 · 3) 81 אֲשֻׁרִים

אִי   coast, border, region (9 · 36) 15 I.

שֵׁשׁ 7 linen (3 · 38) 1058

רִקְמָה   variegated work (8 · 12) 955

מִפְרָשׂ   spread [of canvas as sail] (1 · 2) 831

נֵס   ensign, signal (1 · 21) 651

תְּכֵלֶת   violet fabric (3 · 49) 1067

אַרְגָּמָן   purple thread (2 · 39) 71

אִי   coast, border, region (9 · 36) 15 I.

מְכַסֶּה   covering (1 · 4) 492

שׁוּט 8 to go, rove about (2 · 7 · 13) 1001

חֹבֵל   sailor (4 · 5) 287

בֶּדֶק 9 fissure, rent, breach (2 · 10) 96

אֳנִיָּה   ship (3 · 31) 58

מַלָּח   mariner, sailor (3 · 4) 572

עָרַב   to exchange (2 · 15 · 17) 786

מַעֲרָב   [coll.] merchandise, articles of exchange (9 · 9) 786

כּוֹבַע 10 helmet (2 · 6) 464

תָּלָה   to hang up (2 · 2 · 27) 1067

הָדָר	splendor, honor (2 · 30) 214
מִגְדָּל	11 tower (3 · 49) 153
שֶׁלֶט	perh. shield (1 · 7) 1020
תָּלָה	to hang up (2 · 2 · 27) 1067
כָּלַל	to perfect (2 · 2 · 2) 480
יֳפִי	beauty (10 · 19) 421
סֹחֵר	12 trafficker, trader (7 · 16) 695 סחר
הוֹן	wealth (4 · 26) 223
בְּדִיל	tin (3 · 5) 95
עֹפֶרֶת	lead [metal] (3 · 9) 780
עִזְבוֹנִים	wares (7 · 7) 738 עִזָּבוֹן
רֹכֵל	13 trader (11 · 17[?]) 940 רכל
מַעֲרָב	[coll.] merchandise, articles of exchange (9 · 9) 786
פֶּרֶד	14 mule (1 · 14) 825
עִזְבוֹנִים	wares (7 · 7) 738 עִזָּבוֹן
רֹכֵל	15 trader (11 · 17[?]) 940 רכל
אִי	coast, border, region (9 · 36) 15 I.
סְחֹרָה	merchandise (1 · 1) 695
הוֹבְנִים	ebony (1 · 1) 211 הָבְנִי
אֶשְׁכָּר	gift (1 · 2) 1016
סֹחֵר	16 trafficker, trader (7 · 16) 695 סחר
נֹפֶךְ	perh. ruby or carbuncle (2 · 4) 656
אַרְגָּמָן	purple thread (2 · 39) 71
רִקְמָה	variegated stuff (8 · 12) 955
בּוּץ	byssus [a fine white Egyptian linen] (1 · 8) 101
רָאמוֹת	corals (1 · 3) 910
כַּדְכֹּד	perh. ruby (1 · 2) 461
עִזְבוֹנִים	wares (7 · 7) 738 עִזָּבוֹן
רֹכֵל	17 trader (11 · 17[?]) 940 רכל
חִטָּה	wheat (3 · 30) 334
פַּנַּג	some kind of food (1 · 1) 815
צְרִי	a kind of balsam (1 · 6) 863
מַעֲרָב	[coll.] merchandise, articles of exchange (9 · 9) 786
סֹחֵר	18 trafficker, trader (7 · 16) 695 סחר
הוֹן	wealth (4 · 26) 223
צֶמֶר	wool (3 · 16) 856
צַחַר	reddish grey, tawny (1 · 1) 850

אוּזָל	19 Uzal (1 · 1) 23
עִזְבוֹנִים	wares (7 · 7) 738 עִזָּבוֹן
עָשׁוֹת	[dub.] smooth (1 · 1) 799
קִדָּה	cassia (1 · 2) 869
מַעֲרָב	[coll.] merchandise, articles of exchange (9 · 9) 786
רֹכֵל	20 trader (11 · 17[?]) 940 רכל
חֹפֶשׁ	[dub.] widespread (1 · 1) 344
רִכְבָּה	riding (1 · 1) 939
סֹחֵר	21 trafficker, trader (7 · 16) 695 סחר
כַּר	male lamb (5 · 12) 305 III.
עַתּוּד	male goat (3 · 29) 800
רֹכֵל	22 trader (11 · 17[?]) 940 רכל
בֹּשֶׂם	spice, perfume (1 · 30) 141
יָקָר	precious, rare (2 · 35) 429
עִזְבוֹנִים	wares (7 · 7) 738 עִזָּבוֹן
רֹכֵל	23 trader (11 · 17[?]) 940 רכל
רֹכֵל	24 trader (11 · 17[?]) 940 רכל
מַכְלֻל	gorgeous garment (1 · 1) 483
גְּלוֹם	wrapping, garment (1 · 1) 166
תְּכֵלֶת	violet fabric (3 · 49) 1067
רִקְמָה	variegated stuff (8 · 12) 955
גְּנָזִים	chests (1 · 1) 170
בְּרֹמִים	variegated cloth (1 · 1) 140
חֶבֶל	cord, rope (2 · 49) 286
חבש	to bind, bind on; here ptc. pass. [?] (6 · 28 · 32) 289
אָרוּז	firm, strong (1 · 1) 72
מַרְכֹּלֶת	market place (1 · 1) 940
אֳנִיָּה	25 ship (3 · 31) 58
שָׁרָה	perh. traveler (1 · 1[?]) 1003 I. שׁור
מַעֲרָב	[coll.] merchandise, articles of exchange (9 · 9) 786
שׁוט	26 to go, rove about (2 · 7 · 13) 1001
הוֹן	27 wealth (4 · 26) 223
עִזְבוֹנִים	wares (7 · 7) 738 עִזָּבוֹן
מַעֲרָב	[coll.] merchandise, articles of exchange (9 · 9) 786
מַלָּח	mariner, sailor (3 · 4) 572
חֹבֵל	sailor (4 · 5) 287

בֶּדֶק fissure, rent, breach (2 · 10) 96

עָרַב to exchange (2 · 15 · 17) 786

מַפֶּלֶת overthrow, ruin (6 · 8) 658

זְעָקָה 28 cry, outcry (1 · 18) 277

חֹבֵל sailor (4 · 5) 287

רָעַשׁ to quake, shake (4 · 21 · 29) 950

מִגְרָשׁוֹת open land (1 · 1[?]) 177 מִגְרָשׁ

אֳנִיָּה 29 ship (3 · 31) 58

מָשׁוֹט oar (2 · 2) 1002

מַלָּח mariner, sailor (3 · 4) 572

חֹבֵל sailor (4 · 5) 287

מַר 30 bitterly; bitter (3 · 38) 600 I.

אֵפֶר ashes (2 · 22) 68

הִתְפַּלֵּשׁ perh. to roll in (1 · 4 · 4) 814

הִקְרִיחַ 31 to make a baldness (1 · 1 · 5) 901

קָרְחָה baldness, bald spot (2 · 11) 901

חָגַר to gird on, bind on (3 · 44 · 44) 291

שַׂק sackcloth (2 · 48) 974

מִסְפֵּד wailing (1 · 16) 704

מַר bitter; bitterness (3 · 38) 600 I.

בְּנֵיהֶם 32 בְּ + נִי + suffix; נִי wailing (1 · 1) 624

קִינָה elegy, dirge (9 · 17) 884

קוֹנֵן to chant (4 · 8 · 8) 884

דֻמָּה one silenced, brought to silence; one destroyed [dub.] (1 · 1) 199

עִזְבוֹנִים 33 wares (7 · 7) 738 עִזָּבוֹן

הוֹן wealth (4 · 26) 223

מַעֲרָב wares, merchandise, articles of exchange (9 · 9) 786

הֶעֱשִׁיר to make rich (1 · 14 · 17) 799

מַעֲמַקִּים 34 depths (1 · 5) 771

מַעֲרָב [coll.] merchandise, articles of exchange (9 · 9) 786

אִי 35 coast, border, region (9 · 36) 15 I.

שָׂעַד to bristle (2 · 3 · 3) 972

שַׂעַר horror (2 · 3) 972

רָעַם [dub.] to tremble (1 · 1 · 2) 947

סֹחֵר 36 trafficker, trader (7 · 16) 695 סחר

שָׁרַק to hiss (1 · 12 · 12) 1056

בַּלָּהָה calamity, destruction (3 · 10) 117

Chapter 28

נָגִיד 2 ruler, prince (1 · 44) 617

גָּבַהּ to be haughty (8 · 24 · 34) 146

מוֹשָׁב seat, dwelling (7 · 46) 444

סָתַם 3 ptc. pass. = secret (1 · 10 · 13) 711

עמם to darken, dim (2 · 2 · 2[?]) 770

תְּבוּנָה 4 understanding (1 · 42) 108

רְכֻלָּה 5 traffic (4 · 4) 940

גָּבַהּ to be haughty (8 · 24 · 34) 146

עָרִיץ 7 awe inspiring, terror striking (4 · 20) 792

הֵרִיק to empty out (5 · 17 · 19) 937

יְפִי beauty (10 · 19) 421

יִפְעָה brightness, splendor (2 · 2) 422

שַׁחַת 8 pit (3 · 23) 1001

מָמוֹת death (1 · 2) 560

מְחַלֵּל 9 Piel ptc. = wounding ones (1 · 1 · 7) 319 I. חלל

עָרֵל 10 uncircumcised (16 · 35) 790

קִינָה 12 elegy, dirge (9 · 17) 884

חֹתֵם to seal, seal up (1 · 23 · 27) 367

תָּכְנִית measurement, proportion (2 · 2) 1067

כָּלִיל entire, perfect, whole (3 · 15) 483

יְפִי beauty (10 · 19) 421

גַּן 13 garden (5 · 42) 171

יָקָר precious, rare (2 · 35) 429

מְסֻכָה covering (1 · 1) 697

אֹדֶם carnelian (1 · 3) 10

פִּטְדָה topaz or chrysolite (1 · 4) 809

יַהֲלֹם [dub.] jasper, onyx (1 · 3) 240

תַּרְשִׁישׁ perh. yellow jasper (3 · 7) 1076

שֹׁהַם gem [identity dub.] (1 · 11) 995

יָשְׁפֵה jasper (1 · 3) 448

סַפִּיר sapphire (3 · 11) 705

נֹפֶךְ perh. ruby or carbuncle (2 · 4) 656

בָּרְקַת emerald (1 · 3) 140

תֹּף timbrel, tambourine (1 · 17) 1074

131

נֶקֶב grooves, sockets (1 · 1) 666 I.

נברא to be created (3 · 10 · 48) 135 I.

מִמְשָׁה 14 [dub.] expansion, covering (1 · 1) 603

סכך to screen, cover (2 · 12 · 18) 696 I.

נברא 15 to be created (3 · 10 · 48) 135 I.

עַוְלָה injustice (1 · 32) 732

רְכֻלָּה 16 traffic (4 · 4) 940

סכך to screen, cover (2 · 12 · 18) 696 I.

גָּבַהּ 17 to be haughty (8 · 24 · 34) 146

יֳפִי beauty (10 · 19) 421

יִפְעָה brightness, splendor (2 · 2) 421

עָוֶל 18 injustice, unrighteousness (10 · 21) 732

רְכֻלָּה traffic (4 · 4) 940

אֵפֶר ashes (2 · 22) 68

בַּלָּהָה 19 calamity, destruction (3 · 10) 117

שֶׁפֶט 22 judgment (10 · 16) 1048

דֶּבֶר 23 plague, pestilence (12 · 46) 184

סִלּוֹן 24 brier (2 · 2) 699 סַלּוֹן

מַמְאִיר *Hiph.* ptc. = prick, pain (1 · 4 · 4) 549

קוֹץ thorns (1 · 11) 881

הכאיב to pain, mar (2 · 4 · 8) 456

שָׁאטִים ptc. = one who despises (3 · 3 · 3) 1002 II. שׁוט

בֶּטַח 26 securely (11 · 43) 105

שֶׁפֶט judgment (10 · 16) 1048

שָׁאטִים ptc. = one who despises (3 · 3 · 3) 1002 II. שׁוט

Chapter 29

תַּנִּין 3 sea monster (2 · 15) 1072

רָבַץ to lie down, lie (3 · 24 · 30) 918

חַח 4 hook, ring (4 · 7) 296

לְחִי jaw, jawbone (2 · 21) 534

דָּגָה fish (6 · 15) 185

קַשְׂקֶשֶׂת scale [of fish] (2 · 8) 903

נָטַשׁ 5 to forsake, abandon (4 · 33 · 40) 643

דָּגָה fish (6 · 15) 185

אָכְלָה devouring, eating (10 · 18) 38

מִשְׁעֶנֶה 6 staff (1 · 12) 1044

נָרֹץ 7 to be crushed, broken (1 · 2 · 19) 954

נִשְׁעַן to lean, support oneself (1 · 22 · 22) 1043

מָתְנַיִם loins (12 · 47) 608

חָרְבָּה 9 waste, ruin (14 · 42) 352

חָרְבָּה 10 waste, ruin (14 · 42) 352

חֹרֶב desolation (1 · 16) 351 II.

החרב 12 ptc. = laid waste (2 · 3 · 37) 351 II.

זרה to scatter, disperse (10 · 25 · 38) 279

שְׁבוּת 14 captivity (5 · 26) 986

מְכוּרָה origin (3 · 3) 468 מְכֹרָה

שָׁפָל low (6 · 18) 1050

שָׁפָל 15 low (6 · 18) 1050

המעיט to make small or few, diminish (1 · 13 · 22) 589

רדה to have dominion, rule, dominate (2 · 22 · 23) 921

מִבְטָח 16 confidence (1 · 15) 105

הקרח 18 to be made bald (1 · 1 · 5) 901

מרט to make bare, lay bare (4 · 7 · 14) 598

שָׂכָר hire, wages (2 · 29) 969

שָׁלָל 19 to spoil, plunder (7 · 13 · 15) 1021

בָּזַז to spoil, plunder (5 · 38 · 42) 102

בַּז spoil, booty, plunder (12 · 27) 103

שָׂכָר hire, wages (2 · 29) 969

פְּעֻלָּה 20 wages (1 · 14) 821

הַצְמִיחַ 21 to cause to grow (1 · 14 · 33) 855

פִּתָּחוֹן opening (2 · 2) 836

Chapter 30

הילל 2 to utter, make a howling, give a howl (2 · 30 · 30) 410

הָהּ Alas! (1 · 1) 214

חַלְחָלָה 4 anguish (2 · 4) 298

נהרס to be thrown down, torn down (4 · 10 · 43) 248

132

יְסוֹד foundation, base (2 · 19) 414

עֵרֶב 5 mixed company (1 · 5) 786

סָמַךְ 6 to uphold (2 · 41 · 48) 701

גָּאוֹן pride, exaltation (9 · 49) 144

נחרב 7 *Niph.* ptc. desolate (2 · 2 · 37) 351
II.

עֹזֵר 8 help, helper (2 · 19[?]) 740 עזר

צִי 9 ship (1 · 4) 850

הֶחֱרִיד to drive in terror, rout (3 · 13 · 39) 353

בֶּטַח securely (11 · 43) 105

חַלְחָלָה anguish (2 · 4) 298

עָרִיץ 11 awe inspiring, terror striking (4 · 20) 792

הֵרִיק to empty out (5 · 17 · 19) 937

חָרְבָּה 12 dry ground (1 · 8) 351

מְלֹא fullness (5 · 38) 571

גִּלּוּל 13 idol (39 · 48) 165

אֱלִיל idolatrous worthlessness (1 · 20) 47

יִרְאָה fear, terror (2 · 45) 432

שֶׁפֶט 14 judgment (10 · 16) 1048

מָעוֹז 15 fastness, place of safety (2 · 36) 731

חוּל 16 to be in severe pain, anguish (1 · 30 · 47) 296 I.

בָּחוּר 17 young man (5 · 45) 104

שְׁבִי captivity (3 · 46) 985

חָשַׁךְ 18 to be grow, dark (1 · 26 · 28) 364
חשׁךְ

מוֹטָה bar (2 · 11) 557

גָּאוֹן pride, exaltation (9 · 49) 144

שְׁבִי captivity (3 · 46) 985

שֶׁפֶט 19 judgment (10 · 16) 1048

חבשׁ 21 to be bound up (1 · 2 · 32) 289

רְפֻאָה remedy, medicine (1 · 3) 951

חִתּוּל bandage (1 · 1) 367

חבשׁ to bind up (6 · 28 · 32) 289

זרה 23 to scatter, disperse (10 · 25 · 38) 279

נָאַק 24 to groan (1 · 2 · 2) 611

נְאָקָה groaning (1 · 4) 611

זרה 26 to scatter, disperse (10 · 25 · 38) 279

Chapter 31

דָּמָה 2 to be like, resemble (4 · 13 · 27) 197

גֹּדֶל magnificence (3 · 14) 152

יָפֶה 3 fair, beautiful (3 · 41) 421

עָנָף branch[es], bough[s] (4 · 7) 778

חֹרֶשׁ thicket, shade-giving wood (1 · 3) 361

מֵצַל ptc. = a shadowing (1 · 1 · 2) 853

גָּבֹהַּ high, exalted (6 · 41) 147

קוֹמָה height (8 · 45) 879

עָבֹת interwoven foliage (6 · 24) 721

צַמֶּרֶת treetop (5 · 5) 856

תְּהוֹם 4 deep, sea, abyss (3 · 36) 1062

מַטָּע planting place (3 · 6) 642

תְּעָלָה watercourse (1 · 9) 752

גָּבַהּ 5 to be high, lofty, tall (8 · 24 · 34) 146

קוֹמָה height (8 · 45) 879

סַרְעַפָּה bough (1 · 1) 703

אָרֵךְ to be long (2 · 3 · 34) 73

פֹּארָה bough (6 · 6) 802

סְעַפָּת 6 bough, branch (2 · 2) 703

קָנַן to make a nest (1 · 4 · 5) 890

פֹּארָה bough (6 · 6) 802

יפה 7 to be beautiful (2 · 6 · 8) 421

גֹּדֶל greatness, magnitude (3 · 14) 152

דָּלִיּוֹת branches, boughs (7 · 8) 194

שֹׁרֶשׁ root (5 · 33) 1057

עממ 8 [dub.] to eclipse, darken (2 · 2 · 2 [?]) 770

גַּן garden (5 · 42) 171

בְּרוֹשׁ cypress or fir (symbol of luxuriance) (1 · 20) 141

דָּמָה to be like, resemble (4 · 13 · 27) 197

סְעַפָּת bough, branch (2 · 2) 703

עַרְמוֹן plane tree (1 · 2) 790

פֹּארָה bough (6 · 6) 802

יָפִי	beauty (10 · 19) 421	
יָפֶה	9 fair, beautiful (3 · 41) 421	
דָּלִיּוֹת	branches, boughs (7 · 8) 194	
קָנָא	to be jealous of (2 · 30 · 34) 888	
גַּן	garden (5 · 42) 171	
גָּבַהּ	10 to be high, lofty, tall (8 · 24 · 34) 146	
קוֹמָה	height (8 · 45) 879	
גֹּבַהּ	height (6 · 17) 147	
צַמֶּרֶת	treetop (5 · 5) 856	
עָבֹת	interwoven foliage (6 · 24) 760	
רָם	high (5 · 31[?]) 926 רום	
אַיִל	11 mighty one (>50) 42 II. אֵל	
רֶשַׁע	wickedness (4 · 30) 957	
גָּרַשׁ	to drive out, away (1 · 35 · 48) 176	
עָרִיץ	12 awe inspiring, terror striking (4 · 20) 792	
נָטַשׁ	to forsake, abandon (4 · 33 · 40) 643	
גַּיְא	valley (10 · 47) 161	
דָּלִיּוֹת	branches, boughs (7 · 8) 194	
פֹּארָה	bough (6 · 6) 802	
אָפִיק	channel (7 · 18) 67	
מַפֶּלֶת	13 a ruin (6 · 8) 658	
פֹּארָה	bough (6 · 6) 802	
גָּבַהּ	14 to be high, lofty, tall (8 · 24 · 34) 146	
קוֹמָה	height (8 · 45) 879	
צַמֶּרֶת	treetop (5 · 5) 856	
אַיִל	terebinth [a deciduous tree] (1 · 4) 18 IV.	
גֹּבַהּ	height (6 · 17) 147	
עָבֹת	interwoven foliage (6 · 24) 721	
תַּחְתִּית	lower, lowest (6 · 19) 1066	
הַאֲבִיל	15 to cause to mourn (1 · 1 · 1[?]) 5 I. *Hiph.*	
תְּהוֹם	deep, sea, abyss (3 · 36) 1062	
מָנַע	to withhold (1 · 25 · 29) 586	
נכלא	to be restrained (1 · 3 · 17) 476	
הקדיר	to cause to mourn (3 · 3 · 17) 871	
עֻלְּפֶה	have fainted (1 · 1[?]) 763	

מַפֶּלֶת	16 overthrow, ruin (6 · 8) 658	
הרעיש	to cause to quake (1 · 7 · 29) 950	
תַּחְתִּית	lower, lowest (6 · 19) 1066	
מִבְחָר	choicest, best (4 · 12) 104 I.	
דָּמָה	18 to be like, resemble (4 · 13 · 27) 197	
כָּכָה	thus (2 · 34) 462	
גֹּדֶל	magnificence (3 · 14) 152	
תַּחְתִּית	lower, lowest (6 · 19) 1066	
עָרֵל	uncircumcised (16 · 35) 790	

Chapter 32

קִינָה	2 elegy, dirge (9 · 17) 884	
כְּפִיר	young lion (7 · 31) 498	
נִדְמָה	to be cut off, destroyed, ruined (1 · 13 · 17) 198	
תַּנִּין	sea monster (2 · 15) 1072	
הגיח	you thrust forth, burst forth, (1 · 2 · 5) 161 גיח	
דלח	to stir up, trouble (3 · 3 · 3) 195	
רָפַס	to stamp, tread (2 · 2 · 5) 952	
רֶשֶׁת	3 net (4 · 22) 440	
חֵרֶם	net (4 · 9) 357 II.	
נָטַשׁ	4 to forsake, abandon (4 · 33 · 40) 643	
הֵטִיל	to cast, cast out (1 · 9 · 14) 376	
גַּיְא	5 valley (10 · 47) 161	
רָמוּת	height, lofty stature (1 · 1) 928	
צָפָה	6 outflow (1 · 1) 847	
אָפִיק	channel (7 · 18) 67	
כבה	7 to quench, extinguish (1 · 10 · 24) 459	
הקדיר	to make dark (3 · 3 · 17) 871	
הֵאִיר	to give light; to light up, cause to shine (2 · 34 · 40) 21	
כּוֹכָב	star (1 · 37) 456	
יָרֵחַ	moon (1 · 27) 437	
מָאוֹר	8 light, luminary (1 · 19) 22	
הקדיר	to make dark (3 · 3 · 17) 871	
שֶׁבֶר	9 breaking, shattering (1 · 45) 991	
שער	10 to bristle (2 · 3 · 3) 972	

שַׁעַר	horror (2 · 3) 972	
עוֹפֵף	to cause to fly about, to and fro (1 · 5 · 25) 733	
חָרַד	to tremble (3 · 23 · 39) 353	
רֶגַע	moment (2 · 22) 921	
מַפֶּלֶת	overthrow, ruin (6 · 8) 658	
עָרִיץ	12 awe inspiring, terror striking (4 · 20) 792	
גָּאוֹן	exaltation, majesty, excellence (9 · 49) 144	
דָּלַח	13 to stir up, trouble (3 · 3 · 3) 195	
פַּרְסָה	hoof (2 · 21) 828	
הִשְׁקִיעַ	14 to cause to sink (1 · 2 · 6) 1054	
מָלֵא	15 fullness (5 · 38) 571	
קִינָה	16 elegy, dirge (9 · 17) 884	
קוֹנֵן	to chant (4 · 8 · 8) 884	
נָהָה	18 to lament, wail (1 · 2 · 2[?]) 624	
אַדִּיר	majesty (2 · 27) 12	
תַּחְתִּי	lower, lowest (6 · 19) 1066	
מִמִּי	19 from whom (1 · 2) 566 מִי b.	
נָעֵם	to be pleasant, delightful (1 · 8 · 8) 653	
עָרֵל	uncircumcised (16 · 35) 790	
מָשַׁךְ	20 to draw down (1 · 30 · 36) 604	
אֵל	21 mighty (>50) 42 II.	
עֹזֵר	help, helper (2 · 19[?]) 740	
עָרֵל	uncircumcised (16 · 35) 790	
יַרְכָּה	23 recess, innermost part (5 · 28) 438	
קְבוּרָה	grave (2 · 14) 869	
חִתִּית	terror (8 · 8) 369	
קְבוּרָה	24 grave (2 · 14) 869	
עָרֵל	uncircumcised (16 · 35) 790	
תַּחְתִּי	lower, lowest (6 · 19) 1066	
חִתִּית	terror (8 · 8) 369	
כְּלִמָּה	reproach, ignominy (13 · 30) 484	
מִשְׁכָּב	25 couch, bed (2 · 46) 1012	
עָרֵל	uncircumcised (16 · 35) 790	
חִתִּית	terror (8 · 8) 369	
כְּלִמָּה	reproach, ignominy (13 · 30) 484	
עָרֵל	26 uncircumcised (16 · 35) 790	

מְחֻלָּל	*Pual* ptc. = pierced (1 · 1 · 7) 319 I. חלל	
חִתִּית	terror (8 · 8) 369	
עָרֵל	27 uncircumcised (16 · 35) 790	
חִתִּית	terror (8 · 8) 369	
עָרֵל	28 uncircumcised (16 · 35) 790	
עָרֵל	29 uncircumcised (16 · 35) 790	
נָסִיךְ	30 prince (1 · 6) 651	
חִתִּית	terror (8 · 8) 369	
עָרֵל	uncircumcised (16 · 35) 790	
כְּלִמָּה	reproach, ignominy (13 · 30) 484	
חִתִּית	32 terror (8 · 8) 369	
עָרֵל	uncircumcised (16 · 35) 790	

Chapter 33

צֹפֶה	2 watchman (5 · 19[?]) 859	
הִזְהִיר	3 to warn, give a warning (10 · 13 · 21) 264 II.	
נִזְהַר	4 to take warning (5 · 8 · 21) 264 II.	
נִזְהַר	5 to take warning (5 · 8 · 21) 264 II.	
צֹפֶה	6 watchman (5 · 19[?]) 859	
נִזְהַר	to be warned, received warning (5 · 8 · 21) 264 II.	
צֹפֶה	7 watchman (5 · 19[?]) 859	
הִזְהִיר	to warn, give a warning (10 · 13 · 21) 264 II.	
הִזְהִיר	8 to warn, give a warning (10 · 13 · 21) 264 II.	
הִזְהִיר	9 to warn, give a warning (10 · 13 · 21) 264 II.	
נָמוֹק	10 to pine away (3 · 9 · 10) 596 מקק	
רִשְׁעָה	12 wickedness (5 · 15) 958	
רֶשַׁע	wickedness (4 · 30) 957	
עָוֶל	13 injustice, unrighteousness (10 · 21) 732	
חֲבֹל	15 pledge (3 · 3) 287	
גְּזֵלָה	plunder, spoil (4 · 6) 160	
עָוֶל	injustice, unrighteousness (10 · 21) 732	

נתכן 17 to be adjusted to standard; i.e., right, equitable (9 · 10 · 18) 1067

עָוֶל 18 injustice, unrighteousness (10 · 21) 732

רִשְׁעָה 19 wickedness (5 · 15) 958

נתכן 20 to be adjusted to standard; i.e., right, equitable (9 · 10 · 18) 1067

גָּלוּת 21 exile (3 · 15) 163

פָּלִיט fugitive (7 · 19) 812

פָּלִיט 22 fugitive (7 · 19) 812

נאלם to be dumb (3 · 8 · 9) 47

חָרְבָּה 24 waste, ruin (14 · 42) 352

מוֹרָשָׁה a possession (7 · 9) 440

גִּלּוּל 25 idol (39 · 48) 165

חָרְבָּה 27 waste, ruin (14 · 42) 352

מְצָד stronghold (1 · 11) 844

מְעָרָה cave (1 · 40) 792

דֶּבֶר plague, pestilence (12 · 46) 184

מְשַׁמָּה 28 devastation, waste (5 · 7) 1031

גָּאוֹן pride, exultation (9 · 49) 144

מֵאֵין without (2 · 48[?]) 34 II. אַיִן 6.d.

מְשַׁמָּה 29 devastation, waste (5 · 7) 1031

חַד 30 אֶחָד only here BDB 25

מָבוֹא 31 a coming in (5 · 23) 99

עֲגָבִים [sensuous] love (2 · 2) 721

בֶּצַע unjust gain (3 · 23) 130

עֲגָבִים 32 [sensuous] love (2 · 2) 721

יָפֶה fair, beautiful (3 · 41) 421

נָגֵן to play (1 · 13 · 14) 618

Chapter 34

צֶמֶר 3 wool (3 · 16) 856

בָּרִיא fat (2 · 14) 135

חבש 4 to bind up (6 · 28 · 32) 289

נדח ptc. = banished ones, outcasts (2 · 13 · 43) 623

חָזְקָה force, strength (1 · 6) 306

רדה to have dominion, rule, dominate (2 · 22 · 23) 921

פֶּרֶךְ harshness, severity (1 · 6) 827

מִבְּלִי 5 for lack of (2 · 25) 115

אָכְלָה devouring, eating (10 · 18) 38

שׁגה 6 to err, stray (2 · 17 · 21) 993

רָם high (5 · 31[?]) 926 רום

בַּז 8 spoil, booty, plunder (12 · 27) 103

אָכְלָה devouring, eating (10 · 18) 38

מֵאֵין from lack of (2 · 48[?]) 34

אָכְלָה 10 devouring, eating (10 · 18) 38

בקר 11 to seek (2 · 7 · 7) 133

בַּקָּרָה 12 a seeking (1 · 1) 134

עֵדֶר flock (1 · 39) 727

נפרש perh. to scatter (1 · 1 · 5) 831

בקר to seek (2 · 7 · 7) 133

עֲרָפֶל cloud, heavy cloud (1 · 15) 791

אָפִיק 13 channel (7 · 18) 67

מוֹשָׁב habitable places (7 · 46) 444

מִרְעֶה 14 pasture, pasturage (4 · 13) 945

נָוֶה abode (3 · 45) 627

רבץ to lie down, lie (3 · 24 · 30) 918

שָׁמֵן fertile (2 · 10) 1032

הרביץ 15 to cause to lie down (1 · 6 · 30) 918

נדח 16 ptc. = banished ones, outcasts (2 · 13 · 43) 623

חבש to bind up (6 · 28 · 32) 289

שָׁמֵן stout, robust (2 · 10) 1032

שֶׂה 17 sheep, goat (5 · 45) 961

עַתּוּד male goat (3 · 29) 800

מִרְעֶה 18 pasture, pasturage (4 · 13) 945

רָמַס to trample (2 · 17 · 18) 942

מִשְׁקָע clear (1 · 1) 1054

רפש to stamp, tread (2 · 2 · 5) 952

מִרְמָס 19 trampling place (1 · 7) 942

מִרְפָּשׂ befouled (1 · 1) 952 מִרְפָּשׂ

שֶׂה 20 sheep, goat (5 · 45) 961

בְּרִיָּה fat (2 · 14) 135 בָּרִיא

רָזֶה lean (1 · 2) 931

צַד 21 side (6 · 32) 841

הדף to thrust, push (1 · 11 · 11) 213

נגח to push or thrust at (1 · 6 · 11) 618

136

בַּז 22 spoil, booty, plunder (12 · 27) 103

שֶׂה sheep, goat (5 · 45) 961

בֶּטַח 25 securely (11 · 43) 105 w. לְ

יָשַׁן to sleep, go to sleep (1 · 15 · 16) 445

גֶּשֶׁם 26 rain, shower (5 · 35) 177

יְבוּל 27 produce (1 · 13) 385

בֶּטַח securely (11 · 43) 105 w. לְ

מוֹטָה bar (2 · 11) 557

עֹל yoke (1 · 40) 760

בַּז 28 spoil, booty, plunder (12 · 27) 103

בֶּטַח securely (11 · 43) 105 w. לְ

הֶחֱרִיד to terrify (3 · 16 · 39) 353

מַטָּע 29 planting place (3 · 6) 642

כְּלִמָּה reproach, ignominy (12 · 30) 484

מַרְעִית 31 pasturing, shepherding (1 · 10) 945

Chapter 35

מְשַׁמָּה 3 devastation, waste (5 · 7) 1031

הָרְבָּה 4 waste, ruin (14 · 42) 352

אֵיבָה 5 enmity (2 · 5) 33

הִגִּיר to pour down, hurl down; impf. =
יַגֵּר (1 · 5 · 10) 620

אֵיד calamity, distress (1 · 24) 15

שְׁמָמָה 7 devastation, waste (1 · 1) 1031

גַּיְא 8 valley (10 · 47) 161

אָפִיק channel (7 · 18) 67

קִנְאָה 11 anger (10 · 43) 888

שִׂנְאָה hating, hatred (2 · 17) 971

נֶאָצָה 12 contempt, blasphemy (1 · 3) 611

אָכְלָה devouring, food (10 · 18) 38

הֶעְתִּיר 13 to multiply (1 · 1 · 2) 801

Chapter 36

מוֹרָשָׁה 2 a possession (7 · 9) 448

הֶאָח Aha! (3 · 9) 210

בְּיַעַן 3 by the cause (2 · 3) 774

שָׁאַף to trample on, crush (1 · 14 · 4) 983

מוֹרָשָׁה a possession (7 · 9) 440

דִּבָּה evil report (1 · 9) 179

אָפִיק 4 channel (7 · 18) 67

גַּיְא valley (10 · 47) 161

חָרְבָּה waste, ruin (14 · 42) 352

בַּז spoil, booty, plunder (12 · 27) 103

לַעַג mocking, derision (2 · 7) 541

קִנְאָה 5 anger (10 · 43) 888

מוֹרָשָׁה a possession (7 · 9) 440

שָׁאט despite, contempt (3 · 3) 1002

גֵּרַשׁ to cast out, thrust out (2 · 8 · 48) 176

בַּז spoil, booty, plunder (12 · 27) 103

אָפִיק 6 channel (7 · 18) 67

גַּיְא valley (10 · 47) 161

קִנְאָה anger (10 · 43) 888

כְּלִמָּה reproach, ignominy (13 · 30) 484

כְּלִמָּה reproach, ignominy (13 · 30) 484

עָנָף 8 branch[es], bough[s] (4 · 7) 778

חָרְבָּה 10 waste, ruin (14 · 42) 352

פָּרָה 11 to be fruitful, bear fruit (2 · 22 · 29)
82

קַדְמָה former state (4 · 6) 870

רֹאשָׁה beginning time, early time (1 · 1) 911

שִׁכֵּל 12 to make childless (5 · 18 · 24) 1013

אַתִּי 13 you [old form; fem.] (1 · 7) 61

שִׁכֵּל to make childless (5 · 18 · 24) 1013

שִׁכֵּל 14 to make childless (5 · 18 · 24) 1013

כְּלִמָּה 15 reproach, ignominy (13 · 30) 484

עֲלִילָה 17 deed (8 · 24) 760

טֻמְאָה uncleanness (8 · 37) 380

נִדָּה impurity (5 · 30) 622

גִּלּוּל 18 idol (39 · 48) 165

נֹזְרָה 19 to be scattered, dispersed (2 · 2 · 38)
279

עֲלִילָה deed (8 · 24) 760

חָמַל 21 to spare, have compassion
(7 · 40 · 40) 328

זָרַק 25 to toss, throw (3 · 32 · 34) 284

טֻמְאָה uncleanness (8 · 37) 380

גִּלּוּל idol (39 · 48) 165

טֻמְאָה 29 uncleanness (8 · 37) 380

דָּגָן corn, grain (1 · 40) 186

תְּנוּבָה 30 fruit, produce (1 · 5) 626

מַעֲלָל 31 deed, practice (1 · 41) 760

נקוט to feel loathing (1 · 4 · 7) 876

בִּפְנֵי against (4 · 17) 816

נכלם 32 to be humiliated, ashamed (6 · 26 · 38) 483

חָרְבָּה 33 waste, ruin (14 · 42) 352

הַלֵּזוּ 35 this (1 · 3) 229 הַלָּזֶה

חָרֵב waste, desolate (2 · 10) 351 II.

גַּן garden (5 · 42) 171

נהרס to be thrown down, torn down (4 · 10 · 43) 248

בָּצוּר cut off, made inaccessible (2 · 25) בצר 130

נהרס 36 to be thrown down, torn down (4 · 10 · 43) 248

חָרֵב waste, desolate (2 · 10) 351 II.

Chapter 37

בִּקְעָה 1 plain (5 · 19) 132

בִּקְעָה 2 plain (5 · 19) 132

יָבֵשׁ dry, dried (4 · 9) 386

יָבֵשׁ 4 dry, dried (4 · 9) 386

גִּיד 6 sinew (2 · 7) 161

קרם to spread (2 · 2 · 2) 901

רַעַשׁ 7 earthquake (5 · 17) 950

גִּיד 8 sinew (2 · 7) 161

קרם to spread (2 · 2 · 2) 901

מִלְמָעְלָה above (6 · 24) 751

נפח 9 to breathe, blow (3 · 9 · 12) 655

תִּקְוָה 11 things hoped for, outcome (2 · 32) 876

נִגְזַר to be cut off; i.e., destroyed (1 · 6 · 12) 160

חָבֵר 16 associate, fellow (3 · 12) 288

חָבֵר 19 associate, fellow (3 · 12) 288

מִבֵּין 21 from between (9 · 21) 107 בֵּין 2. d.

נחצה 22 to be divided (1 · 4 · 15) 345

גִּלּוּל 23 idol (39 · 48) 165

שִׁקּוּץ detested thing (8 · 28) 1055

מוֹשָׁב dwelling place (7 · 46) 444

Chapter 38

חָח 4 hook, ring (4 · 7) 296

לְחִי jaw, jawbone (2 · 21) 534

לָבוּשׁ clothed with (9 · 16) 527 לבש

מִכְלוֹל perfection (2 · 2) 483

צִנָּה large shield (4 · 20) 857

כּוֹבַע 5 helmet (2 · 6) 464

אֲגַף 6 bands, armies, hordes (7 · 7) 8

יַרְכָה remote part (5 · 28) 438

נקהל 7 to assemble (1 · 19 · 39) 874

מִשְׁמָר [dub.] reserve, watch (1 · 22) 1038 Lis. ''guard, prison''

חָרְבָּה 8 waste, ruin (14 · 42) 352

בֶּטַח securely (11 · 43) 105

שׁאָה 9 devastation, ruin (1 · 12) 996

אֲגַף bands, armies, hordes (7 · 7) 8

פְּרָזָה 11 open region, hamlet (1 · 3) 826

שָׁקַט to be quiet, undisturbed (2 · 31 · 41) 1052

בֶּטַח securely (11 · 43) 105

בְּאֵין without (1 · 10) 34 II. אַיִן 6. a.

בְּרִיחַ bar (1 · 41) 138

שָׁלַל 12 to spoil, plunder (7 · 13 · 15) 1021

בָּזַז to spoil, plunder (5 · 38 · 42) 102

בַּז spoil, booty, plunder (12 · 27) 103

חָרְבָּה waste, ruin (14 · 42) 352

קִנְיָן acquisition (2 · 9) 889

טַבּוּר navel (1 · 2) 371

סֹחֵר 13 trafficker, trader (7 · 16) 695 סחר

כְּפִיר young lion (7 · 31) 498

שָׁלַל to spoil, plunder (7 · 13 · 15) 1021

בָּזַז to spoil, plunder (5 · 38 · 42) 102

בַּז spoil, booty, plunder (12 · 27) 103

הקהיל to summon an assembly (1 · 20 · 39) 875

138

קִנְיָן	acquisition (2 · 9) 889	
בֶּטַח	14 securely (11 · 43) 105	
יַרְכָּה	15 remote part (5 · 28) 432	
קַדְמוֹנִי	17 former ancient (4 · 10) 870	
קִנְאָה	19 anger (10 · 43) 888	
עֶבְרָה	rage, fury (5 · 34) 720	
רַעַשׁ	earthquake (5 · 17) 950	
רָעַשׁ	20 to quake, shake (4 · 21 · 29) 950	
דָּג	fish (1 · 19) 185	
רֶמֶשׂ	creeping things (2 · 16) 943	
רָמַשׂ	to creep (1 · 16 · 16) 942	
נהרס	to be thrown down, torn down (4 · 10 · 43) 248	
מַדְרֵגָה	steep place, steep (1 · 2) 201	
דֶּבֶר	22 plague, pestilence (12 · 46) 184	
גֶּשֶׁם	rain, shower (5 · 35) 177	
שָׁטַף	to overflow, rinse off, wash off (4 · 28 · 31) 1009	
אֶלְגָּבִישׁ	hail (3 · 3) 38	
גָּפְרִית	brimstone (1 · 7) 172	
הִמְטִיר	to rain, send rain (1 · 16 · 17) 565	
אֲגַף	bands, armies, hordes (7 · 7) 8	

Chapter 39

שׁשׁא	2 to lead on (1 · 1 · 1) 1058	
יַרְכָּה	remote part (5 · 28) 438	
אֲגַף	4 bands, armies, hordes (7 · 7) 8	
עַיִט	bird[s] of prey (1 · 8) 743	
צִפּוֹר	bird, [coll.] (3 · 40) 861	
אָכְלָה	devouring, eating (10 · 18) 38	
אִי	6 coast, border, region (9 · 36) 15 I.	
בֶּטַח	securely (11 · 43) 105	
הִשִּׂיק	9 to make a fire, to burn (1 · 2 · 3) 969	
נֶשֶׁק	equipment, weapons (2 · 10) 676	
צִנָּה	large shield (4 · 20) 857	
מַקֵּל	stick, staff (1 · 18) 596	
רֹמַח	spear, lance (1 · 15) 942	
חטב	10 to cut or gather (1 · 2 · 3) 310	
נֶשֶׁק	equipment, weapons (2 · 10) 676	

שָׁלַל	to spoil, plunder (7 · 13 · 15) 1021	
בָּזַז	to spoil, plunder (5 · 38 · 42) 102	
גַּיְא	11 valley (10 · 47) 161	
קִדְמָה	on the east (1 · 4) 870	
חֹסֶמֶת	ptc. = stop (1 · 2 · 2) 340	
הִבְדִּיל	14 to separate, set apart (3 · 32 · 42) 95	
חקר	to search [for] (1 · 22 · 27) 350	
צִיּוּן	15 signpost, monument (1 · 3) 846	
גַּיְא	valley (10 · 47) 161	
צִפּוֹר	17 bird [coll.] (3 · 40) 861	
כַּר	18 male lamb (5 · 12) 503 III.	
עַתּוּד	male goat (3 · 29) 800	
מְרִיא	fatling (1 · 8) 597	
שָׂבְעָה	19 satiety (3 · 7[?]) 960	
שִׁכָּרוֹן	drunkenness (2 · 3) 1016	
הָלְאָה	22 onward (2 · 13) 229	
מָעַל	23 to act unfaithfully, treacherously (7 · 35 · 35) 591	
טֻמְאָה	24 uncleanness (8 · 37) 380	
שְׁבִית	25 captivity (5 · 26) 986 שְׁבִית	
רָחַם	to have compassion (1 · 42 · 47) 933	
קָנָא	to be zealous (2 · 30 · 34) 888	
כְּלִמָּה	26 reproach, ignominy (13 · 30) 484	
מַעַל	unfaithful, treacherous act (6 · 29) 591	
מָעַל	to act unfaithfully, treacherously (7 · 35 · 35) 591	
בֶּטַח	securely (11 · 43) 105	
הֶחֱרִיד	to terrify (3 · 13 · 39) 353	
כנס	28 to gather (2 · 3 · 11) 488	

Chapter 40

גָּלוּת	1 exile (3 · 15) 163	
עָשׂוֹר	tenth day (3 · 15) 797	
מַרְאָה	2 vision (4 · 12) 909 I.	
גָּבֹהַּ	high, exalted (6 · 41) 147	
מִבְנֶה	structure (1 · 1) 125	
פָּתִיל	3 cord, thread (1 · 11) 836	
פֵּשֶׁת	flax, linen (4 · 16) 833	

139

הֵנָּה 4 hither (1 · 49) 244

טֹפַח 5 span, handbreadth (3 · 9) 381

בִּנְיָן structure (7 · 7) 125

קוֹמָה height (8 · 45) 879

מַעֲלָה 6 step, stair (9 · 47) 752

סַף threshold, sill (7 · 25) 706 II.

תָּא 7 chamber (11 · 13) 1060

סַף threshold, sill (7 · 25) 706 II.

מֵאֵצֶל from beside (2 · 6) 69 I. אֵצֶל

אוּלָם porch (32 · 49) 17 I.

אוּלָם 8 porch (32 · 49) 17 I.

אוּלָם 9 porch (32 · 49) 17 I.

אַיִל pilaster, pillar (21 · 22) 18 II.

תָּא 10 chamber (11 · 13) 1060

מִפּוֹ מִפֹּה repeated = on this side...on that side (33 · 33) 805 פֹּה

אַיִל pilaster, pillar (21 · 22) 18 II.

תָּא 12 chamber (11 · 13) 1060

מִפֹּה on each side (33 · 33) 805 פֹּה

מִפּוֹ repeated = on this side...on that side (33 · 33) 805 פֹּה

גָּג 13 roof (1 · 29) 150

תָּא chamber (11 · 13) 1060

אַיִל 14 pilaster, pillar (21 · 22) 18 II.

אִיתוֹן 15 entrance (1 · 1) 87

אוּלָם porch (32 · 49) 17 I.

פְּנִימִי inner (24 · 33) 819

חַלּוֹן 16 window (12 · 30) 319

אטם ptc. pass. = closed (3 · 8 · 8) 31

תָּא chamber (11 · 13) 1060

אַיִל pilaster, pillar (21 · 22) 18 II.

לִפְנִימָה within (3 · 5) 819 פְּנִימָה

אֵילָם porch (32 · 49) 19

תִּמֹרָה palm figure (13 · 19) 1071

לִשְׁכָּה 17 room, cell (23 · 47) 545

חִיצוֹן outer (18 · 25) 300

רִצְפָה pavement (5 · 7) 954

רִצְפָה 18 pavement (5 · 7) 954

לְעֻמָה side by side with (15 · 31) 769 עֻמָה

תַּחְתּוֹן lower, lowest (6 · 13) 1066

תַּחְתּוֹן 19 lower, lowest (6 · 13) 1066

פְּנִימִי inner (24 · 33) 819

חִיצוֹן 20 outer (18 · 25) 300

תָּא 21 chamber (11 · 13) 1060

מִפּוֹ repeated = on this side...on that side (33 · 33) 805 פֹּה

אַיִל pilaster, pillar (21 · 22) 18 II.

אֵילָם porch (32 · 49) 19

חַלּוֹן 22 window (12 · 30) 319

אֵילָם porch (32 · 49) 19

תִּמֹרָה palm figure (13 · 19) 1071

פְּנִימִי 23 inner (24 · 33) 819

דָּרוֹם 24 south (13 · 17) 204

אַיִל pilaster, pillar (21 · 22) 18 II.

אֵילָם porch (32 · 49) 19

חַלּוֹן 25 window (12 · 30) 319

אֵילָם porch (32 · 49) 19

מַעֲלָה 26 step, stair (9 · 47) 752

אֵילָם porch (32 · 49) 19

תִּמֹרָה palm figure (13 · 19) 1071

מִפּוֹ repeated = on this side...on that side (33 · 33) 805 פֹּה

אַיִל pilaster, pillar (21 · 22) 18 II.

פְּנִימִי 27 inner (24 · 33) 819

דָּרוֹם south (13 · 17) 204

פְּנִימִי 28 inner (24 · 33) 819

דָּרוֹם south (13 · 17) 204

תָּא 29 chamber (11 · 13) 1060

אַיִל pilaster, pillar (21 · 22) 18 II.

אֵילָם porch (32 · 49) 19

חַלּוֹן window (12 · 30) 319

אוּלָם 30 porch (32 · 49) 17 I.

אוּלָם 31 porch (32 · 49) 17 I.

חִיצוֹן outer (18 · 25) 300

תִּמֹרָה palm figure (13 · 19) 1071

אַיִל pilaster, pillar (21 · 22) 18 II.

מַעֲלָה step, stair (9 · 47) 752

מַעֲלָה ascent (3 · 19) 751

פְּנִימִי 32 inner (24 · 33) 819

תָּא 33 chamber (11 · 13) 1060

אַיִל — pilaster, pillar (21 · 22) 18 II.

אֵילָם — porch (32 · 49) 19

חַלּוֹן — window (12 · 30) 319

אֵילָם 34 porch (32 · 49) 19

חִיצוֹן — outer (18 · 25) 300

תִּמְרָה — palm figure (13 · 19) 1071

אַיִל — pilaster, pillar (21 · 22) 18 II.

מִפּוֹ — repeated = on this side...on that side (33 · 33) 805 פֹה

מַעֲלָה — step, stair (9 · 47) 752

מַעֲלֶה — ascent (3 · 19) 751

תָּא 36 chamber (11 · 13) 1060

אַיִל — pilaster, pillar (21 · 22) 18 II.

אֵילָם — porch (32 · 49) 19

חַלּוֹן — window (12 · 30) 319

אַיִל 37 pilaster, pillar (21 · 22) 18 II.

חִיצוֹן — outer (18 · 25) 300

תִּמְרָה — palm figure (13 · 19) 1071

מִפּוֹ — repeated = on this side...on that side (33 · 33) 805 פֹה

מַעֲלָה — step, stair (9 · 47) 752

מַעֲלֶה — ascent (3 · 19) 751

לִשְׁכָּה 38 room, cell (23 · 47) 545

אַיִל — pilaster, pillar (21 · 22) 18 II.

הֵדִיחַ — *Hiph.* to rinse (1 · 4 · 4) 188 דוח

אוּלָם 39 porch (32 · 49) 17 I.

מִפּוֹ מִפֹּה — repeated = on this side...on that side (33 · 33) 805 פֹה

אָשָׁם — trespass offering; offense, guilt (4 · 47) 79

אוּלָם 40 porch (32 · 49) 17 I.

מִפֹּה 41 repeated = on this side...on that side (33 · 33) 805 פֹה

גָּזִית — a cutting, hewing; w/אבן hewn stones (1 · 11) 159

גֹּבַהּ — height (6 · 17) 147

שְׁפַתַּיִם 43 hooks, (1 · 2[?]) 1052

טֹפַח — span, handbreadth (3 · 9) 381

פְּנִימִי 44 inner (24 · 33) 819

לִשְׁכָּה — room, cell (23 · 47) 545

דָּרוֹם — south (13 · 17) 204

זֶה 45 this (1 · 11) 262

לִשְׁכָּה — room, cell (23 · 47) 545

דָּרוֹם — south (13 · 17) 204

לִשְׁכָּה 46 room, cell (23 · 47) 545

קָרֵב — approaching (2 · 11) 898

רבע 47 ptc. = square (2 · 3 · 12) 917

אוּלָם 48 porch (32 · 49) 17 I.

אַיִל — pilaster, pillar (21 · 22) 18 II.

מִפּוֹ מִפֹּה — repeated = on this side...on that side (33 · 33) 805 פֹה

אוּלָם 49 porch (32 · 49) 17 I.

מַעֲלָה — step, stair (9 · 47) 752

אַיִל — pilaster, pillar (21 · 22) 18 II.

מִפֹּה — repeated = on this side...on that side (33 · 33) 805 פֹה

Chapter 41

אַיִל 1 pilaster, pillar (21 · 22) 18 II.

מִפּוֹ — repeated = on this side...on that side (33 · 33) 805 פֹה

מִפּוֹ 2 repeated = on this side...on that side (33 · 33) 805 פֹה

לִפְנִימָה 3 toward the [in]side (3 · 5) 819 פְּנִימָה

אַיִל — pilaster, pillar (21 · 22) 18 II.

צֵלָע 5 side chamber (10 · 39) 854

צֵלָע 6 side chamber (10 · 39) 754

אָחוּז — ptc. pass. fastened, held (2 · 66) 28 אחז

רָחַב 7 to be or grow wide or large (1 · 3 · 25) 931

לְמַעְלָה — upward (8 · 24) 751 מעל 2. c.

צֵלָע — side chamber (10 · 39) 854

מוּסָב — encompassing, surrounding (1 · 1) 687

תַּחְתּוֹן — lower, lowest (6 · 13) 1066

תִּיכוֹן — middle (4 · 12) 1064

גֹּבַהּ 8 height (6 · 17) 147

מִיסָדָה — foundation (1 · 2) 414 מוּסָדָה

141

צֵלָע   side chamber (10 · 39) 854

מְלֹא   fullness (5 · 38) 571

אַצִּיל   to the joining [obscure]; joining, joint (2 · 3) 69

צֵלָע   9 side chamber (10 · 39) 854

בֵּית   between (1 · 3) 108

לִשְׁכָּה   10 room, cell (23 · 47) 545

צֵלָע   11 side chamber (10 · 39) 854

דָּרוֹם   south (13 · 17) 204

בִּנְיָן   12 structure (7 · 7) 125

גִּזְרָה   separation (7 · 8) 160

גִּזְרָה   13 separation (7 · 8) 160

בִּנְיָה   structure, building (1 · 1) 125

גִּזְרָה   14 separation (7 · 8) 160

בִּנְיָן   15 structure (7 · 7) 125

גִּזְרָה   separation (7 · 8) 160

אַתּוּק   gallery, porch (5 · 5) 87   אַתִּיק

מִפּוֹ   repeated = on this side...on that side (33 · 33) 805 פֹּה

פְּנִימִי   inner (24 · 33) 819

אוּלָם   porch (32 · 49) 17 I.

סַף   16 threshold, sill (7 · 25) 706 II.

חַלּוֹן   window (12 · 30) 319

אטם   ptc. pass. = closed (3 · 8 · 8) 31

אַתִּיק   gallery, porch (5 · 5) 87

שָׂחִיף   [dub.] paneled (1 · 1) 965

פְּנִימִי   17 inner (24 · 33) 819

חִיצוֹן   outer (18 · 25) 300

תִּמְרָה   18 palm figure (13 · 19) 1071

תִּמְרָה   19 palm figure (13 · 19) 1071

מִפּוֹ   repeated = on this side...on that side (33 · 33) 805 פֹּה

כְּפִיר   young lion (7 · 31) 498

תִּמְרָה   20 palm figure (13 · 19) 1071

מְזוּזָה   21 door post, gate post (7 · 20) 265

רבע   ptc. pass. = square (2 · 9 · 12) 917

גָּבֹהַּ   22 high, exalted (6 · 41) 147

מִקְצֹעַ   corner post (5 · 12) 893

תִּמְרָה   25 palm figure (13 · 19) 1071

עָב   [dub.] structure of wood; perh.

beam, plank, threshold or projecting roof (2 · 3) 712

אוּלָם   porch (32 · 49) 17 I.

חַלּוֹן   26 window (12 · 30) 319

אטם   ptc. pass. = closed (3 · 8 · 8) 31

תִּמְרָה   palm figure (13 · 19) 1071

מִפּוֹ   repeated = on this side...on that side (33 · 33) 805 פֹּה

אוּלָם   porch (32 · 49) 17 I.

צֵלָע   side chamber (10 · 39) 854

עָב   [dub.] structure of wood; perh. beam, plank, threshold or projecting roof (2 · 3) 712

Chapter 42

הִיצוֹן   1 outer (18 · 25) 300

לִשְׁכָּה   room, cell (23 · 47) 545

גִּזְרָה   separation (7 · 8) 160

בִּנְיָן   structure (7 · 7) 125

פְּנִימִי   3 inner (24 · 33) 819

רִצְפָה   pavement (5 · 7) 954

חִיצוֹן   outer (18 · 25) 300

אַתִּיק   gallery, porch (5 · 5) 87

לִשְׁכָּה   4 room, cell (23 · 47) 545

מַהֲלָךְ   walk (1 · 5) 237

פְּנִימִי   inner (24 · 33) 819

לִשְׁכָּה   5 room, cell (23 · 47) 545

קָצוּר   short (1 · 1[?]) 894

אַתִּיק   gallery, porch (5 · 5) 87

תַּחְתּוֹן   lower, lowest (6 · 13) 1066

תִּיכוֹן   middle (4 · 12) 1064

בִּנְיָן   structure (7 · 7) 125

שִׁלֵּשׁ   6 ptc. = three-storied (1 · 5 · 9) 1026

נֶאֱצַל   to be withdrawn; i.e., shortened or narrowed (1 · 1 · 5) 69

תַּחְתּוֹן   lower, lowest (6 · 13) 1066

תִּיכוֹן   middle (4 · 12) 1064

גָּדֵר   7 wall, fence (3 · 14) 154

לְעֻמָּה   side by side with (15 · 31) 769 עֻמָּה

לִשְׁכָּה		room, cell (23 · 47) 545
חִיצוֹן		outer (18 · 25) 300
לִשְׁכָּה	8	room, cell (23 · 47) 545
חִיצוֹן		outer (18 · 25) 300
לִשְׁכָּה	9	room, cell (23 · 47) 545
חִיצוֹן		outer (18 · 25) 300
גָּדֵר	10	wall, fence (3 · 14) 154
גִּזְרָה		separation (7 · 8) 160
בִּנְיָן		structure (7 · 7) 125
לִשְׁכָּה		room, cell (23 · 47) 545
לִשְׁכָּה	11	room, cell (23 · 47) 545
מוֹצָה		a going forth (4 · 27) 425 I.
לִשְׁכָּה	12	room, cell (23 · 47) 545
דָּרוֹם		south (13 · 17) 204
בִּפְנֵי		in front of (4 · 17) 816 פָּנֶה II. 3.
גְּדֶרֶת		wall (1 · 1[?]) 155 גְּדֵרָה
הָגִין		appropriate, suitable [dub.] (1 · 1) 212
לִשְׁכָּה	13	room, cell (23 · 47) 545
דָּרוֹם		south (13 · 17) 204
גִּזְרָה		separation (7 · 8) 160
אָשָׁם		trespass offering; offense, guilt (4 · 47) 79
חִיצוֹן	14	outer (18 · 25) 300
פְּנִימִי	15	inner (24 · 33) 819
דָּרוֹם	18	south (13 · 17) 204
הִבְדִּיל	20	to make a distinction, separate (3 · 32 · 42) 95
הֹל		profaneness, commonness (4 · 7) 320

Chapter 43

הֵאִיר	2	to light up, cause to shine (2 · 34 · 40) 21
מַרְאָה	3	vision (4 · 12) 909
פְּנִימִי	5	inner (24 · 33) 819
זְנוּת	7	fornication (3 · 9) 276
פֶּגֶר		corpse, carcass (3 · 22) 803
סַף	8	threshold, sill (7 · 25) 706 II.
מְזוּזָה		doorpost, gatepost (7 · 20) 265

זְנוּת	9	fornication (3 · 9) 276
פֶּגֶר		corpse, carcass (3 · 22) 803
נכלם	10	to be humiliated, ashamed (6 · 26 · 38) 483
תָּכְנִית		measurement, proportion (2 · 2) 1067
נכלם	11	to be humiliated, ashamed (6 · 26 · 38) 483
צוּרָה		form, fashion (4 · 5) 849
תְּכוּנָה		arrangement, disposition (1 · 3) 467
מוֹצָה		a going forth (4 · 27) 425 I.
מוֹבָא		entrance (1 · 2) 100
טֹפַח	13	span, handbreadth (3 · 9) 381
חֵיק		bosom [of hollow bottom of altar] (3 · 38) 300
זֶרֶת		span [= ½ cubit] (1 · 7) 284
גַּב		elevation (7 · 13) 146
חֵיק	14	bosom [of hollow bottom of altar] (3 · 38) 300
עֲזָרָה		ledge surrounding (6 · 9) 741
תַּחְתּוֹן		lower, lowest, (6 · 13) 1066
קָטָן		small (3 · 47) 881
אַרְאֵיל	15	hearth, altar hearth (3 · 3) 72 II.
לְמַעְלָה		upward (8 · 34) 751 מַעַל 2. c.
אַרְאֵיל	16	hearth, altar hearth (3 · 3) 72 II.
רבע		ptc. pass. = square (2 · 9 · 12) 917
רֶבַע		pl. = four sides (5 · 7) 917
עֲזָרָה	17	ledge surrounding (6 · 9) 741
רֶבַע		pl. = four sides (5 · 7) 917
חֵיק		bosom [of hollow bottom of altar] (3 · 38) 300
מַעֲלָה		step, stair (9 · 47) 752
זָרַק	18	to toss, throw (3 · 32 · 34) 284
פִּנָּה	20	corner (2 · 30) 819
עֲזָרָה		ledge surrounding (6 · 9) 741
מִפְקָד	21	appointed place (1 · 5) 824
חִטֵּא	22	to purify from sin (>50) 307
מֶלַח	24	salt (2 · 28) 571
הָלְאָה	27	onward (2 · 13) 229

Chapter 44

חִיצוֹן	1	outer (18 · 25) 300
אוּלָם	3	porch (32 · 49) 17 I.
מָבוֹא	5	entering (5 · 23) 99
מוֹצָא		a going forth (4 · 27) 425 I.
מְרִי	6	rebellion (15 · 22) 598
נֵכָר	7	foreignness; נ׳ בֶּן = foreigner (3 · 36) 648
עָרֵל		uncircumcised (16 · 35) 790
הֵפֵר		to break, frustrate (5 · 41 · 44) 830
נֵכָר	9	foreignness; נ׳ בֶּן = foreigner (3 · 36) 648
עָרֵל		uncircumcised (16 · 35) 790
תָּעָה	10	to err (7 · 26 · 50) 1073
גִּלּוּל		idol (39 · 48) 165
פְּקֻדָּה	11	overseer (2 · 32) 824
גִּלּוּל	12	idol (39 · 48) 165
מִכְשׁוֹל		stumbling block (8 · 14) 506
כִּהֵן	13	to act as priest (1 · 23 · 23) 464
כְּלִמָּה		reproach, ignominy (12 · 30) 484
תָּעָה	15	to err (7 · 27 · 50) 1073
פְּנִימִי	17	inner (24 · 33) 819
פֵּשֶׁת		flax, linen (4 · 16) 833
צֶמֶר		wool (3 · 16) 856
פְּאֵר	18	headdress, turban (3 · 7) 802
פֵּשֶׁת		flax, linen (4 · 16) 833
מִכְנָס		undergarments (1 · 5) 488
מָתְנַיִם		loins (12 · 47) 608
חגר		to gird oneself (3 · 44 · 44) 291
יֶזַע		sweat (1 · 1) 402
חִיצוֹן	19	outer (18 · 25) 300
פָּשַׁט		to strip off, put off (2 · 24 · 43) 833
לִשְׁכָּה		room, cell (23 · 47) 545
גִּלַּח	20	to shave, shave off (1 · 18 · 23) 164
פֶּרַע		long hair, locks (1 · 2) 828
כסם		to clip, shear (2 · 2 · 2) 493
פְּנִימִי	21	inner (24 · 33) 819
גרשׁ	22	to cast out, thrust out (2 · 8 · 48) 176
בְּתוּלָה		virgin (2 · 50) 143-144
הוֹרָה	23	to direct, instruct, teach (1 · 45 · 45 [?]) 434 ירה
חֹל		profaneness, commonness (4 · 7) 320
טָהֳרָה	26	cleansing, purification (1 · 13) 372
פְּנִימִי	27	inner (24 · 33) 819
אָשָׁם	29	trespass offering; offense, guilt (4 · 47) 79
חֵרֶם		devoted thing (1 · 29) 356 I.
בִּכּוּרִים	30	firstfruits (1 · 17) 114
עֲרִיסָה		[dub.] course meal (1 · 4) 791
נְבֵלָה	31	carcass, corpse (2 · 48) 615
טְרֵפָה		torn flesh (2 · 9) 383

Chapter 45

רבע	2	ptc. = square (3 · 3 · 12) 917
קָרֵב	4	approaching (2 · 11) 898
לִשְׁכָּה	5	room, cell (23 · 47) 545
לְעֻמָּה	6	side by side with (15 · 31) 769 עמה
מִזֶּה וּמִזֶּה	7	on one side...on the other [idiom] 262 זֶה 6.e.
קֶרֶם		eastward (3 · 26) 870
לְעֻמָּה		side by side with (15 · 31) 769 עמה
הוֹנָה	8	to oppress, maltreat (7 · 14 · 18) 413 ינה
שֹׁד	9	violence, havoc (1 · 25) 994
גְּרוּשָׁה		expulsion, violence (1 · 1) 177
מֹאזְנַיִם	10	balances, scales (2 · 15) 24 מאזן
אֵיפָה		ephah [grain measure] (17 · 39) 35
בַּת		bath [liquid measure] (7 · 13) 144 II.
אֵיפָה	11	ephah [grain measure] (17 · 39) 35
בַּת		bath [liquid measure] (7 · 13) 144 II.
תֹּכֶן		capacity (1 · 2) 1067
מַעֲשֵׂר		tenth part, tithe (2 · 33) 798
חֹמֶר		homer [dry measure] (7 · 13) 330 III.
מַתְכֹּנֶת		measurement, proportion (1 · 5) 1067
גֵּרָה	12	gerah [a weight, 20th part of shekel] (1 · 5) 176
מָנֶה		maneh, mina [measure of weight] (1 · 5) 584

חִטָּה 13 wheat (3 · 30) 334

אֵיפָה ephah [grain measure] (17 · 39) 35

שָׁשָׁה to give a sixth part of (1 · 1 · 1) 995

חֹמֶר homer [dry measure] (7 · 13) 330 III.

שְׂעֹרָה barley (4 · 34) 972

בַּת 14 bath [liquid measure] (7 · 13) 144 II.

מַעֲשֵׂר tenth part, tithe (2 · 33) 798

כֹּר kor [dry measure] (1 · 8) 499

חֹמֶר homer [dry measure] (7 · 13) 330 III.

שֶׂה 15 sheep, goat (5 · 45) 961

מַשְׁקֶה well irrigated (2 · 19) 1052 II.

חָטָא 18 to purify (Piel) (>50) 307

מְזוּזָה 19 doorpost, gate post (7 · 20) 265

פִּנָּה corner (2 · 30) 819

עֲזָרָה ledge surrounding (6 · 9) 741

פְּנִימִי inner (24 · 33) 819

שָׁגָה 20 to commit sin of ignorance (2 · 17 · 21) 993

פֶּתִי simple (1 · 19) 834

פֶּסַח 21 passover (1 · 49) 820

שָׁבוּעַ period of seven, week (1 · 20) 988

אֵיפָה 24 ephah [grain measure] (17 · 39) 35

הִין hin [liquid measure] (6 · 22) 228

Chapter 46

פְּנִימִי 1 inner (24 · 33) 819

אוּלָם 2 porch (32 · 49) 17 I.

מְזוּזָה doorpost, gate post (7 · 20) 265

מִפְתָּן threshold (5 · 8) 837

אֵיפָה 5 ephah [grain measure] (17 · 39) 35

מַתַּת gift (2 · 6) 682

הִין hin [liquid measure] (6 · 22) 228

אֵיפָה 7 ephah [grain measure] (17 · 39) 35

הִין hin [liquid measure] (6 · 22) 228

אוּלָם 8 porch (32 · 49) 17 I.

נֹכַח 9 in front of (5 · 22) 647

אֵיפָה 11 ephah [grain measure] (17 · 39) 35

מַתַּת gift (2 · 6) 682

הִין hin [liquid measure] (6 · 22) 228

נְדָבָה 12 freewill [voluntary] offering (2 · 27) 621

אֵיפָה 14 ephah [grain measure] (17 · 39) 35

הִין hin [liquid measure] (6 · 22) 228

רסס to moisten (1 · 1 · 1) 944

מַתָּנָה 16 gift (5 · 17) 682

מַתָּנָה 17 gift (5 · 17) 682

דְּרוֹר liberty (1 · 7) 204 I.

הוֹנָה 18 to oppress, maltreat (7 · 14 · 18) 413 ינה

מָבוֹא 19 entrance (5 · 23) 99

לִשְׁכָּה room, cell (23 · 47) 545

יַרְכָּה extreme, hinder part (5 · 28) 438

בָּשַׁל 20 to boil (3 · 21 · 28) 143

אָשָׁם trespass offering; offense, guilt (4 · 47) 79

אָפָה to bake (1 · 10 · 13) 66

חִיצוֹן outer (18 · 25) 300

חִיצוֹן 21 outer (18 · 25) 300

מִקְצוֹעַ buttress place (5 · 12) 893

מִקְצוֹעַ 22 buttress place (5 · 12) 893

קטר Qal ptc. pass. = [dub.] enclosed (1 · 1 · 1) 883

מְהֻקְצָעוֹת Hoph. ptc. = cornered, set in corner (1 · 1 · 3[?]) 893

טוּר 23 course, row (1 · 27) 377

מְבַשְּׁלוֹת cooking places (1 · 1) 143

טִירָה row (2 · 7) 377

בָּשַׁל 24 to boil (3 · 21 · 28) 143

Chapter 47

מִפְתָּן 1 threshold (5 · 8) 837

יְמָנִי right, right hand (3 · 33) 412

מִגֶּגֶד in front, opposite, at a distance (1 · 26) 2. c. נֶגֶד 617

פכה 2 to trickle (1 · 1 · 1) 810

145

יְמָנִי right, right hand (3 · 33) 412

קַו 3 line (1 · 17) 876

אֲפָסַיִם soles [of feet] or ankles (1 · 1) 67
אֶפֶס

מָתְנַיִם 4 loins (12 · 47) 608

בֶּרֶךְ knee (3 · 25) 139

גָּאָה 5 to rise up (1 · 7 · 7) 144

שָׂחוּ swimming (1 · 1) 965

מִזֶּה וּמִזֶּה 7 on the one side...on the other 262 זֶה
6. e.

גְּלִילָה 8 circuit, boundary, territory (1 · 6)
327

קַדְמוֹן eastern (1 · 1) 870

שָׁרַץ 9 to swarm (1 · 14 · 14) 1056

דָּגָה fish (6 · 15) 185

דַּוָּג 10 fisher, fisherman (1 · 1) 186

מִשְׁטוֹחַ spreading place (3 · 3) 1009

חֵרֶם net (4 · 9) 357 II.

מִין kind, species (1 · 31) 568

דָּגָה fish (6 · 15) 185

בִּצָּא 11 swamp (1 · 3) 130

גֶּבֶא cistern, pool (1 · 2) 146

מֶלַח salt (2 · 28) 571

מִזֶּה וּנֶזֶּה 12 on the one side...on the other 262 זֶה
6. e.

מַאֲכָל food (3 · 30) 38

יִפּוֹל impf. נָבֵל to droop, wither and fall,
fade (1 · 19 · 23) 615

עָלֶה leaf, leafage (2 · 17) 750

בכר to bear early, new fruit (1 · 2 · 4) 114

תְּרוּפָה healing (1 · 1) 930

חֵבֶל 13 measured portion, lot, part, region
(2 · 49) 286

תִּיכוֹן 16 middle (4 · 12) 1064

מִבֵּין 18 from between (9 · 21) 107 בֵּין 2. d.

קַדְמוֹנִי eastern (4 · 10) 870

תֵּימָן 19 south (4 · 24) 412

נֹכַח 20 in front of (5 · 22) 647

אֶזְרָח 22 [a] native (1 · 17) 280

Chapter 48

תָּעָה 11 to err (7 · 27 · 50) 1073

תְּרוּמִיָּה 12 allotment (1 · 1) 929

לְעֻמָּה 13 side by side with (15 · 31) 769 עֻמָּה

הֵמִיר 14 to exchange (1 · 13 · 14) 558 מור

חֹל 15 profaneness, commonness (4 · 7) 320

מוֹשָׁב dwelling place (7 · 43) 444

לְעֻמָּה 18 side by side with (15 · 31) 769 עֻמָּה

תְּבוּאָה product, yield (1 · 43) 100

לְעֻמָּה 21 side by side with (15 · 31) 769 עֻמָּה

תֵּימָן 28 south (4 · 24) 412

מַחֲלֹקֶת 29 division, part (1 · 35) 324

תּוֹצָאָה 30 outskirts (1 · 23) 426

HOSEA

Chapter 1

תְּחִלָּה 2 beginning; ת׳דבר יהוה = when Yhwh first spoke (1 · 22) 321

זְנוּנִים fornication (6 · 12) 276

הָרָה 3 to conceive, become pregnant (3 · 38 · 40) 247

מַמְלָכוּת 4 dominion, royal power, kingdom, reign (1 · 9) 575

הָרָה 6 to conceive, become pregnant (3 · 38 · 40) 247

רְחַם to have compassion, be compassionate (4 · 42 · 47) 933

רְחַם 7 to have compassion, be compassionate (4 · 42 · 47) 933

גָּמַל 8 to wean; to deal adequately with, deal out to; to ripen (1 · 34 · 37) 168

הָרָה to conceive, become pregnant (3 · 38 · 40) 247

Chapter 2

חוֹל 1 sand (1 · 22) 297

רְחַם 3 to be shown compassion (3 · 4 · 47) 933

זְנוּנִים 4 fornication (6 · 12) 276

נַאֲפוּף adultery (1 · 1) 610

שַׁד female breast (2 · 21) 994

מִבֵּין from between (1 · 21) בין w. preps. d. 107

הִפְשִׁיט 5 to strip, strip off (1 · 15 · 43) 832

עָרוֹם naked (1 · 16) 736

הִצִּיג to set, exhibit, place (1 · 15 · 16) 426

צִיָּה drought, dryness (1 · 16) 851

צָמָא thirst (1 · 17) 854

רְחַם 6 to have compassion, be compassionate (4 · 42 · 47) 933

זְנוּנִים fornication (6 · 12) 276

הָרָה 7 to conceive, become pregnant Lis. 435 has הרה ''mother'' (1 · 3) 247

מְאַהֵב ptc. = lover, friend (5 · 16) 12-13

צֶמֶר wool (2 · 16) 856

פֵּשֶׁת flax, linen (2 · 16) 833

שִׁקּוּי drink (1 · 3) 1052

שָׂךְ 8 שׂוך to hedge up, fence up (1 · 2 · 2) 962

סִיר thorn, hook (1 · 5) 696

גָּדַר to wall up or off, build a wall (1 · 7 · 7) 154

גָּדֵר wall, fence (1 · 14) 154

נְתִיבָה path, course of life (1 · 21) 677

מְאַהֵב 9 ptc. = lover, friend (5 · 16) 12-13

הִשִּׂיג to overtake, reach (2 · 49 · 49) 673

מֵעַתָּה from now, henceforth; but here comparative = ''than now'' עתה para. 2.e. BDB 774

דָּגָן 10 corn, grain of cereals (6 · 40) 186

תִּירוֹשׁ must, fresh or new wine (6 · 38) 440

יִצְהָר fresh oil (2 · 23) 844

דָּגָן 11 corn, grain of cereals (6 · 40) 186

תִּירוֹשׁ must, fresh or new wine (6 · 38) 440

צֶמֶר wool (2 · 16) 856

פֵּשֶׁת flax, linen (2 · 16) 833

נַבְלוּת 12 immodesty, shamelessness (1 · 1) 615

מְאַהֵב ptc. = lover, friend (5 · 16) 12-13

מָשׂוֹשׂ 13 exultation, rejoicing (1 · 17) 965

תְּאֵנָה 14 fig tree, fig (2 · 39) 1061

אֶתְנָה hire (1 · 1) 1071

מְאַהֵב ptc. = lover, friend (5 · 16) 12-13

עדה 15 to ornament, deck oneself (1 · 8 · 8) 725

נֶזֶם ring (1 · 17) 633

חֶלְיָה jewelry (1 · 1) 318

מְאַהֵב ptc. = lover, friend (5 · 16) 12-13

פתה 16 to persuade, entice, deceive (1 · 17 · 27) 834

תִּקְוָה 17 hope (1 · 32) 876

147

נְעוּרִים   youth, early life (1 · 46) 655

רֶמֶשׂ   20 [coll.] creeping things, moving things (1 · 16) 943

בֶּטַח   with לְ securely; quietness and security (1 · 43) 105

אָרַשׂ   21 to betroth (3 · 6 · 11) 77

רַחֲמִים   compassion (1 · 38) 933

אָרַשׂ   22 to betroth (3 · 6 · 11) 77

דָּגָן   24 corn, grain of cereals (6 · 40) 186

תִּירוֹשׁ   must, fresh or new wine (6 · 38) 440

יִצְהָר   fresh oil (2 · 23) 844

רָחַם   25 to have compassion, be compassionate (4 · 42 · 47) 933

רחם   to be shown compassion (3 · 4 · 47) 933

Chapter 3

נאף   1 to commit adultery (4 · 14 · 31) 610

אֲשִׁישָׁה   [pressed] raisin-cake (1 · 5) 84

עֵנָב   grape, grapes (2 · 19) 772

כרה   2 to get by trade, buy (1 · 4 · 4) 500

חֹמֶר   homer, dry measure (1 · 13) 330

שְׂעֹרָה   barley; pl. = barley grains (*1 · 33) 972 *occurs two times here; Lis. 1381 missed it.

לֶתֶךְ ,לֵתֶךְ   a barley measure (1 · 1) 547

מַצֵּבָה   4 pillar (3 · 36) 663

אֵפוֹד   ephod, means of consulting deity, priestly garment (1 · 49) 65

תרף ,תְּרָפִים   kind of idol, object of reverence and means of divination (1 · 15) 1076

פָּחַד   5 to be in dread, in awe (1 · 22 · 25) 808

טוּב   good things (2 · 32) 375

Chapter 4

אָלָה   2 to swear, take an oath, curse (2 · 3 · 6) 46

כָּחַשׁ   to deceive, act deceptively (2 · 19 · 22) 471

רָצַח   to murder, slay (1 · 35 · 41) 953

גנב   to steal, take by stealth (1 · 30 · 39) 170

נאף   to commit adultery (1 · 17 · 31) 610

פָּרַץ   to use violence, break through, into, out, etc. (2 · 46 · 49) 829

אָבַל   3 to mourn, lament (2 · 18 · 38) 5

אֻמְלַל   to be or grow feeble, to languish (1 · 15 · 15) 51

דָּג   fish (1 · 19) 185

דמה   5 to cause to cease, cut off (1 · 4 · 16) 198

נִדְמָה   6 to be cut off, destroyed, ruined (4 · 12 · 16) 198

מִבְּלִי   from want of, unawares (1 · 25) 115

כֹּהֵן   to minister as a priest, be or become a priest (1 · 23 · 23) 464

רבב   7 [inf. constr.] to become many, much (3 · 23 · 24) 912

קָלוֹן   ignominy, shame (2 · 17) 885-886

הֵמִיר   to exchange, change (1 · 13 · 14) 558

מַעֲלָל   9 deed, practice, evil practice (5 · 41) 760

פָּרַץ   10 to break over [limits], increase; to break through, into, out, etc. (2 · 46 · 49) 829

זְנוּת   11 fornication (2 · 9) 276

תִּירוֹשׁ   must, fresh or new wine (6 · 38) 440

מַקֵּל   12 wand, staff, rod (1 · 18) 596

זְנוּנִים   fornication (5 · 11) 276

הִתְעָה   to cause to err, mislead, wander about (1 · 21 · 50) 1073

מִתַּחַת   from under, from beneath para. III.2.a. תחת 1066

אַלּוֹן 13 oak tree, oak (1 · 9) 47

לִבְנֶה poplar (1 · 2) 527

אֵלָה ,אַלָּה terebinth, a deciduous tree with pinnate leaves and red berries (1 · 17) 18

כַּלָּה young wife, bride; daughter-in-law (2 · 34) 483

נאף to commit adultery (4 · 14 · 31) 610

כַּלָּה 14 young wife, bride; daughter-in-law (2 · 34) 483

נאף to commit adultery (4 · 14 · 31) 610

פרד to make a separation (1 · 1 · 26) 825

זוֹנָה ptc. = harlot (1 · 33) 275

קָדֵשׁ temple prostitute (1 · 11) 873

נלבט to be thrust down, away (1 · 3 · 3) 526

אָשַׁם 15 to be [become] guilty, be held guilty, do a wrong (5 · 33 · 35) 79

פָּרָה 16 heifer, cow (1 · 26) 831

סָרַר to be stubborn, rebellious (3 · 17 · 17) 710

מֶרְחָב broad or roomy place (1 · 6) 932

חבר 17 to unite, be joined, come as allies (1 · 11 · 28) 287

עָצָב idol (4 · 17) 781

סֹבֶא 18 drink, liquor (1 · 3) 685

הֵבוּ imper. of אהב pp 12-13; G.K.

קָלוֹן ignominy, shame (2 · 17) 885-886

מָגֵן shield (1 · 4); but Lis. 749 has sep. word = insolent. 171

הֵ 19 all by itself [?] - text prob. no refs in G.K.; K and D; Davidson Grammar (Syntax)

Chapter 5

הִקְשִׁיב 1 to give attention (1 · 45 · 46) 904

הַאֲזִין to hear, give ear, listen (1 · 41 · 41) 24

פַּח bird trap (2 · 25) 809

רֶשֶׁת net (2 · 22) 440

שַׁחֲטָה 2 [mng. dub.] slaughtering (1 · 1) 1006

שֵׂט סֵט swerver, revolter; deeds that swerve (1 · 2) 962

הֶעְמִיק to make deep (2 · 8 · 9) 770

מוּסָר chastening, discipline (1 · 50) 416

נכחר 3 to be hidden (1 · 11 · 32) 470

מַעֲלָל 4 bad practice, deed, practice (5 · 41) 760

זְנוּנִים fornication (5 · 11) 276

גָּאוֹן 5 exaltation, majesty, excellence, pride (2 · 49) 144-145

בִּפְנֵי in the face of (2 · 17) para. II.3.a. פָּנֶה 816

חָלַץ 6 to withdraw; draw off or out (1 · 5 · 27) 322

בגד 7 to act or deal treacherously, faithlessly, deceitfully (2 · 49 · 49) 93

חֲצֹצְרָה 8 clarion, wind instrument (1 · 29) 348

הריע to sound a signal for war or march, raise a shout, give a blast (1 · 40 · 44) 929

שַׁמָּה 9 appalling waste (1 · 39) 1031

תּוֹכֵחָה rebuke, correction (1 · 4) 407

הִסִּיג 10 to displace, move back, remove (1 · 7 · 25) 690

עֶבְרָה overflowing rage, fury; overflow (2 · 34) 720

עָשַׁק 11 to oppress, wrong; ptc. = oppressed (2 · 36 · 37) 798-799

רצץ to crush, oppress (1 · 11 · 19) 954

הוֹאִיל to be determined, resolved; to acquiesce; to undertake (1 · 18 · 18) 383

צַו [mng. dub.] command, ordinance (1 · 9) 846

עָשׁ 12 moth (1 · 7) 799

רָקָב rottenness, decay (1 · 5) 799

חֳלִי 13 sickness (1 · 24) 318

יָרֵב let him contend (2 · 2) 937

149

מָזוֹר   wound, injury (2 · 3) 267

גהה   to depart, be cured, healed (1 · 1 · 1) 155

שַׁחַל   14 lion (2 · 7) 1006

כְּפִיר   young lion (1 · 31) 498

טָרַף   to tear, rend (2 · 19 · 24) 382

אָשַׁם,אָשֵׁם   15 to be held guilty, bear punishment, be guilty (5 · 33 · 35) 79

צַר   straits, distress (0 · 20) 865 Lis. 1227 missed entry

שׁחר   to look early for, look diligently for (1 · 12 · 13) 1007

גְּדוּד   marauding band, troop (2 · 33) 151

חֶבֶר   company, band, association, society (1 · 7) 288

רצח   to murder, assassinate (1 · 3 · 41) 953

זִמָּה   wickedness, evil device; plan, purpose (1 · 28) 273

שַׁעֲרִירִיָה   10 read שַׁעֲרוּרִיָה, שַׁעֲרוּרִי horror, horible thing (1 · 2) 1045

זְנוּת   fornication (2 · 9) 276

קָצִיר   11 what is harvested, harvesting, time of harvest (1 · 49) 894

שְׁבוּת   captivity (1 · 26) 986

Chapter 6

טָרַף   1 to tear, rend (2 · 19 · 24) 382

יַךְ   *Hiph.* imperf. of נכה Lis. 929

חבש   to bind up, bind, bind on (1 · 28 · 32) 289

שַׁחַר   2 dawn (2 · 23) 1007

מוֹצָא   a going forth; that which goes forth; place of going forth (1 · 27) 425

גֶּשֶׁם   rain, shower (1 · 35) 177

מַלְקוֹשׁ   latter rain, spring rain (1 · 8) 545

יוֹרֶה   early rain from last of Oct. to first of Dec. (2 · 2 · 3); BDB lists as noun (Lis. 639 as hiph. verb form ''to sprinkle'') 435

טַל   4 dew, night mist (3 · 31) 378

חצב   5 to hew in pieces; hew, hew out (1 · 14 · 17) 345

אֵמֶר   utterance, word (1 · 48) 56

בגד   7 to act or deal treacherously, faithlessly, deceitfully (2 · 49 · 49) 93

קִרְיָה   8 town, city (1 · 28) 900

עָקֹב   foot-tracked; insidious; deceitful (1 · 3) 784

חִכָּה   9 to wait, to tarry, to wait for (1 · 13 · 14) 314

Chapter 7

גַּנָּב   1 thief (1 · 17) 170

פָּשַׁט   to put off [one's shelter]; i.e., to make a dash, to strip off (1 · 24 · 43) 832-833

גְּדוּד   marauding band, troop (2 · 33) 151

מַעֲלָל   2 practice, deed (5 · 41) 760

כַּחַשׁ   3 lying, untruthfulness (3 · 6) 471

נאף   4 to commit adultery (4 · 14 · 31) 610

תַּנּוּר   portable stove, fire pot (3 · 15) 1072

אֹפֶה   ptc. = baker (2 · 12) 66

לוּשׁ   to knead (1 · 5 · 5) 534

בָּצֵק   dough (1 · 5) 130

חָמֵץ   to be leavened, soured (1 · 3 · 4) 329

מָשַׁךְ   5 BDB says text prob. corrupt; to draw, drag, draw out; LXX, AV, RV, to stretch out (2 · 30 · 36) 604

לוֹצֵץ   *Po 'lel* ptc. מ dropped = scorner (1 · 1 · 12) 539

תַּנּוּר   6 portable stove, fire pot (3 · 15) 1072

אֹרֵב   ambush, intrigue (1 · 2) 70

יָשֵׁן   asleep, sleeping (1 · 9) 653

אֹפֶה   ptc. = baker (2 · 12) 66

לֶהָבָה   flame (1 · 19) 529

חַם, חמם   7 to be [grow] warm (1 · 23 · 26) 328

תַּנּוּר   portable stove, fire pot (3 · 15) 1072

הִתְבֹּלֵל   8   to mix oneself (1 · 1 · 43) 232

עֻגָה   disc or cake of bread (1 · 7) 728

בְּלִי   adv. of negation, not (3 · 23) 115

שֵׂיבָה   9   gray hair, hoary head, old age (1 · 20) 966

זָרַק   to be profuse, toss or scatter abundantly (1 · 1 · 1) [note Lis.458 has as sep. verb "to be white"] 248

גָּאוֹן   10   exaltation, majesty, excellence, pride (2 · 49) 144-145

בִּפְנֵי   in the face of, against (2 · 17) para. II.3. פָּנֶה p. 816

יוֹנָה   11   dove (2 · 33) 401

פתה   to be open-minded, simple; to be enticed, deceived (1 · 5 · 27) 834

רֶשֶׁת   12   net (2 · 22) 440

הִיסִיר   to chasten (1 · 1 · 38) 415

שֵׁמַע   hearing, report (1 · 17) 1034

אוֹי   13   Woe! [an impassioned expression of grief and despair] (2 · 25) 17

נדד   to flee, depart, wander (2 · 20 · 24) 622

שֹׁד   devastation, ruin, violence (4 · 25) 994

פָּשַׁע   to transgress, rebel (3 · 40 · 41) 833

כָּזָב   lie, falsehood, deceptive thing (2 · 31) 469

הֵילִל   14   to howl, give a howl in distress (1 · 30 · 30) 410

מִשְׁכָּב   couch, bed (1 · 46) 1012

דָּגָן   corn, grain (6 · 40) 186

תִּירוֹשׁ   must, fresh or new wine (6 · 38) 440

הִתְגּוֹרֵר   Lis. has under גור; *Hithpol.* = to stay, loaf about as a client (1 · 3 · 83) Lis. 319; BDB lists as dub. under גור; to assemble themselves; and II גור to excite themselves [pp. 157-158] or even התגדד to cut oneself [p. 151].

יָסַר   15   to discipline, correct (1 · 27 · 38) 416

עַל   16   height, upward (2 · 8 as subst.) 752

רְמִיָּה   deceit, treachery (1 · 15) 941

זַעַם   indignation (1 · 22) 276

זוֹ   this (1 · 2) 262

לַעַג   mocking, derision (1 · 7) 541

Chapter 8

חֵךְ   1   palate, roof of mouth, gums (1 · 18) 335

נֶשֶׁר   griffon-vulture, eagle (1 · 26) 676

פָּשַׁע   to transgress, rebel (3 · 40 · 41) 833

זָנַח   3   to reject, spurn (2 · 16 · 19) 276

הִשִּׂיר   4   to make [i.e., appoint] princes (1 · 1 · 8) 979

עָצָב   idol (4 · 17) 781

זָנַח   5   to reject, spurn (2 · 16 · 19) 276

עֵגֶל   calf (3 · 35) 722

עַד־מָתַי   how long[?] (1 ·   ) 607

נִקָּיוֹן   freedom from punishment; innocency (1 · 5) 667

חָרָשׁ   6   graver, artificer (2 · 38) 360

שְׁבָבִים   splinters (1 · 1) 985

עֵגֶל   calf (3 · 35) 722

סוּפָה   7   storm wind (1 · 15) 693; see G.K. para. 90f. p. 250 for old accusative form הֵ

קָצַר   to reap, harvest (3 · 24 · 24) 894

קָמָה   standing grain (1 · 10) 879

צֶמַח   sprouting, growth (1 · 12) 855

בְּלִי   adverb of negation, not (3 · 23) 115

קֶמַח   flour, meal (1 · 14) 887

אוּלַי   if perchance, peradventure (1 · 45) 19

בָּלַע   to swallow up, engulf, swallow down (1 · 20 · 41) 118

נִבְלַע   8   to be swallowed (1 · 1 · 41) 118

חֵפֶץ   delight, pleasure (1 · 39) 343

פֶּרֶא   9   wild ass (1 · 10) 825

בדד to be separate, isolated (1 · 3 · 3)
94

התנה to hire [lovers] (1 · 1 · 3) 1071

אַהַב love, amour (1 · 2) 13

גַּם כִּי 10 yea though, yea when, even when
[idiom] גַּם para. 6 169

תנה to hire; to hire [a lover] (1 · 2 · 3)
1071

מַשָּׂא load, burden; BDB says read משה
w. LXX (1 · 45) 672

רְבּוֹ, רְבּוֹא 12 ten thousand, myriad (1 · 11) 914

הַבְהָב 13 gift [dub.] (1 · 1) 396

רָצָה to accept, be pleased with
(1 · 42 · 50) 953

עֹשֶׂה 14 ptc. = maker (1 · 24) 793

בֹּצֵר, בָּצוּר ptc. pass. = cut off, made inaccessible, fortified (1 · 25) 131

אַרְמוֹן citadel, castle, palace (1 · 33) 74

Chapter 9

גִּיל 1 rejoicing (1 · 8) 162

אֶתְנַן hire of harlot (1 · 11) 1072

גֹּרֶן threshing floor (3 · 34) 175

דָּגָן corn, grain (6 · 40) 186

גֹּרֶן 2 threshing floor (3 · 34) 175

יֶקֶב wine vat (1 · 16) 428

תִּירוֹשׁ must, fresh or new wine (6 · 38)
440

כָּחַשׁ to act deceptively, deceive
(1 · 19 · 22) 471

נָסַךְ 4 to pour out libations, pour out, cast
metal images (1 · 7 · 24) 650

ערב to be sweet, pleasing (1 · 8 · 8) 787

אֹנֶה, אָוֶן BDB אָוֶן trouble, sorrow, mourning;
Lis. mourning (1[?] · 2[?]) 19-20

שֹׁד 6 violence, havoc, devastation, ruin;
BDB read אשׁור (4 · 25) 994

מַחְמָד desirable thing, precious thing
(2 · 13) 326

קִמּוֹשׁ [coll.] thistles or nettles (1 · 3) 888

חוֹחַ brier, bramble; hook, ring (1 · 11)
296

פְּקֻדָּה 7 visitation = punishment; oversight,
charge; store (1 · 32) 824

שִׁלֵּם requital, retribution, reward (1 · 3)
1024

אֱוִיל foolish (1 · 26) 17

שׁגע to be mad; Pu. ptc. = maddened
[Lis. 1404 "sad"] (1 · 5 · 7) 993

רַבָּה to be or become much or many;
BDB read רב (3 · 23 · 24) 912

מַשְׂטֵמָה animosity (2 · 2) 966

צפה 8 to look out, spy; ptc. = watchman
(1 · 9 · 18) 859

פַּח bird trap (2 · 25) 809

יָקוֹשׁ יָקוֹשׁ bait layer, fowler (1 · 4) 430

מַשְׂטֵמָה animosity (2 · 2) 966

הֶעֱמִיק 9 to make deep, to be in the depth of
[sq. vb.] (2 · 8 · 9) 770

עֵנָב 10 grape[s] (2 · 19) 772

בִּכּוּרָה first ripe fig, early fig (1 · 4) 114

תְּאֵנָה fig tree, fig (2 · 39) 1061

נזר to devote or dedicate oneself, hold
sacredly aloof from (1 · 4 · 10) 634

בֹּשֶׁת shameful thing, shame (1 · 30) 102

שִׁקּוּץ detested thing (1 · 28) 1055

אֹהַב love, loved object; amour [carnal]
(1 · 2) 13

הִתְעוֹפֵף 11 to fly away (1 · 1 · 25) 733

לֵדָה [inf. cstr.] to bring forth, bringing
forth (1 · 4) 408

הֵרָיוֹן conception, pregnancy (1 · 2) 248

שִׁכֵּל 12 to make childless, cause barrenness
(1 · 18 · 23) 1013

כִּי־גַם for even [idiom] para. 6 גַּם 169

אוֹי Woe! [an impassioned expression
of grief and dispair] (2 · 25) 17

שׁתל 13 to transplant [Lis. 1503 "plant"]
(1 · 10 · 10) 1060

נָוֶה	meadow, abode of shepherds; habitation (1 · 45) 627	מַצֵּבָה	a pillar as a memorial, either personal or sacred (3 · 36) 663
רֶחֶם 14	womb (1 · 33) 933	אלה 4	to swear, take an oath (2 · 3 · 6) 46
הִשְׂכִּיל	to miscarry; ptc. = miscarrying (1 · 2 · 23) 1013	פָּרַח	to bud, sprout, send out shoots (3 · 28 · 33) 827
שַׁד	female breast (2 · 21) 994	רוֹשׁ, רֹאשׁ	a bitter and poisonous herb (1 · 12) 91
צמק	to dry up, shrivel (1 · 1 · 1) 855	תֶּלֶם	furrow (2 · 5) 1068
רֹעַ 15	evil, badness (1 · 19) 947-948	שָׂדַי	field, land (2 · 13) 961
מַעֲלָל	practice, deed, evil practice (5 · 41) 760	עֶגְלָה 5	heifer, young cow (2 · 12) 722
גרשׁ	to drive out, drive away (1 · 35 · 48) 176	גור	to be afraid, but BDB reads ינודו lament (1 · 10) 158
סָרַר	to be stubborn, rebellious (3 · 17 · 17) 710	שָׁכֵן	inhabitant, neighbor (1 · 20) 1015
שֹׁרֶשׁ 16	root (2 · 33) 1057	אָבַל	to mourn, lament (2 · 18 · 38) 5
בְּלִי	[בל] adv. of negation, not (3 · 23) 115	כֹּמֶר	idol-priest (1 · 3) 485
גַּם כִּי	yea though, yea when, even when [idiom] גַּם para. 6. 169	גִּיל	to tremble, rejoice (1 · 45 · 45) 162
מַחְמַד	desirable thing, precious thing (2 · 13) 326	הוּבַל 6	to be borne along, carried; to be led, conducted (2 · 11 · 18) 384
נדד 17	to wander, stray; retreat, flee, depart (2 · 20 · 24) 622	יָרֵב	let him contend (2 · 2) 937
		בָּשְׁנָה	shame (1 · 1) 292
		נִדְמָה 7	to be cut off, destroyed, ruined (4 · 13 · 17) 198
		קֶצֶף	[prob.] splinter (1 · 1) 893

Chapter 10

בקק 1	to be luxuriant; II root = to lay waste (1 · 4 · 7) 132	קוֹץ 8	thornbush, thorns (1 · 11) 881
		דַּרְדַּר	thistles [coll.] (1 · 2) 205
שׁנה	to make, produce [one time]; to set, place (1 · 5 · 5) 1001	הִשִּׂיג 9	to overtake, reach (2 · 49 · 49) 673
רבב	Lis. 1310 as inf. cstr. = to be [become] many, much; BDB רב (3 · 23 · 24) 1310	עַלְוָה	BH³ reads עולה Lis. 1070 ''injustice'' violent deed of injustice (1 · 1) 732
מַצֵּבָה	pillar as a memorial, either personal or sacred (3 · 36) 663	אַוָּה 10	desire, will (1 · 7) 16
חָלַק 2	to be smooth, slippery (1 · 2 · 9) 325	יסר	to discipline, chasten, admonish (1 · 4 · 38) 415
אָשַׁם	to be held guilty, bear punishment, to be guilty (5 · 33 · 35) 79	עוֹנָה	BDB - no def. given; read עָוֹן iniquity, guilt; Lis. 1036 furrows [dub.] (1 · 1) 733,730
ערף	to break the neck [of an animal] (1 · 6 · 6) 791	עֶגְלָה 11	heifer, young cow (2 · 12) 722
		דּוֹשׁ דָּשׁ	to thresh, tread on, trample on (1 · 13 · 16) 190

153

טוֹב	fairness, beauty, good things, goodness (2 · 32) 375
צַוָּאר	neck, back of neck (1 · 41) 848
חרשׁ	to plow, cut in, engrave (2 · 23 · 26) 360
שׂדד	to harrow (1 · 3 · 3) 961
קצר 12	to reap, harvest (3 · 24 · 24) 894
ניר	to break up, freshly till (1 · 2 · 2) 644
נִיר	untilled ground, tillable ground (1 · 3) 644
הוֹרה	to throw water, rain; to throw, shoot (2 · 2 · 3) Lis. sep. root "to sprinkle" 434
חרשׁ 13	to plow, cut in, engrave (2 · 23 · 26) 360
רֶשַׁע	wickedness (1 · 30) 957
עַוְלָה	injustice, unrighteousness, wrong (1 · 32) 732
קצר	to reap, harvest (3 · 24 · 24) 894
כַּחַשׁ	lying, falsehood; leanness (3 · 6) 471
שָׁאוֹן 14	din, crash, roar (1 · 18) 981
מִבְצָר	fortress, stronghold (1 · 37) 131
שֹׁד	devastation, ruin (4 · 25) 994; but BDB reads inf. to devastate
רטשׁ	to be dashed in pieces (2 · 4 · 6) 936
כָּכָה 15	thus (1 · 34) 462
שַׁחַר	dawn [obscure use] (2 · 23) 1007
נדְמָה	to be cut off, destroyed, ruined (4 · 13 · 17) 198

Chapter 11

פָּסִיל 2	idol, image (1 · 23) 820
תרגל 3	Tiph. verb form = to teach to walk (1 · 1 · 15) 920
קחם	BDB p. 542 reads אכחם w. LXX, τ, etc. from vb. לקח
חֶבֶל 4	cord, band; humanely, kindly (1 · 49) 286
מָשַׁךְ	to draw, lead [in love] (2 · 30 · 36) 604

עֲבֹת	cord, rope (1 · 24) 721
עֹל	yoke (1 · 40) 760
לְחִי	jaw, jawbone, cheek (1 · 21) 534
מֵאֵן 5	to refuse (1 · 46 · 46) 549
חוּל	to whirl, whirl about, dance, writhe (1 · 6 · 9) 296-297 Lis. 468 2 roots
בַּד	gate bar, rod, pole (1 · 41) 94
מוֹעֵצָה	counsel, plan, principle (1 · 7) 420
תלא 7	to hang; but Ho 117 prob. corrupt [hung to my backsliding = [?] (1 · 3 · 3) 1067
מְשׁוּבָה	turning back, apostasy (2 · 12) 1000
עַל	subst. "height" as adv. upward w. אל (2 · 8) 752
יַחַד	all together, altogether (2 · 44) 403
מגן 8	to deliver up (1 · 3 · 3) 171
יַחַד	all together, altogether (2 · 44) 403
נכמר	to grow warm and tender, grow hot (1 · 4 · 4) 485
נחום,נחמים	compassion, comfort (1 · 3) 637
חָרוֹן 9	[burning of] anger (1 · 41) 354
עִיר	agitation (1 · 2) 735
אַרְיֵה 10	lion (1 · 45) 71
שׁאג	to roar (2 · 20 · 20) 980
חָרַד	to go or come trembling; to tremble, be anxiously careful (2 · 23 · 39) 353
חָרַד 11	to go or come trembling; to tremble, be anxiously careful (2 · 23 · 39) 353
צִפּוֹר	bird, birds (1 · 40) 861-862
יוֹנָה	dove (2 · 33) 401

Chapter 12

כַּחַשׁ 1	lying, falsehood; leanness (3 · 6) 471
מִרְמָה	deceit, treachery (2 · 39) 941
רָד ,רוד	to wander restlessly, roam; but BDB says crpt. (1 · 2 · 4) 923

כָּזָב 2 lie, falsehood, deceptive thing (2 · 31) 469

שֹׁד violence, havoc, devastation, ruin (4 · 25) 994

הוּבַל to be borne along, carried; to be led, conducted (2 · 11 · 18) 384-385

מַעֲלָל 3 deed, practice, bad practice (5 · 41) 760

עָקַב 4 to attack at the heel, follow at the heel; to overreach (1 · 3 · 3) 784 Lis. 1109 2 rts.

אוֹן vigor, strength, wealth (2 · 10) 20

שָׂרָה to persevere, persist, exert oneself (1 · 2 · 2) 975

שָׂרָה, שׂוּר 5 to persevere, persist, exert oneself (1 · 1 · 1) 975

זֵכֶר 6 memorial, remembrance (2 · 23) 271

קַוֵּה 7 to wait or look eagerly for (1 · 39 · 45) 875

כְּנַעַן 8 merchant; Canaan (1 · 4) 488

מֹאזֵן balances (1 · 15) 24-25

מִרְמָה deceit, treachery (2 · 39) 941

עָשַׁק to practice extortion, oppress, wrong (2 · 36 · 37) 798

עָשַׁר 9 to be [become] rich (1 · 2 · 17) 799

אוֹן wealth; vigor; strength (2 · 10) 20

יְגִיעַ product, produce, acquired property (1 · 16) 388

חֵטְא sin, guilt of sin, punishment for sin (1 · 33) 307-308

חָזוֹן 11 divine communication in a vision, oracle, prophecy; vision (1 · 35) 302-303

דִּמָּה to use comparisons or similitudes; to liken, compare, think (*1 · 13 · 27) 197 *Lis. missed this entry

גַּל 12 heap, wave, billow (1 · 20) 164

תֶּלֶם furrow (2 · 5) 1068

שָׂדַי field:land (2 · 13) 961

תַּמְרוּר 15 bitterness (1 · 3) 601

נָטַשׁ to leave, forsake, permit (1 · 33 · 40) 643-644

Chapter 13

רְתֵת 1 trembling (1 · 1) 958

אָשַׁם to be [become] guilty, do wrong (5 · 33 · 35) 79

מַסֵּכָה 2 molten metal or image; libation (1 · 25) 651

תְּבוּנָה act of understanding, faculty of understanding, object of knowledge (1 · 42) 108

עֹצֶב idol (4 · 17) 781

חָרָשׁ graver, artificer, worker in metal (2 · 38) 360

עֵגֶל calf, image of calf (3 · 35) 722

נָשַׁק to kiss (1 · 26 · 32) 676

טַל 3 dew, night mist (3 · 31) 378

מֹץ chaff (1 · 8) 558

סֹעַר to be storm-driven (1 · 1 · 7) 704

גֹּרֶן threshing floor (3 · 34) 175

עָשָׁן smoke (1 · 25) 798

אֲרֻבָּה lattice, latticed opening, window, sluice (1 · 9) 70

זוּלָה 4 except, besides (1 · 16) 265

מוֹשִׁיעַ ptc. = savior (1 · 27) 446

בִּלְתִּי after a preceding negation, not [= except]; not (1 · 24) 116

תַּלְאֻבוֹת, תַּלְאֵבָה 5 drought [Lis. 1519 fever] (1 · 1) 520

מַרְעִית 6 pasturage, pasturing (1 · 10) 945

שַׁחַל 7 lion (2 · 7) 1006

נָמֵר leopard (1 · 6) 649

שׁוּר to watch, lie in wait (2 · 16 · 16) 1003

פָּגַשׁ 8 to meet, encounter (1 · 10 · 14) 803

דֹּב — bear (1 · 12) 179

שַׁכּוּל — bereaved, robbed of offspring (1 · 6) 1014

סְגוֹר — enclosure, encasement (1 · 2) 689

לָבִיא — lion, lioness (1 · 11) 522

עֹזֵר — 9 one who helps, help (1 · 21) 740

אֱהִי — 10 where[?] (3 · 3) 13

אֵפוֹא — enclitic part. = then (1 · 15) 66

עֶבְרָה — 11 overflowing rage, fury; overflow (2 · 34) 720

צָפַן — 12 to hide, lie hidden, lurk (1 · 24 · 29)

חֵבֶל — 13 pains of travail, pain (1 · 7) 286

מַשְׁבֵּר, מִשְׁבָּר — breach, mouth of womb (1 · 3) 991

אֱהִי — 14 where[?] (3 · 3) 13

דֶּבֶר — pestilence, plague (1 · 3) 184

קֹטֶב — destruction (1 · 4) 881

נֹחַם — sorrow, repentance (1 · 1) 637

הפרה, הפריא — 15 to show fruitfulness, bear fruit (1 · 1 · 1) 826 Lis. sep. root פרא p.1183

מָקוֹר — spring, fountain [= source of life and vigor] (1 · 18) 881

חרב — to be dried up, be dry (1 · 17 · 37) 351

מַעְיָן — spring (1 · 23) 745-746

שסה — to spoil, plunder (1 · 4 · 5) 1042

חֶמְדָּה — desire, delight (1 · 16) 326

Chapter 14

אָשַׁם — 1 to be or become guilty (5 · 33 · 35) 79

מָרָה — to be disobedient, rebellious (1 · 21 · 43) 598

עוֹלָל, עוֹלֵל — child (1 · 11) 760

רטש — to be dashed in pieces (2 · 3 · 6) 936

הָרִיָה, הָרָה — pregnant (1 · 15) 248

רחם — 4 to be shown compassion (3 · 4 · 47) 933

יָתוֹם — orphan (1 · 42) 450

מְשׁוּבָה — 5 turning back, apostasy (2 · 12) 1000

נְדָבָה — voluntariness (1 · 26) 621

טַל — 6 dew, night mist (3 · 31) 378

פָּרַח — to bud, sprout, send out shoots (3 · 28 · 33) 827

שׁוֹשַׁנָּה, שׁוּשַׁן — lily, lilylike flower (1 · 17) 1004

שֹׁרֶשׁ — root (2 · 33) 1057

יוֹנֶקֶת — 7 young shoot, twig (1 · 6) 413

זַיִת — olive tree, olives (1 · 38) 278

הוֹד — splendor, majesty (1 · 24) 217

דָּגָן — corn, cereal grain (6 · 40) 186

פָּרַח — to bud, sprout, send out shoots (3 · 28 · 33) 827

זֵכֶר — memorial, remembrance (2 · 23) 271

מַה־לּוֹ — 9 [idiom] formula of repudiation or emphatic denial (XXXX) מה para. 1.d. (c) 553

עָצָב — idol (4 · 17) 781

שׁוּר — to regard, observe; to watch, lie in wait (2 · 16 · 16) 1003

בְּרוֹשׁ — cypress, fir (1 · 20) 141

רַעֲנָן — luxuriant, fresh (1 · 19) 947

נָבוֹן — 10 ptc. = understanding, discerning (1 · 21) 106

פָּשַׁע — to transgress, rebel, revolt (3 · 40 · 41) 833

JOEL

Chapter 1

הַאֲזִין 2 to hear, give ear, listen (1 · 41 · 41) 24

גָּזָם 4 [coll.] locusts (2 · 3) 160

אַרְבֶּה a kind of locust, locust swarm (3 · 24) 916

יֶלֶק a kind of locust (3 · 9) 410

חָסִיל a kind of locust (2 · 6) 340

הֵקִיץ 5 to awake (1 · 22 · 23) 884

שִׁכּוֹר drunken; drunken one (1 · 13) 1016

הֵילִל to utter or make a howling, howl (3 · 30 · 30) 410

עָסִיס sweet wine (2 · 5) 779

עָצוּם 6 mighty, strong in numbers (4 · 31) 783

אַרְיֵה lion (1 · 45) 71

מְתַלְּעוֹת teeth, incisors (1 · 4) 1069

לָבִיא lion (1 · 11) 522

שַׁמָּה 7 appalling waste (1 · 39) 1031

תְּאֵנָה fig tree; fig (3 · 39) 1061

קְצָפָה a snapping or splintering (1 · 1) 893

חָשַׂף to strip, lay bear (2 · 10 · 10) 362

הִלְבִּין to show whiteness, grow white, make white (1 · 4 · 5) 526

שָׂרִיג tendril, twig (1 · 3) 974

אלה 8 to wail (1 · 1 · 1) 46

בְּתוּלָה virgin (1 · 50) 143

חגר to gird on, bind on (2 · 44 · 44) 291

שַׂק sackcloth, sack (2 · 48) 974

נְעוּרִים youth, early life (1 · 46) 655

אָבַל 9 to mourn, lament (2 · 18 · 38) 5

אָבַל 10 to mourn, lament (2 · 18 · 38) 5

דָּגָן corn, cereal grain (3 · 40) 186

תִּירוֹשׁ must, fresh or new wine (3 · 38) 440

אֻמְלַל to be or grow feeble, languish (2 · 15 · 15) 51

יִצְהָר fresh oil (3 · 23) 844

אִכָּר 11 plowman, husbandman (1 · 7) 38

הֵילִל to utter or make a howling, howl (3 · 30 · 30) 410

כֹּרֵם ptc. = vinedresser (1 · 5) 501

חִטָּה wheat (1 · 30) 334

שְׂעֹרָה barley (1 · 33) 972

קָצִיר what is harvested, crop; harvesting; time of harvest (2 · 49) 894

תְּאֵנָה 12 fig tree, fig (3 · 39) 1061

אֻמְלַל to be or grow feeble, languish (2 · 15 · 15) 51

רִמּוֹן pomegranate (1 · 32) 941

תָּמָר palm tree, date palm (1 · 12) 1071

תַּפּוּחַ apple tree, apple (1 · 6) 656

שָׂשׂוֹן exultation, joy (1 · 22) 965

חגר 13 to gird on, bind on (2 · 44 · 44) 291

ספד to wail, lament (1 · 28 · 30) 704

הֵילִל to utter or make a howling, howl (3 · 30 · 30) 410

שַׂק sackcloth, sack (2 · 48) 974

נִמְנַע to be withheld (1 · 4 · 29) 586

צוֹם 14 fast, fasting (3 · 26) 847

עֲצָרָה sacred assembly, assembly (2 · 11) 783

אֲהָהּ 15 [interj.] alas! (1 · 15) 13

שֹׁד devastation, ruin (1 · 25) 994

שַׁדַּי name of God = (1) self-sufficient, (2) almighty, or (3) my sovereign (1 · 48) 994-995

אֹכֶל 16 food (1 · 44) 38

גִּיל rejoicing (1 · 8) 162

עבשׁ 17 to shrivel (1 · 1 · 1) 721

פְּרֻדָה grain of seed; Lis. 1184 "dried fig" (1 · 1) 825

מֶגְרָפָה shovel (1 · 1) 175

נהרס to be thrown down, torn down (1 · 10 · 43) 248

מַמְּגֻרָה storehouse, granary (1 · 1) 158

דָּגָן corn, cereal grain (3 · 40) 186

נאנח 18 to sigh, groan (1 · 12 · 12) 58

157

נָבוֹךְ (בוך) to be confused, in confusion (1 · 3 · 3) 100

עֵדֶר flock, flocks and herds, herds (2 · 37) 727

מִרְעֶה pasturage, pasture (1 · 13) 945

נאשם to suffer punishment (1 · 1 · 35) 79

נָוֶה, נָוֶה 19 pasture, meadow (3 · 45) 627

לֶהָבָה flame (2 · 19) 529

לִהַט to set ablaze (2 · 9 · 11) 529

ערג 20 to long for (1 · 3 · 3) 788

אָפִיק channel, streambed, ravine (2 · 18) 67

נָוֶה, נָוֶה pasture, meadow (3 · 45) 627

Chapter 2

הריע 1 to sound a signal for war or march, to raise a shout (1 · 40 · 44) 929

רָגַז to quake, quiver, be excited, perturbed (2 · 30 · 41) 919

אֲפֵלָה 2 darkness (1 · 10) 66

עֲרָפֶל cloud, heavy cloud (1 · 15) 791

שַׁחַר dawn (1 · 23) 1007

עָצוּם mighty, strong in numbers (4 · 31) 783

דּוֹר וָדוֹר duration to come, future ages 189

לִהַט 3 to set ablaze (2 · 9 · 11) 529

גַּן garden, enclosure (1 · 41) 171

פְּלֵיטָה escaped remnant; escape, deliverance (2 · 28) 812

מֶרְכָּבָה 5 chariot (1 · 44) 939

רקד to dance, leap (1 · 5 · 9) 955

לַהַב flame; blade (1 · 12) 529

קַשׁ stubble, chaff (1 · 16) 905

עָצוּם mighty, strong in numbers (4 · 31) 783

חוּל, חִיל 6 to twist, writhe, dance (1 · 30 · 47) 297

פָּארוּר to gather a glow [dub.] (1 · 2) 802

עבט 7 lend on pledge [dub.], most read

עבת (1 · 1 · 1) Lis. 1018 "to change" 716

דחק 8 to thrust, crowd, oppress (1 · 1 · 1) 191

מְסִלָּה raised way, highway (1 · 27) 700

שֶׁלַח missile, weapon (1 · 8) 1019

בצע to cut off, break off (1 · 10 · 16) 130

שקק 9 to run, run about, rush (1 · 5 · 6) 1055

חַלּוֹן window (1 · 30) 319

גַּנָּב thief (1 · 30) 319

רָגַז 10 to quake, quiver, be excited, perturbed (2 · 30 · 41) 919

רעש to quake, shake (2 · 21 · 29) 950

יָרֵחַ moon (3-27) 437

קָדַר to be dark (2 · 13 · 17) 871

כּוֹכָב star (2 · 37) 456

נֹגַהּ brightness (2 · 19) 618

עָצוּם 11 mighty, strong in numbers (4 · 31) 783

נוֹרָא ptc. = awful, fearful (2 · 44) 431

הכיל to sustain, endure; to contain (1 · 12 · 38) 465   כול, כיל

צוֹם 12 fast, fasting (3 · 26) 847

בְּכִי weeping (1 · 30) 113

מִסְפֵּד wailing (1 · 16) 704

חַנּוּן 13 gracious (1 · 13) 337

רַחוּם compassionate (1 · 13) 933

אָרֵךְ long (1 · 15) 74

צוֹם 15 fast, fasting (3 · 26) 847

עֲצָרָה sacred assembly, assembly (2 · 11) 783

עוֹלָל 16 child (1 · 9) 760

יוֹנֵק ptc. = suckling, babe (1 · 11) 413

שַׁד female breast (1 · 21) 994

חָתָן bridegroom; daughter's husband (1 · 20) 368

חֶדֶר chamber, room (1 · 37) 293

כַּלָּה bride; daughter-in-law (1 · 34) 483

חֻפָּה canopy, chamber (1 · 3) 342

אֵילָם, אוּלָם porch (1 · 49) 17

חוּס to pity, look upon with compassion (1 · 24 · 24) 299

אַיֵּה where? (1 · 44) 32

קָנָא 18 to be zealous, jealous, envious (1 · 18 · 32) 888

חָמַל to spare, have compassion (1 · 40 · 40) 328

דָּגָן 19 corn, cereal grain (3 · 40) 186

תִּירוֹשׁ must, fresh or new wine (3 · 38) 440

יִצְהָר fresh oil (3 · 23) 844

צְפוֹנִי 20 northern one, northerner (1 · 1) 861

הִדִּיחַ to thrust out, banish (1 · 27 · 43) 623

צִיָּה dryness, drought (1 · 16) 851

קַדְמֹנִי eastern; former, ancient (1 · 10) 870

סוֹף end, conclusion (1 · 5) 693

בְּאֹשׁ stench (1 · 3) 93

צַחֲנָה stench (1 · 1) 850

גִּיל 21 to rejoice (2 · 45 · 45) 162

שָׂדַי 22 field, land (1 · 13) 961

דָּשָׁא to sprout, shoot, grow green (1 · 1 · 2) 205

נָוֶה, נָוֶה pasture, meadow (3 · 45) 627

תְּאֵנָה fig tree, fig (3 · 39) 1061

גִּיל 23 to rejoice (2 · 45 · 45) 162

מוֹרֶה [early] rain (1 · 2) 435

גֶּשֶׁם rain, shower (1 · 35) 177

מַלְקוֹשׁ latter rain, spring rain, showers of Mar.-Apr. (1 · 8) 545

גֹּרֶן 24 threshing floor (1 · 34) 175

בַּר grain, corn (1 · 14) 141

הֵשִׁיק to overflow (2 · 2 · 3) 1003

יֶקֶב wine vat (2 · 16) 428

תִּירוֹשׁ must, fresh or new wine (3 · 38) 440

יִצְהָר fresh oil (3 · 23) 844

אַרְבֶּה 25 a kind of locust, locust swarm (3 · 24) 916

יֶלֶק a kind of locust (3 · 9) 410

חָסִיל a kind of locust (2 · 6) 340

גָּזָם [coll.] locusts (2 · 3) 160

הִפְלִיא 26 to do wonderfully, wondrously; to do a hard thing (1 · 10 · 24) 810

Chapter 3

אַחֲרֵי־כֵן 1 afterwards (1 · [?]) para. 3.a. כֵּן 486

חָלַם to dream (1 · 27 · 29) 321

בָּחוּר young man (1 · 45) 104

חִזָּיוֹן vision, divine communication in a vision (1 · 9) 303

מוֹפֵת 3 wonder, sign, portent

תִּימָרָה [palmlike] column (1 · 2) 1071

עָשָׁן smoke (1 · 25) 798

יָרֵחַ 4 moon (3 · 27) 437

נוֹרָא awful, fearful (2 · 44) 431

פְּלֵיטָה escaped remnant; escape, deliverance (2 · 28) 812

שָׂרִיד survivor (1 · 28) 975

Chapter 4

שְׁבוּת 1 captivity, captives (1 · 26) 986

פִּזַּר 2 to scatter (1 · 7 · 10) 808

יַדַּד 3 to cast (1 · 3 · 3) 391

זוֹנָה ptc. = harlot (1 · 33) 275

יַלְדָּה girl, damsel (1 · 3) 409

גְּלִילָה 4 circuit, boundary, territory (1 · 6) 165

גְּמוּל recompense, dealing (3 · 19) 168

גָּמַל to recompense, deal fully with; wean; ripen (1 · 34 · 37) 168

קַל swift, swiftly; light (1 · 13) 886

מְהֵרָה haste; hastily (1 · 20) 555

מַחְמַד 5 desirable, precious things; desire (1 · 13) 326

גְּמוּל 7 recompense, dealing (3 · 19) 168

כָּתַת 10 form = imv. masc. pl., to beat, hammer, crush (1 · 5 · 17) 510

אֵת a cutting instrument of iron, plowshare (1 · 5) 88

מַזְמֵרָה pruning knife (1 · 4) 275

רֹמַח spear, lance (1 · 15) 942

חַלָּשׁ weak (1 · 1) 325

עוּשׁ 11 to lend aid, come to help [dub.] (1 · 1 · 1) 736

מִסָּבִיב on every side, from round about (2 · 42) 687

הַנְחִית to bring down; imv., on form sep. G.K. para. 64 h.3. (1 · 1 · 8) 639

מִסָּבִיב 12 on every side, from round about (2 · 42) 687

מַגָּל 13 sickle (1 · 2) 618

בָּשַׁל to boil, cook (1 · 2 · 27) 143

קָצִיר what is reaped, harvested; harvesting; time of harvest (2 · 49) 894

רדה Lis. 1318 to tread; BDB ירד (1 · 22 · 22) 921.432

גַּת winepress (1 · 5) 178

הֵשִׁיק to overflow (2 · 2 · 3) 1003

יֶקֶב wine vat (2 · 16) 428

חָרוּץ 14 strict decision (2 · 4) 358

יָרֵחַ 15 moon (3 · 27) 437

קָדַר to be dark (2 · 13 · 17) 871

כּוֹכָב star (2 · 37) 456

נֹגַהּ brightness (2 · 19) 618

שָׁאַג 16 to roar (1 · 20 · 20) 980

רעשׁ to quake, shake (2 · 21 · 29) 950

מַחֲסֶה refuge, shelter (1 · 20) 340

מָעוֹז refuge, place of safety (1 · 36) 731-732

נטף 18 to drip, drop (1 · 9 · 18) 642

עָסִיס sweet wine (2 · 5) 779

חָלָב milk (1 · 44) 316

אָפִיק channel, streambed, ravine (2 · 18) 67

מַעְיָן spring (1 · 23) 745

נָקִיא 19 innocent (1 · 43) 667

דּוֹר, נָדוֹר 20 duration to come; future ages 189

נקה 21 to leave unpunished (1 · 16 · 41) 667

160

AMOS

Chapter 1

נֹקֵד 1 sheep-raiser, -dealer, -tender (1 · 2) 667

רַעַשׁ earthquake, quaking, shaking (1 · 17) 950

שָׁאַג 2 to roar (3 · 20 · 20) 980

אָבַל to mourn, lament (3 · 18 · 20) 5

נָוֶה, נָוָה pasture, meadow (1 · 45) 627

דּוּשׁ, דָּשׁ 3 to thresh, tread on (1 · 13 · 15) 190

חָרוּץ sharp (1 · 4) 358

אַרְמוֹן 4 castle, palace (12 · 33) 74

בְּרִיחַ 5 bar, gate bar (1 · 41) 138

בִּקְעָה plain, valley (0 · 19) 132

תָּמַךְ to wield, grasp, lay hold of (2 · 20 · 21) 1069

קִיר prop. noun

גָּלוּת 6 exiles, exile (2 · 15) 163

שָׁלֵם full, complete; at peace (2 · 28) 1023

אַרְמוֹן 7 castle, palace (12 · 33) 74

תָּמַךְ 8 to wield, grasp, lay hold of (2 · 20 · 21) 1069

גָּלוּת 9 exiles, exile (2 · 15) 163

שָׁלֵם full, complete; at peace (2 · 28) 1023

אַרְמוֹן 10 castle, palace (12 · 33) 74

רַחֲמִים 11 compassion (1 · 38) 933

טָרַף to tear, rend (1 · 19 · 24) 383

עֶבְרָה overflowing rage, fury; overflow, arrogance (1 · 34) 720

נֵצַח everlastingness, ever (2 · 43) 664

אַרְמוֹן 12 castle, palace (12 · 33) 74

הָרָה, הָרֶה 13 pregnant woman, pregnant (1 · 15) 248

הִרְחִיב to enlarge, make large (1 · 21 · 25) 931

הִצִּית 14 to kindle (1 · 17 · 27) 428

אַרְמוֹן castle, palace (12 · 33) 74

תְּרוּעָה war cry, shout or blast of war (2 · 36) 929-930

סַעַר tempest (1 · 8) 704

סוּפָה storm wind (1 · 15) 693

גּוֹלָה 15 exile, exiles (1 · 42) 163

Chapter 2

שִׂיד 1 lime, whitewash (1 · 4) 966

אַרְמוֹן castle, palace (12 · 33) 74

שָׁאוֹן roar, din (1 · 18) 980

תְּרוּעָה war cry, shout or blast of war (2 · 36) 929-930

הִתְעָה 4 cause to err, mislead (1 · 21 · 50) 1073

כָּזָב lie, falsehood (1 · 31) 469

אַרְמוֹן 5 castle, palace (12 · 33) 74

בַּעֲבוּר 6 for the sake of, on account of, in order that (2 · 45) 721

נַעַל sandal, shoe (2 · 22) 653

שָׁאַף 7 to trample on, crush (2 · 14 · 14) 983

דַּל reduced, weak, helpless (4 · 48) 195

עָנָו poor and weak, needy (1 · 21) 776

חָבַל 8 to hold by a pledge (1 · 13 · 14) 286

עָנַשׁ to punish; ptc. pass. = those fined (1 · 6 · 9)

גֹּבַהּ 9 height; exaltation, grandeur; haughtiness (2 · 9) 147

חָסֹן strong (1 · 2) 340

אַלּוֹן oak (1 · 9) 47

מִמַּעַל above (1 · 29) 751 מַעַל para. 1.

שֹׁרֶשׁ root (1 · 33) 1057

בָּחוּר 11 young man (3 · 45) 104

נָזִיר devotee (2 · 16) 634

נָזִיר 12 devotee (2 · 16) 634

הֵעִיק 13 [dub.] read הָפִיק to totter, cause to totter (2 · 2 · 2) 734

עֲגָלָה cart (1 · 25) 722

עָמִיר swath, row of fallen grain (1 · 4) 771

מָנוֹס 14 place of escape, refuge; flight
(1 · 8) 631

קַל light, swift, fleet (2 · 13) 886-887

אָמֵץ to make firm, strengthen, assure,
harden (1 · 19 · 41) 54-55

קַל 15 light, swift, fleet (2 · 13) 886-887

אַמִּיץ 16 mighty (1 · 6) 55

עָרוֹם naked (1 · 16) 736

Chapter 3

בִּלְתִּי אִם 3 save that, except (2 · 24) 116, 50

נוֹעַד to meet by appointment (1 · 18 · 28)
416

שָׁאַג 4 to roar (3 · 20 · 20) 980

אַרְיֵה lion (2 · 45) 71

טֶרֶף prey (1 · 17) 383

כְּפִיר young lion (1 · 31) 498

מְעֹנָה den, lair, refuge (1 · 9) 733

בִּלְתִּי אִם save that, except (2 · 24) 116, 50

צִפּוֹר 5 bird; [coll.] birds (1 · 40) 862

פַּח bird trap (2 · 25) 809

מוֹקֵשׁ bait, lure (1 · 27) 430

חָרַד 6 to be startled, tremble, be terrified
(1 · 23 · 39) 353

סוֹד 7 secret counsel, counsel, council
(1 · 21) 691

אַרְיֵה 8 lion (2 · 45) 71

שָׁאַג to roar (3 · 20 · 20) 980

אַרְמוֹן castle, palace (12 · 33) 74

מְהוּמָה tumult, confusion (1 · 12) 223

עֲשׁוּקִים oppression, extortion (1 · 3) 799

נָכֹחַ 10 straightforwardness, honesty;
straight, right (1 · 8) 647

אָצַר to store up (1 · 3 · 5) 69

שֹׁד violence, havoc; ruin (3 · 25) 994

אַרְמוֹן castle, palace (12 · 33) 74

נבז 11 to be spoiled, plundered (1 · 3 · 41)
102-103

אַרְמוֹן castle, palace (12 · 33) 74

אֲרִי 12 lion (2 · 35) 71

כְּרָעִים, כְּרָע leg, legs (1 · 9) 502

בְּדַל piece, severed piece (1 · 1) 95

מִטָּה couch, bed (2 · 29) 641

דְּמֶשֶׁק [meaning dub.] (1 · 1) 200

עֶרֶשׂ couch, divan (2 · 11) 793

הֵעִיד 13 to cause to testify, to take as witness, bear witness (1 · 38 · 43) 729-
730

נִגְדַּע to be hewn off (1 · 7 · 22) 154

חֹרֶף 15 harvest time, autumn; w. בית = autumn house or palace (1 · 7) 358

קַיִץ summer, summer fruit (3 · 20) 884

סוּף to come to an end, cease (1 · 4 · 8)
692

Chapter 4

פָּרָה 1 heifer, cow (1 · 26) 831

עָשַׁק to oppress, wrong (1 · 36 · 37) 798

דַּל reduced, poor, weak (4 · 48) 195

רצץ to crush, oppress (1 · 11 · 19) 954

צִנָּה, צֵן 2 hook or barb (1 · 3) 856

סִיר hook, thorn (1 · 5) 696

דּוּגָה fishing, fishery (1 · 1) 186

פֶּרֶץ 3 breach, bursting forth, outburst
(2 · 19) 829

הַרְמוֹן [meaning dub.] perh. a proper loca-
tion (1 · 1) 248

פָּשַׁע 4 to transgress, rebel (2 · 40 · 41) 833

מַעֲשֵׂר tithe, payment of tenth part (1 · 33)
798

חָמֵץ 5 that which is leavened (1 · 11) 329

תּוֹדָה thank offering, thanksgiving (1 · 32)
392

נְדָבָה free will or voluntary offering,
voluntariness (1 · 26) 621

נִקָּיוֹן 6 cleanness [though perh. קהיון
''bluntness''], innocency (1 · 5) 667

חֹסֶר want, lack (1 · 3) 341

מָנַע 7 to withhold, hold back (1 · 25 · 29) 586

גֶּשֶׁם rain, shower (1 · 35) 177

בְּעוֹד within yet (1 · 20) עוד 2.a. 729

קָצִיר harvesting; harvest; time of harvest (1 · 49) 894

הִמְטִיר to send rain; rain (3 · 16 · 17) 565

חֶלְקָה portion of ground (2 · 24) 324

נמטר to be rained on (1 · 1 · 17) 565

נוע 8 to totter, go tottering; to wave (2 · 22 · 38) 631

שִׁדָּפוֹן 9 smut [on crops] (1 · ה) 995

יֵרָקוֹן rust, mildew, paleness (1 · 6) 439

גַּנָּה garden, orchard (2 · 16) 171

תְּאֵנָה fig tree, fig (1 · 39) 1061

זַיִת olive tree, olive (1 · 38) 268

גָּזָם [coll.] locusts (1 · 3) 160

דֶּבֶר 10 plague, pestilence (1 · 46) 184

בָּחוּר young man (3 · 45) 104

שְׁבִי act of capture; captivity; captives (2 · 49) 985

בְּאֹשׁ stench (1 · 3) 93

מַהְפֵּכָה 11 overthrow (1 · 6) 246

אוּד brand, firebrand (1 · 3) 15

שְׂרֵפָה burning (1 · 13) 977

עֵקֶב 12 because, as a consequence of (1 · 15) 784

יָצַר 13 to form, fashion (2 · 41 · 44) 427

בָּרָא to shape, fashion, create (1 · 38 · 48) 135

שֵׂחַ thought (1 · 1) 967

עֹשֶׂה ptc. = maker (2 · 24) 793

שַׁחַר dawn (1 · 23) 1007

עֵיפָה darkness (1 · 2) 734

Chapter 5

קִינָה 1 elegy, dirge (2 · 17) 884

בְּתוּלָה 2 virgin (2 · 50) 143-144

נטש to be forsaken (1 · 6 · 40) 643

כבה 6 to quench, extinguish (1 · 10 · 24) 459

לַעֲנָה 7 wormwood (2 · 8) 542

עֹשֶׂה 8 ptc. = maker (2 · 24) 793

כִּימָה Pleiades (1 · 3) 465

כְּסִיל Orion (1 · 4) 493

צַלְמָוֶת deep shadow, death shadow (1 · 18) 853

הֶחְשִׁיךְ to make dark, cause darkness (2 · 6 · 17) 364-365

הִבְלִיג 9 to cause to burst or flash; to smile, look cheerful (1 · 4 · 4) 114

שֹׁד devastation, ruin, violence, havoc (3 · 25) 994

עַז mighty one; mighty, strong (1 · 22) 738

מִבְצָר fortress, stronghold (1 · 37) 131

תעב 10 to regard as an abomination (1 · 15 · 22) 1073

בושס 11 to trample; [inf.] trampling (1 · 1 · 1) 143

דַּל reduced, poor, weak (4 · 48) 195

מַשְׂאָה, מַשָּׂאת portion, present, offering; that which rises; utterance; burden (1 · 16) 673

בַּר grain, corn (3 · 14) 141

גָּזִית cutting, hewing (1 · 11) 159

חֶמֶד desire, delight (1 · 5) 326

עָצוּם 12 numerous, countless (1 · 31) 783

צָרַר to show hostility toward, vex; ptc. = vexer, harasser (1 · 10 · 10) 865

כֹּפֶר the price of a life, ransom (1 · 13) 497

דמם 13 to be silent, be still (1 · 23 · 30) 198-199

כֵּן 14 emphasis of agreement כֵּן 2.d. or right, honest (1 · 24) 486, 487

הִצִּיג 15 to set up, establish; to place (1 · 15 · 16) 426

אוּלַי   peradventure, perhaps (1 · 45) 19

רְחוֹב, רְחֹב   16 broad open place, plaza (1 · 43) 932

מִסְפֵּד   wailing (3 · 16) 704

הוֹ   [interj.] Ah! (1 · 1) 214

אִכָּר   plowman, husbandman (1 · 7) 38

אֵבֶל   mourning (3 · 24) 5

נְהִי   mourning song, lamentation (1 · 7) 7

מִסְפֵּד   17 wailing (3 · 16) 704

הִתְאַוָּה   18 to desire, long for, lust after (1 · 16 · 27) 16

אֲרִי   19 lion (2 · 35) 71

פָּגַע   to meet, light upon, encounter (1 · 40 · 46) 803

דֹּב   bear (1 · 12) 179

סָמַךְ   to lean, lay, rest, support (1 · 41 · 48) 701

נָשַׁךְ   to bite (2 · 10 · 12) 675

נָחָשׁ   fleeing serpent, serpent (2 · 31) 638

אָפֵל   20 gloomy (1 · 1) 66

נֹגַהּ   brightness (1 · 19) 618

הֵרִיחַ   21 to smell or perceive odor; here metaph. = delight in (1 · 11 · 14) 926

עֲצָרָה   assembly, sacred assembly (1 · 11) 783

רָצָה   22 to accept favorably, be pleased with (1 · 42 · 50) 953

מְרִיא   fatling, fatlings (1 · 8) 597

זִמְרָה   23 melody, song (1 · 4) 274

נֶבֶל   harp, lute, guitar (2 · 27) 614

נגול   24 to roll, roll up, roll along (1 · 2 · 17) 164

אֵיתָן   ever-flowing, steady flow, permanent (1 · 14) 450

סִכּוּת   26 n. pr. div. Sakkut (1 · 1) 696

כִּיּוּן   n. pr. dei. Saturn (1 · 1) 475

צֶלֶם   image, likeness (1 · 17) 853

כּוֹכָב   star (1 · 37) 456

מֵהָלְאָה   27 out there, onward, further (1 · 3) 229

     הָלְאָה

Chapter 6

הוֹי   1 [interj.] Ah! (2 · 51) 222-223

שַׁאֲנָן   at ease, careless, wanton, arrogant; secure (1 · 11) 983

נָקוֹב   ptc. = noted, distinguished, to prick off, designate; pierce (1 · 13 · 19) 666

נדה   3 to thrust off, exclude, put away (1 · 2 · 2) 622

מִטָּה   couch, bed (2 · 29) 641

סרה   to go free, be unrestrained; to exceed, overhang (1 · 3 · 4) 710

שֶׁבֶת   seat, place of sitting (1 · 7) 443

עֶרֶשׂ   4 couch, divan (2 · 11) 793

כַּר   he-lamb (1 · 12) 503

עֵגֶל   calf (1 · 35) 722

מַרְבֵּק   stall, calves from stall = fattened calves (1 · 4) 918

פרט   5 [dub.] to chant, scatter, stammer (1 · 1 · 1) 827

נֶבֶל   harp, lute, guitar (2 · 27) 614

מִזְרָק   6 bowl, basin (1 · 32) 284

שֵׁבֶר   breaking, fracture (1 · 45) 991

מִרְזַח   7 cry, cry of mourning (1 · 2) 931

סָרוּחַ   ptc. pass. = sprawler (1 · 3) 710

תאב   8 to loathe (1 · 1 · 1) 1060

גָּאוֹן   exaltation, majesty, excellence, pride (2 · 49) 144-145

אַרְמוֹן   castle, palace (12 · 33) 74

מְלֹא   fullness, that which fills, entire contents (1 · 38) 571

סרף   10 ptc. = burner, one who burns something (1 · 1 · 1) 977

לַאֲשֶׁר   to him who, to that which, to those who (1 · 38) 82

יַרְכָּה, יְרֵכָה   recess, innermost part; side, flank (1 · 28) 438

הָס   [interj.] Hush! Keep silent! (2 · 6) 245

רָסִיס	11	fragment (1 · 1) 944
בָּקִיעַ, בקע		fissure, breach (1 · 2) 132
חרשׁ	12	to plow, cut in, engrave (2 · 23 · 26) 360
רוֹשׁ, רֹאשׁ		a bitter and poisonous herb, venom (1 · 12) 912
לַעֲנָה		wormwood (2 · 8) 542
שָׂמֵחַ	13	one showing joy; joyful, glad (1 · 21) 970
לֹא		without (1 · 11) לא 4.e. 520
חֹזֶק		strength (1 · 5) 305
לָחַץ	14	to oppress, squeeze, press (1 · 14 · 15) 537

Chapter 7

יָצַר	1	to form, fashion (2 · 41 · 44) 427-428
גֹּבַי		[coll.] locusts (1 · 2) 146
תְּחִלָּה		beginning (1 · 22) 321
לֶקֶשׁ		aftergrowth, spring crop (2 · 2) 545
גֵּז		shearing, mowing (1 · 4) 159
עֵשֶׂב	2	herb, herbage (1 · 33) 793
סלח		to forgive, pardon (1 · 33 · 40) 699
תְּהוֹם	4	deep; deep sea, abyss (1 · 36) 1062
אֲנָךְ	7	plummet, plum bob (4 · 4) 59
אֲנָךְ	8	plummet, plum bob (4 · 4) 59
חרב	9	to be waste, desolate (1 · 9 · 37) 351
קָשַׁר	10	to league together, conspire, bind (1 · 35 · 43) 905
הכיל		to sustain, endure; to contain, hold in (1 · 12 · 38) 465
חֹזֶה	12	seer (1 · 17) 302
בּוֹקֵר	14	herdsman (1 · 1) 133
בלס		ptc. = gatherer of or gathering figs or sycamore fruit (1 · 1 · 1) 118
שִׁקְמָה		sycamore tree (1 · 7) 1054
הטיף	16	to discourse; to drip (2 · 9 · 18) 642-643

חֶבֶל	17	measuring cord, line, band; measured portion, region (1 · 49) 28

Chapter 8

כְּלוּב	1	basket, cage (2 · 3) 477
קַיִץ		summer fruit, summer (3 · 20) 884
כְּלוּב	2	basket, cage (2 · 3) 477
קַיִץ		summer fruit, summer (3 · 20) 884
הֵילִל	3	to become howlings, make a howling, howl (1 · 30 · 30) 410
שִׁירָה		song (1 · 13) 1010
פֶּגֶר		corpse, carcass (1 · 22) 803
הָס, הַס		[inter.] Hush! Keep silent! (2 · 6) 245
שָׁאַף	4	to trample on, crush (2 · 14 · 14) 983
לשבית		= ל = השבית; see G.K. para. 53.q. 991
ענו		poor, afflicted (1 · 21) 776
מָתַי	5	when[?] (1 · 42) 607
השׁביר		to sell grain (2 · 5 · 21) 991
שֶׁבֶר		corn, grain (1 · 9) 991
בַּר		grain, corn (3 · 14) 141
הקטין		to make small (1 · 1 · 4) 881
אֵיפָה		receptacle holding an ephah, ephah, a certain quantity (1 · 39) 35
עוה		to make crooked, falsify, pervert (1 · 9 · 11) 736
מֹאזְנַיִם, מאזן		balances, scales (1 · 15) 24-25
מִרְמָה		deceit, treachery (1 · 39) 941
דַּל	6	reduced, poor, weak (4 · 48) 195
בַּעֲבוּר		for the sake of, on account of, in order that (2 · 45) 721
נַעַל		sandal, shoe (2 · 22) 653
מַפָּל		fallings, refuse; hanging part (1 · 2) 658
בַּר		grain, corn (3 · 14) 141
השׁביר		to sell grain (2 · 5 · 21) 991

גָּאוֹן	7	exaltation, majesty, excellence, pride (2 · 49) 144-145
נֶצַח		everlastingness, ever, w. ל = for-ever (2 · 43) 664
רָגַז	8	to quake, be disquieted, perturbed, excited (1 · 30 · 41) 919
אָבַל		to mourn, lament (3 · 18 · 20) 5
אֹר		Nile
נִגְרַשׁ		to be driven, tossed (1 · 3 · 48) 176
נשקה		Q נשקע to sink (1 · 1 · 6) 1054
יְאוֹר		Nile
צָהֳרַיִם	9	noon, midday (1 · 23) 843-844
הֶחְשִׁיךְ		to cause darkness, make darkness (2 · 6 · 17) 364-365
אֵבֶל	10	mourning (3 · 24) 5
קִינָה		elegy, dirge (2 · 17) 884
מָתְנַיִם		loins (1 · 47) 608
שַׂק		sackcloth, sack (1 · 48) 974
קָרְחָה		bald spot, baldness (1 · 11) 901
יָחִיד		only one, one (1 · 12) 402
מַר		bitterness; bitter (1 · 38) 600
צָמָא	11	thirst (2 · 17) 854
נוע	12	to totter, go tottering; to wave, quiver (2 · 22 · 38) 631
שׁוֹטֵט		to go eagerly, quickly, to and fro (1 · 5 · 13) 1001-1002
הִתְעַלֵּף	13	to enwrap oneself, swoon away (1 · 3 · 5) 763
בְּתוּלָה		virgin (2 · 50) 143-144
יָפֶה		fair, beautiful (1 · 41) 421
בָּחוּר		young man (3 · 45) 104
צָמָא		thirst (2 · 17) 854
אַשְׁמָה		becoming guilty, doing wrong (1 · 19) 80

Chapter 9

כַּפְתּוֹר	1	capital, knob, bulb (1 · 16) 499
רַעַשׁ		to quake, shake (1 · 21 · 29) 950
סַף		threshold, sill (1 · 25) 706

בָּצַע		to cut off, break off (1 · 10 · 16) 130
פָּלִיט		escaped one, fugitive (1 · 19) 812
חָתַר	2	to dig into; to row (1 · 8 · 8) 369
נֶחְבָּא	3	to hide oneself (1 · 16 · 34) 285
חפשׂ		to search for, search through (1 · 8 · 23) 344
מִנֶּגֶד		from before, in front of, opposite (1 · 26) 617
קַרְקַע		floor (1 · 7) 903
נָחָשׁ		serpent (2 · 31) 638
נָשַׁךְ		to bite (2 · 10 · 12) 675
שְׁבִי	4	state of captivity, captives, act of capture (2 · 49) 985
מוּג	5	to melt, faint (1 · 4 · 17) 556
אָבַל		to mourn, lament (3 · 18 · 20) 5
יְאֹר		Nile
שָׁקַע		to sink, sink down (1 · 3 · 6) 1054
מַעֲלָה	6	story, step, stair, ascent (1 · 47) 752
אֲגֻדָּה		vault; band, bunch (1 · 4) 8
יסד		to found, establish (1 · 20 · 41) 413-414
חַטָּא	7	sinful; sinner (2 · 19) 308
אֶפֶס כִּי	8	save that, yet (1 · 4) 67
הֵנִיעַ	9	to shake, cause to totter (1 · 14 · 38) 631
נְנוֹעַ		to be tossed about (1 · 2 · 38) 631
כְּבָרָה		sieve; netlike implement (1 · 1) 460
צְרוֹר		bundle, parcel, pouch (1 · 2) 865
חַטָּא	10	sinner; sinful (2 · 19) 308
הִקְדִּים		to come in front of (1 · 2 · 26) 869-870
סֻכָּה	11	booth, thicket (1 · 31) 697
גָּדַר		to wall up, build a wall (1 · 7 · 7) 154
פֶּרֶץ		breach, bursting forth, outburst (2 · 19) 829
הֲרִיסָה		ruin (1 · 1) 249
חָרַשׁ	13	to plow; ptc. = plowman; to cut in, engrave (2 · 23 · 26) 360
קָצַר		ptc. = reaper (1 · 10) 894

עֵנָב   grapes, grape (1 · 19) 772

מָשַׁךְ   to trail, draw along, draw, draw out, drag (1 · 30 · 36) 604

הטיף   to drip; to discourse (2 · 9 · 18) 642-643

עָסִיס   sweet wine, pressed-out juice (1 · 5) 779

התמוגג   to melt, flow (1 · 3 · 17) 556

שְׁבוּת   14 captivity, captives (1 · 26) 986

גַּנָּה   garden, orchard (2 · 16) 171

נתש   15 to be rooted up, pulled up (1 · 4 · 21) 684

OBADIAH

Chapter 1

חָזוֹן	1	vision (1 · 35) 302-303
שְׁמוּעָה		report (1 · 27) 1035
צִיר		envoy, messenger (1 · 6) 851
בָּזָה	2	to despise; ptc. pass. = despised (1 · 31 · 42) 102
זָדוֹן	3	presumptuousness, presumption, insolence (1 · 10) 268
הִשִּׁיא		to beguile (2 · 15 · 16) 674
חָגוּ		place of concealment, retreat (1 · 3) 291
הִגְבִּיהַ	4	to make high, exalt (1 · 10 · 34) 146-147
נֶשֶׁר		griffon vulture, eagle (1 · 26) 676-677
כּוֹכָב		star (1 · 37) 456-457
קֵן		nest (1 · 13) 890
גַּנָּב	5	thief (1 · 17) 170
נִדְמָה		to be cut off, destroyed, ruined (1 · 13 · 17) 198
גנב		to take by stealth, steal (1 · 30 · 39) 170
דַּי		sufficient for + suffix (1 · 12) 191
בצר		to gather grapes; ptc. = grape gathering or gatherer (1 · 7 · 7) 130-131
עֹלֵלוֹת עֹלֵלוֹת		gleaning (1 · 6) 760
נחפשׂ	6	ptc. = searched out (1 · 1 · 23) 344
נבעה		to be searched out (1 · 2 · 4) 126
מַצְפֻּן		hidden treasure, treasure (1 · 1) 861
הִשִּׁיא	7	to beguile (2 · 15 · 16) 674
מָזוֹר		[dub.] net, fetter, stumbling block (1 · 1) 561
תְּבוּנָה		act of understanding, faculty of understanding (2 · 42) 108
תְּבוּנָה	8	faculty of understanding, act of understanding (2 · 42) 108
קֶטֶל	9	slaughter (1 · 1) 881
בּוּשָׁה	10	shame (1 · 4) 102
מִנֶּגֶד	11	from or at a distance, in front of (1 · 26) נגד 2.c. 617
שׁבה		to take captive (1 · 30 · 38) 985
נָכְרִי		foreigner; foreign (1 · 45) 648
ידד		to cast a lot (1 · 3 · 3) 391
נֵכֶר, נֶכֶר	12	misfortune, calamity (1 · 2) 648
אֵיד	13	calamity, distress (3 · 24) 15
פֶּרֶק	14	parting of ways; plunder (1 · 2) 830
שָׂרִיט		escaped one, fugitive (1 · 19) 812
שָׂרִיד		survivor (2 · 28) 975
גְּמוּל	15	recompense; dealing; benefit (1 · 19) 168
לוע, לעע	16	to swallow, swallow down (1 · 1 · 1) 534
כְּלוֹא		as though (1 · 1) לא 4.d. 520
פְּלֵיטָה	17	escaped remnant; escape (1 · 28) 812
מוֹרָשׁ		possession (1 · 2) 440
לֶהָבָה	18	flame (1 · 19) 529
קַשׁ		stubble, chaff (1 · 16) 905
דלק		to burn, hotly pursue (1 · 7 · 9) 196
שָׂרִיד		survivor (2 · 28) 975
שְׁפֵלָה	19	lowland (1 · 20) 1050
גָּלוּת, גָּלֻת	20	exiles, exile (2 · 15) 163
חֵיל, חֵל		fortress, rampart (1 · 9) 298
מוֹשִׁיעַ	21	ptc. = savior, deliverer (1 · 27) 446
מְלוּכָה		kingship, kingly office, royalty (1 · 24) 574

JONAH

Chapter 1

אֲנִיָּה 3 ship, merchant ship (3 · 31) 58

שָׂכָר passage money, fare, hire, wages (1 · 28) 969

הֵטִיל 4 to cast, cast out, hurl (4 · 9 · 14) 376

סַעַר tempest (2 · 8) 704

אֲנִיָּה ship, merchant ship (3 · 31) 58

מַלָּח 5 mariner, sailor (1 · 4) 572

הֵטִיל to cast, cast out, hurl (4 · 9 · 14) 376

אֲנִיָּה ship, merchant ship (3 · 31) 58

יַרְכָה dual recess, extreme parts (1 · 28) 438

סְפִינָה vessel, ship (1 · 1) 706

נִרְדָּם to be or fall fast asleep (2 · 7 · 7) 922

חֹבֵל 6 sailor (1 · 5) 287

נִרְדָּם to be or fall fast asleep (2 · 7 · 7) 922

אוּלַי perhaps, peradventure (1 · 45) 19

הִתְעַשֵּׁת to think, give a thought to (1 · 1 · 1) 799

בְּ שֶׁל מִי 7 on account of (1 · 1) שׁ para. 4.d. 980

בַּאֲשֶׁר לְמִי 8 [idiom] on account of me (1 · 1) מִי (1 · 20) לְמִי (1 · 19) בַּאֲשֶׁר 85 בַּאֲשֶׁר b. 566

מֵאַיִן so there is no, so there is not (1 · 48) אִין 6.d. 35

אֵי where? אֵי־מִזֶּה ה whence? (1 · 39) 32

יַבָּשָׁה 9 dry land, dry ground (3 · 14) 387

יִרְאָה 10 fear, terror (2 · 45) 432

שָׁתַק 11 to be quiet (2 · 4 · 4) 1060

סָעַר to storm, rage (2 · 3 · 7) 704

הֵטִיל 12 to cast, cast out, hurl (4 · 9 · 14) 376

שָׁתַק to be quiet (2 · 4 · 4) 1060

בְּשֶׁל on account of (1 · [?]) שׁ para. 4.d. 980

סַעַר tempest (2 · 8) 704

חָתַר 13 to row, dig (1 · 8 · 8) 369

יַבָּשָׁה dry land, dry ground (3 · 14) 387

סָעַר to storm, rage (2 · 3 · 7) 704

אָנָּה 14 strong particle of entreaty, I [we] beseech (2 · 6) 58

נָקִיא, נָקִי innocent (1 · 43) 667

הֵטִיל 15 to cast, cast out, hurl (4 · 9 · 14) 376

זַעַף raging, storming; rage (1 · 7) 277

יִרְאָה 16 fear, terror (2 · 45) 432

נָדַר to vow (2 · 31 · 31) 623

Chapter 2

מִנָּה 1 to appoint, ordain (4 · 9 · 28) 584

דָּג fish (3 · 19) 185

בָּלַע to swallow down, swallow up (1 · 20 · 41) 118

מֵעֶה internal organ; here = stomach, belly (2 · 32) 588-589

מֵעֶה 2 internal organ; here = stomach, belly (2 · 32) 588-589

דָּגָה fish (1 · 15) 185

שׁוּעַ 3 to cry for help (1 · 21 · 21) 1002

מְצוּלָה 4 deep, deep sea, depth (1 · 12) 846-847

מִשְׁבָּר breaker of sea; i.e., big wave (1 · 5) 991

גַּל wave, roller, billow, heap (1 · 16) 164

נִגְרַשׁ 5 to be driven, tossed (1 · 3 · 48) 176

מִנֶּגֶד from before, in front of, opposite (1 · 26) 617

אָפַף 6 to encompass, surround (1 · 5 · 5) 67

תְּהוֹם sea, deep sea; primeval (1 · 36) 1062-1063

סוּף rushes, reeds (1 · 4) 693

חָבַשׁ to bind, bind on or up; ptc. = bound (1 · 28 · 32) 289

קֶצֶב 7 extremity, bottom; shape, cut (1 · 3) 891

169

בְּרִיחַ   bar (1 · 41) 138

שַׁחַת   pit (1 · 23) 1001

הִתְעַטֵּף   8 to faint, faint away (1 · 6 · 11)

תּוֹדָה   10 thanksgiving in song, thanksgiving (1 · 32) 392

נָדַר   to vow (2 · 31 · 31) 623

דָּג   11 fish (3 · 19) 185

הֵקִיא   to vomit up (1 · 7 · 9) 883

יַבָּשָׁה   dry land, dry ground (3 · 14) 387

Chapter 3

קְרִיאָה   2 proclamation (1 · 1) 896

מַהֲלָךְ   3 journey, walk (2 · 5) 237

מַהֲלָךְ   4 journey, walk (2 · 5) 237

צוֹם   5 fast, fasting (1 · 26) 847

שַׂק   sackcloth, sack (3 · 48) 974

קָטֹן   insignificant, small (1 · 47) 881-882

אַדֶּרֶת   6 mantle, cloak; glory (1 · 12) 12

שַׂק   sackcloth, sack (3 · 48) 974

אֵפֶר   ashes (1 · 22) 68

טַעַם   7 decision, decree; judgment, taste (1 · 13) 381

טָעַם   to taste, perceive (1 · 11 · 11) 380-381

מְאוּמָה   anything (1 · 32) 548

שַׂק   8 sackcloth, sack (3 · 48) 974

חָזְקָה   severely, sharply; strength, force (1 · 6) 306

חָרוֹן   9 anger, burning of anger (1 · 41) 354

Chapter 4

אָנָּה   2 strong particle of entreaty, I or we beseech thee (2 · 6) 58

קָדַם   to be beforehand, go before, be in front; to meet, confront (1 · 24 · 26) 869-870

חַנּוּן   gracious (1 · 13) 337

רַחוּם   compassionate (1 · 13) 938

אֶרֶךְ   long, slow (1 · 15) 74

סֻכָּה   5 booth, temporary shelter (1 · 31) 697

מָנָה   6 to appoint, ordain (4 · 9 · 28) 584

קִיקָיוֹן   plant, perh. bottle-gourd (5 · 5) 884

מִנָּה   7 to appoint, ordain (4 · 9 · 28) 584

תּוֹלַעַת   worm, grub, vine weevil (1 · 41) 1069

שַׁחַר   dawn (1 · 23) 1007

מָחֳרָת   the morrow, day following a past day (1 · 32) 564

קִיקָיוֹן   plant, perh. bottle-gourd (5 · 5) 884

זָרַח   8 to rise, come forth, appear (1 · 18 · 18) 280

מִנָּה   to appoint, ordain (4 · 9 · 28) 584

חֲרִישִׁי   [meaning dub.] silent, still, sultry (1 · 1) 362 Lis. 531 "sharp, hot"

הִתְעַלֵּף   to swoon away; enwrap oneself (1 · 3 · 5) 763

קִיקָיוֹן   9 plant, perh. bottle-gourd (5 · 5) 884

חוּס   10 to look upon with compassion (2 · 24 · 24) 299

קִיקָיוֹן   plant, perh. bottle-gourd (5 · 5) 884

עָמַל   to labor, toil (1 · 11 · 11) 765

חוּס   11 to look upon with compassion (2 · 24 · 24) 299

רִבּוֹ   ten thousand, myriad (1 · 11) 914

MICAH

Chapter 1

הִקְשִׁיב	2 to give attention (1 · 45 · 46) 904
מְלֹא	fullness, that which fills, entire contents (1 · 38) 571
נָמֵס	4 niph. מסס, to melt, dissolve (1 · 19 · 21) 587
דּוֹנַג	wax (1 · 4) 200
הֻגַּר	hoph. נגר to be poured out, melted (1 · 1 · 10) 620
מוֹרָד	descent, slope (1 · 5) 434
עִי	6 ruin, heap of ruins (2 · 5) 730
מַטָּע	planting place; act of planting (1 · 6) 642
הִגִּיר	to pour down, hurl down (1 · 5 · 10) 620
גַּיְא	valley (1 · 47) 161
יְסוֹד	foundation (1 · 19) 414
פָּסִיל	7 idol, image (2 · 23) 820-821
הֻכַּת	hoph. כתת to be crushed, beat in pieces (1 · 4 · 17) 510
אֶתְנַן	hire of harlot (3 · 11) 1072
עָצָב	idol (1 · 17) 781
זוֹנָה	ptc. = harlot (2 · 33) 275-276
סָפַד	8 to wail, lament (1 · 28 · 30) 704
הֵילִל	to utter or make a howling, give a howl (1 · 30 · 30) 410
שִׁילָל	Q שׁוֹלָל barefoot (1 · 3) 1021
עָרוֹם	naked (1 · 16) 736
מִסְפֵּד	wailing (2 · 16) 704
תַּן	jackal (1 · 14) 1072
אֵבֶל	mourning (1 · 24) 5
יַעֲנָה	[dub.] greed (1 · 8) 419 Lis. 617 ostrich
אָנוּשׁ	9 ptc. pass. = incurable (1 · 8) 60
מַכָּה	wound, beating, blow (1 · 48) 646
הִתְפַּלֵּשׁ	10 to do an act of mourning; perh. roll in dust (1 · 4 · 4) 814

עֶרְיָה	11 nakedness (1 · 6) 789
בֹּשֶׁת	shame (1 · 30) 102
מִסְפֵּד	wailing (2 · 16) 704
עֶמְדָּה	standing ground (1 · 1) 765
חוּל, חִיל	12 to twist or writhe in anxious longing; to writhe, dance (1 · 3 · 5) 296-297 Lis. has sep. rt. 488
רְתֹם	13 to bind, attach (1 · 1 · 1) 958
מֶרְכָּבָה	chariot (2 · 44) 939
רֶכֶשׁ	steeds, horses (1 · 3) 940
שִׁלּוּחִים	14 sending away, parting gift (1 · 3) 1019
אַכְזָב	deceptive, disappointing (1 · 2) 469
יוֹרֵשׁ	15 ptc. = heir, possessor, captor (1 · 5) 439
קָרַח	16 to make a baldness, make bald (1 · 2 · 5) 901
גָּזַז	to shear, cut off (1 · 14 · 15) 159
תַּעֲנוּג	daintiness, luxury, exquisite delight (2 · 5) 772
הִרְחִיב	to make large, enlarge (1 · 21 · 25) 931
קָרְחָה	baldness, bald spot (1 · 11) 901
נֶשֶׁר	griffon vulture, eagle (1 · 26) 676-677

Chapter 2

מִשְׁכָּב	1 couch, bed; act of lying (1 · 46) 1012
אֵל	strength, power (1[?] · 5[?]) 7. אֵל 43
חָמַד	2 to desire, take pleasure in (1 · 16 · 21) 326
גָּזַל	to take violent possession of, to tear away, seize (2 · 29 · 30) 159
עָשַׁק	to oppress, wrong (1 · 36 · 37) 798
הֵמִישׁ	[Lis. Qal.] to remove, take away (2 · 20 · 20) 559
צַוָּאר	neck, back of neck (1 · 41) 848
רוֹמָה	haughtily (1 · 1) 928

מָשָׁל 4 prophetic figurative discourse, proverb, by-word, parable (1 · 39) 605

נָהָה to lament, wail (1 · 2 · 2) 624

נְהִי wailing, lamentation, mourning song (1 · 7) 624

הֵמִיר to change, alter, exchange (1 · 13 · 14) 558

הֵמִישׁ [Lis. *Qal.*] to remove, take away (2 · 20 · 20) 559

שׁוֹבֵב apostate, turning back (1 · 3) 1000

חֶבֶל 5 measuring cord, line, cord; measured portion (1 · 49) 286

הִטִּיף 6 to discourse; to drip (5 · 9 · 18) 642-643

נָסוֹג to turn oneself or itself away, hence = cease (1 · 14 · 25) 690-691

כְּלִמָּה insult, reproach, ignominy (1 · 30) 484

קָצַר 7 to be short, impatient (1 · 12 · 14) 894

מַעֲלָל deed, practice, act (3 · 41) 760

אֶתְמוּל 8 yesterday, w. מִן = already; formerly (1 · 8) 1069-1070

מִמּוּל from the front of, off the front of, in front of (1 · 9) 557

שַׂלְמָה wrapper, mantle; but BDB reads שׁלמה ''him at peace with him'' (1 · 16) 971

אֶדֶר mantle, cloak, glory, magnificence (1 · 2) 12

הִפְשִׁיט to strip off, strip, flay (2 · 15 · 43) 832-833

בֶּטַח securely; security (1 · 43) 105

גרשׁ piel., to drive out, drive away (1 · 35 · 48) 176-177

תַּעֲנוּג daintiness, luxury, exquisite delight (2 · 5) 772

עוֹלָל child (1 · 9) 760

הָדָר honor, glory, splendor, majesty, ornament (1 · 30) 214

מְנוּחָה 10 resting place, rest (1 · 21) 629

בַּעֲבוּר for the sake of, on account of, in order that (1 · 45) 721

טֻמְאָה uncleanness (1 · 37) 380 Lis. puts w. טֻמְאָה

חבל to ruin, destroy (1 · 6 · 11) 287

חֶבֶל destruction (1 · 2) 287

נמרץ to be sick; ptc. = grievous (1 · 3 · 4) 599

לוּ 11 if, O that (1 · 19) 530

כָּזַב to lie, tell a lie (1 · 12 · 16) 469

הִטִּיף to discourse; to drip (5 · 9 · 18) 642-643

שֵׁכָר intoxicating drink, strong drink (1 · 22) 1016

יַחַד 12 together (1 · 44) 403

בָּצְרָה enclosure; i.e., [sheep]fold (1 · 1) 131

עֵדֶר flock, herd (3 · 37) 727

דֹּבֶר pasture (1 · 2) 184

ההים to mutter, show disquietude (1 · 2 · 6) 223

פָּרַץ 13 to break through, break down, break out, burst out (2 · 46 · 49) 829

Chapter 3

קָצִין 1 ruler, man in authority, chief, dictator (2 · 11) 892

גָּזַל 2 to take violent possession of, to tear away, seize (2 · 29 · 30) 159

שְׁאֵר flesh (2 · 17) 984-985

שְׁאֵר 3 flesh (2 · 17) 984-985

הִפְשִׁיט to strip off, strip, flay (2 · 15 · 43) 832-833

פצח to break in pieces (1 · 1 · 1) 822 Lis. has sep. root 1178

סִיר pot, household utensil for boiling (1 · 29) 696

קַלַּחַת caldron (1 · 2) 886

מַעֲלָל 4 practice, deed, act (3 · 41) 760

הִתְעָה 5 to cause to err, mislead; to be made to wander about (1 · 21 · 50) 1073

נָשַׁךְ to bite (1 · 10 · 12) 675

חָזוֹן 6 vision (1 · 35) 303

חָשַׁךְ to be [grow] dark (1 · 11 · 17) 364-365

קסם to practice divination (2 · 11 · 11) 890

קָדַר to be dark (1 · 13 · 17) 871

חֹזֶה 7 seer (1 · 17) 302

חפר to be abashed, ashamed (1 · 13 · 17) 344

קֹסֵם ptc. = diviner, practicing divination (1 · 9) 890

עָטָה to wrap, envelop oneself (1 · 11 · 14) 741

שָׂפָם moustache (1 · 5) 974

מַעֲנֶה answer, response (1 · 6) 775

אוּלָם 8 but, but indeed (1 · 19) 19

קָצִין 9 ruler, man in authority, chief, dictator (2 · 11) 892

תעב piel. to regard as an abomination, abhor (1 · 15 · 22) 1073

עקש to twist (1 · 3 · 5) 786

עַוְלָה 10 violent deeds of injustice; unrighteousness, wrong (1 · 32) 732

שֹׁחַד 11 present, bribe (1 · 23) 1005

מְחִיר hire, price (1 · 15) 564

הורה to teach, instruct, direct (2 · 45 · 45) 435

קסם to practice divination (2 · 11 · 11) 890

נִשְׁעַן to lean, support oneself (1 · 22 · 22) 1043

בִּגְלַל 12 on account of, for the sake of (1 · 10) 164

נחרש to be plowed (1 · 2 · 26) 360

עִי ruin, heap of ruins (2 · 5) 730

Chapter 4

נהר 1 to flow, stream (1 · 3 · 3) 625

הורה 2 to teach, instruct, direct (2 · 45 · 45) 435

עָצוּם 3 mighty, strong in numbers (2 · 31) 783

כָּתַּת to beat, hammer, crush (1 · 5 · 17) 510

אֵת a cutting instrument of iron, plowshare (1 · 5) 88

חֲנִית spear (1 · 47) 333

מַזְמֵרָה pruning knife (1 · 4) 275

תְּאֵנָה 4 fig tree, fig (1 · 39) 1061

הֶחֱרִיד to terrify, drive in terror, rout (1 · 16 · 39) 353

צלע 6 to limp (2 · 4 · 4) 854

נִדְחָה to be thrust out, banished; ptc. = banished one, outcast (1 · 13 · 43) 623

צלע 7 to limp (2 · 4 · 4) 854

נהלא ptc. removed far off (1 · 1 · 1) 229

עָצוּם mighty, strong in numbers (2 · 31) 783

מִגְדָּל 8 tower, מ־עֵדֶר shepherd's watch-tower near Bethlehem (1 · 49) 153-154

עֵדֶר flock, herd (3 · 37) 727

עֹפֶל mound, hill (1 · 8) 779

אָתָה to come, come upon (1 · 19 · 21) 87

מֶמְשָׁלָה rule, dominion (1 · 17) 606

הֵרִיעַ 9 to cry out in distress, to shout a war cry, to shout in triumph (1 · 40 · 44) 929

רֵעַ shouting, roar (1 · 3) 929

יוֹעֵץ ptc. = counselor, adviser (1 · 22) 419

חִיל anguish, writhing (1 · 6) 297

חִיל, חוּל 10 to twist, writhe, dance, whirl (1 · 30 · 47) 296-297

גִּיחַ to thrust forth, bring forth, draw forth, burst forth (1 · 3 · 5) 161

קִרְיָה town, city (1 · 30) 900

חָנֵף 11 to be polluted; to be profane (1 · 7 · 11) 337-338

עָמִיר 12 swath, row of fallen grain (1 · 4) 771

גֹּרֶן threshing floor (1 · 34) 175

דָּשׁ, דּוֹשׁ 13 to tread, thresh, trample (1 · 13 · 16) 190

פַּרְסָה hoof (1 · 21) 828

נְחוּשָׁה bronze, copper (1 · 10) 639

הֵדַק to make dust of, pulverize (1 · 8 · 13) 200

הַחֲרִים to devote to [for sacred use]; to devote to destruction, exterminate (1 · 48 · 51) 355-356

בֶּצַע gain made by violence, unjust gain (1 · 23) 130

הִתְגֹּדֵד 14 to gather in troops or bands; to cut oneself (1 · 7 · 8) 151

גְּדוּד troops, marauding band; foray, raid (1 · 33) 151

מָצוֹר siege, siege enclosure, siege works (1 · 25) 848-849

לְחִי cheek, jaw, jawbone (1 · 21) 534

Chapter 5

צָעִיר 1 little, insignificant; young, younger (1 · 22) 859

אֶלֶף family, thousand (1 · 12) 48-49 Lis. 102 has 2 rts

מֹשֵׁל ptc. = when one rules, ruler (1 · 24) 605

מוֹצָאָה origin; place of going out to, privy (1 · 2) 426

גָּאוֹן 3 exaltation, majesty, excellence, pride (1 · 49) 144-145

אֶפֶס end, extremity (1 · 27) 67

אַרְמוֹן 4 citadel, castle, palace (1 · 33) 74

נָסִיךְ prince (1 · 6) 651 BDB has 2 roots Lis. 932 has 1 root

טַל 6 dew, night mist (1 · 31) 378

רְבִיבִים copious showers (1 · 6) 914

עֵשֶׂב herb; herbage, incl. grass (1 · 33) 793

קִוָּה to lie in wait for, to wait for, look eagerly for (1 · 39 · 45) 875

יָחַל Piel. to wait, tarry (1 · 25 · 42) 403-404

אַרְיֵה 7 lion (1 · 45) 71

כְּפִיר young lion (1 · 31) 498

עֵדֶר flock, herd (3 · 37) 727

רָמַס to trample down, trample (1 · 17 · 18) 942

טָרַף to tear, rend (1 · 19 · 24) 382

מֶרְכָּבָה 9 chariot (2 · 44) 939

הָרַס 10 to throw down, tear down, break down (1 · 30 · 43) 248

מִבְצָר fortress, stronghold, fortication (1 · 37) 131

כֶּשֶׁף 11 sorcery (1 · 6) 506

עוֹנֵן to practice soothsaying (1 · 10 · 11) 778

פָּסִיל 12 idol, image (2 · 23) 820-821

מַצֵּבָה sacred pillar, pillar used as personal or sacred memorial (1 · 36) 663

נָתַשׁ 13 to pull up, pluck up, root out (1 · 16 · 21) 684

אֲשֵׁרָה sacred tree or pole representing Canaanite goddess (1 · 40) 81

נָקָם vengeance (1 · 17) 668

Chapter 6

אֵתָן, אֵיתָן 2 ever-enduring, permanent, ever-flowing (1 · 14) 450-451

מוֹסָד foundation (1 · 13) 414

הלאה 3 to weary, make weary, exhaust (1 · 6 · 19) 521

בַּמָּה 6 wherewith[?] by what[?] (1 · 29) מה 4.a. 552

קדם to come to meet; to confront; to go before (2 · 24 · 26) 869-870

נכף niph. to bow oneself (1 · 1 · 5) 496

עֵגֶל calf (1 · 35) 722

רָצָה 7 to accept, be pleased with, make acceptable (1 · 42 · 50) 953

רְבָבָה ten thousand, myriad, multitude (1 · 16) 914

הַצְנֵעַ 8 to make humble; w. הלך = to show a humble walk (1 · 1 · 1) 857

תּוּשִׁיָּה 9 abiding success; sound and efficient wisdom (1 · 12) 444

יעד to appoint, assign (1 · 5 · 28) 416

רֶשַׁע 10 wickedness (2 · 30) 957

אֵיפָה ephah, grain measure (1 · 39) 35

רָזוֹן scantness, leanness; wasting (1 · 3) 931

זָעַם to denounce, curse; to be indignant (1 · 11 · 12) 276

זכה 11 to be clear, justified, regarded as just; to be clean, pure (1 · 4 · 8) 269

מֹאזְנַיִם balances, scales (1 · 15) 24

רֶשַׁע wickedness (2 · 30) 957

כִּיס bag, purse (1 · 5) 476

מִרְמָה deceit, treachery (1 · 39) 941

עָשִׁיר 12 the rich, rich (1 · 23) 799

רְמִיָּה deceit, treachery (1 · 15) 941

יֶשַׁח 14 emptiness [dub.] (1 · 1) 445

הסיג to remove, carry away; to displace, move back (1 · 7 · 25) 690-691

הפליט to bring into security (1 · 2 · 27) 812

פלט to bring into security, cause to escape (1 · 24 · 27) 812

קצר 15 to reap, harvest (1 · 24 · 24) 894

זַיִת olive, olives, olive tree (1 · 38) 268

סוּךְ to anoint oneself, to anoint, to be poured (1 · 7 · 9) 691-692

תִּירוֹשׁ must, new wine (1 · 38) 440

מוֹעֵצָה 16 counsel, plan, principle, device (1 · 7) 760

שַׁמָּה horror, state of being appalled; a waste (1 · 39) 1031

שְׁרֵקָה [object of derisive] hissing (1 · 7) 1056-1057

Chapter 7

אַלְלַי 1 Alas! Woe! (1 · 2) 47

אֹסֶף gathering (1 · 3) 63

קַיִץ summer fruit, summer (1 · 20) 884

עוֹלֵלוֹת gleaning (1 · 6) 760

בָּצִיר vintage (1 · 7) 131

אֶשְׁכּוֹל cluster (1 · 9) 79

בִּכּוּרָה first ripe fig, early fig (1 · 4) 114

אִוָּה to desire (1 · 11 · 27) 16

חָסִיד 2 pious man, godly man; kind, pious (1 · 32) 339

אָרַב to lie in wait, ambush (1 · 20 · 23) 70

צוּד to hunt (1 · 13 · 17) 844

חֵרֶם net (1 · 9) 357

שַׁלֵּם, שָׁלוֹם reward, bribe, requital (1 · 3) 1024

הַוָּה desire; engulfing ruin, destruction (1 · 3) 217

עבת to wind, weave [dub.] (1 · 1 · 1) 721

חֵדֶק 4 brier (1 · 2) 293

מְסוּכָה hedge (1 · 1) 692

צפה to watch, look forth; ptc. = watchman (2 · 9 · 18) 859

פְּקֻדָּה visitation; oversight; mustering; store (1 · 32) 824

מְבוּכָה confusion, confounding (1 · 2) 100

אַלּוּף 5 friend, intimate; tame, docile (1 · 9) 48

חֵיק   bosom, fold of garment at breast (1 · 38) 300

נבל   6 to regard or treat as a fool (1 · 4 · 25) 614

כַּלָּה   daughter-in-law (1 · 34) 483

חָמוֹת   husband's mother (1 · 11) 327

צפה   7 to watch, look forth (2 · 9 · 18) 859

הוֹחִיל   to wait for, hope for (1 · 15 · 42) 403-404

יֵשַׁע   salvation, safety, welfare (1 · 36) 447

זַעַף   9 raging, rage, storming (1 · 7) 277

בּוּשָׁה   10 shame (1 · 4) 102

אַי   where? (1 · 39) 32

מִרְמָס   trampling, trampling place (1 · 7) 942

טִיט   mud, mire (1 · 13) 376

גָּדֵר   11 wall, fence (1 · 14) 154-155

לְמִן   12 from (2 · 14) מִן 9.b. 583

מַעֲלָל   13 practice, deed, act (3 · 41) 760

בָּדָד   14 isolation, separation (1 · 11) 94-95

כַּרְמֶל   garden land or n. pr. Carmel (1 · 14) 502

נִפְלָאוֹת   15 *Niph.* ptc. = wonderful acts (1 · 43) 810

חרשׁ   16 to be silent (1 · 7 · 46) 361

לחך   17 to lick; w. עפר = sign of humiliation (1 · 5 · 6) 535

נָחָשׁ   serpent (1 · 31) 638

זחל   to crawl away, shrink back (1 · 3 · 3) 267

רָגַז   to come quivering, to quake, be excited, be perturbed (1 · 30 · 41) 919

מִסְגְּרוֹת   fastness, border, rim (1 · 17) 689

פָּחַד   to turn in dread, be in dread, be in awe (1 · 22 · 25) 808

רָחַם   19 to have compassion, be compassionate (1 · 42 · 47) 933

כבשׁ   to subdue, dominate, tread down, bring into bondage (1 · 8 · 14) 461

מְצוּלָה   depth, deep (1 · 12) 846

NAHUM

Chapter 1

מַשָּׂא 1 utterance, prophetic utterance, oracle (1 · 21) 672

חָזוֹן vision, divine communication in a vision (1 · 35) 302-303

קַנּוֹא 2 jealous (1 · 2) 888

נקם to avenge, take vengeance (3 · 13 · 35) 667-668

בַּעַל חֵמָה [idiom] a possessor of fury = furious חמה para. 2.c. 404

נטר to keep, maintain; to keep, guard (1 · 5 · 5) 643 Lis. 924 "to be angry"

אָרֵךְ 3 long, א׳אפים = slow to anger (1 · 15) 74

נקה to leave unpunished; to hold innocent, acquit (2 · 16 · 41) 667

סוּפָה storm wind (1 · 15) 693

שְׂעָרָה storm (1 · 2) 973

אָבָק dust (1 · 6) 7

גָּעַר 4 to rebuke (1 · 14 · 14) 172

הֶחֱרִיב to dry up (1 · 13 · 37) 351

אֻמְלַל to be or grow weak, feeble, to languish (2 · 15 · 15) 51

פֶּרַח sprout, bud (1 · 17) 827

רעש 5 to quake, shake (1 · 21 · 29) 950

הִתְמוֹגֵג to melt, flow (1 · 3 · 17) 556

תֵּבֵל world (1 · 35) 385

זַעַם 6 indignation (1 · 22) 276

חָרוֹן anger, [burning of] anger (1 · 41) 354

נִתַּךְ to be poured out, poured forth, poured (1 · 8 · 21) 677

נתץ to be pulled down, broken down (1 · 3 · 42) 683

מָעוֹז 7 refuge, place of safety or protection (2 · 36) 732

חָסָה to seek refuge (1 · 37 · 37) 340

שֶׁטֶף 8 flood (1 · 6) 1009

כָּלָה complete destruction, annihilation; completion (2 · 22) 478

כָּלָה 9 complete destruction, annihilation; completion (2 · 22) 478

סִיר 10 thorn, hook (1 · 5) 696

סבך to interweave, ptc. pass. = interwoven, entangled (1 · 1 · 2) 687

סֹבֶא liquor, drink (1 · 3) 685

סבא to imbibe, drink largely; ptc. act. = drunkard (1 · 2 · 2) 684-685

קַשׁ stubble, chaff (1 · 16) 905

יָבֵשׁ dry, dried (1 · 9) 386

יוֹעֵץ 11 ptc. = advising, counseling; counselor (1 · 22) 419

בְּלִיַּעַל ruin, destruction, worthlessness (2 · 27) 116

שָׁלֵם 12 full, perfect, complete; safe; peace (1 · 28) 1023-1024

נָגוֹז Niph. to be cut off (1 · 1 · 15) 159

מוֹט 13 bar of yoke, pole (1 · 4) 557

מוֹסֵר band, restraining band or bond (1 · 12) 64

נתק to tear apart, snap; to tear out or away (1 · 11 · 27) 683

פֶּסֶל 14 idol, image (1 · 31) 820

מַסֵּכָה molten metal or image; libation (1 · 25) 651

Chapter 2

מְבַשֵּׂר 1 heralding or herald of glad tidings; gladdening with good tidings (1 · 9) 142

חגג to keep a pilgrim feast; to behave as at a feast (1 · 16 · 16) 290

בְּלִיַּעַל man of ruin, destroyer; worthlessness (2 · 27) 116

הֵפִיץ, מֵפִיץ 2 to scatter; but BDB as noun scatterer, disperser (1 · 36 · 65) 807

מְצוּרָה rampart, siege works (1 · 8) 849

צפה to watch, look forth (1 · 9 · 18) 859

מָתְנַיִם loins (2 · 47) 608

אָמֵץ to make firm, strengthen, secure, harden (1 · 19 · 41) 54-55

גָּאוֹן 3 exaltation, majesty, excellence (2 · 49) 144-145

בקק to empty, lay waste (2 · 5 · 8) 132

זְמוֹרָה twig, branch, shoot (1 · 5) 274

אדם 4 pu. ptc. reddened (1 · 7 · 10) 10

תלע 4 to be clad in scarlet (1 · 1 · 1) 1069

פְּלָדָה iron, steel (1 · 1) 811

בְּרוֹשׁ cypress, fir; here fig. for spear shafts (1 · 20) 141

הרעל to be made to quiver, to be made to shake (1 · 1 · 1) 947

הִתְהוֹלֵל 5 to act madly or like a madman (1 · 6 · 14) 237-239 Lis. 426 has 2 rts

הִשְׁתַּקְשֵׁק hitpalp. to rush to and fro (1 · 1 · 6) 1055

רְחוֹב broad open place, plaza (1 · 43) 932

לַפִּיד torch (1 · 13) 542

בָּרָק lightning, lightning flash (2 · 21) 140

אַדִּיר 6 majestic one; majestic (2 · 27) 12

הֲלִיכָה going, walking; traveling company (1 · 6) 237

סֹכֵךְ protector, a shielding structure (1 · 1) 697

נָמוֹג 7 to melt away; fig. for helplessness (1 · 8 · 17) 556 niph. מוג

נהג 8 to moan, lament (1 · 1 · 1) 624

יוֹנָה dove (1 · 33) 401

תּוֹפֵף ptc. = twittering (1 · 1 · 2) 1074

בְּרֵכָה 9 pool, pond (1 · 17) 140

בָּזַז 10 to spoil, take as spoil, plunder (2 · 38 · 42) 102

קָצֶה end (3 · 5) 892

תְּכוּנָה preparation, things prepared, supply; arrangement; fixed place (1 · 3) 467

חֶמְדָּה desire, thing desired, precious thing (1 · 16) 326

בּוּקָה 11 emptiness (1 · 1) 101

מְבוּקָה void, emptiness (1 · 1) 101

בלק ptc. = devastated city (1 · 1 · 2) 118

נָמֵס niph. to melt = to faint, grow fearful; melt (1 · 19 · 21) 587

פֵּק tottering, staggering (1 · 1) 807

בֶּרֶךְ knee (1 · 25) 139

חַלְחָלָה anguish (1 · 4) 298

מָתְנַיִם loins (2 · 47) 608

פָּארוּר [dub.] glow (1 · 2) 802

אַיֵּה 12 where? (1 · 44) 32

מָעוֹן lair, refuge, dwelling (1 · 18) 732

אֲרִי lion (1 · 35) 71

מִרְעֶה pasture, pasturage (1 · 13) 945

כְּפִיר young lion (2 · 31) 498

אַרְיֵה lion (3 · 45) 71

לָבִיא lion (1 · 11) 522

גּוֹר, גּוּר whelp (1 · 7) 158

הֶחֱרִיד to drive in terror; ptc. = one to terrify (1 · 16 · 39) 353

אַרְיֵה 13 lion (3 · 45) 71

טָרַף to tear, rend (1 · 19 · 24) 382

בְּדֵי for what suffices for, for the need of; in the abundance of; as often as (1 · 6) דַּי 2.a. 191

גּוּר whelp (1 · 2) 158

חנק to strangle (1 · 1 · 2) 338

לָבָאה, לְבִי lion (1 · 1) 522

טֶרֶף prey, food; leaf (3 · 17) 383

חֹר, חוֹר hole, hole as a den (1 · 7) 359

מְעֹנָה den, lair, refuge, habitation (1 · 9) 733

טְרֵפָה animal torn [by wild beasts] (1 · 9) 383

עָשָׁן 14 smoke (1 · 25) 798

כְּפִיר young lion (2 · 31) 498

טֶרֶף prey, food; leaf (3 · 17) 383

Chapter 3

כַּחַשׁ 1 lying; leanness (1 · 6) 471

פֶּרֶק plunder; parting of ways (1 · 2) 830

המישׁ, מָשׁ to depart, leave its place; remove (1 · 20 · 20) 559

טֶרֶף prey, food; leaf (3 · 17) 383

שׁוֹט 2 whip, scourge (1 · 6) 1002

רַעַשׁ earthquake, shaking of earth; trembling, shaking, quivering (1 · 17) 950

אוֹפַן wheel (1 · 35) 66

דהר to rush, dash (1 · 1 · 1) 187

מֶרְכָּבָה chariot (1 · 44) 939

רקד to dance, leap; here = jolting of chariot (1 · 5 · 9) 955

לַהַב 3 flashing point; blade; flame (1 · 12) 529

בָּרָק lightning, glitter (2 · 21) 140

חֲנִית spear (1 · 47) 333

כֹּבֶד mass, abundance; weight; vehemence (1 · 4) 458

פֶּגֶר corpse, carcass (1 · 22) 803

קֵצֶה end (3 · 5) 892

גְּוִיָּה dead body, corpse, body (2 · 13) 156

זְנוּנִים 4 fornication (2 · 12) 276

זוֹנָה ptc. = harlot (1 · 33) 275

בַּעֲלָה sorceress, mistress (1 · 4) 128

כֶּשֶׁף sorcery; fig. for seductive and corruptive influence (2 · 6) 506

שׁוּל 5 skirt of robe, train (1 · 11) 1002

מַעַר bare, naked place (1 · 2) 789

קָלוֹן ignomy, dishonor, disgrace (1 · 17) 885-886

שֶׁקֶץ, שִׁקּוּץ 6 detested thing (1 · 28) 1055

נבל to treat as a fool (1 · 4 · 25) 614

רֳאִי sight, [warning] spectacle; appearance; seeing (1 · 4) 909

נדד 7 to retreat, flee; to depart, wander, stray (1 · 20 · 24) 622

נָד, נוד to show grief, lament [by shaking the head]; to move to and fro, wander, flutter (1 · 20 · 27) 626

מֵאַיִן whence[?] (1 · 48[?]) אַיִן 32

חֵיל 8 rampart, little wall of outer fortification, fortress (1 · 9) 298

עֹצֶם 9 might; bones (1 · 4) 782 end (3 · 5) 892

עֶזְרָה help, one who helps (1 · 26) 740-741

גּוֹלָה 10 [coll.] exiles, exile (1 · 42) 163

שְׁבִי state of captivity; act of capture; [coll.] captives (1 · 49) 985

עוֹלֵל child (1 · 9) 760

רטשׁ to be dashed in pieces (1 · 4 · 6) 936

ידד to cast a lot (1 · 3 · 3) 391

רתק to be bound (1 · 1 · 2) 958

זֵק, זִקִּים fetters (1 · 4) 279

שׁכר 11 to become drunken, be drunk (1 · 9 · 18) 1016

נעלם to be obscured, concealed (1 · 11 · 29) 761

מָעוֹז place of safety, protection (2 · 36) 731-732

מִבְצָר 12 fortress, stronghold, fortification (2 · 37) 131

תְּאֵנָה fig tree, fig (1 · 39) 1061

בִּכּוּרִים firstfruits (1 · 17) 114

ננוע niph. to be tossed about (1 · 2 · 38) 631

בְּרִיחַ 13 bar of city gate, bar (1 · 41) 138

מָצוֹר 14 siege, siege works (1 · 25) 848-849

שׁאב to draw [water] (1 · 14 · 14) 980

מִבְצָר fortress, stronghold, fortification (2 · 37) 131

טִיט   clay, mud (1 · 13) 376

רָמַס   to trample (1 · 17 · 18) 942

חֹמֶר   mortar, cement, clay, mire (1 · 17) 330

מַלְבֵּן   brick mold, quadrangle (1 · 3) 527

יֶלֶק   15 kind of locust (3 · 9) 410

אַרְבֶּה   kind of locust (2 · 24) 916

רֹכֵל   16 ptc. = trafficker, trader (1 · 18) 940

כּוֹכָב   star (1 · 37) 456-457

יֶלֶק   kind of locust (3 · 9) 410

פָּשַׁט   to strip off; make a dash (1 · 24 · 43) 832-833

עוּף   to fly away, fly (1 · 18 · 25) 733

מִנְזָר,מִנְזָרִים   17 consecrated ones, princes; Lis. 829 "guardsmen" (1 · 1) 634

אַרְבֶּה   kind of locust (2 · 24) 916

טִפְסָר   scribe, marshal (1 · 2) 381

גּוֹב   [coll.] locust (1 · 1) 146

גּוֹבַי   swarm of locusts; [coll.] locusts (1 · 1) 146

גְּדֵרָה   wall, hedge (1 · 8) 155

קָרָה   cold, coldness (1 · 5) 903

זָרַח   to rise, come forth (1 · 18 · 18) 280

נֹדַד   to be chased away (1 · 1 · 24) 622

אֵי   where? (1 · 39) 32

נוּם   18 to be drowsy, slumber (1 · 6 · 6) 630

אַדִּיר   majestic one; majestic (2 · 27) 12

נפוֹשׁ   *Niph.* to be scattered (1 · 1 · 1) 807

כֵּהָה   19 lessening, alleviation (1 · 1) 462

שֶׁבֶר   breaking, shattering, crashing; breaking = solution (1 · 45) 991

נַחְלָה   *Niph.* ptc. = diseased, severe, sore (1 · 5) 317-318

מַכָּה   beating, scourging, blow, slaughter; defeat (1 · 48) 646-647

שֵׁמַע   report, hearing (1 · 17) 1034

HABAKKUK

Chapter 1

מַשָּׂא 1 revelation, utterance, oracle (1 · 21) 672

אָנָה 2 wither? עַד־אָנָה = how long? (1 · 39) 33

שׁוּע to cry out for help (1 · 21 · 21) 1002

שֹׁד 3 violence, havoc (2 · 25) 994

לְנֶגֶד in the sight of (1 · 32) נֶגֶד 2.b. 617

מָדוֹן strife, contention (1 · 12) 193

פּוּג 4 to grow numb; w. תּוֹרָה = to be ineffective (1 · 3 · 4) 806

נֶצַח everlastingness, ever; לָנֶצַח = forever (1 · 43) 664

הִכְתִּיר to throw out; to surround (1 · 3 · 6) 509

עָקֵל to be bent out of shape, crooked (1 · 1 · 1) 785

הִתְתַּמַּהּ 5 to astonish [your]selves, be astounded (1 · 1 · 9) 1069

תָּמַהּ to be astounded (1 · 8 · 9) 1069

פֹּעַל deed, thing done (2 · 37) 821

מַר 6 fierce, bitter (1 · 38) 600

מֶרְחָב broad, roomy place; מ׳אֶרֶץ expanses of the earth (1 · 6) 932

אָיֹם 7 terrible, dreadful (1 · 3) 33

נוֹרָא Niph. ptc. = fearful, dreadful (1 · 44) 431

שְׂאֵת dignity, exaltation; swelling, uprising (1 · 7) 673

נָמֵר 8 leopard (1 · 6) 649

חָדַד to be sharp, keen (1 · 1 · 6) 292

זְאֵב wolf (1 · 8) 255

פּוּשׁ to spring about [dub.] Lis. 115 "to paw" (1 · 3 · 3) 807

מֵרָחוֹק to a distance (1 · 34) רָחוֹק 2.(3) 935

עוּף to fly (1 · 18 · 25) 733

נֶשֶׁר griffon vulture, eagle (1 · 26) 676

חָשׁ, חוּשׁ to make haste (1 · 15 · 21) 301

מְגַמָּה 9 uncertain meaning, Lis. 748 "striving" [dub.] (1 · 1) 169 poss. "assembling" of faces directed forward

חוֹל sand (1 · 22) 297

שְׁבִי captives, captivity (1 · 49) 985

הִתְקַלֵּס 10 to mock, deride (1 · 3 · 4) 887

רֹזֵן ptc. = ruler (1 · 6) 931

מִשְׂחָק object of derision (1 · 1) 966

מִבְצָר fortress, stronghold (1 · 37) 131

שָׂחַק to laugh (1 · 19 · 36) 965

צבר to heap up (1 · 7 · 7) 840

חָלַף 11 to move or sweep on, pass on, pass through (1 · 14 · 26) 322

אָשֵׁם to be or become guilty (1 · 33 · 35) 79

זוּ this, which (1 · 15) 262

יָסַד 12 to found, establish (1 · 20 · 41) 413

בָּגַד 13 to act treacherously (2 · 49 · 49) 93

הֶחֱרִישׁ to be silent (1 · 38 · 46) 361

בִּלַּע to swallow up, engulf, confuse, confound (1 · 20 · 41) 118

דָּג 14 fish (1 · 19) 185

רֶמֶשׂ creeping things (1 · 16) 943

מֹשֵׁל ptc. = ruler (1 · 24) 605

חַכָּה 15 fishhook (1 · 3) 335

גרר to drag away (1 · 3 · 4) 176

חֵרֶם net (3 · 9) 357

מִכְמֶרֶת net, fishing net (2 · 3[?]) 485

גִּיל to rejoice (2 · 45 · 45) 162

חֵרֶם 16 net (3 · 9) 357

מִכְמֶרֶת net, fishing net (2 · 3[?]) 485

שָׁמֵן fat, rich (1 · 10) 1032

מַאֲכָל food (1 · 30) 38

בָּרִיא fat (1 · 14) 135

הֵרִיק 17 to empty out (1 · 17 · 19) 937-938

חֵרֶם net (3 · 9) 357

חָמַל to spare, have compassion (1 · 40 · 40) 328

181

Chapter 2

הִתְיַצֵּב 1 to station oneself, take one's stand (1 · 48 · 48) 426

מָצוֹר rampart, siege works (1 · 25) 848-849

צפה to watch closely (1 · 9 · 18) 859

תּוֹכַחַת argument, impeachment, reproof (1 · 24) 407

חָזוֹן 2 vision, divine communication in a vision (2 · 35) 302-303

בֵּאֵר to make distinct, plain (1 · 3 · 3) 91

לוּחַ tablet, board, plate (1 · 43) 531

חָזוֹן 3 vision, divine communication in a vision (2 · 35) 302-303

הפוח, הפיח to pant, puff; here = to haste (1 · 12 · 13) 806

כָּזַב to disappoint, fail; to lie (1 · 12 · 16) 469

הִתְמַהְמַהּ *Hithpael*, to linger, tarry, wait (1 · 9 · 9) 554

חִכָּה to wait for (1 · 13 · 14) 314

אָחַר to delay (1 · 15 · 17) 29

עפל 4 to be swollen; but subst. needed (1 · 1 · 2) 779

יָשַׁר to be upright, right (1 · 13 · 25) 448

אַף כִּי 5 furthermore, indeed, indeed that (1 · 20) 65

בגד to act treacherously (2 · 49 · 49) 93

יָהִיר proud, haughty (1 · 2) 397

נוה to abide, dwell (1 · 1 · 1) 627

הִרְחִיב to enlarge, make large (1 · 21 · 25) 931

מָשָׁל 6 proverb, parable (1 · 39) 605

מְלִיצָה satire, mocking poem (1 · 2) 539

חִידָה riddle, enigma (1 · 17) 295

מָתַי when[?] עַד־מָתַי = until when[?] how long[?] (1 · 42) 607

עַבְטִיט weight of pledges, heavy debts (1 · 1) 716

פֶּתַע 7 suddenness; suddenly (1 · 7) 837

נָשַׁךְ to bite; to charge interest (1 · 10 · 12) 675

יקץ to awake, become suddenly active (1 · 11 · 11) 429

זעזע *Pilp.* to shake violently (1 · 1 · 3) 266

מְשִׁסָּה plunder, spoil (1 · 6) 1042

שָׁלַל 8 to spoil, plunder (2 · 13 · 15) 1021

קִרְיָה town, city (3 · 30) 900

בצע 9 to gain by violence, cut off (1 · 10 · 16) 130

בֶּצַע unjust gain, gain made by violence (1 · 23) 130

קֵן nest (1 · 13) 890

בֹּשֶׁת 10 shame (1 · 30) 102

קצה to cut off (1 · 1 · 5) 891

כָּפִיס 11 some beam in a house, perh. rafter or girder (1 · 1) 496

קִרְיָה 12 town, city (3 · 30) 900

עַוְלָה violent deeds of injustice, injustice (1 · 32) 732

יגע 13 to toil or labor for (בְּ), grow weary (1 · 20 · 26) 388

בְּדֵי what suffices for para. 2a דַּי (2 · 6) 191

לְאֹם people (1 · 35) 522

רִיק emptiness, vanity (1 · 12) 938

יעף to be or grow weary (1 · 8 · 9) 419

ספח 15 to join, attach to (1 · 1 · 5) 705

שׁכר to make drunken (1 · 4 · 18) 1016

מָעוֹר nakedness (1 · 1) 735

קָלוֹן 16 ignominy, dishonor (1 · 17) 885-886

נערל to be counted uncircumcised (1 · 1 · 2) 790

כּוֹס cup (1 · 31) 468

קִיקָלוֹן 17 disgrace (1 · 1) 887

שֹׁד devastation, ruin (2 · 25) 994

קִרְיָה town, city (3 · 30) 900

הוֹעִיל 18 to profit, benefit (1 · 23 · 23) 418

פֶּסֶל idol, image (1 · 31) 820

פָּסַל to hew, hew into shape (1 · 6 · 6) 820

יָצַר to form, fashion (2 · 41 · 44) 427

מַסֵּכָה molten metal, image (1 · 25) 651

הוֹרָה, מוֹרֶ to teach, instruct [ptc. = teacher (1[?] · 9[?])] (2[?] · 45[?] · 45[?]) 434

יֵצֶר form [of a graven image] (1 · 9) 428

אֱלִיל insufficiency, worthlessness; אלילים = worthless gods, idols (1 · 20) 47

אִלֵּם dumb (1 · 6) 48

הֵקִיץ 19 to awake (1 · 22 · 23) 884

דּוּמָם silence (1 · 3) 189

הוֹרָה to teach, instruct (2[?] · 45[?] · 45[?]) 434

הַס 20 Hush! (1 · 6) 245

Chapter 3

שִׁגָּיוֹן 1 [meaning dub.] prob. a title (1 · 2) 993

שֵׁמַע 2 report (1 · 17) 1034

פֹּעַל deed, thing done (2 · 37) 821

רֹגֶז raging, wrath (1 · 7) 919

רִחַם to have compassion (1 · 42 · 47) 933

תֵּימָן 3 district of Edom, south country (1 · 24[?]) 412

הוֹד splendor, majesty (1 · 24) 217

נֹגַהּ 4 brightness (2 · 19) 618

חֶבְיוֹן hiding, hiding place, veil (1 · 1) 285

דֶּבֶר 5 plague, pestilence (1 · 46) 184

רֶשֶׁף fire-bolt, flame (1 · 7) 958

מוֹדֵד 6 *Pol.* to measure; Lis. מוד to shake up (1 · 1 · 1) מדד 556, 551

הִתִּיר to cause to spring or start up (1 · 5 · 7) 684

הִתְפֹּצֵץ *Hithpo.* to be shattered (1 · 1 · 3) 822-823, 1126

עַד perpetuity (1 · 53) 723

שׁחה be bowed down, humbled (1 · 12 · 18) 1005

הֲלִיכָה going; of goings = doings, ways (1 · 6) 237

רָגַז 7 to quake (3 · 30 · 41) 919

עֶבְרָה 8 overflowing rage, fury (1 · 34) 720

מֶרְכָּבָה chariot (1 · 44) 939

עֶרְיָה 9 nakedness (1 · 6) 789

נֵעוֹר to be exposed, bare (1 · 1 · 1) 735

שְׁבוּעָה oath [dub. here] (1 · 30) 989-990

אֹמֶר, אֵמֶר word, appointment [dub.] (1 · 6) 56-57

חוּל, חִיל 10 to writhe, be in anguish (1 · 30 · 47) 296

זֶרֶם flood of rain, downpour (1 · 9) 281

תְּהוֹם deep, sea (1 · 36) 1062-1063

רוֹם adv. on high (1 · 1) 927

יָרֵחַ 11 moon (1 · 27) 437

זְבֻל height, lofty abode (1 · 5) 259

נֹגַהּ brightness, glitter (2 · 19) 618

בָּרָק lightning; fig. of flashing arrow-head (1 · 21) 140

חֲנִית spear, spearhead (1 · 47) 333-334

זַעַם 12 indignation (1 · 22) 276

צָעַד to step, march (1 · 7 · 8) 857

דּוּשׁ, דָּשׁ to trample on, thresh (1 · 13 · 16) 190

יֵשַׁע 13 deliverance, salvation (3 · 36) 447

מָשִׁיחַ anointed (1 · 39) 603

מָחַץ to smite through, shatter (1 · 14 · 14) 563

עָרָה to lay bare (1 · 9 · 15) 788

יְסוֹד foundation (1 · 19) 414

צַוָּאר neck, back of neck (1 · 41) 848

נָקַב 14 to pierce, bore (1 · 13 · 19) 666

פֶּרֶז warriors, leaders [dub.] (1 · 1) 826

סָעַר to storm (1 · 3 · 7) 704

עֲלִיצוּת exultation (1 · 1) 763

מִסְתָּר hiding place (1 · 10) 712

חָמַר 15 to ferment, foam up (1 · 1*) 330
*Lis. 508 חֹמֶר "foaming waters"

רָגַז 16 to quake, come quivering
(3 · 30 · 41) 919

צלל to quiver, tingle (1 · 4 · 4) 852

רָקָב rottenness, caries (1 · 5) 955

גוד to invade, attack (1 · 3 · 3) 156

תְּאֵנָה 17 fig tree (1 · 39) 1061

פָּרַח to send out shoots, bud (1 · 28 · 33) 827

יְבוּל produce (1 · 13) 385

כָּחֵשׁ to disappoint, fail (1 · 19 · 22) 471

זַיִת olive tree (1 · 38) 268

שְׁדֵמָה field (1 · 6) 995

אֹכֶל food (1 · 44) 38

גָּזַר to cut off, destroy (1 · 6 · 12) 160

מִכְלָה enclosure, fold (1 · 3) 476

רֶפֶת stable, stall (1 · 1) 952

עלז 18 to exult, triumph (1 · 16 · 16) 759

גִּיל to rejoice (2 · 45 · 45) 162

יֵשַׁע deliverance, salvation (3 · 36) 447

אַיָּלָה 19 hind, doe (1 · 11) 19

נְגִינָה music (1 · 14) 618

ZEPHANIAH

Chapter 1

הֵסִיף 2 to make an end of (3 · 4 · 8) 692

הֵסִיף 3 to make an end of (3 · 4 · 8) 692

דָּג   fish (2 · 19) 185

מַכְשֵׁלָה   stumbling block = idol [dub.] overthrown mass (1 · 2) 506

שְׁאָר 4 rest, residue, remainder (1 · 26) 984

כֹּמֶר   [idol-] priest (1 · 3) 485

גָּג 5 roof, top (1 · 29) 150

נָסוֹג 6 to turn oneself away, turn back = prove faithless (1 · 14 · 25) 690-691

הַס 7 [interj.] Hush! Keep silence! (1 · 6) 245

מַלְבּוּשׁ 8 raiment, attire (1 · 8) 528

נָכְרִי   foreign, alien (1 · 45) 648

דִּלֵּג 9 to leap; ptc. = one leaping (1 · 1 · 5) 194

מִפְתָּן   threshold (1 · 8) 837

מִרְמָה   treachery, deceit (1 · 39) 941

צְעָקָה 10 cry of distress, cry, outcry (1 · 21) 858

דָּג   fish (2 · 19) 185

יְלָלָה   howling (1 · 5) 410

מִשְׁנֶה   second quarter, second district; double, copy, second (1 · 36) 1041

שֶׁבֶר   crashing, breaking, fracture (1 · 45) 991

הֵילִל 11 to utter or make a howling (1 · 30 · 30) 410

מַכְתֵּשׁ   mortar, hollow resembling a mortar; here = a part of Jerusalem [not in Lis.] 509

נִדְמָה   to be cut off, destroyed, ruined (1 · 13 · 17) 198

כְּנַעַן   merchant, merchants (1 · 4) 448

נָטִיל   laden (1 · 1) 642

חִפֵּשׂ 12 to search through, search for (1 · 8 · 23) 344

נֵר   lamp (1 · 45) 632

קָפָא   to thicken, condense, congeal; here fig. of easygoing men (1 · 2 · 3) 891

שֶׁמֶר   pl. lees, dregs (1 · 5) 1038

מְשִׁסָּה 13 booty, plunder (1 · 6) 1042

מַר 14 bitter; bitterness (1 · 38) 600

צָרַח   to roar, cry (1 · 1 · 2) 863

עֶבְרָה 15 overflowing rage, fury; overflow (2 · 34) 720

מְצוּקָה   straits, stress (1 · 6) 848

שֹׁאָה   devastation, ruin (1 · 13) 996

מְשׁוֹאָה   desolation (1 · 3) 996

אֲפֵלָה   darkness, gloominess, calamity (1 · 10) 66

עֲרָפֶל   cloud, heavy cloud (1 · 15) 791

תְּרוּעָה 16 alarm of war, war-cry, blast for march, shout of joy (1 · 36) 929

בָּצוּר   ptc. pass. = cut off, made inaccessible, fortified (1 · 25) 130-131

פִּנָּה   corner (2 · 30) 819

גָּבֹהַּ   high, lofty, tall, exalted, haughty (1 · 41) 147

עִוֵּר 17 blind (1 · 26) 734

לָחוּם   intestines, bowels (1 · 2) 535-536

גָּלָל   dung (1 · 2) 165

עֶבְרָה 18 overflowing rage, fury; overflow (2 · 34) 720

קִנְאָה   ardor of anger, zeal, jealousy (2 · 43) 888

כָּלָה   complete destruction (1 · 22) 478

נִבְהַל   to be disturbed, dismayed, terrified; ptc. as adj. = "terrible" (1 · 24 · 39) 96

Chapter 2

הִתְקוֹשֵׁשׁ 1 to gather oneself together (1 · 1 · 8) 905

קוֹשׁ   to gather together (1 · 1 · 8) 905

נִכְסַף   to long [for], turn pale [dub.] (1 · 4 · 6) 493-494

185

בְּטֶרֶם 2 before (3 · 39) 382

מֹץ chaff (1 · 8) 558

חָרוֹן [burning of] anger (1 · 41) 354

עָנָו 3 poor and weak, afflicted (1 · 21) 776

עֲנָוָה humility, meekness (1 · 4) 776

אוּלַי perhaps, peradventure (1 · 45) 19

צָהֳרַיִם 4 midday, noon (1 · 23) 843

גרש to drive out, drive away (1 · 35 · 48) 176-177

נעקר to pluck up, root up (1 · 1 · 7) 785

חֶבֶל 5 measured portion, lot; cord, rope (3 · 49) 286

מֵאֵין without, so that not (2 · 48[?]) para. 6. (d.) אין 35

חֶבֶל 6 measured portion, lot; cord, rope (3 · 49) 286

נָוֶה ,נָוָה pasture, meadow (1 · 45) 627

כָּרָה cistern, well (1 · 1) 500

גְּדֵרָה wall, hedge (1 · 8) 155

חֶבֶל 7 measured portion, lot; cord, rope (3 · 49) 286

רָבַע to lie down, lie (3 · 24 · 30) 918

שְׁבוּת ,שְׁבִית captivity, captives (1 · 6) 986

גִּדּוּף 8 pl. revilings, reviling words (1 · 3) 154

חֵרֵף to reproach, say sharp things about (2 · 34 · 38) 357

מִמְשָׁק 9 possession, place of possession, place possessed by (1 · 1) 606

חָרוּל a kind of weed, perh. chickpea (1 · 3) 355

מִכְרֵה pit [dub.] (1 · 1) 500

מֶלַח salt (1 · 28) 571

בָּזַז to plunder, dispoil, take as spoil (1 · 38 · 42) 102

גָּאוֹן 10 pride, exaltation (1 · 49) 144-145

חֵרֵף to reproach, say sharp things about (2 · 34 · 38) 357

נוֹרָא 11 Niph. ptc. = awe-inspiring, fearful (1 · 44) 431

רָזָה to be [grow] lean (1 · 1 · 2) 930

אִי coast, region; islands (1 · 36) 15-16

צִיָּה 13 drought, dryness (1 · 16) 851

רָבַץ 14 to lie down, lie (3 · 24 · 30) 918

עֵדֶר flock, herd (1 · 37) 727

קָאַת bird, usu. pelican but improb; Lis. 1231 owl [?] (1 · 5) 866

קִפֹּד porcupine (1 · 3) 891

כַּפְתּוֹר capital [of pillar]; knob, bulb (1 · 16) 499

חַלּוֹן window (1 · 30) 319

חֹרֶב desolation (1 · 16) 351

סַף threshold, sill (1 · 25) 706

אַרְזָה cedar panels, cedar work (1 · 1) 72

עֵרָה to lay bare (1 · 9 · 15) 788

עַלִּיז 15 exultant, jubilant (2 · 7) 759

בֶּטַח security; as adv. = securely (1 · 43) 105

אֶפֶס part. of negation, cessation; אֲנִי אֶפְעוֹד prob. = "I am and there is none besides" (1 · 27) 67

שַׁמָּה horror, an appalling thing (1 · 39) 1031

מַרְבֵּץ lying down, place of lying down (1 · 2) 918

שָׁרַק to hiss; perh. also whistle (1 · 12 · 12) 1056

הֵנִיעַ to shake, cause to totter, wag (1 · 14 · 38) 631

Chapter 3

מָרָה → מרא 1 ptc. f.s. = disobedient, rebelling (1 · 1 · 1) 598

נגאל to be defiled; ptc. = defiled, pol-luted one (1 · 3 · 11) 146

ינה to suppress; ptc. f. coll. = oppres-sors (1 · 4 · 18) 413

מוּסָר 2 discipline, correction (2 · 50) 416

אֲרִי 3 lion (1 · 35) 71

שָׁאַג roar (1 · 20 · 20) 980

זְאֵב wolf (1 · 8) 255

גרם to reserve [dub.], cut off (1 · 1 · 3) 175

פחז 4 to be wanton, reckless (1 · 2 · 2) 808

בֹּגְדוֹת pl. abst. treachery (1 · 1) 93

חמס to treat violently, wrong (1 · 7 · 8) 329

עַוְלָה 5 violent deeds of injustice (2 · 21) 732

נֶעְדָּר to be lacking, to fail (1 · 5 · 6) 727

עַוָּל unjust, unrighteous one (1 · 5) 732

בֹּשֶׁת shame, shameful thing (2 · 30) 102

פִּנָּה 6 corner (2 · 30) 819

הֶחֱרִיב to lay waste, make desolate (1 · 13 · 37) 351

מִבְּלִי so that there is no; from want of (2 · 25) para 3.c. בְּלִי 115

נצדה to be laid waste (1 · 1 · 1) 841

מֵאֵין so that not, without; from lack of (2 · 48[?]) para. 6.d. אַיִן 35

מוּסָר 7 discipline, correction (2 · 50) 416

מָעוֹן dwelling [but difficult in context] (1 · 18) 732-733

אָכֵן but in fact, but indeed; surely, truly (1 · 18) 38

עֲלִילָה evil deeds; deed, wantonness (2 · 24) 760

חִכָּה 8 to wait for, await, wait (1 · 13 · 14) 314

עַד booty, prey (1 · 3) 723

זַעַם indignation (1 · 22) 276

חָרוֹן [burning of] anger (1 · 41) 354

קִנְאָה ardor of anger; zeal, jealousy (2 · 43) 888

בָּרוּר 9 ptc. pass. = purified (1 · 2) 140

שְׁכֶם shoulder (1 · 22) 1014

עָתָר 10 suppliant, worshiper [dub.] (1 · 1) 801

הֵבִיל to bear along, conduct, carry away (1 · 7 · 18) 384-385

עֲלִילָה 11 evil deeds, evil deed, wantonness (2 · 24) 760

פָּשַׁע to transgress, rebel (1 · 40 · 41) 838

עַלִּיז exultant, jubilant (2 · 7) 759

גַּאֲוָה pride, haughtiness, majesty (1 · 19) 144

גָּבַהּ to be lofty, [in bad sense] haughty; to be high, exalted (1 · 24 · 34) 146-147

דַּל 12 reduced, poor, weak, thin (1 · 48) 195

חָסָה to seek refuge (1 · 37 · 37) 340

עַוְלָה 13 violent deeds of injustice, unrighteousness (2 · 21) 732

כָּזָב lie, falsehood (1 · 31) 469

תַּרְמִית deceitfulness (1 · 5) 941

רָבַץ to lie down, lie (3 · 24 · 30) 918

הֶחֱרִיד to drive in terror, rout; ptc. = one who terrifies (1 · 16 · 39) 353

הֵרִיעַ 14 to shout in triumph, raise a shout or war-cry (1 · 40 · 44) 929

עלז to exult, triumph (1 · 16 · 16) 759

רפה 16 to sink down; [idiom] w. יָד = to lose heart or energy (1 · 14 · 44) 951

שִׂישׂ, שׂוּשׂ 17 to exult, display joy (1 · 27 · 27) 965

הֶחֱרִישׁ to be silent, make silent (1 · 38 · 46) 361

גִּיל to rejoice (1 · 45 · 45) 162

רִנָּה ringing cry in joy, proclamation, etc. (1 · 33) 943

נוגה 18 Niph. ptc. = grieved (1 · 2 · 8) 387

מַשְׂאֵת burden, portion carried; that which rises; oracle (1 · 16) 673

צלע 19 to limp (1 · 4 · 4) 854

נדח to be thrust out, banished (1 · 13 · 43) 623

בֹּשֶׁת shame, shameful thing (2 · 30) 102

שְׁבִית, שְׁבוּת captivity, captives (1 · 6) 986

HAGGAI

Chapter 1

פֶּחָה 1 governor (4 · 27) 808

סָפַן 4 to cover; ptc. pass. = paneled (1 · 6 · 6) 706

חָרֵב, שָׂבְעָה, waste, desolate (2 · 10) 351

שָׂבְעָה 6 inf. abs. sated, satisfied (1 · 7) 959

שָׁכַר to become drunken, be drunk (1 · 9 · 18) 1016

חמם, חַם to be [grow] warm (1 · 23 · 26) 328

הִשְׂתַּכֵּר to earn wages (2 · 2 · 20) 968

צְרוֹר bundle, pouch (1 · 7) 865

נקב to pierce (1 · 13 · 19) 666

רָצָה 8 to be pleased with, favorable to (1 · 42 · 50) 953

נפח 9 to breathe, blow (1 · 5 · 12) 655

חָרֵב waste, desolate (2 · 10) 351

כלא 10 to withhold, restrain, shut up (2 · 14 · 17) 476

טַל night mist, dew (1 · 31) 378

יְבוּל produce (1 · 13) 385

חֹרֶב 11 drought, dryness, heat (1 · 16) 351

דָּגָן corn, cereal grain (1 · 40) 186

תִּירוֹשׁ must, fresh or new wine (1 · 38) 440

יִצְהָר fresh oil (1 · 23) 844

יְגִיעַ product, produce, acquired property (1 · 16) 388

מַלְאֲכוּת 13 message (1 · 1) 522

פֶּחָה 14 governor (4 · 27) 808

Chapter 2

פֶּחָה 2 governor (4 · 27) 808

כְּאַיִן 3 as nothing (1 · 7) 1. 34

הרעיש 6 to cause to quake (1 · 7 · 29) 950

חָרָבָה dry ground (1 · 8) 351

הרעיש 7 to cause to quake (1 · 7 · 29) 950

חֶמְדָּה desire, delight (1 · 16) 326

נָזִיד 12 thing sodden, or boiled, pottage (1 · 6) 268

מַאֲכָל food (1 · 30) 38

מַעְלָה 15 upward, onward (1 · 53) 751

מִטֶּרֶם from before (1 · 1) 382

עֲרֵמָה 16 heap (1 · 11) 790

יֶקֶב wine vay (1 · 16) 428

חָשַׂף to take from the surface, skim, strip off (1 · 10 · 10) 362

פּוּרָה wine press (1 · 2) 807

שִׁדָּפוֹן 17 smut (1 · 5) 995

יֵרָקוֹן rust, mildew (1 · 6) 439

בָּרָד hail (1 · 29) 135

לְמִן 18 from (1 · 14) מן 9.b. 577

יָסַד to be founded, laid (1 · 6 · 41) 413

מְגוּרָה 19 storehouse, granary (1 · 2) 158

תְּאֵנָה fig tree, fig (1 · 39) 1061

רִמּוֹן pomegranate (1 · 32) 941

זַיִת olive tree, olives (1 · 38) 268

פֶּחָה 21 governor (4 · 27) 808

הרעיש to cause to quake (1 · 7 · 29) 950

חֹזֶק 22 strength (1 · 5) 305

מֶרְכָּבָה chariot (1 · 44) 939

חוֹתָם 23 seal, signet ring (1 · 14) 368

ZECHARIAH

Chapter 1

קָצַף 2 to be angry (3 · 28 · 34) 893

קֶצֶף   wrath (3 · 28) 893

מַעֲלָל 4 practice, deed (2 · 41) 760

הִקְשִׁיב   to give attention (2 · 45 · 46) 904

אַיֵּה 5 where[?] (1 · 44) 32

הִשִּׂיג 6 to overtake, reach, attain to (1 · 49 · 49) 673

זָמַם   to purpose, devise, consider (3 · 13 · 13) 273

מַעֲלָל   practice, deed (2 · 41) 760

הֲדַס 8 myrtle [tree] (3 · 6) 213

מְצֻלָה   basin, hollow [dub.] (2 · 12) 847

אָדֹם   red (3 · 9) 10

שָׂרֹק   sorrel [dub.], Lis. 1389 ''bright red'' (1 · 2) 977

לָבָן   white (3 · 29) 526

הֲדַס 10 myrtle [tree] (3 · 6) 213

הֲדַס 11 myrtle [tree] (3 · 6) 213

שָׁקַט   to be quiet, undisturbed (1 · 31 · 41) 1052-1053

עַד־מָתַי 12 until when? how long? (idiom) 607 מתי (1 · 42) 607

רִחַם   to have compassion, be compassionate (2 · 42 · 47) 933

זָעַם   to be indignant, have indignation (1 · 11 · 12) 276

נִחֻמִים 13 comfort, compassion (1 · 3) 637

קִנֵּא 14 to be zealous, jealous (3 · 18 · 32) 888

קִנְאָה   zeal, ardor of zeal, jealousy (2 · 43) 888

קֶצֶף 15 wrath (3 · 28) 893

קָצַף   to be angry (3 · 28 · 34) 893

שַׁאֲנָן   at ease; here with collateral qualities of carelessness, wantonness, and arrogance (1 · 11) 983

רַחֲמִים 16 compassion (2 · 38) 933

קָו ,קַו קרה   line, measuring line (1 · 25) 876

פּוּץ 17 to overflow (2 · 13 · 65*) 807

  *BDB has sep. root

Chapter 2

זרה 2 to scatter, disperse (3 · 25 · 38) 279-280

חָרָשׁ 3 graver, artificer (1 · 38) 360

זרה 4 to scatter, disperse (3 · 25 · 38) 279-280

כְּפִי   in such proportion that, according to, according to the mouth of (1 · 16) פה 6.b. 805

הֶחֱרִיד   to drive in terror, rout (1 · 16 · 39) 353

ידה   piel. = to cast down (1 · 2 · 3) 392

חֶבֶל 5 measuring cord, line, rope; territory (1 · 49) 286

אָנָה 6 where? whither? (2 · 39) 33

כַּמֶּה, כַּמָּה   how much? how many? how often? (3 · 13) para. 4.c. מה 553

הַלָּז 8 synonym of זה this (1 · 7) 229

פְּרָזָה, פְּרָזוֹת   open region, hamlet (1 · 3) 826

שָׁלַל 12 to spoil, plunder (1 · 13 · 15) 1021

בָּבָה   [dub.] apple, opening, baby (1 · 1) 93

הֵנִיף 13 to shake, wave, brandish; shed abroad (1 · 32 · 34) 631-632

נִלְוָה 15 to join oneself, be joined (1 · 11 · 12) 530-531

הַס 17 Hush! Keep silence! (1 · 6) 245

מָעוֹן   dwelling, refuge (1 · 18) 732

189

Chapter 3

שָׂטָן 1 adversary, Satan (3 · 26) 966

שׂטן to be [act as] adversary (1 · 6 · 6) 966

שָׂטָן 2 adversary, Satan (3 · 26) 966

גָּעַר to rebuke (2 · 14 · 14) 172

אוּד brand, firebrand (1 · 3) 15

לָבוּשׁ,לָבֵשׁ 3 ptc. pass. = clothed with (1 · 16) 527-528

צֹאִי filthy (2 · 2) 844

צֹאִי 4 filthy (2 · 2) 844

מַחֲלָצָה,מַחֲלָצוֹת robe of state (1 · 2) 323

צָנִיף 5 turban (2 · 5) 857

הֵעִיד to exhort solemnly, admonish, charge, warn, protest; to testify, cause to testify (1 · 38 · 43) 729-730

דָּן,דִּין 7 to govern, judge (1 · 23 · 24) 192

מַהֲלָךְ walk, journey, going (1 · 5) 237

מוֹפֵת 8 sign, token, wonder (1 · 36) 68-69

צֶמַח sprout, growth (2 · 12) 855

פִּתַּח 9 to engrave (1 · 8 · 9) 836

פִּתּוּחַ engraving (1 · 11) 836

מָשׁ,מוֹשׁ to depart, remove (2 · 20 · 20) 559

תְּאֵנָה 10 fig tree, fig (1 · 39) 1061

Chapter 4

שֵׁנָה שׁנה 1 sleep (1 · 23) 446

מְנוֹרָה 2 lampstand (2 · 40) 633

גֻּלָּה bowl; here = oil receptacle of lamp (2 · 15) 165

נֵר lamp (2 · 45) 632

מוּצֶקֶת,מוּצָקָה pipe [through which oil is poured] (1 · 2) 427

זַיִת 3 olive tree, olives (5 · 38) 268

גֻּלָּה bowl; here = oil receptacle of lamp (2 · 15) 165

מִישׁוֹר 7 level country, tableland, plain; uprightness (1 · 23) 449

רֹאשָׁה top (1 · 1) 911

תְּשֻׁאָה noise (1 · 4) 996

יָסַד 9 to found, establish (1 · 10 · 41) 413-414

בִּצַּע to cut off; here = to finish, complete (1 · 6 · 16) 130

בַּז,בּוּז 10 to despise (1 · 14 · 14) 100

קָטֹן small, unimportant, young (1 · 47) 881-882

בְּדִיל tin, alloy; הָאבן הב׳ = plummet (1 · 5) 95

שׁוֹטֵט to go eagerly, quickly to an fro (1 · 5 · 13) 1001-1002

זַיִת 11 olive tree, olives (5 · 38) 268

מְנוֹרָה lampstand (2 · 40) 633

שִׁבֹּלֶת 12 ear of grain (1 · 20) 987

זַיִת olive tree, olives (5 · 38) 268

צַנְתְּרוֹת pipes (1 · 1) 857

רִיק to pour out (1 · 17 · 19) 938

יִצְהָר 14 fresh oil, anointing oil; בני י׳ = anointed ones (1 · 23) 844

Chapter 5

מְגִלָּה 1 roll, writing, book (2 · 21) 166

עוּף to fly (2 · 18 · 25) 733

מְגִלָּה 2 roll, writing, book (2 · 21) 166

עוּף to fly (2 · 18 · 25) 733

אָלָה 3 curse, oath (1 · 36) 46

גנב to steal, take by stealth (1 · 30 · 39) 170

נִקָּה to be cleaned out, purged out (2 · 24 · 41) 667

גַּנָּב 4 thief (1 · 17) 170

אֵיפָה 6 receptacle holding an ephah; i.e., 40 liters (5 · 39) 35

עֹפֶרֶת 7 lead; כבר ע׳ a round wt. of lead (2 · 9) 780

190

אֵיפָה   receptacle holding an ephah; i.e., 40 liters (5 · 39) 35

רִשְׁעָה   8 wickedness (1 · 15) 958

אֵיפָה   receptacle holding an ephah; i.e., 40 liters (5 · 39) 35

עֹפֶרֶת   lead (2 · 9) 780

חֲסִידָה   9 stork (1 · 6) 339

אֵיפָה   receptacle holding an ephah; i.e., 40 liters (5 · 39) 35

אָנָה   10 whither[?] (2 · 39) אָן 33

אֵיפָה   receptacle holding an ephah; i.e., 40 liters (5 · 39) 35

מְכוֹנָה   11 base or stand (1 · 25) 467

Chapter 6

מֶרְכָּבָה   1 chariot (5 · 44) 939

מִבֵּין   from between (2 · 21) 107

מֶרְכָּבָה   2 chariot (5 · 44) 939

אָדֹם   red (3 · 9) 10

שָׁחֹר   black (2 · 6) 1007

מֶרְכָּבָה   3 chariot (5 · 44) 939

לָבֵן   white (3 · 29) 526

בָּרֹד   spotted, marked (2 · 4) 136

אָמֹץ   strong (2 · 2) 55

הִתְיַצֵּב   5 to set or station oneself; c. לִפְנֵי = present oneself before (1 · 48 · 48) 426

שָׁחֹר   6 black (2 · 6) 1007

לָבֵן   white (3 · 29) 526

בָּרֹד   spotted, marked (2 · 4) 136

תֵּימָן   south, southern quarter (2 · 24) 412

אָמֹץ   7 strong (2 · 2) 55

גּוֹלָה   10 exile, exiles (2 · 42) 163

עֲטָרָה   11 crown, wreath (2 · 23) 742

צֶמַח   12 sprout, growth (2 · 12) 855

צָמַח   to sprout, spring up (1 · 15 · 33) 855

הוֹד   13 splendor, majesty (2 · 24) 217

עֲטָרָה   14 crown, wreath (2 · 23) 742

זִכָּרוֹן   memorial, reminder (1 · 24) 272

Chapter 7

נָזַר   3 *Niph.*, to devote, dedicate oneself (1 · 4 · 10) 634

כַּמֶּה   how many? how much, how often (3 · 13) para. 4.c. מָה 553

צוֹם   5 to fast, abstain from food (2 · 20 · 20) 847

סָפַד   to wail, lament (3 · 28 · 30) 704

שָׁלֵוָה   7 quiet, at ease, prosperous (1 · 8) 1017

שְׁפֵלָה   lowland, strip of land west of Judean mts. (1 · 20) 1050

רַחֲמִים   9 compassion (2 · 38) 933

יָתוֹם   10 orphan (1 · 42) 450

עָשַׁק   to oppress, wrong (1 · 36 · 37) 798

מֵאֵן   11 to refuse (1 · 46 · 46) 549

הִקְשִׁיב   to give attention (2 · 45 · 46) 904

סָרַר   to be stubborn, rebellious (1 · 17 · 17) 710-711

שָׁמִיר   12 adamant, flint; thorn[s] (1 · 11) 1038-1039

קֶצֶף   wrath (3 · 28) 893

סָעַר   14 *Piel.*, to storm away, hurl by storm wind (1 · 1 · 7) 704

חֶמְדָּה   desire, delight (1 · 16) 326

שַׁמָּה   appalling waste (1 · 39) 1031

Chapter 8

קָנָא   2 to be zealous, jealous (3 · 18 · 32) 888

קִנְאָה   zeal, ardor of zeal, jealousy (2 · 43) 888

רְחוֹב ,רָחָב   4 broad open place (3 · 43) 932

מִשְׁעֶנֶת ,מַשְׁעֵנָה   staff, support (1 · 12) 1044

191

רְחֹב, רְחוֹב 5 broad open place (3 · 43) 932

יַלְדָּה girl, damsel (1 · 3) 409

שָׂחַק to play, jest, make sport (1 · 16 · 36) 965-966

נִפְלָא 6 to be beyond one's power, difficult to do; to be extraordinary (2 · 13 · 24) 810

מָבוֹא 7 entrance, entering; w. שֶׁמֶשׁ west (1 · 23) 99-100

יֻסַּד 9 to be founded, laid (1 · 6 · 41) 413-414

שָׂכָר 10 hire, wages (4 · 28) 969

יְבוּל 12 produce (1 · 13) 385

טַל night mist, dew (1 · 31) 378

קְלָלָה 13 curse (1 · 33) 887

זָמַם 14 to purpose, devise (3 · 13 · 13) 237

הִקְצִיף to provoke to wrath (1 · 5 · 34) 893

זָמַם 15 to purpose, devise (3 · 13 · 13) 273

שְׁבוּעָה, שָׁבַע 16 oath (1 · 30) 989-990

צוֹם 19 fasting, fast (4 · 26) 847

שָׂשׂוֹן exultation, joy (1 · 22) 965

עָצוּם 22 mighty, strong in numbers (1 · 31) 783

Chapter 9

מַשָּׂא 1 utterance, oracle (2 · 21) 672-673

מְנוּחָה resting place (1 · 21) 629-630

גָּבַל 2 to bound, border (1 · 3 · 5) 148

חָכַם to be or become wise, act wisely (1 · 18 · 26) 314

מָצוֹר 3 rampart; siege works, siege (2 · 25) 848-849

צָבַר to heap up (1 · 7 · 7) 840

חָרוּץ gold (1 · 6) 359

טִיט mud, mire (2 · 13) 376

חֵיל 4 rampart (1 · 9) 298

חוּל, חִיל 5 to be in severe pain, twist, writhe (2 · 30 · 47) 296-297

מַבָּט expectation, object of hope or confidence (1 · 3) 613-614

מַמְזֵר 6 bastard, child of incest (1 · 2) 561

גָּאוֹן exaltation, majesty, excellence (3 · 49) 144-145

שִׁקּוּץ, שֶׁקֶץ 7 detested thing (1 · 28) 1055

מִבֵּין from between (2 · 21) 107

מֵעֹבֵר וּמִשָּׁב 8 [idiom] from those going to and fro para. 3. a. עבר p. 717

נֹגֵשׂ ptc. = exactor [of tribute], oppressor, tyrant (2 · 15) 620

גִּיל 9 to rejoice (2 · 45 · 45) 162

הֵרִיעַ to shout in triumph, raise a shout, sound a signal for war or march (1 · 40 · 44) 929

עַיִר male donkey [young and vigorous] (1 · 9) 747

אָתוֹן female donkey (1 · 33) 87

מָשַׁל 10 dominion (1 · 2) 606

אֶפֶס end, extreme limit (1 · 27) 67

אָסִיר 11 bondman, prisoner, captive (2 · 17) 64

בִּצָּרוֹן 12 stronghold (1 · 1) 131

אָסִיר bondman, prisoner, captive (2 · 17) 64

תִּקְוָה hope (1 · 32) 876

מִשְׁנֶה double, double portion (1 · 36) 1041

בָּרָק 14 lightning (1 · 21) 140

סְעָרָה tempest, storm wind (1 · 16) 704

תֵּימָן south, southern quarter (2 · 24) 412

גָּנַן, הֵגֵין to defend (2 · 8 · 8) 170-171

כָּבַשׁ 15 to subdue, dominate, bring into bondage (1 · 8 · 14) 461

קֶלַע sling (1 · 6) 8

הָמָה to be boisterous, turbulent; to murmur, growl, roar (1 · 33 · 33) 242

מִזְרָק bowl, basin (2 · 32) 284

192

זָוִית corner (1 · 2) 265

נֵזֶר 16 crown, consecration (1 · 23) 643

הִתְנֹסֵס [dub.] to be raised, prominent
(1 · 2 · 3) 651

טוּב 17 fairness, beauty, good things,
goods (1 · 32) 375

יֳפִי beauty (1-19) 421

דָּגָן corn, cereal grain (1 · 40) 186

בָּחוּר young man (1 · 45) 104

תִּירוֹשׁ must, fresh or new wine (1 · 38) 440

נוֹבֵב to make flourish (1 · 1 · 4) 626

בְּתוּלָה virgin (1 · 50) 143-144

Chapter 10

מָטָר 1 rain (2 · 38) 564

מַלְקוֹשׁ latter rain, spring rain (1 · 8) 545

חֲזִיז thunderbolt, lightning flash (1 · 3)
304

גֶּשֶׁם rain, shower (2 · 35) 177

עֵשֶׂב herbage, herb (1 · 33) 793

תְּרָפִים 2 a kind of idol (1 · 15) 1076

קֹסֵם ptc. = one who practices divination (1 · 9) 890

עַתּוּד male goat (1 · 29) 800

עֵדֶר flock (1 · 37) 727

הוֹד majesty, splendor (2 · 24) 217

פִּנָּה 4 corner (2 · 30) 819

יָתֵד tent pin; peg, pin (1 · 23) 450

נֹגֵשׂ oppressor, tyrant (2 · 15) 620

בּוּס 5 to tread down, trample (1 · 7 · 12)
100

טִיט mud, mire (2 · 13) 376

גבר 6 to make strong, strengthen
(2 · 3 · 25) 149

רחם to have compassion, be compassionate (2 · 42 · 47) 933

זָנַח to reject, spurn (1 · 16 · 19) 276

גִּיל 7 to rejoice (2 · 45 · 45) 162

שָׁרַק 8 to hiss (1 · 12 · 12) 1056

מֶרְחָק 9 distant place, far country, distance
(1 · 18) 935

גַּל 11 wave, roller; billow, heap (1 · 16)
164

מְצוּלָה depth (2 · 12) 847

גָּאוֹן exaltation, majesty, excellence
(3 · 49) 144-145

גבר to make strong, strengthen
(2 · 3 · 25) 149

Chapter 11

הֵילִל 2 to utter or make a howling
(2 · 30 · 30) 410

בְּרוֹשׁ cypress or fir (1 · 20) 141

אַדִּיר majestic one; majestic (1 · 27) 12

אַלּוֹן oak (1 · 9) 47

בָּצִיר→בָּצוֹר vintage; but BDB reads kt. cut off,
made inaccessible (1 · 1) 130, 131

יְלָלָה 3 howling (1 · 5) 410

אַדֶּרֶת glory, magnificence; cloak (2 · 12)
12

שְׁאָגָה roaring, cry (1 · 7) 980

כְּפִיר young lion (1 · 31) 498

גָּאוֹן majesty, exaltation, excellence
(3 · 49) 144-145

חֲרֵגָה slaughter (2 · 5) 247

קֹנֶה 5 ptc. = owner (1 · 7) 888-889

אָשַׁם to be held guilty, be guilty
(1 · 33 · 35) 79

הֶעֱשִׁיר to gain riches, make rich
(1 · 14 · 17) 779

חָמַל to spare, have compassion
(2 · 40 · 40) 328

חָמַל 6 to spare, have compassion
(2 · 40 · 40) 328

בָּתַת to beat or crush fine, hammer
(1 · 5 · 17) 510

הֲרֵגָה 7 slaughter (2 · 5) 247

193

מַקֵּל rod, staff (3 · 18) 596

נֹעַם delightfulness, pleasantness (2 · 7) 653

חֶבֶל ,חֹבְלִים to bind symbol of fraternity; to pledge (2 · 2) 286

הִכְחִיד 8 to efface, annihilate; hide (1 · 6 · 32) 470

יֶרַח month (1 · 12) 437

קָצַר to be short, impatient (1 · 12 · 14) 894

בָּחַל to feel loathing (1 · 1 · 1) 103

נִכְחָד 9 to be effaced, destroyed; to be hidden (3 · 11 · 32) 470

רְעוּת fellow (1 · 6) 946

מַקֵּל 10 rod, staff (3 · 18) 596

נֹעַם delightfulness, pleasantness (2 · 7) 653

גָּדַע to hew, cut in two (2 · 5 · 22) 154

הֵפֵר ,הָפֵר to break, violate; to fustrate (2 · 42 · 45) 830

הֻפַר 11 Hoph., to be broken; to be fustrated (1 · 3 · 45) 830

יהב 12 to give, set, ascribe (1 · 33 · 33) 396

שָׂכָר hire, wages (4 · 28) 969

שָׁקַל to weigh out, to weigh (1 · 19 · 22) 1053

יוֹצֵר 13 ptc. = potter (2 · 17) 427

אֶדֶר glory, magnificence; mantle, cloak (1 · 2) 12

יְקָר price, preciousness; honor (1 · 17) 430

יקר to be appraised, valued; to be precious, highly valued, esteemed (1 · 9 · 11) 429

גָּדַע 14 to hew, cut in two (2 · 5 · 22) 154

מַקֵּל rod, staff (3 · 18) 596

חֶבֶל to bind symbol of fraternity; to pledge (2 · 2) 286

הֵפִיר ,הֵפֵר to break, violate; to frustrate (2 · 42 · 45) 830

אַחֲוָה brotherhood (1 · 1) 27

אֱוִלִי 15 foolish (1 · 1) 17

נִכְחַד 16 to be effaced, destroyed; to be hidden (3 · 11 · 32) 470

נַעַר shaking, scattering [dub. text] (1 · 1) 654

כִּלְכֵּל to sustain, support; to contain (1 · 24 · 38) 465

בָּרִיא fat (1 · 14) 135

פַּרְסָה hoof (1 · 21) 828

פרק Piel, to tear off (1 · 3 · 10) 830

אֱלִיל 17 worthlessness, insufficiency (1 · 20) 47

כהה to grow dim, faint (2 · 6 · 10) 462

Chapter 12

מַשָּׂא 1 utterance, oracle (2 · 21) 672-673

יָסַר to found, establish (1 · 20 · 41) 413

יָצַר ,יוֹצֵר to form, fashion (1 · 41 · 44) 427

סַף 2 goblet, basin (1 · 6) 706

רַעַל reeling (1 · 1) 947

מָצוֹר siege, siege works (2 · 25) 848-849

מַעֲמָסָה 3 load, burden (1 · 1) 770

עמס to carry a load, carry as a load; to load (1 · 7 · 9) 770

שָׂרַט to incise, scratch (1 · 2 · 3) 976

נִשְׂרַט to be scratched (1 · 1 · 3) 976

תִּמָּהוֹן 4 bewilderment (1 · 2) 1069

שִׁגָּעוֹן madness (1 · 3) 993

פָּקַח to open eyes and [once] ears (1 · 17 · 20) 824

עִוָּרוֹן blindness (1 · 2) 734

אַמְצָה 5 strength (1 · 1) 55

כִּיּוֹר 6 pot, basin (1 · 23) 468

לַפִּיד torch (1 · 13) 542

עָמִיר swath, row of fallen grain (1 · 4) 771

תִּפְאָרָה	7	glory, honor, beauty (2 · 50) 802
גָּנַן, הֵגֵין	8	to defend (2 · 8 · 8) 170-171
תַּחֲנוּן	10	pl. abstr. = supplication for favor (1 · 18) 337
דָּקַר		to pierce, pierce through (2 · 7 · 11) 201
סָפַד		to wail, lament (3 · 28 · 30) 704
מִסְפֵּד		wailing (3 · 16) 704
יָחִיד		only one, solitary (1 · 12) 402
הֵמַר		*Hiph.*, to make bitter, show bitterness (2 · 5 · 16) 600
מִסְפֵּד	11	wailing (3 · 16) 704
בִּקְעָה		valley (1 · 19) 132
סָפַד	12	to wail, lament (3 · 28 · 30) 704

Chapter 13

מָקוֹר	1	spring, fountain (1 · 18) 881
נִדָּה		impure thing (1 · 30) 622
עָצָב	2	idol (1 · 30) 781
טֻמְאָה		uncleanness (1 · 37) 380
דָּקַר	3	to pierce, pierce through (2 · 7 · 11) 201
חִזָּיוֹן	4	vision, divine communication in a vision (1 · 9) 303
אַדֶּרֶת		mantle, cloak; glory, magnificence (2 · 12) 12
שֵׂעָר		hair (1 · 27) 972
כָּחַשׁ		to deceive, act deceptively (1 · 19 · 22) 471
נְעוּרִים	5	youth, early life (1 · 46) 655
מַכָּה	6	beating, scourging; blow, stripe; slaughter (1 · 48) 646-647
מְאַהֵב		*Piel.* ptc. = friend (1 · 16) 12-13
עָמִית	7	fellow, associate, relation (1 · 12) 765
צָעַר		to be [grow] insignificant (1 · 3 · 3) 858
פִּי	8	[idiom] portion para. 5. b. פֶּה 805
גָּוַע		to expire, perish, die (1 · 23 · 23) 157

צָרַף	9	to smelt, refine, test (2 · 19 · 22) 864
בָּחַן		to try, test, prove (2 · 25 · 29) 103

Chapter 14

נָשַׁס, נָשַׁסס	2	to be plundered, rifled (1 · 2 · 5) 1042
נִשְׁגַּל		to be violated, ravished (1 · 2 · 4) 993
גּוֹלָה		exile, exiles (2 · 42) 163
קְרָב	3	battle, war (1 · 8) 898
זַיִת	4	olives, olive tree (5 · 38) 268
מִקֶּדֶם		eastward (1 · 26) 869
גַּיְא		valley (3 · 47) 161
מָשׁ, מוּשׁ		to depart; remove (2 · 20 · 20) 559
גַּיְא	5	valley (3 · 47) 161
רַעַשׁ		earthquake, shaking (1 · 17) 950
יָקָר	6	precious, rare, splendid, weighty; but BDB reads וְקָרוֹת ''cold'' (1 · 35) 429-430
קָפָא		to be condensed, thickened; to congeal (0 · 2 · 3) 891
קִפָּאוֹן		*Q.* congelation (1 · 1) 891
קַדְמֹנִי	8	eastern; former, ancient (1 · 10) 870
קַיִץ		summer season, summer fruit (1 · 20) 884
חֹרֶף		harvest time, autumn (1 · 7) 358
רָאַם	10	to rise (1 · 1 · 1) 910
פִּנָּה		corner (2 · 30) 819
מִגְדָּל		tower (1 · 49) 153-154
יֶקֶב		wine vat (1 · 16) 428
חֵרֶם	11	devotion, ban; devoted thing (1 · 29) 356
בֶּטַח		securely; security (1 · 43) 105
מַגֵּפָה	12	plague, pestilence, slaughter, blow (4 · 26) 620
נָגַף		to strike, smite (2 · 25 · 48) 619
צָבָא		to wage war (1 · 12 · 14) 838

הֵמִיק	to cause to rot (1 · 1 · 10) 596	
נמק, נמקק	to rot, rot away, pine away (2 · 9 · 10) 596	
חֹר, חוֹר	hole; w. עַיִן = eye socket (1 · 7) 359	
מְהוּמָה	13 tumult, confusion, turmoil (1 · 12) 223	
מַגֵּפָה	15 plague, pestilence, slaughter, blow (4 · 26) 620	
פֶּרֶד	mule (1 · 14) 825	
מִדֵּי	16 as often as (1 · 15) דֵּי 2.c. 191	
שָׁנָה בְשָׁנָה	year by year (1 · [?]) 1040	
חגג	to keep a pilgrim feast (3 · 16 · 16) 290	
סֻכָּה	booth (3 · 31) 697	
גֶּשֶׁם	17 rain, shower (2 · 35) 177	

מַגֵּפָה	18 plague, pestilence, slaughter, blow (4 · 26) 620	
נָגַף	to strike, smite (2 · 25 · 48) 619	
חגג	to keep a pilgrim feast (3 · 16 · 16) 290	
סֻכָּה	booth (3 · 31) 697	
חגג	19 to keep a pilgrim feast (3 · 16 · 16) 290	
סֻכָּה	booth (3 · 31) 697	
מְצִלָּה	20 bell (1 · 1) 853	
סִיר	pot (2 · 29) 696	
מִזְרָק	bowl, basin (2 · 32) 284	
סִיר	21 pot (2 · 29) 696	
בשׁל	to boil (1 · 21 · 28) 143	
כְּנַעֲנִי	trader, merchant (1 · 4) 489	

MALACHI

Chapter 1

מַשָּׂא 1 utterance, oracle (2 · 21) 672-673

בַּמָּה 2 whereby[?] by what means[?] מה 4.a. 553

תַּן 3 jackal (1 · 14) 1072

רשש 4 to be beaten down (1 · 1 · 2) 958

חָרְבָּה waste, ruin (1 · 42) 352

הָרַס to throw down, tear down; to break down, break through (1 · 30 · 43) 248

רִשְׁעָה wickedness (3 · 15) 958

זָעַם to be indignant, have indignation (1 · 11 · 12) 276

אַיֵּה 6 where? (3 · 44) 32

מוֹרָא reverence, object of reverence, fear (2 · 12) 432

בָּזָה to despise, regard with contempt (2 · 31 · 42) 102

בַּמֶּה whereby[?] by what means[?] מה 4.a. 553

גאל ,מְגֹאָל 7 Pual, to be desecrated (2 · 4 · 11) 146

בַּמֶּה whereby[?] by what means[?] מה 4.a. 553

גאל Piel, to pollute, desecrate (1 · 1 · 11) 146

נבזה to be despicable, contemptible, despised, vile (3 · 10 · 42) 102

עִוֵּר 8 blind (1 · 26) 734

פִּסֵּחַ lame (2 · 14) 820

פֶּחָה governor (1 · 27) 808

רָצָה to be pleased with, favorable to (3 · 42 · 50) 953

הֵאִיר 10 to light, give light, make shine (1 · 34 · 40) 21

חִנָּם for no purpose, in vain, gratis, for nothing (1 · 32) 336

חֵפֶץ delight, desire, good pleasure (2 · 39) 343

רָצָה to accept, be pleased with, favorable to (3 · 43 · 50) 953

מֻקְטָר 11 Lis. Ho. ptc.; but BDB incense (1 · 2 · 115) 883

מָבוֹא entrance, entering; w. שֶׁמֶשׁ = west (1 · 23) 99-100

גאל 12 Pual, to be desecrated (2 · 4 · 11) 146

נִיב fruit (1 · 2) 626

נבזה to be despicable, contemptible, despised, vile (3 · 10 · 42) 102

אֹכֶל food (1 · 44) 38

תְּלָאָה 13 weariness, hardship (1 · 5) 521

הפיח to sniff at [in contempt], cause to breathe out (1 · 2 · 12) 655-656

גָּזַל to tear away, rob, seize (1 · 29 · 30) 159

פִּסֵּחַ lame (2 · 14) 820

רָצָה to accept, be pleased with, favorable to (3 · 42 · 50) 953

נכל ,נוֹכֵל 14 to be crafty, deceitful, knavish; ptc. = knave (1 · 1 · 4) 647

עֵדֶר flock, herd (1 · 37) 727

נָדַר to row (1 · 31 · 31) 623

נוֹרָא inspiring reverence, awe; fearful (2 · 44) 431

Chapter 2

מְאֵרָה 2 curse (2 · 5) 76

גָּעַר 3 to rebuke (2 · 14 · 14) 172

זרה to scatter, disperse (1 · 25 · 38) 279-280

פֶּרֶשׁ offal; i.e., contents of stomach area (2 · 7) 831

מוֹרָא 5 object of reverence; reverence, fear (2 · 12) 432

עַוְלָה 6 injustice, unrighteousness, wrong (1 · 32) 732

מִישׁוֹר   uprightness; level place (1 · 23) 449

נִבְזֶה   9 to be despicable, contemptible, despised, vile (3 · 10 · 42) 102

שָׁפָל   humiliated, low (1 · 18) 1050

כְּפִי   according as (1 · 16) פֶּה 6.b. 805

בָּרָא   10 to shape, fashion, create (1 · 38 · 48) 135

בגד   to act or deal treacherously, faithlessly (5 · 49 · 49) 93

בגד   11 to act or deal treacherously, faithlessly (5 · 49 · 49) 93

בָּעַל   to marry, rule over (1 · 10 · 12) 127

נֵכָר   that which is foreign, foreignness (1 · 36) 648

דִּמְעָה   13 [coll.] tears (1 · 23) 199

בְּכִי   weeping (1 · 30) 113

אֲנָקָה   crying, groaning (1 · 4) 60

מֵאֵין   so that there is no (1 · 48) אֵין 6.d. 35

הֵעִיד   14 to testify, bear witness, cause to testify, affirm solemnly, warn (1 · 38 · 43) 729

נְעוּרִים   youth, early life (2 · 46) 655

בגד   to act or deal treacherously, faithlessly (5 · 49 · 49) 93

חֲבֶרֶת   consort; i.e., wife (1 · 1) 289

שְׁאָר   15 remnant, rest, residue (1 · 26) 984

נְעוּרִים   youth, early life (2 · 46) 655

בגד   to act or deal treacherously, faithlessly (5 · 49 · 49) 93

לְבוּשׁ   16 garment, clothing (1 · 31) 528

בגד   to act or deal treacherously, faithlessly (5 · 49 · 49) 93

הוֹגִיעַ   17 to make to toil, make weary (2 · 4 · 26) 388

בַּמֶּה   whereby[?] by what means[?] מה 4.a. 553

Chapter 3

פִּתְאֹם   1 suddenly; suddenness (1 · 25) 837

חָפֵץ   delighting in, having pleasure in (1 · 12) 343

כִּלְכֵּל   2 to support, endure, to sustain; to contain (1 · 24 · 38) 465

צרף   *Piel* ptc. = a refiner (2 · 2 · 22) 864

בֹּרִית   lye, alkali, potash, soap (1 · 2) 141

צרף   3 *Piel* ptc. = a refiner (2 · 2 · 22) 864

זִקֵּק   to purify (1 · 1 · 7) 279

ערב   4 to be sweet, pleasing (1 · 8 · 8) 787

קַדְמֹנִי   former, ancient (1 · 10) 870

כִּשֵּׁף   5 to practice sorcery (1 · 6 · 6) 506

נאף   *Piel,* to commit adultery (1 · 14 · 31) 610

עָשַׁק   to oppress, wrong (1 · 36 · 37) 798

שָׂכָר   hire, wages (1 · 28) 969

שָׂכִיר   hired (1 · 18) 969

יָתוֹם   orphan (1 · 42) 450

שָׁנָה   6 to change (1 · 14 · 26) 1039

בַּמֶּה   7 whereby[?] by what means[?] מה 4.a. 553

קָבַע   8 to rob [dub.] (4 · 6 · 6) 867

בַּמֶּה   whereby[?] by what means[?] מה 4.a. 553

מַעֲשֵׂר   tithe, payment of tenth part, tenth part (2 · 33) 789

מְאֵרָה   9 curse (2 · 5) 76

קָבַע   to rob [dub.] (4 · 6 · 6) 867

מַעֲשֵׂר   10 tithe, payment of tenth part, tenth part (2 · 33) 798

טֶרֶף   food, prey (1 · 4) 383

בָּזֹאת   by or through this (1 · 4) זה 6. b. 261

בחן   to prove, test, try (2 · 25 · 29) 103

אֲרֻבָּה   lattice, latticed opening, window, sluice (1 · 9) 70

הֵרִיק   to pour out or down, to empty or draw out (1 · 17 · 19) 937-938

עַד־בְּלִי till there be no (1 · 2) para. d.
"with preps." d. בְּלִי 116 בְּלִי
(1 · 23)   115

דַּי sufficiency; w. idiom above = forever (1 · 12) דַּי 1. 191

גָּעַר 11 to rebuke (1 · 14 · 14) 172

שִׁכֵּל to show abortion, cause barrenness,
be made childless (1 · 18 · 23) 1013

אִשֵּׁר 12 to pronounce happy, call blessed;
to go straight on (2 · 7 · 9) 80

חֵפֶץ delight, pleasure (2 · 39) 343

בֶּצַע 14 profit, gain made by violence
(1 · 23) 130

קְדֹרַנִּית adv. as mourners (1 · 1) 871

אִשֵּׁר 15 to pronounce happy, call blessed;
to go straight on (2 · 7 · 9) 80

זֵד insolent, presumptuous (2 · 13) 267

רִשְׁעָה wickedness (3 · 15) 958

בֹּחַן to prove, test, try (2 · 25 · 29) 103

הִקְשִׁיר 16 to give attention (1 · 45 · 46) 904

זִכָּרוֹן memorial, reminder (1 · 24) 272

יָרֵא vb. adj.; but BDB vb. = to fear,
reverence, honor (3 · 45) 431

סְגֻלָּה 17 valued property, peculiar treasure
(1 · 8) 688

חָמַל to spare, have compassion
(2 · 40 · 40) 328

תַּנּוּר 19 fire pot, portable stove (1 · 14) 1072

זֵד insolent, presumptuous (2 · 13) 267

רִשְׁעָה wickedness (3 · 15) 958

קַשׁ stubble, chaff (1 · 16) 905

לָהַט to set ablaze (1 · 9 · 11) 529

שֹׁרֶשׁ root (1 · 33) 1057

עָנָף branch[es], bough[es] (1 · 7) 778

זרח 20 to rise, come forth (1 · 18 · 18) 280

יָרֵא vb. adj.; but BDB vb. = to fear,
reverence, honor (3 · 45) 431

מַרְפֵּא health, healing, cure (1 · 13) 951

פּוּשׁ [apparently] to spring about
(1 · 3 · 3) 807

עֵגֶל calf (1 · 35) 722

מַרְבֵּק stall, place where calves are fattened (1 · 4) 918

עסס 21 to press, crush (1 · 1 · 1) 779

אֵפֶר ashes (1 · 22) 68

נוֹרָא 23 inspiring reverence, awe; fearful
(2 · 44) 431

חֵרֶם 24 devotion, ban, devoted thing
(1 · 29) 356

APPENDIX

Words occurring more than fifty times

APPENDIX

1. This list includes all words occurring over fifty times in the Old Testament, excluding proper nouns and numerals.

2. The number with the definition is the page number in BDB where the word occurs. E.g., "בְּאֵר well (24·38) 91" indicates that בְּאֵר can be found on page 91 of BDB.

3. The first definition listed for verbs is always the Qal meaning. E.g., אָבַד means "to perish" in the Qal stem.

4. Meanings for stems other than Qal are listed normally only if they differ from the following:

Niph.	=	passive of *Qal*
Piel	=	intensive of *Qal*
Pual	=	passive of *Piel*
Hiph.	=	causative of *Qal*
Hoph.	=	passive of *Hiph.*
Hithp.	=	reflexive of *Qal*

5. The occurrence of the stem with the meaning shown in item 4 above is indicated by an asterisk (*).

APPENDIX

אָב	father 3
אָבַד	to perish 1
	Pi. to cause to perish
	Hiph. to destroy, put to death
אָבָה	to be willing, consent 2
אֶבְיוֹן	in want, needy, poor 2
אֶבֶן	stone 6
אָדוֹן	lord (see BDB for explanation of אֲדֹנִי, אֲדֹנָי, אֲדֹנָי) 10
אָדָם	man, mankind 9
אֲדָמָה	ground, land 9
אֶדֶן	base, pedestal 10
אָהֵב	to love 12
	Niph. ptc. =lovely, lovable 2 S 1:23
	Pi. ptc.=friends Zech. 13:6; lovers
אַהֲבָה	love 13
אֹהֶל	tent 13
אוֹ	or 14
אָוֶן	trouble, sorrow, wickedness 19
אוֹצָר	treasure, store, treasury, storehouse 69
אוֹר	light 21
אוֹת	sign 16
אָז	at that time, then 23
אֹזֶן	ear 23
אָח	brother 26
אָחוֹת	sister 27
אחז	to grasp, take hold, take possession 28
	Pi. to enclose, overlay Job 26:9
	Hoph. to be fastened to 2 Chron. 9:18
אֲחֻזָּה	possession 28
אַחַר	behind, after 29
אַחֵר	another 29
אַחֲרוֹן	coming after, behind 30
אַחֲרִית	after-part, end 31
אֹיֵב	(ptc. of איב) enemy 33
אֵיךְ	how? how! 32
אַיִל	ram 17
אַיִן	subst., nothing, naught 34
	part of negation, is not, are not
אִישׁ	man 35
אַךְ	surely, howbeit 36
אָכַל	to eat 37

אַל	Adv. of negation 39
אֵל	god, God; power (5t) 42
אֶל	to, towards 39
אֱלוֹהַּ	god, God 43
אַלּוּף	chief 49
אַלְמָנָה	widow 48
אֶלֶף	thousand 48
אִם	hypoth. part., interrog. part. 49
אֵם	mother 51
אָמָה	maid, hand maid 51
אַמָּה	cubit 52
אֱמוּנָה	firmness, steadfastness, fidelity 53
אמן	to confirm, support 52
	Hiph. to stand firm, to trust, believe
אָמַר	to utter, say 55
	Niph. to be called
	Hiph. to avow Deut. 26:17, 18
	Hithp. to act proudly, boast Ps. 94:4, Isa. 61:6
אֱמֶת	firmness, faithfulness, truth 54
אֲנַחְנוּ	we 59
אֲנִי	I 58
אָנֹכִי	I 59
אָסַף	to gather, remove 62
	Pi. ptc. as subst.=rearguard, rearward
אסר	to tie, bind, imprison, to harness 63
	Pu. to be taken prisoner Isa. 22:3
אַף	nose, nostril, face, anger 60
אַף	also, yea 64
אֵצֶל	in proximity to, beside 69
אָרוֹן	chest, ark 75
אֶרֶז	cedar 72
אֹרַח	way, path 73
אֹרֶךְ	length 73
אֶרֶץ	earth, land 75
ארר	to curse 76
	Hoph. to be cursed Num. 22:6
אֵשׁ	fire 77
אִשָּׁה	woman, wife, female 61
אִשֶּׁה	an offering made by fire 77
אֲשֶׁר	part. of relation 81
אֵת	mark of the accusative 84
אֵת	with 85
אַתְּ	you (sing. fem.) 61
אַתָּה	you (sing. masc.) 61

אַתֶּם you (pl. masc.) 61

בְּ in, at, by, with 88

בֶּגֶד garment, covering 93

בְּהֵמָה beast, animal, cattle 96

בּוֹא to come in, come, go in, go 97

בּוֹר pit, cistern, well 92

בּוֹשׁ to be ashamed 101

Po'lel to delay Exod. 32:1 Judg. 5:28
Hithpo'l to be ashamed before one another Gen. 2:25

בָּחַר to choose 103

Pu. to be chosen, selected Eccl. 9:4

בֶּטֶן belly, body, womb 105

בָּטַח to trust 105

בִּין to discern, understand 106

Niph. to be intelligent, discerning, have understanding
Po'l. to attentively consider Deut. 32:10
*Hiph. to understand
Hithpo'l. to show oneself attentive, consider diligently
to get understanding Jer. 23:20; Job 26:14; Ps. 119:104
to show oneself to have understanding Ps. 119:100

בֵּין in the interval of, between 107

בַּיִת house, מִבַּיִת = on the inside, מִבֵּית = within 108

בָּכָה to weep, bewail 113

Pi. to lament Jer. 31:25
to bewail Ezek. 8:14

בְּכֹר, בְּכוֹר first born 114

בַּל Adv., not 115

בָּמָה high place 119

בֵּן son 119

בָּנָה to build 124

בַּעַד away from, behind, about, on behalf of 126

בַּעַל owner, lord, husband, citizens 127

בער to burn, consume 128

*Pi. to kindle, light
Pu. to burn Jer. 36:22

בָּקַע to cleave, break open or through 131

Pu. to be ripped open Josh. 9:4 Ezek. 26:10 Hos. 14:1

Hoph. to be broken into Jer. 39:2
Hithp. to burst (themselves) open Josh. 9:13
to cleave asunder Mic. 1:4

בָּקָר cattle, herd, ox 133

בֹּקֶר morning 133

בקשׁ Pi. to seek 134

Pu. to be sought Jer. 50:20 Esth. 2:23 Ezek. 26:21

בַּרְזֶל iron 137

בָּרַח to go through, flee 137

*Hiph. to pass through Ex. 26:28

בְּרִית covenant 136

ברך to kneel, bless 138

Niph. to bless oneself Gen. 12:3, 18:18, 28:14
Pi. to bless; to salute, greet
Pu. to be prospered
to have prosperity invoked Num. 22:6
Hiph. to cause to kneel Gen. 24:11

בְּרָכָה blessing 139

בָּשָׂר flesh 142

בַּת daughter 123

גָּאַל to redeem, act as kinsman 145

*Niph. to redeem oneself Lev. 25:49

גְּבוּל border, boundary, territory 147

גִּבּוֹר strong, mighty 150

גְּבוּרָה strength, might 150

גִּבְעָה hill 148

גֶּבֶר man 149

גָּדוֹל great 152

גָּדַל to grow up, become great 152

Pi. to cause to grow
to make great, powerful
to magnify
Pu. to be brought up Ps. 144:12
Hiph. to make great
to magnify
to do great things
Hithp. to magnify oneself Isa. 10:15 Ezek. 38:23 Dan. 11:36

גּוֹי nation, people 156

גּוּר to sojourn 157

Hithpo'l. to seek hospitality with 1 Kings 17:20 (Hos. 7:14 dub.)

גּוֹרָל lot 174

גָּלָה to uncover, remove 162
*Niph. to uncover oneself
*Pi. to disclose, lay bare
to make known, reveal
Hiph. to carry away into exile,
take into exile
Hithp. to be uncovered Gen. 9:21
to reveal oneself Prov. 18:2

גַּם also, moreover, yea 168

גָּמָל camel 168

גֶּפֶן vine 172

גֵּר sojourner 158

דָּבֵק to cling, cleave, keep 179
Pu. to be joined together Job 38:38,
41:9
*Hiph. to pursue closely
to overtake
Hoph. to be made to cleave Ps. 22:16

דבר to speak 180
Niph. to speak with one another
Hiph. to lead, or put to flight Ps. 18:48,
47:4
Hithp. to speak

דָּבָר speech, word; saying, utterance;
matter, affair 182

דְּבַשׁ honey 185

דּוֹד beloved, love, uncle 187

דּוֹר period, generation;
dwelling Isa. 38:12 Ps. 49:20 189

דֶּלֶת door 195

דָּם blood 196

דַּעַת knowledge 395

דָּרַךְ to tread, march
*Hiph. to tread, tread down 201

דֶּרֶךְ way, road, distance, journey, manner 201

דָּרַשׁ to resort to, seek 205
Niph. to let oneself be inquired of
to be required Gen. 42:22
to be sought out 1 Chron. 26:31

הַ, הָ, הַ (def. art.) the 206

הַ, הָ, הַ interrog· part. 209

הֶבֶל vapor, breath 210

הוּא (3rd pers. sing. pron.) he, she (in
Pent.), it; with art. = that 214 216

הוֹי ah, alas, ha 222

הִיא (3rd pers. sing. pron.) she, it; with
art. = that 214–216

הָיָה to be, become, come to pass, fall out
224

הֵיכָל palace, temple 228

הָלַךְ to go, come, walk 229
Niph. to be gone Ps. 109:23
Hithp. to walk, walk about, move to
and fro

הלל to be boastful 237
Pi. to praise
Hithpa. to make one's boast Ps. 10:3
44:9
Hithpa. to glory, boast, make one's
boast
Po'el. to make fool of Isa. 44:25 Job
12:17 Eccl. 7:7
Po'al. to be mad Ps. 102:9, Eccl. 2:2
Hithpo. to act madly, like a madman

הֵם, הֵמָּה (3rd pers. pl. masc. pron.; as neuter,
rarely) they; with art=those (not
defined in BDB) 241

הָמוֹן sound, murmur, roar, crowd,
abundance 242

הֵן lo! behold! 243

הֵנָּה fem. of הֵמָּה (see above) 241

הִנֵּה lo! behold! 243

הָפַךְ to turn, overturn 245
*Niph. to turn oneself, turn, turn
back
Hithp. to turn this way and that Gen.
3:24 Judg. 7:13 Job 37:12
to transform oneself Job 38:14
Hoph. to be turned (upon) Job 30:15

הַר mountain, hill, hill country 249

הָרַג to kill, slay 246
Pu. to be slain Is. 27:7

וָ, וּ, וְ (adv., conj.) so, then, and, and also,
but, both . . . and (וְ . . . וְ), consecutive
verb formations, (cohort.) so that
(introduces apodosis after כִּ, אִם) then
251–255

זֹאת fem, of זֶה (see below)

זָבַח to slaughter for sacrifice 256

Pi. to sacrifice

זֶבַח   sacrifice 257

זֶה   (demonstr. sing. masc. pron. [fem., זֹאת] and adv.) this, here; also used idiomatically with prepositions 260–262

זָהָב   gold 262

זָכַר   to remember 269

זָכָר   male 271

זָנָה   to commit fornication, to be a harlot 275

Pu. Ezek. 16:34 ז' לֹא=fornication was not done

Hiph. to cause to commit fornication to commit fornication

זעק   to cry, cry out, call 277

Niph. to be called together.

to assemble

to join

Hiph. to call, call out, or together

to make a crying Job 35:9 (וי ז' ויאמר)

to have proclamation made Jonah 3:7

to call out to, or at Zech. 6:8

זָקֵן   old 278

זר   strange (adj.), stranger (noun) BDB under זור 266

זְרֹוצַ   arm, shoulder, strength 283

זָרַע   to sow, scatter seed 281

Niph. to be made pregnant Num. 5:28

Pu. to be sown Isa. 40:24

Hiph. to produce seed Gen. 1:11, 12

to bear a child Lev. 12:2

זֶרַע   sowing, seed, offspring 282

חַג   festive-gathering, feast 290

חָדַל   to cease 292

Hoph. to be made to leave Judg. 9:9, 11, 13

חָדָשׁ   new 294

חֹדֶשׁ   new moon, month 294

חֹומָה   wall 327

חוּץ   the outside, a street 299

חָזָה   to see, behold 302

חָזַק   to be or grow firm, strong, strengthen 304

Pi. to make strong, firm, hard

to strengthen

Hiph. to prevail

to take or keep hold, seize, grasp

Hithp. to strengthen oneself

to put forth strength

to withstand 2 Chron. 13:7, 8

to hold strongly with

חָזָק   strong, stout, mighty 305

חָטָא   to miss, go wrong, sin 306

Hiph. to miss the mark Judg. 20:16

to bring into guilt, condemnation

Hithp. to miss or lose oneself Job 41:17

to purify oneself

חַטָּאת   sin, sin offering 308

חַי   alive, living 311

חָיָה   to live 310

Pi. to preserve alive, let live

to give life Job 33:4

to quicken, revive, refresh

Hiph. to preserve alive, let live

to quicken, revive

חַיָה   living thing, animal; life (some poetry); appetite Job 38:39; revival, renewal Isa. 57:10, 312

חַיִּים   life 313

חַיִל   strength, efficiency, wealth, army 298

חָכָם   wise 314

חָכְמָה   widsom 315

חֵלֶב   fat 316

חָלָה   to be weak, sick 317

Niph. to make oneself sick Jer. 12:13

to be made sick Dan. 8:27 Amos 6:6; Ptc.=diseased

Pi. to make sick Deut. 29:21 Ps. 77:11,

to appease, entreat the favor of

Pu. to be made weak Isa. 14:10

Hithp. to make oneself sick 2 Sam. 13:2, 5, 6

Hiph. to become sick Hos. 7:5

חֲלֹום   dream 321

חלל   *Niph.* to pollute, defile oneself Lev. 21:4, 9, 320

to be polluted, defiled

Pi. to defile, pollute

to dishonor

to violate

to treat as common

Pu. to be profaned Ezek. 36:23

Hiph. to allow to be profaned Ezek. 39:7, 20:9

to begin

Hoph. to be begun Gen. 4:26

חָלָל pierced 319

חָלַק to divide, share 323

*Niph. to divide oneself Gen. 14:15

to assign, distribute 1 Chron. 23:6, 24:3 (see Pi.)

*Pi. to assign, distribute 1 Chron. 23:6, 24:3 (see Niph.)

to scatter Gen. 49:7 Lam. 4:16

Pu. to be divided Isa. 33:23 Amos 7:17 Zech. 14:1

Hiph. to receive a portion Jer. 37:12

Hithp. to divide among themselves Josh. 18:5

חֵלֶק portion, tract, territory 324

חֵמָה heat, rage 404

חֲמוֹר he-ass, male donkey 331

חָמָס violence, wrong 329

חֵן favor, grace 336

חָנָה to decline, bend down, encamp 333

חָנַן to show favor, be gracious 335

Niph. to be pitied Jer. 22:23

Pi. to make gracious Jer. 26:25

Po'el to direct favor to Ps. 102:15 Prov. 14:21

Hoph. to be shown favor Isa. 26:10 Prov. 21:10

Hithp. to seek or implore favor

חֶסֶד goodness, kindness 338

חָפֵץ to delight in 342

חֵץ arrow 346

חֲצִי half 345

חָצֵר enclosure, court 346

חֹק something prescribed, a statute, decree, ordinance 349

חֻקָּה something prescribed, enactment, statute 349

חֶרֶב sword 352

חָרָה to burn, be kindled (of anger) 354

Niph. to be angry Isa. 41:11, 45:24 Song of Sol. 1:6

Hiph. to be burned (?) Neh. 3:20

to cause to be kindled Job 19:11

Hithp. to heat oneself in vexation Ps. 37:1, 7, 8, Prov. 24:19

to hotly contend (dub.) Jer. 12:5

to strive eagerly (dub.) Jer. 22:15

הֶרְפָּה reproach 357

חָשַׁב to think, account, reckon 362

Hithp. to reckon oneself Num. 23:9

חֹשֶׁךְ darkness, obscurity 365

חתת to be shattered, dismayed 369

Niph. to be put in awe Mal. 2:5

Pi. to dismay, scare Job 7:14

to be shattered (?) Jer. 51:56

טָהוֹר clean, pure 373

טָהֵר to be clean, pure 372

Pi. to cleanse, purify

to pronounce clean *Pu.* to be cleansed 1 Sam. 20:26 Ezek. 22:24

Hithp. to purify oneself

to present oneself for purification

טוֹב pleasant, agreeable, good 373

טָמֵא to be, become unclean 379

Niph. to defile oneself, be defiled

to be regarded as unclean Job 18:3

Pi. to defile

to pronounce unclean

Hithp. to defile oneself

Hothp. to be defiled Deut. 24:4

טָמֵא unclean 379

יְאֹר stream, canal; stream of Nile 384

יָבֵשׁ to be dry, dried up, withered 386

Pi. to make dry, dry up

*Hiph. to exhibit dryness

יָד hand 388

ידה to shoot Jer. 50:14, 392

Pi. to cast Lam. 3:53 Zech. 2:4

Hiph. to give thanks, laud, praise

to confess

Hithp. to confess

to give thanks 2 Chron. 30:22

יָדַע to know 393

*Niph. to make oneself known

to be perceived Gen. 41:21 Ps. 74:5

to be instructed Jer. 31:19

Pi. to cause to know Job 38:12 Ps. 104:19(?)

Po. to cause to know 1 Sam. 21:3

Pu. ptc: known Isa. 12:5 as subst.=acquaintance (remaining Pu.)

Hithp. to make oneself known Gen. 45:1 Num. 12:6

יוֹם day 398

יוֹמָם daytime, by day 401

יַחְדָּו together 403

יטב to be good, well, glad, pleasing 405

יַיִן wine 406

יכח *Hiph.* to decide, adjudge, prove 406

Hoph. to be chastened Job. 33:19

Niph. to reason together Isa. 1:18

to reason Job 23:7

to be set right, justified Gen. 20:16

Hithp. to argue Mic. 6:2

יָכֹל to be able, have power, prevail, endure 407

יָלַד to bear, bring forth, beget 408

Pi. to cause (or help) to bring forth Exod. 1:16

Ptc. as subst. = midwife

Pu. to be born

Hiph. to beget

Hithp. to declare pedigree Num. 1:18

יֶלֶד child, son, boy, youth 409

descendants Isa. 29:23

יָם sea, freq. indicates western point of compass, west 410

יָמִין right hand 411

יָסַף to add 414

*Niph. to join oneself to Exod. 1:10

יַעַן on account of, because 774

יָעַץ to advise, counsel 419

Niph. to consult together, exchange

counsel

Hithp. to conspire Ps. 83:4

יַעַר wood, forest, thicket 420

יָצָא to go or come out 422

יָצַק to pour, cast, flow 427

Hiph. to pour out

Hoph. ptc.=cast, molten firmly established Job 11:15

יָרֵא to fear 431

Pi. to make afraid, terrify

יָרַד to come or go down, descend 432

יְרִיעָה curtain 438

יָרַשׁ take possession of, inherit, dispossess 439

Niph. to be impoverished

Pi. to take possession of, devour Deut. 28:42

*Hiph. to take possession of Num. 14:24

יֵשׁ is, are 441

יָשַׁב to sit, remain, dwell 442

Pi. to set Ezek. 25:4

*Hiph. to cause to be inhabited Ezek. 36:33 Isa. 54:3

to marry (only Ezra and Nehemiah)

Hoph. to be made to dwell Isa. 5:8

to be inhabited Isa. 44:26

יְשׁוּעָה salvation; victory 447

ישׁע *Hiph.* to deliver 446

Niph. to be liberated, saved

יָשָׁר straight, right 449

יתר *Qal* ptc. = remainder 1 Sam. 15:15, 45

Niph. to be left over, remain over

Hiph. to leave over, leave

to excel, show preeminence Gen. 49:4

to show excess=have more than enough Exod. 36:7

to make abundant Deut. 28:11; 30:9

יֶתֶר remainder, excess, preeminence 451

כְּ the like of, like, as 453

כַּאֲשֶׁר according as, as, when 455

כָּבֵד to be heavy, weighty, burdensome, honored 457

Niph. to be made heavy Prov. 8:24

to be honored, enjoy honor

to get oneself glory

Pi. to make heavy, insensible 1 Sam. 6:66

to make honorable

to honor, glorify

Pu. to be made honorable, honored Isa. 58:13 Pr. 13:18, 27:18

*Hiph. to display honor

Hithp. to make oneself heavy Nah. 3:15

to honor oneself Prov. 12:9

כָּבוֹד   abundance, honor, glory 458

כבס   to wash, ptc. only = fuller, washer 460

Pu. to be washed Lev. 13:58, 15:17

Hothp. to be washed out Lev. 13:55, 56

כֶּבֶשׂ   lamb 461

כֹּה   thus, here 462

כֹּהֵן   priest 463

כּוּן   *Niph.* to be set up, established, fixed 465

to be directed aright

to be prepared, ready

Hiph. to establish, set up

to fix, make ready

to direct

to arrange, order 2 Chron. 29:19, 35:20

Po'lel to set up, establish

to constitute, make

to fix

to direct Job 8:8

Po'lal to be established Ps. 37:23

to be prepared Ezek. 28:13

Hithpo'l to be established

כֹּחַ   strength, power 470

כִּי   that, for, when, because, since 471

כִּכָּר   a round; hence

1. a round district

2. a round loaf

3. a round weight, talent

כֹּל   whole, all 481

כָּלָה   to be complete, at an end, finished, accomplished, spent 477

Pi. to complete, bring to an end, finish

accomplish

to cause to cease Num. 17:25, Ps. 78:33

to exhaust, use up

to consume Lev. 26:16

to destroy

Pu. to be finished, ended Ps. 72:20

to be complete Gen. 2:1

כְּלִי   article, utensil, vessel 479

כְּמוֹ   like, as, when 455

כֵּן   so, thus 485

כָּנָף   wing, extremity 489

כִּסֵּא (כִּסֵּה)   seat of honor, throne 490

כסה   to conceal, cover, ptc. only: Act.= conceal Prov. 12:16, 23 491

Pass.="covered" Ps. 32:1

Niph. to be covered Jer. 51:42 Ezek. 24:8

*Pual to be clothed 1 Chron. 21:16 Eccl. 6:4

כְּסִיל   stupid fellow, fool 493

כֶּסֶף   silver, money 494

כָּעַס   to be vexed, angry 494

Pi. to be angered 1 Sam. 1:6 Deut. 32:21

כַּף   hollow, flat of hand, palm, sole, pan 496

כְּפִי   according to the command of, according to the mouth of, in proportion to (of, that) 805

כָּפַר   *Pi.* to cover over, pacify, make propitiation, atone 497

Hithp. to be covered 1 Sam. 3:14

Nithp. to be covered Deut. 21:8

כְּרוּב   cherub 500

כֶּרֶם   vineyard 501

כָּרַת   to cut off, cut down 503

*Niph. to be chewed Num. 11:33

Pual to be cut off Ezek. 16:4

to be cut down Judg. 6:28

*Hiph. to take away 1 Sam. 20:15

to permit to perish 1 Kings 18:5

כָּשַׁל   to stumble, stagger, totter 505

Niph. (= Qal)

to be tottering, feeble Isa. 40:30, 1 Sam.

2:4. Zech. 12:8

Pi. Ezek. 36:14 only (but see BDB)

*Hiph. to make feeble, weak Lam. 1:14

Hoph. ptc. only=the ones who have stumbled Jer. 18:23 Ezek. 21:20(?)

כָּתַב   to write 507

Pi. to write Isa. 10:1

כָּתֵף   shoulder, shoulder-blade; side; support 1 Kings 7:30, 34 509

לְ   to, for, in regard to 510

לֹא, לוֹא   Adv., not 518

לֵב   inner man, mind, will, heart 524

לֵבָב   inner man, mind, will, heart 523

לְבַד   in a state of separation, alone, by itself 94

לְבַד מִן   besides, apart from 94

לְבִלְתִּי   so as not, in order not (to) 116

לָבֵשׁ   to put on, wear, clothe, be clothed 527

Pu. ptc. only=arrayed

לחם   to fight, do battle Ps. 35:1, 56:2, 3 535

Niph. to engage in battle, wage war

לֶחֶם   bread, food 536

לַיִל, לַיְלָה   night 538

לוּן, לִין   to lodge, pass the night 533

Hiph. to cause to rest, lodge 2 Sam. 17:8

Hithpo'l to dwell, abide Job 39:28 Ps. 91:1

לָכַד   to capture, seize, take 539

Hithp. to grasp each other Job 41:9 to compact Job 38:30

לָכֵן   therefore 486

לָמַד   to exercise in, learn 540

Pi. to teach

לָמָה, לָמָּה   why? 554

לְמַעַן   for the sake of, on account of, to the intent that, in order that 775

לְפִי   according to (as) 805

לִפְנֵי   at the face of or front of, in the presence of, before 816

לָקַח   to take 542

Pu. to be taken Gen. 2:23 3:19, 23 Jer. 29:22

to be stolen Judg. 17:2

to be taken captive Jer. 48:46

to be taken away, removed 2 Kings 2:10 Isa. 53:8

Hoph. to be taken, brought

Hithp. to take hold of oneself Exod. 9:24 Ezek. 1:4

לָשׁוֹן   tongue 546

מְאֹד   muchness, force, abundance, exceedingly 547

מֵאַחַר   from after 29

מָאַס   to reject, refuse, despise 549

מָגֵן   shield 171

מִגְרָשׁ   common, common land, open land 177

מִדְבָּר   wilderness 184

מָדַד   to measure 551

Pi. to extend, continue Job 7:4

to measure, measure off 2 Sam. 8:2 Ps. 60:8, 108:8

Po. to be measured Hab. 3:6

Hithpo. to measure himself 1 Kings 17:21

מִדָּה   measure, measurement 551

garment Ps. 133:2

size Jer. 22:14

stature 1 Chron. 11:23, 20:6

מַדּוּעַ   wherefore? on what account? 396

מְדִינָה   province 193

מָה, מֶה   what? how? aught? 552

מהר   *Niph.* to be hurried, hasty 554

Pi. to hasten, make haste

Inf. Abs. מַהֵר quickly, speedily

מַהֵר   quickly, speedily 555

מוֹעֵד   appointed time, place, meeting 417

מות   to die 559

Po'lel to kill, put to death

*Hoph. to die prematurely Prov. 19:16

מָוֶת   death 560

מִזְבֵּחַ   altar 258

מִזְמוֹר   melody 274

מִזְרָח   place of sunrise, east 280

מַחֲנֶה encampment, camp 334

מָחָר tomorrow, in time to come 563

מַחֲשָׁבָה thought, device 364

מַטֶּה staff, rod, shaft; tribe, branch Ezek. 19:11, 12, 14 641

מִי who? 566

מַיִם (pl. of מֵי) pl. only; water, waters 565

מָכַר to sell 569

*Niph. to sell oneself

מָלֵא to be full, fill 569

*Niph. to be accomplished, ended Exod. 7:25 Job 15:32

*Pi. to confirm 1 Kings 1.14

Pu. ptc.=set Song of Sol. 5:14

Hithp. to mass oneself Job 16:10

מָלֵא full 570

מַלְאָךְ messenger 521

מְלָאכָה occupation, work; workmanship; property; service, use; public business 521

מִלְחָמָה battle, war 536

מלט Niph. to slip away 1 Sam. 20:29 2 Sam. 4:6 572

to escape

to be delivered

Pi. to lay (eggs) Isa. 34:15

to let escape 2 Kings 23:18

to deliver

Hiph. to give birth to Isa. 66:7

to deliver Isa. 31:5

Hithp. to slip forth, escape Job 41:11

to escape Job 19:20

מָלַךְ to be, become, king or queen, to reign 573

Hoph. to be made king Dan. 9:1

מֶלֶךְ king 572

מַלְכוּת royalty, royal power, reign, kingdom 574

מִלִּפְנֵי from before, because 817

מַמְלָכָה kingdom, sovereignty, dominion, reign 575

מִן out of, from, on account of, off, on the side of, since, above, than, so that not 577

מִנְחָה gift, tribute, offering 585

מְנַצֵּחַ Pi. ptc. of נצח; in Psalms=perh. musical director, choir master; elsewhere=director 663

מִסְפָּר number; recounting Judg. 7:15 708

מְעַט a little, fewness, a few 589

מַעַל above, upwards 751

מֵעַל from upon, from over, from by (beside) 758–759

מַעְלָה upwards 751

מֵעִם from with or beside; away from, from 768

מַעֲשֶׂה deed, work 795

מִפְּנֵי from the face or presence of, from before, because 818

מָצָא to attain to, find 592

to learn, devise Eccl. 7:27, 27, 29

to experience Ps. 116:3 Eccl. 7:14

to find out

to come upon, light upon

to hit Deut. 19:5 1 Sam. 31:3 1 Chron. 10:3

*Niph. to be gained; secured Ho. 14:9

to be left

to be present

to prove to be 1 Chron. 24:4 2 Chron. 2:16

to be sufficient Josh. 17:16

*Hiph. to cause to encounter 2 Sam. 3:8 Zech. 11:6

to present Lev. 9:12, 13, 18

מַצָּה unleavened bread or cake(s) 595

מִצְוָה commandment 846

מִקְדָּשׁ sacred place, sanctuary 874

מָקוֹם standing place, place 879

מִקְנֶה cattle 889

מַרְאֶה sight, appearance, vision 909

מָרוֹם height 928

מָשַׁח to smear, anoint 602

מִשְׁכָּן dwelling place, 'tabernacle' 1015

מָשַׁל to rule, have dominion, reign 605

Hiph. to cause to rule Ps. 8:7 Dan. 11:39

to exercise dominion Job 25:2

מִשְׁמֶרֶת guard, watch; charge, function 1038

מִשְׁפָּחָה clan 1046

מִשְׁפָּט judgment, justice, right manner, fitting 1 Kings 5:8; fitness Isa. 28:26; 40:14 1048

מֵת dead one. corpse 559 (מוּת)

מִתַּחַת from under, from beneath, from 1066

נָא part. of entreaty of exhortation, I pray, now 609

נְאֻם utterance, declaration 610

נבא *Niph.* to prophesy 612
Hithp. to prophesy

נבט *Pi.* to look Isa. 5:30 613
Hiph. to look
to regard, show regard

נָבִיא spokesman, speaker, prophet 611

נֶגֶב south country, Negeb, south 616

נגד *Hiph.* to declare, tell 616
to avow, acknowledge, confess Isa. 3:9 Ps. 38:19
Hoph. to be told, announced, reported

נֶגֶד in front of, in sight of, opposite to 617

נָגַע to touch, reach, strike 619
Niph. to be stricken, defeated Josh. 8:15
Pi. to strike Gen. 12:17 2 Kings 15:5 2 Chron. 26:20
Pu. to be stricken Ps. 73:5
*Hiph. to reach, extend
to approach
to befall

נֶגַע stroke, plague, mark 619

נגש to draw near, approach 620
Niph. (as Qal)
Hoph. to be brought near 2 Sam. 3:34 Mal. 1:11
Hithp. to draw near Isa. 45:20

נֶדֶר vow 623

נָהָר stream, river 625

נוּחַ to rest 628
Hiph. to leave
to abandon Jer. 14:9 Ps. 119:121
to permit

Hoph. to be caused to rest La. 5:5 Zech. 5:11
ptc. as subst=space left, open space Ezek. 41:9, 11

נוּס to flee, escape 630
Po'lel to cause to flee, to drive Isa. 59:19
Hithpo'l to take flight Ps. 60:6
Hiph. to put to flight Deut. 32:30
to drive hastily Exod. 9:20
to cause to disappear, hide Judg. 6:11

נָחַל to get or take as a possession 635
Pi. to divide for a possession

נַחַל torrent, torrent valley, wady 636

נַחֲלָה possession, property, inheritance 635

נחם *Niph.* to be sorry 636
to comfort oneself
Pi. to comfort, console
Pual to be relieved, consoled Isa. 54:11, 66:13
Hithp. to be sorry, have compassion Deut. 32:36 Ps. 135:14
to rue Num. 23:19
to comfort oneself, be relieved Gen. 37:35 Ps. 119:52
to ease oneself Ezek. 5:13 Gen. 27:42

נָחֹשֶׁת copper, bronze, (dual) fetter of copper or bronze 638

נָטָה to stretch out, spread out, extend, incline, bend 639
Niph. to be stretched out Num. 24:6 Zech. 1:16
to stretch themselves out Jer. 6:4
Hiph. to stretch out Isa. 31:3 Jer. 6:12, 15:6
to spread out 2 Sam. 16:22, 21:10 Isa. 54:2
to turn, incline

נטע to plant 642
Niph. to be planted Isa. 40:24

נכה *Niph.* to be smitten 2 Sam. 11:15 645
Pu. to be smitten Exod. 9:31, 32
Hiph. to smite, strike

נֶסֶךְ drink-offering; molten images 651

נָסַע to pull out or up, set out, journey 652
Niph. to be pulled up Isa. 38:12 Job 4:21

נַעַר boy, lad, youth; servant 654

נַעֲרָה girl, damsel 655

נָפַל to fall, lie 656
Pi'lel Ezek. 28:23 But BDB="rd. וְנִפַּל"

נֶפֶשׁ soul, living being, life, self, person, desire, appetite, emotion, passion 659

נצב *Niph.* to take one's stand, stand 662
Hiph. to station, set, set up
Hoph. to be fixed, determined Gen. 28:12 Judg. 9:6 Nah. 2:8

נצל *Niph.* to deliver oneself, be delivered 664
Pi. to strip off, spoil 2 Chron. 20:25 Exod. 3:22, 12:36
to deliver Ezek. 14:14
Hiph. to snatch away, deliver
Hoph. to be plucked out Amos. 4:11 Zech. 3:2
Hithp. to strip oneself Exod. 33:6

נצר to watch, guard, keep 665

נָשָׂא to lift, carry, take 669

נָשִׂיא a chief, prince 672

נָתַן to give, put, set 678
Hoph. (as *Niph.*)

סָבַב to turn about, go around, surround 685
Niph. to turn oneself
to be turned over Jer. 6:12
Pi. to change 2 Sam. 14:20
Po. to encompass, surround

סָבִיב circuit, round about 686

סָגַר to shut, close 688
Pi. to deliver up
Pu. to be shut up
Hiph. to deliver up
to shut up

סוּס horse 692

סֹפֵר secretary, muster officer, scribe 708

סוּר to turn aside 693

Po'lel to turn aside Lam. 3:11
Hiph. to put aside

סֶלָה (a benediction[?]) see BDB 699

סֶלַע crag, cliff 700

סֹלֶת fine flour 701

סָפַר to count 707
Pi. to recount, rehearse, declare

סֵפֶר document, writing, book 706

סָתַר *Niph.* to hide oneself 711
to be hid, concealed
Pi. to carefully hide Isa. 16:3
Pu. to be carefully concealed Prov. 27:5
Hithp. to hide oneself
Hiph. to conceal, hide

עָבַד to work, serve 712
Niph. to be tilled Deut. 21:4 Ezek. 36:9, 34
ptc.=cultivated Eccl. 5:8 (dub.)
Pu. to be worked Deut. 21:3 Isa. 14:3

עֶבֶד servant, slave, subject 713

עֲבֹדָה labor, service 715

עָבַר to pass over, through, by, on 716
Niph. to be forded Ezek. 47:5
Pi. to impregnate Job 21:10
to cause to pass across 1 Kings 6:21

עֵבֶר region across or beyond, side 719

עַד as far as, even to, up to, until, while 723

עֵד witness 729

עֵדָה congregation 417

עֵדוּת testimony 730

עוֹד still, yet, again, besides 728

עוֹלָם forever, always, everlasting; ancient, old; age 761

עָוֹן iniquity, guilt; punishment of iniquity 730

עוֹף coll. birds, fowl; flying insects 733

עוּר to rouse oneself, awake 734
Po'l to rouse, incite
Pilp. to rouse, (raise?) Isa. 15:5
Hithpo'l to be excited Job 31:29, 17:8
to rouse oneself Isa. 64:6
Hiph. to rouse
to act aroused Ps. 35:23, 73:20

Appendix

עוֹר skin, hide 736

עֵז she-goat; pl. subst.=goat's hair 777

עֹז strength, might 738

עָזַב to leave, forsake, loose 736
Pu. to be deserted Isa. 32:14 Jer. 49:25

עוֹזר to help 740
Hiph. (dub.) as Qal 2 Sam. 18:3 2 Chron. 28:23

עַיִן eye; surface Exod. 10:5, 15 Num. 22:5, 11
appearance Lev. 13:5, 37, 55 Num. 11:7 1 Sam. 16:7(?), gleam, sparkle Ezek. 1 (5t), 8:2, 10:9 Dan. 10:6 Prov. 23:31 744

עִיר city, town; fortress 746

עַל on, on the ground of, according to, on account of, on behalf of, concerning, besides, in addition to, together with, beyond, above, over, by, onto, toward, to, against 752–759

עָלָה to go up, ascend, climb 748
Niph. to take oneself away 2 Sam. 2:27
to be exalted Ps. 47:10, 97:9
Hiph. to take away Ps. 102:25 Job 36:20
Hoph. to be carried away Nah. 2:8
to be taken up 2 Chron. 20:34
to be offered Judg. 6:23
Hithp. to lift oneself Jer. 51:3

עֹלָה whole burnt offering 750

עֶלְיוֹן upper, high, highest 751

עַם, עָם people, nation 766

עִם with 767

עָמַד to take one's stand, stand; to arise, appear
to be appointed Ezek. 10:14
to grow flat, insipid Jer. 48:11 763
Hiph. to station, set
to have a fixed look עֵ׳ אֶת-פָּנָיו 2 Kings 8:11
to restore Ezra 9:9
to raise Dan. 11:11, 13

עַמּוּד pillar, column 765

עָמָל trouble, mischief, toil 765

עֵמֶק valley, lowland 770

עָנָה to answer, respond 772
Niph. to make answer Ezra 14:4, 7
Hiph. ptc. Eccl. 5:19 (dub.) See BDB

ענה to be put down or become low Isa. 25:5 776
to be depressed, down cast Isa. 31:4
to be afflicted Ps. 116:10, 119:67 Zech. 10:2
Niph. to humble oneself Exod. 10:3
to be afflicted Isa. 53:7, 58:10 Ps. 119:107
Pi. to humble, afflict
Pu. to be afflicted Ps. 119:71, 132:1 Isa. 53:4
to be humbled Lev. 23:29
Hiph. to afflict 1 Kings 8:35 2 Chon. 6:26
Hithp. to humble oneself Gen. 16:9 Ezek. 8:21 Dan. 10:12
to be afflicted 1 Kings 2:26 Ps. 107:17

עָנִי poor, afflicted, humble 776

עָנָן cloudmass, cloud 777

עָפָר dry earth, dust; ore Job 28:2 779

עֵץ tree, trees, wood 781

עֵצָה counsel, advice 420

עֶצֶם bone, substance; self (same) 782

עֶרֶב evening; night Job 7:4 787

עֲרָבָה desert plain, steppe 787

עֶרְוָה nakedness, pudenda 788

עָרַךְ to arrange, set in order
to compare Isa. 40:18 Ps. 40:6
to be comparable Ps. 89:7 Job 28:17, 19 789
Hiph. to value, tax

עָשָׂה to do, work
to make
to acquire
to use 1 Sam. 8:16 Exod. 38:24
to spend, pass. Eccl. 6:12 793
Pu. to be made Ps. 139:15

עֵת time; experiences, fortunes Isa. 33:6 Ps. 31:16 1 Chron. 29:30 773

עַתָּה   now 773

פֵּאָה   corner, side 802

פָּדָה   to ransom 804

פֶּה   mouth; end 2 Kings 10:21, 21:16
Ezra. 9:11
portion Deut. 21:17 2 Kings 2:9 Zech.
13:8 804

פּוּץ   to be dispersed, scattered 806
Niph. (as Qal)

פָּלַל   *Pi.* to mediate, arbitrate, interpose 813
Hithp. to pray, intercede

פֶּן   lest 814

פָּנָה   to turn, turn and look, look 815
Pi. to turn away, put out of the way
Hiph. to turn Judg. 15:4 1 Sam. 10:9
Jer. 48:39
to make a turn
Hoph. to be turned Jer. 49:8 Ezek. 9:2

פָּנֶה   face 815

פָּעַל   to do, make 821

פַּעַם   once, time, step, now; anvil 821

פָּקַד   to attend to, visit, muster, appoint 823
Niph. to be missed, lacking
Pi. to muster Isa. 13:4
Pu. to be passed in review Exod. 38:21
to be caused to miss Isa. 38:10
Hithp. to be mustered Judg. 20:15, 17, 21:9
Hothp. (as Hithp.)
Hiph. to set, make overseer
to commit, entrust
to deposit
Hoph. to be visited Jer. 6:6
to be deposited Lev. 5:23
to be made overseer

פַּר   young bull, steer 830

פְּרִי   fruit 826

פַּרְעֹה   Pharaoh 829

פָּרַשׂ   to spread out, spread 831
Niph. to be scattered Ezek. 17:21, 34:12

פָּרָשׁ   horseman; horse 832

פֶּשַׁע   transgression; guilt of transgression; punishment for transgression; Dan. 8:12, 13, 9:24; offering for transgression Mic. 6:7 833

פתח   to open 834

פֶּתַח   doorway, opening, entrance 835

צֹאן   (coll.) small cattle, sheep and goats, flock, flocks 838

צָבָא   army, host; war, warfare, service 838

צַדִּיק   just, righteous 843

צֶדֶק   rightness, righteousness 841

צְדָקָה   righteousness 842

צוה   *Pi.* to lay charge (upon), give charge (to), charge, command, order 845

צוּר   rock, cliff 849

צֵל   shadow, shade 853

צלח   to rush
to be successful, prosper 852
Hiph. to show experience, prosperity

צָעַק   to cry, cry out 858
Niph. to be summoned
Hiph. to call together 1 Sam. 10:17
Pi. to cry aloud 2 Kings 2:12

צָפוֹן   north 860

צַר   adversary, foe 865

צָרָה   straits, distress 865

צרר   to bind, tie up
to be scant, cramped 864
Pu. to be tied up Josh. 9:4
Hiph. to make narrow, press hard, cause distress

קָבַץ   to gather, collect, assemble 867
Niph. (as Qal)
Hithp. to gather together, be gathered together

קָבַר   to bury 868

קֶבֶר   grave, tomb 868

קָדוֹשׁ   sacred, holy 872

קָדִים   East, east wind 870

קֶדֶם   front, east; ancient, of old; beginning Prov. 8:22, 23 869

קָדַשׁ   to be set apart, consecrated 872
Niph. to show oneself sacred, majestic

to be honored
to be consecrated Exod. 29:43
Pi. to consecrate, dedicate;
to keep sacred
to honor as sacred, hallow
Hiph. (as Pi.)
Hithp. to be observed as holy Isa. 30:29
to consecrate oneself

קֹדֶשׁ   apartness, sacredness 871

קָהָל   assembly, company, congregation 874

קוֹל   sound, voice 876

קוּם   to arise, stand up, stand
to be fulfilled 877
Pi. to fulfil Ezek. 13:6 Ps. 119:106
to confirm, ratify Ruth 4:7
to establish Ps. 119:28
to impose Esth. 9 (7 times)
Po'l. to raise up
Hithpo'l to rise up
Hiph. to raise, set up

קָטֹן   small, insignificant 882

קטר   *Pi.* to make sacrifices smoke 882
Pu. to be fumigated Song of Sol. 3:6
Hiph. to make (sacrifices) smoke
Hoph. to be made to smoke Lev. 6:15 Mal. 1:11

קְטֹרֶת   incense, sweet smoke of sacrifice 1 Sam. 2:28 (?) Isa. 1:13 Ps. 66: 15, 141:2 882

קִיר   wall 885

קָלַל   to be slight, swift, trifling 886
Niph. to show oneself swift Isa. 30:16
to be, appear trifling
to be lightly esteemed 2 Sam. 6:22
Pi. to curse
Hiph. to make light, lighten
to treat with contempt
Pilp. to shake Ezek. 21:26
to whet Eccl. 10:10
Hithpalp. to shake oneself Jer. 4:24

קָנָה   to get, acquire; buy 888

קָנֶה   stalk, reed; shoulder joint Job 31:22 889

קֵץ   end 893

קָצֶה   end; border, outskirts 892

קָרָא   to call, proclaim, read 894
Niph. to call oneself Isa. 48:2

קרא   to encounter, befall, often
with ל (לִקְרַאת) = toward, against
Niph. to meet unexpectedly Exod. 5:3
Deut. 22:6 2 Sam. 18:9, 20:1
Hiph. to cause to befall Jer. 32:23

קָרַב   to approach, come near 897
Niph. to be brought Exod. 22:7 Josh. 7:14
Pi. to cause to approach, bring near

קֶרֶב   inward part, midst 899

קָרְבָּן   offering, oblation 898

קָרוֹב   near 898

קֶרֶן   horn; hill Isa. 5:1; rays Hab. 3:4 901

קָרַע   to tear 902

קֶרֶשׁ   board, coll. boards Ezek. 27:6 903

קֶשֶׁת   bow 905

רָאָה   to see 906
to select 2 Kings 10:3 1 Sam. 16:1
to provide, furnish Deut. 33:21 Gen. 22:8, 14
to consider, reflect Eccl. 7:14
Niph. to appear
Pu. to be seen, detected Job 33:21
Hiph. to cause to experience Hab. 1:3 Ps. 60:5 71:20 85:8
Hithp. = reciprocal

ראש   head, top; beginning, first; chief; sum 910

רִאשׁוֹן   former, first, chief; before, formerly 911

רֵאשִׁית   beginning, first, chief 912

רַב   much, many, great, chief 912

רֹב   multitiude, abundance 913

רבה   to be, become, much, many, great 915
Pi. to increase, enlarge Judg. 9:29 Ps. 44:13
to bring up, rear Lam. 2:22 Ezek. 19:2
Hiph. הַרְבֵּה greatly, exceedingly

רֶגֶל   foot 919

רָדַף   to pursue, chase, persecute 922
Hiph. to chase Judg. 20:43

רוּחַ   breath, wind, spirit; quarter, side
Ezek. 42:16, 17, 18, 19, 20 1 Chron.
9:24 Jer. 52:23 924

רוּם   to be high, exalted, rise 926
Po'lel to cause to rise
to erect, raise, exalt
Hoph. to be taken off Lev. 4:10
be abolished Dan. 8:11
Hithpo'l to exalt oneself Isa. 33:10
Dan. 11:36

רוּץ   to run 930
Po'lel to run swiftly, dart Nah. 2:5

רֹחַב   breadth, width 931

רָחוֹק   distant, far; distance 935

רָחַץ   to wash 934
Pu. to be washed Prov. 30:12 Ezek.
16:4
Hithp. to wash oneself Job 9:30

רָחַק   to be or become far, distant 934
Pi. to send far away

רִיב   to strive, contend 936
Hiph. ptc.=displaying contention 1
Sam. 2:10 Hos. 4:4

רִיב   strife, dispute 936

רֵיחַ   scent, odor 926

רָכַב   to ride, mount and ride 938

רֶכֶב   chariots; upper millstone Deut. 24:6
Judg. 9:53 2 Sam. 11:21 riders, troop 2
Kings 7:14 Isa. 21:7, 9, 22:6 939

רנן   to give ringing cry 943
Pu. "no ringing cry shall be given" Isa.
16:10

רַע   bad, evil; distress, misery, injury,
calamity 948

רֵעַ   friend, companion, fellow 945

רָעָב   famine, hunger 944

רָעָה   to pasture, tend, graze 944

רָעָה   evil, misery, distress, injury 949

רֹעֶה   shepherd, herdsman 945 (רָעָה)

רעע   to be evil, bad 949
Niph. to suffer hurt Prov. 11:15, 13:20

Hiph. to do an injury, hurt to do evil,
wickedly

רָפָא   to heal 950
Hithp. Inf. cstr. to get healed 2 Kings
8:29, 9:15 2 Chron. 22:6

רצה   to be pleased with, to accept 953
to be pleased Ps. 40:14 1 Chron.
28:4
to make acceptable
Niph. to be accepted
Pi. to seek favor Job 20:10
Hiph. to pay off Lev. 25:34
Hithp. to make oneself acceptable
1 Sam. 29:4

רָצוֹן   goodwill, favor, acceptance, will 953

רַק   only, altogether, surely 956

רָשָׁע   wicked, criminal; guilty 957

שָׂבַע   to be sated, satisfied, surfeited 959
Niph. ptc. sated Job 31:31
Pi. to satisfy Ezek. 7:19 Ps. 90:14

שָׂדֶה   field, land 961

שִׂים, שׂוּם   to put, place, set 962
Hiph. (see BDB) Ezek. 14:8, 21:21 Job
4:20
Hoph. to be set Gen. 24:33

שָׂכַל   to be prudent 1 Sam. 18:30 968
Hiph. to look at Gen. 3:6
to consider, ponder
to have insight
to cause to consider
to give insight
to act prudently
to prosper
to cause to prosper Deut. 29:8 1 Kings
2:3

שְׂמֹאל   the left 969

שָׂמַח   to rejoice, be glad 970
Pi. to cause to rejoice
Hiph. (=*Pi.*) Ps. 89:43

שִׂמְחָה   joy, gladness, mirth 970

שָׂנֵא   to hate 971
Niph. to be hated Prov. 14:17, 20
Pi. ptc. only, enemy

שָׂעִיר   he-goat, buck 972

שָׂפָה   lip, speech, edge 973

שַׂר   chief, ruler, official, captain, prince 978

שָׂרַף   to burn 976

Pi. ptc. one burning Amos 6:10

Pu. to be burnt up Lev. 10:16

שָׁ, שֶׁ, שַׁ   who, which, that 979

שְׁאוֹל   sheol, hades 982

שָׁאַל   to ask, inquire 981

Niph. to ask for oneself 1 Sam. 20:6, 28 Neh. 13:6

Pi. to inquire carefully 2 Sam. 20:18 to beg Ps. 109:10

Hiph. to grant, make over to 1 Sam. 1:28, 2:20(?) Exod. 12:36

שָׁאַר   to remain, be left over 1 Sam. 16:11 983

Niph. (as Qal)

שְׁאֵרִית   rest, residue, remnant, remainder 984

שֵׁבֶט   rod, staff, club, sceptre; tribe 986

שבע   *Qal* ptc. pass. those sworn Ezek. 21:28 989

Niph. to swear

Hiph. to cause to swear

to adjure

שָׁבַר   to break, break in pieces 990

Hiph. to cause to break out Isa. 66:9

Hoph. to be broken, shattered Jer. 8:21

שָׁבַת   to cease, desist, rest 991

Niph. to cease

Hiph. to cause to fail Lev. 2:13 Jer. 48:35 Ruth 4:14

שַׁבָּת   Sabbath 992

שדד   to deal violently with, despoil, devastate, ruin 994

Niph. to be utterly ruined Mic. 2:4

Pi. to assault Prov. 24:15, 19:26

Pu. to be devastated

Po'el to violently destroy Hos. 10:2

Hoph. to be devastated Hos. 10:14 Isa. 33:1

שָׁוְא   emptiness, vanity 996

שׁוּב   to turn back, return 996

Po'l. to bring back

to restore Ps. 23:3 Isa. 58:12

to lead away Ezek. 38:4, 39:2 Isa. 47:10

to apostatize Jer. 8:5

Pu. to be restored Ezek. 38:8

שׁוֹפָר   horn 1051

שׁוֹר   a head of cattle (without reference to sex); bullock, ox 1004

שׁחה   to bow down Isa. 51:23 1005

Hiph. to depress Prov. 12:25

Hithpa'lel to bow down, prostrate oneself

שָׁחַט   to slaughter, beat 1006

Niph. to be slaughtered Num. 11:22 Lev. 6:18

שחת   *Niph.* to be marred, spoiled Jer. 13:7, 18:4 1007

to be injured Exod. 8:20

to be corrupted, corrupt Gen. 6:11, 12 Ezek. 20:44

Pi. to spoil, ruin

to pervert, corrupt

Hiph. (=*Pi.*)

Hoph. ptc. spoiled, ruined Prov. 25:26 Mal. 1:14

שׁיר   to sing 1010

Po'l. to sing

Hoph. to be sung Isa. 26:1

שִׁיר   song 1010

שִׁית   to put, set

to make 1011

Hoph. to be imposed Exod. 21:30

שָׁכַב   to lie down 1011

שָׁכַח   to forget 1013

Pi. to cause to forget Lam. 2:6

Hiph. (=*Pi.*) Jer. 23:27

Hithp. to be forgotten Eccl. 8:10

שׁכם   *Hiph.* to start early, rise early 1014

שָׁכֵן   to settle down, abide, dwell 1014

Pi. to make settle down, establish

to make to dwell Num. 14:30 Jer. 7:3, 7

Hiph. to lay Ps. 7:6

to place, set, establish Gen. 3:24 Josh. 18:1

to cause to settle Ezek. 32:4

to cause to dwell Ps. 78:55

שָׁלוֹם peace, completeness, soundness, welfare 1022

שָׁלַח to send, stretch out

to let loose Ps. 50:19 1018

Pi. to send away

to let go, set free

to shoot forth

to let down Jer. 38:6, 11

to shoot 1 Sam. 20:20

Hiph. to send

שֻׁלְחָן table 1020

שָׁלַךְ *Hiph.* to throw, fling, cast 1020

שָׁלָל prey, spoil, plunder, booty 1021

שׁלם to be complete, sound Job 9:4 1022

Pi. to complete, finish 1 Kings 9:25

to make whole

to make safe Job 8:6

to make good

to reward, recompense

Pu. to be performed Ps. 65:2

to be repaid, requited Jer. 18:20 Prov. 11:31, 13:13

Hiph. to make and end of Isa. 38:12, 13

to complete, perform Job 23:14 Isa. 44:26, 28

שֶׁלֶם peace offering; sacrifice for alliance or friend 1023

שָׁם there, thither 1027

שֵׁם name 1027

שׁמד *Niph.* to be exterminated, destroyed 1029

Hiph. to annihilate, exterminate to destroy

שָׁמַיִם heavens, sky 1029

שׁמם to be desolated, appalled 1030

Niph. (as Qal)

Po'. to be appalled Ezra 9:3, 4

to be appalling, causing horror

Hithpo. to be appalled

to cause oneself desolation, ruin Eccl. 7:16

שְׁמָמָה devastation, waste 1031

שֶׁמֶן fat, oil 1032

שָׁמַע to hear 1033

Niph. to grant hearing 2 Chron. 30:27

Pi. to cause to hear 1 Sam. 15:4, 23:8

שָׁמַר to keep, watch, preserve 1036

Niph. to be on one's guard

to keep oneself, refrain 1 Sam. 21:5

to be kept, guarded Hos. 12:14 Ps. 37:28

Pi. to pay regard Jonah 2:9

Hithp. to keep oneself from Ps. 18:24 2 Sam. 22:24 Mic. 6:16

שֹׁמֵר watchman 1036 (שָׁמַר)

שֶׁמֶשׁ sun; pinnacle, battlement 1039

שֵׁן tooth, ivory 1042

שָׁנָה year 1040

שַׁעַר gate 1044

שִׁפְחָה maid, maid-servant 1046

שָׁפַט to judge, govern 1047

Niph. to enter into controversy, plead

to be judged Ps. 9:20, 37:33, 109:7

Po'el ptc. opponent-at-law Job 9:15 Zeph. 3:15 Ps. 109:31

שֹׁפֵט judge 1047 (שָׁפַט)

שָׁפַךְ to pour out, pour 1049

Pu. to be poured out, shed Zeph. 1:17 Num. 35:33

to be caused to slip Ps. 73:2

Hithp. to pour oneself out Job 30:16 Lam. 4:1, 2:12

שׁקה *Hiph.* to cause to drink, give to drink 1052

Pu. to be watered Job 21:24

שֶׁקֶל shekel 1053

שֶׁקֶר deception, falsehood 1055

שרת *Pi.* to minister, serve 1058

שָׁתָה to drink 1059

Niph. to be drunk Lev. 11:34

תְּהִלָּה praise, song of praise; renown, fame 239

תָּוֶךְ midst 1063

תּוֹעֵבָה   abomination 1072

תּוֹרָה   direction, instruction, law; custom, manner 2 Sam. 7:19 435

תַּחַת   underneath, below, instead of 1065

מִתַּחַת   from under, from beneath 1066

תָּמִיד   continually, continuity 556

תָּמִים   complete, whole, sound, healthful, wholesome, innocent 1071

תמם   to be complete. finished 1070

תִּפְאָרָה   beauty, glory 802

תִּפִלָּה   prayer 813

תָּפַשׂ   to lay hold of, seize, grasp 1074
Pi. to grasp Prov. 30:28

תָּקַע   to thrust, clap, give a blow 1075
Niph. to be blown Amos. 3:6 Isa. 27:13 to strike oneself into (pledge oneself) Job 17:3

תְּרוּמָה   contribution, offering 929